Studies in Diplomacy and International Relations

Series Editors
Donna Lee
Manchester Metropolitan University
Manchester, West Yorkshire, UK

Paul Sharp
College of Liberal Arts, Rm 302A
University of Minnesota
Duluth, MN, USA

Marcus Holmes
College of William & Mary
Williamsburg, VA, USA

More information about this series at
http://www.palgrave.com/gp/series/14471

Paul Soyez

Australia and France's Mutual Empowerment

Middle Powers' Strategies for Pacific and Global Challenges

Paul Soyez
University of Melbourne
Parkville, VIC, Australia

Studies in Diplomacy and International Relations
ISBN 978-3-030-13448-8   ISBN 978-3-030-13449-5   (eBook)
https://doi.org/10.1007/978-3-030-13449-5

Library of Congress Control Number: 2019931935

© The Editor(s) (if applicable) and The Author(s), under exclusive license to Springer
Nature Switzerland AG 2019
This work is subject to copyright. All rights are solely and exclusively licensed by the
Publisher, whether the whole or part of the material is concerned, specifically the rights
of translation, reprinting, reuse of illustrations, recitation, broadcasting, reproduction
on microfilms or in any other physical way, and transmission or information storage and
retrieval, electronic adaptation, computer software, or by similar or dissimilar methodology
now known or hereafter developed.
The use of general descriptive names, registered names, trademarks, service marks, etc. in this
publication does not imply, even in the absence of a specific statement, that such names are
exempt from the relevant protective laws and regulations and therefore free for general use.
The publisher, the authors and the editors are safe to assume that the advice and
information in this book are believed to be true and accurate at the date of publication.
Neither the publisher nor the authors or the editors give a warranty, express or implied,
with respect to the material contained herein or for any errors or omissions that may have
been made. The publisher remains neutral with regard to jurisdictional claims in published
maps and institutional affiliations.

Cover credit: DANIEL MUNOZ/Stringer/Getty Images

This Palgrave Macmillan imprint is published by the registered company Springer Nature
Switzerland AG
The registered company address is: Gewerbestrasse 11, 6330 Cham, Switzerland

To my mother

To beautiful memories
in Europe and in the South Pacific

Contents

1 Introduction   1

2 Methodological and Theoretical Frameworks   23

3 Economic Diplomacy, an Innovative Force of the French–Australian Relationship   55

4 Threatening Australia's Backyard? French–Australian Tensions on Nuclear Policies and Their Resolution   101

5 Global Security as a Central Objective of the Bilateral Partnership   137

6 New Caledonia, Cornerstone of an Ambiguous French–Australian Relationship   179

7 An Appeased Neighbourhood: French–Australian Cooperation in the South Pacific Region   211

8 Conclusion   261

Appendix—List of Archives 269

Bibliography 285

Index 297

ABBREVIATIONS

AD	*Archives diplomatiques françaises*/French Diplomatic Archives
AN	*Archives nationales de France*/French National Archives
ANZUS	Australia New Zealand United States
APEC	Asia-Pacific Economic Cooperation
ASEAN	Association of Southeast Asian Nations
CAP	Common Agricultural Policy
DFAT	Department of Foreign Affairs and Trade
EEC	European Economic Community
EEZ	Economic Exclusive Zone
EU	European Union
FANC	*Forces armées de la Nouvelle-Calédonie*/Armed Forces of New Caledonia
FRANZ	France Australia New Zealand
FTA	Free Trade Agreement
INTERFET	International Force East Timor
IORA	Indian Ocean Rim Association
NAA	National Archives of Australia
NATO	North Atlantic Treaty Organization
PC	Pacific Community (former South Pacific Community—SPC)
PICs	Pacific Island Countries
PIF	Pacific Islands Forum (former South Pacific Forum)
PNG	Papua New Guinea
RAMSI	Regional Assistance Mission to Solomon Islands
TPP	Trans-Pacific Partnership Agreement
UN	United Nations
UNDP	United Nations Development Programme

x   ABBREVIATIONS

UNGA   United Nations General Assembly
UNSC   United Nations Security Council
US   United States

LIST OF TABLES

Table 2.1	List of Australian interviewees	36
Table 2.2	List of French interviewees	37
Table 3.1	French–Australian merchandise trade in December 2018	71
Table 3.2	Type of merchandise traded by France and Australia	72
Table 3.3	French–Australian trade of services in 2018	72
Table 3.4	French–Australian cross-investments in 2017	78
Table 7.1	New Caledonia in the French state's budget in 2011	229

xi

CHAPTER 1

Introduction

Since April 2016, Australia and France have been married. Their wedding present consisted of twelve submarines, which engaged both countries in a fifty-year union. This metaphor, created by former Australian Prime Minister Malcolm Turnbull and former French President François Hollande, represents the deep level of strategic cooperation in which Paris and Canberra have engaged since 2012 and the signature of the French–Australian Strategic Partnership. How did these two countries reach such a high level of commitment to each other, when only about two decades ago, a group of Australians bombed the French consulate in Perth to protest against French nuclear testing in the Pacific? This book aims to investigate the dynamics behind this historically ambiguous relationship.

More precisely, this study explains why and how France and Australia are currently engaged in a process of strategic and economic mutual empowerment and how this rapprochement has been possible, owing to thirty years of diplomatic efforts to overcome ongoing culturally and historically constructed misunderstandings and conflicts. Employing an approach based on constructive theories and Joseph Nye's doctrine of "smart power" to analyse this evolution, this book investigates how two very different Western powers have adapted to the twenty first century's "international disorder" (Beeson and Hameri 2017). The concept of empowerment, now used in International Relations, originally comes from the field of psychology. Zimmerman and Perkins define the concept

© The Author(s) 2019
P. Soyez, *Australia and France's Mutual Empowerment,*
Studies in Diplomacy and International Relations,
https://doi.org/10.1007/978-3-030-13449-5_1

1

as "a construct that links individual strengths and competencies, natural helping systems, and proactive behaviours to social policy and social change" (1995, p. 569). Moreover, they add that "empowerment suggests that participation with others to achieve goals, efforts to gain access to resources, and some critical understandings of the socio-political environment are basic components of the construct" (1995, p. 571). This book was primarily designed to understand why, since the end of the Cold War, the bilateral relationship between France and Australia has dramatically improved. In fact, during the Cold War and until the last French nuclear testing in the South Pacific in 1996, relations between Paris and Canberra were regularly stormy, and French and Australian foreign policy-makers perceived a genuine mutual mistrust. Therefore, the aim of this study has been to understand which interests, which personalities, which elements of the global context have led France and Australia to engage in a regional and global rapprochement, and what have been the human, economic and political prerequisites which enabled it. This book demonstrates how French and Australian foreign policy-makers have understood that, in regard to their numerous common interests, both countries had to mutually empower each other in order to strengthen their own power, regionally and globally. This book is the first to propose an answer to these questions. It argues that these inclusive dynamics of empowerment constitute the response of two diverse middle powers to current global threats and represent a tool suitable for modernising the strategies and practices of both countries' diplomacies.

Australian and French foreign policies have been challenged by the global reconfigurations of the twenty first century. As Joseph Nye explains, "power always depends on a context". In the current context, power can be considered three-dimensional: military, economic and the "realm of transnational relations that cross borders outside of government control" (2011, pp. xiv–xv). The year 2017 has witnessed the completion of the globalising shift away from the international order that was established after the end of World War II, as demonstrated by US President Donald Trump's negative attitude towards the North Atlantic Treaty Organization (NATO). Populist parties have gained power in many Western democracies, threatening the current international order but highlighting some of the destructive consequences of globalisation.

This book understands globalisation in the context of two of its definitions. According to Neil Brenner, globalisation constitutes the "accelerated circulation of people, commodities, capital, money, identities and images through global space", leading to "disembedding social, economic and political relations from their local-territorial preconditions" (1999, p. 431). Moreover, Jan Nederveen Pieterse perceives "globalisation as hybridisation: structural hybridisation, or the emergence of new, mixed forms of cooperation, and cultural hybridisation, or the development of translocal mélange cultures" (1994, p. 161). Decades of rapid globalisation have forced actors in the field of International Relations, official and non-governmental, to redefine their foreign policies and actions in order to adapt to a world influenced by increasing insecurities. While the United States remains a "hyperpower", defined by Hubert Védrine as the state "predominant in all areas of power: economic, technological, military, monetary, linguistic and cultural", global affairs seem less and less controlled by Washington's order. Therefore, according to Nye, "two great shifts are occurring in this century: a power transition among states and a power diffusion away from all states to nonstate actors" (2011, p. xv). More precisely, the most important factor of this power transition has been, since the end of the Cold War, the economic, followed by the diplomatic, rise of Asia. The rapid and extraordinary development of the Asian continent, symbolised by the current global weight of China and India, has significantly reshuffled global dynamics. The rise of Asia has had a tremendous impact of the French–Australian bilateral relationship, as this book demonstrates.

Globalisation, as with any process, is neither simply positive nor negative. However, the globalisation of the economy and its political, social and cultural consequences have challenged international actors differently with respect to their identity, security and interests. In fact, while globalisation does not automatically lead to an Americanisation of the world,[1] "the United States has ruled as the supreme chief of globalisation because it has ruled in a system which it has imposed and which primarily benefits itself" (Védrine 2001, p. 3). Many countries, such as France, have felt deeply threatened by such global dynamics, which are often perceived as an accelerating factor of a potential European decline. Countries such as Australia, on the other hand, have demonstrated more confidence in the outcome they can attain thanks to the internationalisation of the economy. Moreover, from what was once a bipolar division of the world, international relations are increasingly led in a multipolar context. While these dynamics have often been perceived as contributing to insecurities, they have also made it possible for countries such as France and Australia to develop a more independent foreign policy regarding some significant global and regional issues. Therefore, such tangible and significant modifications of the international order have impacted the traditional conceptualisation of power. This book adopts Hubert Védrine's classification of powers, which provides the most relevant hierarchy for analysing the French–Australian bilateral relationship (2001, p. 4). According to Védrine, states can be classified according to five categories of power. On top of this hierarchy, the United States maintains its global influence as "hyperpower". Next, seven countries constitute "globally influential powers": China, France, Germany, India, Japan, Russia and the United Kingdom. Védrine opens the question as to whether the EU could be included in this category or not, since power cannot be reduced to hard power alone but must also include soft power. At a third level there are between twenty and thirty countries, considered by Védrine as "powers", some of them having a regional influence, for example, Australia, Brazil, Canada, Indonesia, Iran, Italy, Mexico, Saudi Arabia and Turkey. The fourth category encompasses countries "without power and often influenced by a power", and the fifth group is composed by "pseudo-states", which have originated from the proliferation of sovereignties and are not able to exercise their own sovereignty without becoming failed states. Both the second and third groups can be considered middle powers, but with different levels of diplomatic reach. Diplomats interviewed for this research in Paris and in Canberra define France as a "global middle power" and Australia as a "regional middle power", a distinction adopted by this book.

Specialists in International Relations have also witnessed the progressive multiplication and diversification of actors involved in international policies since the end of the Cold War. These state and nonstate actors are not just international but also transnational, such as multinational companies, international organisations and migrants. Another factor is the development of an international civil society in addition to the traditional concept of national ones.[2] This international public opinion, even very diverse, deeply influenced by the media as this book illustrates, particularly regarding Pacific issues, encompasses "generosity, devotion, networks, militancy, interests, lobbies, beliefs and a fair amount of disguised real power" (Védrine 2001, p. 8). "Nonstate actors now crowd the stage" (Nye 2011, p. xvi). The diversification of actors involved in foreign policy raises new issues without having made the old ones disappear. It has also reinforced existing balances of power, which means that globalisation has become neither fairer nor more democratic. As Joseph

Nye asserts, "in an information-based world of cybersecurity, power diffusion may be a greater threat than power transition" amongst great states (Nye 2011, p. xiii). Consequently, decision-making processes have become more complex, because they have had to take into account more and more diverse interests. Foreign policy discourses and strategies have to be based on new political narratives, as the French–Australian relationship illustrates, in order to remain legitimate and, therefore, to reinforce themselves. This book highlights all the different types of actors who have been involved in the evolution of the French–Australian bilateral relationship since the end of the Cold War.

Finally, the transformation of international affairs since the end of the Cold War, visible through both a transition and a diffusion of power, has led to an increasing interdependence between states which share interests, values and cultural links. The progressive French–Australian rapprochement and the constitution of their strategic partnership takes place within this context. Facing increasing challenges to their power, economy and identity, states often cannot reach their international objectives alone: "On many transnational issues, empowering others can help us to accomplish our own goals" (Nye 2011, p. xvii). This book demonstrates the ways in which Australia and France have fully integrated this logic. As Martine Piquet highlighted, "the two countries' difficulties in finding their place in a rapidly changing world. [...] France and Australia have had to reconsider their positions on the international scene, and in the process, to reconstruct self-images, while not necessarily liking the image of themselves mirrored in the other's criticisms" (2000).

Therefore, this book asserts as its main argument that the transformation of the French–Australian bilateral relationship since 1985, and the constitution of their genuine strategic partnership since 2012, has been conceived by Australian and French policy-makers as a process of mutual empowerment. Canberra and Paris have constructed this mutual support to help each of them to modernise their own diplomacy, with the aid of a new alliance and new practises, and to answer together new regional and global challenges. Moreover, this book argues that this progressive empowerment has not only been possible because of the settlement of three main conflicts between France and Australia—the Common Agricultural Policy (CAP), the French nuclear testing issue and Australia's opposition to French policies in New Caledonia—but also because French and Australian policy-makers have implemented supports for dialogue to help overcome their ongoing misperceptions and misunderstandings and to align their approach to regional and world issues.

Since the study of International Relations must be conducted within its historical context, this book analyses the evolution and dynamics of French–Australian relations since the end of the Cold War. This study starts in 1985–1986, an historic moment understood according to Nicolas Offenstadt's "diachronic" and "synchronic" approaches (2006, pp. 42–44). A diachronic approach studies moments according to which elements they keep from the past and which they open up for the future. A synchronic one focuses on the variation between understandings of individual moments depending on the actors. Therefore, by combining both approaches, Offenstadt proposes that, in order to apprehend the historiographical significance of a singular moment, one must compare it within a series of moments. Such a comparison enables one to draw conclusions about both the event itself and its long-term structures. Arlette Farge's plea for the largest periodization of the historical moment (2002, p. 67), in order to make it as inclusive as possible, reinforces the proposal of this study for a liberal delineation of the end of the Cold War. In fact, Farge demonstrates that historians should include ensembles of thoughts and mental categories within the concept of "moment". She explains that this intellectual meaning of the moment enables one to comprehend its core elements: the intentions of the actors and above all their vision of the future. The anticipations of the moment's consequences are part of the moment itself. Globally, John Matlock, former US Ambassador to Moscow, argues that the Cold War ended gradually beginning in 1985 (Brown 2010, p. 245). Regarding the French–Australian relationship, the second half of the 1980s presented a series of intense conflicts regarding France's nuclear testing, the Rainbow Warrior affair and France's management of the violent tensions in New Caledonia (1985–1986). However, the election of a new government in Paris led by Michel Rocard in 1988, with a drastic change in France's Pacific strategy, enabled a fast and genuine improvement of the French–Australian bilateral relationship. Moreover, following Frank's approach (2009), we can argue that the acceleration of regional processes in Europe and Asia in the second half of the 1980s present moments that mirrored the end of the bipolar order that defined the Cold War. Therefore, in order to fully understand the new mindset of policy-makers and public opinion in the post-Cold War world, this book chooses 1985 as described above as a starting point for the study. This moment represents the beginning of the disruption of the previous order and the establishment of new relationships, logics, tensions and agreements. Because of the diversity of issues and actors involved in the Australian–French relationship since 1985, drawing an absolute and exhaustive periodization of the bilateral relation in the last thirty years is impossible. However, the evolution of the relationship can be understood through three consecutive sequences. Firstly, during the 1980s and 1990s, the Australian–French relationship was characterised by a mutual indifference and sometimes mistrust regarding trade regulation and nuclear strategies. From Paris, Australia's full support to the United States led to the idea that French policy-makers did not have much to gain from developing relations with Canberra. However, at the end of the 1990s and early 2000s, this position evolved and both countries realised that they could gain from increasing their diplomatic relations. This improvement was led by economic interests of French companies based in Australia and of Australian companies trading with France. Moreover, this rapprochement can also be explained by the development of work migration from young French professionals to Australia, which became a very attractive destination in France. Lastly, since 2012, the Australian–French relationship has been characterised by a continuous deepening of the political, diplomatic and strategic ties between Canberra and Paris.

Setting the Scene: The Role of History and Geography

French Diplomacy: What Future for France as a Global Middle Power?

As the 2017 French Presidential elections have demonstrated, French society is currently engaged in a deep questioning of its political, economic, social, cultural and diplomatic model. Regarding foreign policy, Paris' goal is to maintain certain prior elements of its secular diplomatic tradition while modernising its means of influence in order to face the current challenges previously mentioned. France's core diplomatic tradition is often described as a *"certaine idée de la France"* (a certain idea of what France is), as summarised by Charles De Gaulle in order to explain France's *politique de grandeur*. This depiction, fully embedded in the French national identity, illustrates the fact that French policy-makers are perfectly aware that their power is limited compared to that of Washington or Beijing. However, French public opinion and policy-makers believe that France remains a significant and useful power and that Paris should not take orders from any other state. Overseas, this vision has in the past often been dismissed as arrogant, particularly by many Australian policy-makers, themselves perhaps arrogantly expecting Paris to align with an American order simply because it is dominant.

This *politique de grandeur* has constituted a constant feature of France's foreign policy in the last sixty years. In fact, French foreign policy-making is characterised by its strict continuity under both left and right-wing governments. French foreign policy-makers believe that there is a "global French foreign policy" and that France has "the ability and the duty to play a major geopolitical role". Védrine describes this singular French ambition as "the willingness to be different", the absence of fear to oppose the foreign policy of the United States, the desire to fight for countries and causes in the world that no other power cares about, the dismissal of strict realism and the promotion of constructivism, which enables the French to preserve French culture against American standardisation (2001, p. x).

Even if this conception remains part of the French identity, the *politique de grandeur* has had to be adapted to the new challenges of the twenty first century. To begin, French policy-makers have developed a strategy to elucidate Paris's position and to attempt to counter the perception of arrogance. The study of the French–Australian bilateral relationship illustrates perfectly this new attitude, which aims to enable France to develop new partnerships in the face of current international threats. As Nye explains, "contextual intelligence, the ability to understand an evolving environment and capitalize on trends, will become a crucial skill in enabling leaders to convert power into successful strategies" (2011, p. xvii). In fact, France perceives itself as deeply affected by the negative effects of globalisation: the focus on economic neoliberalism, on the increasing need for individuality and flexibility and the pre-eminence of the English language. Therefore, French policy-makers have called at numerous times for a stronger response to globalisation, by promoting the work of multilateral organisations which can serve this economic and strategic interest. This threatening context has led French policy-makers to debate further about appropriate foreign policy and which narrative Paris should implement in order to maintain its power.

Thierry De Montbrial and Gomart (2017) argues that the first aim of any foreign policy is the long-term survival of the political unit producing it. Because of the primary aim of survival, security and identity constitute crucial issues for any foreign policy. However, as the rise of the far-right party *Front National* has demonstrated in the last ten years, France's understanding of its identity has been deeply challenged by economic, cultural and migratory globalisation. According to Montbrial, France's lack of confidence in its identity has weakened its diplomacy in the last fifteen years, because French policy-makers and public opinion have questioned France's role in international relations. Montbrial claims that the solution to this challenge lies in a foreign policy which would strongly assert the primary goal of securing national interests, defined as the operational translation of survival, identity and integrity. The analyst explains that France should always prioritise its national interest. The latter must be defended by partnerships with its allies, traditional or new, without contradicting its universal values as a leading nation in the fight for human rights.

Regardless of whether one believes that France should focus on its national interest more than on its values, Thierry de Montrial's analysis illustrates the ongoing French debate pertaining to France's diplomatic response to these challenges and opportunities inherent in globalisation. Further examining this debate, this book argues that, especially in the last five years, France's foreign policy has already shifted towards the promotion of its national interests on a few innovative and specific issues, such as solidifying its presence in the Indo-Pacific region through a bilateral relationship with Australia. The recent development of the French–Australian partnership is indicative of France's effort to modernise its diplomatic narrative and, consequently, to enhance its global diplomatic network and influence. In fact, this book demonstrates that, by forging a strong partnership with Australia, France intends to strengthen its Indo-Pacific identity, the modernisation of its economic diplomacy, and therefore, its role as an influential global middle power.

Finally, French foreign policy cannot be understood without taking into account its European Union (EU) dimension. Paris's primary focus has been the reinforcement of its own security and that of its closest allies, the other member-states of the EU. Moreover, the EU, as a global economic and political power itself composed of a few strong middle powers with global reach, has interests not only in the European continent but also all around the world. While the idea of a tangible common European defence has lingered and been delayed for more than fifty years, the protection of European interests—at least the ones which have suited Paris—has always constituted a significant element of

France's global foreign policy. It is worth noting that French President Emmanuel Macron has been elected in 2017 partly on the promise to develop the EU's common defence, supported by German Chancellor Angela Merkel. This book demonstrates that the European factor has played a crucial role in the development of the French–Australian bilateral relationship. France intends to represent European interests in the Indo-Pacific region, and conversely the interests of this region in European institutions. In this manner, France can reinforce its strategic narrative in the South Pacific and, therefore, its own global influence and power. Moreover, France's actions to reinforce and secure EU's interests are likely to increase due to the new political context. US President Donald Trump's unreliability and France's new President Emmanuel Macron, whose diplomatic program is centred around the solidification of European defence, highlight the importance of the European component of France's foreign policy-making.

A More Independent Australian Foreign Policy?

Unlike France, Australia's key strategic challenge since the end of the Cold War has been to reconcile its history with its geography in order to benefit from both. In short, in an increasingly multilateral world, Australia's traditional alignment with the United States must be questioned in order to enable Australia to further benefit from its regional environment, especially from Asia's economic growth. This approach necessarily raises questions concerning Australia's identity and perception of itself. Despite its multicultural society, Australia's identity has remained mostly Anglo-Saxon, and some components of Australian society show reluctance to accept its new Asian elements, while at the same time Asian countries don't generally recognise Australia as one of themselves. Therefore, as with France, the current process of globalisation has challenged Australia's identity and its understanding of the world and has modified its global strategy. This tension has also been exacerbated by Australian domestic politics, with the Australian Labour Party often more supportive of Canberra's regional involvement than Liberal governments, which are more inclined to promote Western alliances. Moreover, despite the partisan unanimity of support for multilateral engagement in the early decades after 1945, since toward the end of the 1990s, conservative Australian governments have tended to be more sceptical about the UN and the parties have also regularly differed on their focus regarding multilateral versus bilateral approaches. This debate has become more significant in Australia than in France, which has traditionally favoured multilateral negotiations.

Australian foreign policy and practice have been less bipartisan than in France and Liberal and Labor governments have followed significantly different traditions. According to John Langmore et al. (2014, pp. 19–38), such opposition has not only pertained to Australian foreign policy practices and outcomes but, more broadly, to Australian values, identity and to its vision of the global order. Josh Frydenberg claims that the Liberal tradition in Australian foreign policy is based on the strength of Canberra's commitment to the United States, as demonstrated by Australia's engagement in wars led by Washington and Canberra's dependence on US protection. He also asserts that Liberal Australian policy-makers have favoured bilateral relationships with their Asian partners in order to assist Australia so it can benefit from Asia's economic growth. Therefore, Frydenberg criticises Labor governments for committing to multilateral organisations out of principle, when he claims that Liberal policy-makers have intended to use multilateral negotiations only when they enabled the pursuit of Australian national interests. On the other hand, John Langmore and Melissa Parke define the Labor tradition in Australian foreign policy by "Australia's distinctive middle-power pursuit of international security, peace, human rights, and economic and social equity" (2014, p. 20). They attribute the development of Australia's independent foreign policy to the Curtin and Chifley Labor governments, which forged articulation of Australia's own national interests. Moreover, Labor policy-makers have favoured Australia's engagement with the United Nations and the rule of law over a strict commitment to the American alliance in order to achieve the goal of international rule of law. Their policies have been dedicated to making Australia a "global good citizen", for example by supporting Gareth Evans' concept of the 'responsibility to protect' or by increasing Australia's aid to development programs. Lastly, Langmore and Parke assert that Labor governments have worked at integrating Australia into its regional environment earlier and deeper than Liberal policy-makers did, as demonstrated since the time of Whitlam's abrogation of the White Australia Policy and establishment of official relations with China in 1972. This focus on Australia's regional integration has been prioritised by all Labor government, as demonstrated by Julia Gillard's commissioning of a White Paper on *Australia in the Asian Century* in 2012

(2014, pp. 30–35). Such tangible differences between Liberal and Labor governments remain noticeable and highlight broader strategic debates amongst specialists in Australian foreign policy.

Geostrategic debates are not new in Australia. One can find their origin in what Geoffrey Blainey described as "the tyranny of distance" (1983) to explain Australia's zealous demonstrations of belonging to the Anglo-Saxon world in order to compensate for its distance from London and Washington and its proximity with Asia, which has often been perceived as a threat. Therefore, unlike France's global strategy based on independence, Australia's security strategy has always been framed by the desire for protection from a powerful guarantor. This role of protector was played by the British Empire until 1942. Since then, Australia has progressively reduced its connection to the United Kingdom, especially after London's entry into the European Economic Community in 1973, nevertheless maintaining a special relationship with its former colonial power. From a defence and security point of view, Australia has sought protection by the United States since World War II, an alliance symbolised in the Pacific through the ANZUS Treaty of 1951. Australia's participation in all American-led wars, even in Iraq in 2003, and the development of American military bases within its territory serve as tangible manifestations of this alignment. However, such a strong Australian reliance on the United States to maintain Canberra's security and frame its foreign policy has made Australia's regional integration more complex. Derek McDougall claims that "throughout the evolution of the Australia-US relationship a central theme has been the way in which Australian sees the relationship contributing to its role in the Asia-Pacific region" (2009, p. 52).

Alongside their security strategy of alignment with the United States, Australian policy-makers have also conducted a strategy of integration with Asia. Mark Beeson has highlighted the manner in which the implementation of both these strategies, based on a hard and unstable equilibrium, is often ambiguous in what he and Shahar Hameri call an "international disorder" (2017). On numerous occasions, Australian policy-makers have sought to implement concrete strategies to integrate Australia's regional environment, such as by establishing institutional frameworks for regional dialogue with the creation of the Asia-Pacific Economic Cooperation (APEC) in 1989, or by its rapprochement with Asia-Pacific institutions, such as with the Association of Southeast Asian Nations (ASEAN) Regional Forum. Australia's multiple free trade agreements (FTAs) with Asian economic powers, such as its support for a Trans-Pacific Partnership (TPP), can be analysed through this integrating lens. The creation of Australia's White Paper *Australia and the Asian Century* in 2012 has also demonstrated this will to engage further in this region. However, the current context of powers in Asia has partly been perceived as constituting a threat to Australia's regional assertion: "Perhaps the most obvious transformation worrying Australian foreign policy-makers is the apparent weakening of the US-centred security order in East Asia and the re-emergence of China as a major power in the region" (Beeson and Hameiri 2017, p. 1). This book demonstrates the concern of Australian foreign policy-makers with the diplomatic emergence of China, which challenges the norms that underpin a global international order based on Western values, and its consequences on Canberra's relationship with Paris.

Australian policy-makers have also started to focus on revising Australia's regional strategy in order to develop a narrative potentially leaving Canberra less open to the accusation of being an "awkward partner". Philomena Murray, Alex Warleigh-Lack and Baogang He have pointed out Australia's "awkward" relationship with Asia, when "awkwardness refers to an uncomfortable state of affairs in which one party strives to participate in a region but lacks full belonging and commitment to the goal of the latter" (2014, p. 280). This book also argues that, like France, Australia can be considered an awkward partner with the Pacific Island Countries (PICs) as much as with Asia. Australian policy-makers try to accommodate the fact that Australia still perceives itself as an Anglo-Saxon country, isolated in Southeast Asia from its natural Western partners, while its economic and geopolitical interest are increasingly located within Asia. Australia's foreign policy is deeply divided by this dichotomy, and its policy-makers strive to find the right balance in order to benefit from association with both worlds. Specialists of Australian foreign policy regularly debate about the level of engagement Australia should implement with its Asian partners, as opposed or alongside its strong commitment to the United States. In *Australian Foreign Policy, Controversies and Debates* (2014, pp. 136–153), Rémy Davison and Shamsul Khan juxtapose powerful arguments. Davison asserts that "the US alliance remains central to Australia across numerous issues areas, including regional security, defence procurement and trade" when, on the other hand, "Chinese foreign policy in practice is frequently diametrically opposed to Australian regional and global interests, as it partners and protects regimes that threaten regional stability" (2014, p. 136). Therefore, he claims that it would not be in Canberra's interest to distance itself from the United States in order to become closer to China. While Shamsul Khan does not call for a significant rapprochement with China, he proposes that Australian policy-makers should partly withdraw from the American alliance, which he considers obsolete. This would enable Australia to avoid being caught up in the Sino-American rivalry by implementing "the pursuance of independent foreign and security policies without any formal security alliances, and involvement in the Asian regional system through multiple complex connections, both multilateral and bilateral" (2014, p. 136).

Hugh White goes further regarding this debate, arguing that Australia's strategic dichotomy between Washington and Beijing cannot be ignored any longer. He asserts that Australian policy-makers will have to choose either a strategy focused on the protection of Australian security by the US or another strategy favouring Australia's economic interests in Asia (2017). White even claims: "It is possible that Australian policy during 2011-2015 may actually have helped quicken the pace of escalating major-power rivalry by encouraging each side to believe they had Australia's support" (2017, p. 105). Refusing to take a side would be counterproductive for Australia in the conflict which, according to White, is doomed to happen between Washington and Beijing. Instead, White asserts that Australian policy-makers should fully acknowledge the rise of China and its consequences, implement a genuine debate regarding the position Canberra should adopt, meanwhile also establishing new global partnerships so as not to face this dilemma alone. Therefore, this book claims that Australia's commitment to building a genuine strategic partnership with France is a major component of Canberra's strategy to reduce its awkwardness when engaging with the Indo-Pacific region and to find new sources of support with regard to the tensions between Washington and Beijing.

South Pacific, Oceania, Indo-Pacific and Outre-Mer: *What Geographic Level for Which Interest?*

This study analyses the development of the French–Australian bilateral relationship, not only globally but also in the region where France and Australia are neighbours, the South Pacific. It refers to different spaces and territories, two very different concepts. In Lévy and Lussault's

Dictionnaire de la géographie et de l'espace des sociétés, Jean-Paul Ferrier defines territories as humanised spaces, structured around social practices which provide them with an identity (2009, pp. 907–912). Moreover, according to Guy Di Méo, territories come from the economic, ideological, political and social appropriation of spaces by groups aware of their own symbols and history (1996, p. 40). Therefore, by referring to the concept of *Outre-mer,* this book refers to a very significant territory within the French Republic. In fact, the French *Outre-mer* does not only encompass France's twelve overseas territories in North and South America, in the Atlantic, Indian, Pacific and Antarctic Oceans.[3] The concept of *Outre-mer* also gathers specific political, historical, economic, ideological and emotional ties between the 2.6 million French citizens living in these territories and metropolitan France. The *Outre-mer* also constitutes a crucial support for France's foreign policy, for its global strategy and its identity as a global middle power. Additionally, as this book also demonstrates, the *Outre-mer* corresponds to a history of debates around legitimacy and sovereignty, of contestation of France and of administrative innovation in order to maintain France's presence far from Europe.

This book also refers to three spaces which must be demarcated: the South Pacific, Oceania and the Indo-Pacific region. The South Pacific represents one of the sub-regions of the Pacific region, which covers the seas between North and South America and the Indian Ocean, and ranging from the Artic to the Antarctic. The Asia-Pacific is another sub-region of the Pacific, excluding its American shores (Antheaume and Bonnemaison 1988, p. 9). This study argues, following the study of Nathalie Mrgudovic (2008, p. 33) that the South Pacific corresponds to the French notion of *Océanie,* Oceania in English, which encompasses the PICs, New Zealand and Australia. This delimitation, even if it does not correspond to Antheaume and Bonnemaison's geographic definition of the South Pacific which excludes Australia and New Zealand, is the one shared by the actors of the South Pacific, as demonstrated by the composition of the Pacific Islands Forum (PIF). The South Pacific is itself divided into three cultural ensembles: Melanesia, Micronesia and Polynesia.[4] Moreover, Nathalie Mrgudovic defines the PICs as the states of the South Pacific, Australia and New Zealand excluded, which can be independent or not, corresponding to small archipelagos with specific political and judicial regimes (2008, p. 34).

More recently, Australian as well as French policy-makers have increasingly relied on the geographic concept of an Indo-Pacific region in order

16   P. SOYEZ

to build their strategic narratives. This new trans-regional ensemble encompasses the Indian Ocean, South East Asia and the South Pacific. This concept does not have a strong geographic coherence. What geographic commonalities would justify gathering within one ensemble the shores of Kenya alongside Tahiti? However, the Indo-Pacific space finds its coherence in the increasing interdependence of the Indian and Pacific Oceans, connected by common security issues and trade routes. This concept follows a new geopolitical approach which has been forged to support the ambitions of states, primarily Australia and France, which desire to link the defence of their interest in the Indian and Pacific Oceans within one strategic narrative supporting a new integrated regional foreign policy. Moreover, this concept also enables Australian policy-makers to promote a new space of which Australia constitutes the centre (Beeson 2014).

Overview of the Book

This book seeks to analyse the development of the French–Australian bilateral relationship since the end of the Cold War by conducting a method never before implemented on this topic, which will be presented in Chapter 2. This section introduces the theoretical research framework, which combines Joseph Nye's doctrine of "smart power" with a constructivist approach. The development of a genuine dialogue between French and Australian policy-makers requires the support of the constructivist theory because it deals with the question of their evolving mutual understanding, grounded in social, historical and cultural backgrounds. The theoretical framework also encompasses interpretative theories in order to study French and Australian diplomatic actors' perception of their policies. Chapter 2 introduces the methodology, based on the close reading analysis of hundreds of French and Australian archival documents and the conducting of interviews with experts in both countries. This section finishes with an examination of the existing academic literature pertaining to the topic and explains how this research fills an important gap in the bibliography pertaining to France and Australia. The outline which follows from this research combines thematic and chronological approaches.

The third chapter is dedicated to the analysis of the economic relationship developed by France and Australia since the end of the Cold War. This book argues that economic actors have been the primary protagonists of the French–Australian rapprochement, therefore economic aspects of the relationship must be studied before others. This section analyses the settlement of tensions between Paris and Canberra regarding agricultural free trade and the European CAP, which was one of the three prerequisites for the construction of the French–Australian strategic partnership. France and Australia currently agree on the norms which should underpin international trade. This book demonstrates the manner in which Australia's economic diplomacy has influenced French economic diplomacy, not only in terms of structures but also because Australia is one of the few countries chosen by French policy-makers to start implementing France's economic diplomacy. The attempt to develop innovative economic diplomacies has had a strong influence on the smart power strategies of France and Australia. Additionally, French–Australian economic cooperation is currently expanding, thanks to the support of both Paris and Canberra for an EU–Australia FTA, which this chapter also analyses.

Chapters 4 and 5 study the evolution of the French–Australian relationship with respect to their security strategies at a global level. In Chapter 4, the book investigates the ideologies and mechanisms behind French and Australian strategies pertaining to nuclear deterrence and armament. This research highlights their complete disagreement on this crucial aspect of global security. Chapter 4 is also dedicated to the analysis of French–Australian tensions regarding France's nuclear testing program in the South Pacific. This book argues that, while opposition to France's nuclear program represented a factor of regional integration in the South Pacific, Australian policy-makers also tried to become mediators between Paris and the PICs in order to protect both Canberra's global interests, through the Western alliance and Australia's regional leadership. This book also claims that the settlement of French–Australian tensions pertaining to nuclear deterrence constituted the second prerequisite to their strategic alignment, studied in Chapter 5.

After their economic interests, the pursuit of national and international security in response to shared global threats has been the second factor enabling French–Australian rapprochement. In the fifth chapter, this research provides an analysis of the global cooperation implemented by Canberra and Paris in order to secure their mutual interests. This book argues that, in order to coordinate both countries' security strategies, French and Australian policy-makers primarily had to develop what Karl Deutsch (1968) describes as a "we-feeling", defined as the reduction of their mutual misunderstanding and the alignment of their vision of the world thanks to a genuine strategic dialogue. Therefore, Chapter 5 also encompasses a study of the frames of dialogue which have enabled this rapprochement, such as Australia's presence as an elected member of the UN Security Council. Paris and Canberra have developed, since 2012, a genuine strategic partnership to secure their global interests against common threats, mainly the fight against terrorism. This alliance has been cemented by numerous armament contracts between the two countries, most recently Australia's purchase in 2016 of new submarines from the French company Naval Group (formerly called DCNS).

Chapters 6 and 7 investigate the logic underpinning the increasing French–Australian regional cooperation in the South Pacific, which combines hard and soft powers. As a third prerequisite for their rapprochement, France and Australia have had to arrive at a conciliatory position regarding France's management of its decolonising process in New Caledonia, which is studied in Chapter 6. This section critically analyses the extent to which New Caledonia has proven to be, at the same time, the source of vivid tensions between Canberra and Paris and the mirror of their own strategic ambiguities. This book offers an understanding that, more than being concerned about New Caledonia's future, both countries were mostly in disagreement with respect to their vision of sovereignty, political legitimacy and decolonisation. This analysis focuses on the very ambiguous positions of both France and Australia regarding the future of the archipelago, another manifestation of their regional awkwardness. This chapter also assesses thirty years of territorial innovations implemented by France since the Matignon-Oudinot Accords, which have provided more autonomy to New Caledonia, and the consequences of New Caledonia's referendum in 2018 on the French–Australian partnership. This book argues that the French–Australian tensions regarding New Caledonia represented a broader sense of competition between the two countries regarding Oceanian leadership.

Finally, the seventh chapter of this book analyses the mechanisms and ambitions which have motivated Australia and France to become significant partners for the security and development of the South Pacific in order to reinforce their own leadership and reduce their regional "awkwardness". This chapter also examines the regional contestations of this strategic partnership and the numerous levels of cooperation established by French and Australian policy-makers to convince the region to accept their influence. This section focuses on France's smart power strategy to strengthen its presence in the South Pacific, based on the elaboration of a new strategic narrative and the regional integration of its overseas territories. This analysis also investigates how Australia's regional interests have increasingly converged with the French interests in order to protect Australia's regional leadership from the increasing presence of new powers in the South Pacific, especially China. This chapter presents an accurate assessment of the political and diplomatic benefits of French–Australian academic and military cooperation in the South Pacific and the manner in which this cooperation provides a model for their shared actions in the Indian Ocean. Such rationales enable France and Australia to develop a close strategy for the Indo-Pacific region as a whole. Chapter 8 concludes this book by providing the main answers to its research questions and proving how, on each issue presented above, France and Australia have tried to implement smart power strategies in order to maintain their global and regional influence, through their bilateral empowerment and their multilateral engagements.

Notes

1. From a French point of view, the concept of Americanisation commonly refers to the increasing influence of American cultural, social and economic practices and norms onto the French society, enabled by the United States' status of hyperpower and its economic leadership. However, as Jean-Marie Guéhenno explains, "this Americanization/globalization is also a severe shock to historical, memory-based communities and it is fragmenting societies" (1999, p. 7).
2. The rise of an international civil society and its consequences on International Relations has especially been analysed by Alejandro Colás in *International Civil Society, Social Movements in World Politics* (2002).
3. France's *Outre-mer* is comprised of French Guyana in South America; Saint-Pierre and Miquelon off the shores of Canada; the archipelagos of Guadeloupe, Martinique, Saint-Martin and Saint-Barthélemy in the Caribbean; Mayotte and La Réunion in the Indian Ocean, the *Terres Australes and Antarctiques Françaises* in the Antarctic Ocean; New Caledonia, French Polynesia and Wallis and Futuna in the Pacific Ocean. See http://www.outre-mer.gouv.fr/les-territoires.
4. According to Antheaume and Bonnemaison (1988, p. 113), Melanesia is comprised of Papua New Guinea (PNG), the Solomon Islands, Fiji, Vanuatu and New Caledonia. Micronesia encompasses the Federated States of Micronesia, the Northern Mariana Islands, Guam, Palau, Kiribati

and Nauru. Polynesia is composed of the Cook Islands, Samoa, American Samoa, Tonga, Tuvalu, Niue, Pitcairn, French Polynesia and Wallis and Futuna.

REFERENCES

Archives Nationales, Pierrefitte, France.

National Archives of Australia, Canberra, Australia.

Antheaume, B & Bonnemaison, J 1988, *Atlas des îles des États du Pacifique Sud*, GIP Reclus/Publisud, Paris.

Beeson, M 2014, 'The Rise of the Indo-Pacific', *The Conversation*, 3 May, viewed 30 October 2017, http://theconversation.com/the-rise-of-the-indo-pacific-26271.

Beeson, M & Hameiri, S 2017, *Navigating the New International Disorder, Australia in World Affairs 2011–2015*, Oxford Press, Oxford.

Blainey, G 1983, *The Tyranny of Distance*, Sun Books, Sydney.

Brenner, N 1999, 'Globalisation as Reterritorialization: The Re-scaling of Urban Governance in the European Union', *Urban Studies*, vol. 36, no. 3, pp. 431–451.

Brown, A 2010, 'The Gorbachev Revolution and the End of the Cold War', in MP Leffler & OA Westad (eds), *The Cambridge History of the Cold War, Endings*, Vol III, Cambridge University Press, Cambridge, pp. 244–266.

Davison, R & Khan, S 2014, 'ANZUS and the Rise of China', in D Baldino, A Carr & AJ Langlois (eds), *Australian Foreign Policy, Controversies and Debates*, Oxford University Press, Oxford, pp. 136–154.

De Montbrial, T & Gomart, T 2017, *Notre intérêt national, quelle politique étrangère pour la France?* Odile Jacob, Paris.

Deutsch, K 1968, *The Analysis of International Relations*, Prentice Hall International, Englewood Cliffs.

Di Méo, G 1996, *Les territoires du quotidien*, L'Harmattan, Paris.

Farge, A 2002, 'Penser et définir l'événement en histoire. Approche des situations et des acteurs sociaux', *Terrain*, vol. 38, pp. 69–78.

Frank, R, Haba, K & Momose, H 2009, *The End of the Cold War and the Regional Integration*, Aoyama Gakuin University Press, Tokyo.

Guéhenno, J-M 1999, 'Américanisation du monde ou mondialisation de l'Amérique?' *Politique Étrangère*, vol. 64, no. 1, pp. 7–20.

Langmore, J, Frydenberg, J & Parke, M 2014, 'The Liberal/Labor Tradition', in D Baldino, A Carr & AJ Langlois (eds), *Australian Foreign Policy, Controversies and Debates*, Oxford University Press, Oxford, pp. 19–38.

Lévy, J & Lussault, M 2009, *Dictionnaire de la géographie et de l'espace des sociétés*, Belin, Paris.

McDougall, D 2009, *Australian Foreign Relations, Entering the 21st Century*, Pearson, Sydney.

Mrgudovic, N 2008, *La France dans le Pacifique sud: les enjeux de la puissance*, L'Harmattan, Paris.

Murray, P, Warleigh-Lack, A & He, B 2014, 'Awkward States and Regional Organisations: The United Kingdom and Australia Compared', *Comparative European Politics*, vol. 12, no. 3, pp. 279–300.

Nederveen Pieterse, J 1994, 'Globalisation as Hybridization', *International Sociology*, vol. 9, no. 2, pp. 161–184.

Nye, JS 2011, *The Future of Power*, Public Affairs, New York.

Offenstadt, N 2006, *Les mots de l'historien*, Presses Universitaires du Mirail, Toulouse.

Perkins, DD & Zimmerman, MA 1995, 'Empowerment Theory, Research and Application', *American Journal of Community Psychology*, vol. 23, no. 5, pp. 569–579.

Piquet, M 2000, *Cold War in Warm Waters: Reflections on Australian and French Mutual Misunderstandings in the Pacific*, The University of Melbourne Press, Melbourne.

Védrine, H 2001, *France in an Age of Globalisation*, Brookings Institution Press, Washington.

White, H 2017, 'The United States or China: "We Don't Have to Choose"', in M Beeson & S Hameiri (eds), *Navigating the New International Disorder, Australia in World Affairs 2011–2015*, Oxford Press, Oxford, pp. 93–108.

CHAPTER 2

Methodological and Theoretical Frameworks

The study of Australian and French diplomacy, of the construction of their bilateral relationship and of their involvement in global affairs, has to be understood within the context of the current theoretical debates that shape the field of International Relations. Several theoretical interpretations of world policies are useful to this book, but "smart power", postmodern constructivism and interpretive theory seem to unmask the most pertinent answers to its research questions. Joseph Nye's doctrine of "smart power" and postmodern constructivism provide a framework for understanding the broad and global issues of this book. Interpretive theories form a relevant lens through which to understand the arguments and representations elaborated by the actors of foreign policy-making. However, this research is conducted following an approach that is equally empirical and theoretical.

THEORETICAL FRAMEWORK AND CONTRIBUTIONS TO IDEAS

Theorizing the Renewal of Power Relations Through a Constructivist Lens

Analysing the transformation of the French–Australian bilateral relationship primarily requires engaging with the crucial debates pertaining to the concept of power and its current transformations. When studying the interests and processes that have led French and Australian policy-makers

© The Author(s) 2019   23
P. Soyez, *Australia and France's Mutual Empowerment*,
Studies in Diplomacy and International Relations,
https://doi.org/10.1007/978-3-030-13449-5_2

to overcome decades of tensions in order to develop a genuine strategic partnership, Joseph Nye's doctrine of "smart power" diplomacy provides a relevant framework. This book demonstrates that France and Australia have acted as smart powers in their diplomatic efforts toward mutual engagement in order to protect their shared interests, whether they are global or situated in the Indo-Pacific region. In *The Future of Power*, Nye defines smart power as "the combination of the hard power of coercion and payment with the soft power of persuasion and attraction" (2011, p. xiii). According to Mai'a Davis Cross, "smart power can be redefined as the strategic and simultaneous use of coercion and co-option" (2011, p. 698). More precisely, actors of International Relations—whether they are official or not—implement smart power strategies when, depending on the context, they utilise military, economic, cultural and scientific tools in order to achieve an objective. Moreover, Joseph Nye explains that smart power strategies seek to achieve five goals. A strategy, defined as a drive "relating means to ends, and that requires clarity about goals (preferred outcomes), resources, and tactics", must answers five questions to correspond to smart power: (1) "what goals or outcomes are preferred?"; (2) "What resources are available and in which context?"; (3) "What are the positions and preferences of the targets of influence attempts?"; (4) "Which forms of power behaviour are most likely to succeed?" and (5) "What is the probability of success?" (Nye 2011, p. 208). This book demonstrates that the renewal of French and Australian diplomacies since the end of the Cold War, mirrored in the development of their bilateral strategic partnership, corresponds to the smart power doctrine on all five questions. Moreover, "any actor that aspires to enhance its position on the world stage has to build strategies around these news fundamentals of 'smartness'. [...] A final reason for the hunt for smart power today is that target populations have become 'smarter'" (Wilson 2008, p. 113). In their ongoing effort to improve and modernize their foreign policy, France and Australia have been engaged in a process of assessment of their diplomatic, economic and cultural tools in order to increase their influence and support their interests. Then, both countries have sought to develop new partnerships with nations sharing common interests and a common vision of global security which benefits from complementary resources. This study argues and demonstrates that the construction of the French–Australian partnership follows this 'smart' strategy. "Achieving smart power requires artfully combining conceptual, institutional, and political elements into a reform movement capable of sustaining foreign policy innovation into the future" (Wilson 2008, p. 120). This research analyses France's and Australia's joint reform movement.

This study of the transformation of the Australian-French bilateral relationship demonstrates the limitations of the realist approach to middle powers' diplomatic strategies. This book demonstrates that the development of the French–Australian Strategic Partnership is a positive evolution; more complex than a "diplomatic transformation" as defined by Nicholas J. Wheeler: "a process in which two adversaries go through a series of steps of de-escalation which progressively reduce the role that the threat or the use of force plays in their relationship" (2013, p. 479). The complex logics driving this evolution are explored here.

The deep rapprochement that Paris and Canberra have implemented at a fast pace since 2012 should not be limited to a rationalist and conjunctural security strategy in the Indo-Pacific region. This study has revealed the importance of the current security, diplomatic and economic shifts in the Indo-Pacific region, in particular in the South Pacific. Paris and Canberra's mutual empowerment does not constitute simply the least dangerous strategy to reach security for both powers, nor does not only mitigate past tensions between France and Australia, whether they pertained to international trade regulation, nuclear strategy or sovereignty. The recent French–Australian mutual empowerment has necessitated a global reconceptualisation of France and Australia's presence, role and identity in the Indo-Pacific, encompassing the vast diversity of French and Australian actors of their Pacific presence. These actors, increasingly interconnected, pursue different interests. Therefore, French and Australian policy makers have had to develop new political and identity narratives encompassing all these dimensions in order to reassert together their country's legitimacy and role in the region. This long, complex and ongoing intellectual process goes much further than a realist, short term diplomatic move in order to reduce a potential threat. This diplomatic shift has been difficult to implement individually and in cooperation, firstly because of the sources of tension analysed in this book but also because of the profound misunderstanding affecting French and Australian policy-makers' judgement.

The strategic, intellectual, identity-related, legitimising and mutual empowerment implemented by Paris and Canberra must be analysed through the smart power doctrine because of its englobing dimension. This process is firstly based on increasingly diverse French and Australian communities in the Indo-Pacific region, smartly interconnected between themselves but also within a globalised public opinion. Smart power goes further than a realist approach to states' strategies because it requires an innovative and inclusive reconceptualization of the state's identity, legitimacy, objectives, social components and tools, as demonstrated by France's institutional process in New Caledonia. A French–Australian smart mutual empowerment capitalises on the social dynamics and interactions of the French and Australian communities in the Indo-Pacific.

Consequently, this book goes further than Booth and Wheeler's concept of the security dilemma sensibility (2008) because it does not limit itself to security strategies; it extends the study of the transformation of conflict into cooperation to include identity, in all its components. In fact, this study starts following Wheeler's definition of the diplomatic transformation and of its three stages. It also acknowledges Wheeler's useful studies of the importance of the interpersonal level in trust-building between states (2013). In *Investigating diplomatic transformations*, Wheeler asserts that "a key precondition for the growth of trust at the 'highest level' of diplomacy is a capacity to empathize with the other side's security fears and motivations, [...] the 'security dilemma sensibility'" (2013, p. 478). This study supports this assertion but goes further. While Wheeler claims that trust can exist between policy-makers but not communities (who would simply 'cooperate') (2013, p. 480), this book proves the contrary. While highlighting that interpersonal links between French and Australian policy-makers have played a crucial role in improving the bilateral relationship by enabling these leaders to walk away from their mutual misconceptions, this book argues that this empathy "at the highest level" was only possible because of the primary improvement of the French–Australian people-to-people relationships. These inter-community relationships opened the way and forced officials to empathise. In summary, the renewal of the French–Australian bilateral relationship has gone beyond a "de-escalation" from conflicts as described by Wheeler, to an inclusive, smart and mutual empowerment.

Moreover, according to Arnold Wolfers, power has two goals. The first one, which he calls "possession goal", pushes an actor to use and increase its power to reach a tangible objective, such as taking possession of resources. The second goal of power is a "milieu goal", which, according to Wolfers, is intangible and structural. The milieu goal pushes states to create an international environment that will suit their national interests, where other states will work, consciously or not, for another states' objectives. This contextual and structural objective is a fundamental component of power (Wolfers 1962, pp. 73–77). Therefore, by conducting smart power diplomacies in the Indo-Pacific region, Australian and French policy-makers have implemented a strategy analysed by Wolfers as the pursuit of "milieu goals".

Even if the constructivist approach to International Relations may not be as broadly accepted as the realist approach, this theoretical corpus has developed an understanding of the world that is quite relevant to the study of Australian and French diplomacies and their interactions. German scholar Alexander Wendt is considered the key actor of this theoretical current. His article 'Anarchy is what States make of it: the social construction of power politics' (1992) was the first statement of his position, which was developed further in 1999 in *Social Theory of International Politics* (1999). Wendt argues that, even if the world is characterised by a global anarchy and states constitute the fundamental units of International Relations, this anarchy has been socially constructed and should not be considered an inherent feature of human nature. Therefore, policies can deeply impact this international anarchy. The constructivist approach has not been developed in total opposition to previous theories, especially with relation to realist theories, since both constructivists and realists recognise that the international system is characterised by an anarchical dynamic in which states, recognised in both approaches as the fundamental unit of the system, have to interact. This book will establish that the evolution of the French–Australian bilateral relationship must be analysed through a constructivist lens because its mechanisms have been deeply impacted not only by conjectural interest but also by cultural and identity-related elements. The ways in which Australia and France culturally understand the world and international relations have become more similar since the end of the Cold War. This book argues that this intellectual coming together was the primary enabler of the development of their strategic partnership, to a greater degree than merely shared security interests.

Although Wendt was the first systematic definer of constructivist theories, such theories find their roots in the work of Karl Deutsch's theory of national identity in International Relations (1968). Deutsch's approach to national identities is crucial to this book because his theory provides a useful framework for understanding the processes that have enabled French and Australian policy-makers to improve their personal relationships in order to enhance their countries' bilateral diplomacy.

Deutsch argued that states gather around 'plural security communities', alliances between several independent entities that share the same issues of security and believe that international agreements can peacefully resolve international conflicts. According to Deutsch, in order to build a plural security community, states need three key factors: they must have the capacity to predict each other's position, they have to trust each other—the 'we-feeling'—and their elites must have compatible fundamental values. National identities are a crucial component of the creation of such communities and have played a tangible role in the tumultuous improvement of the French–Australian bilateral relationship.

Constructivist theories are also relevant for this topic because they enable the researcher to consider a range of factors broader than the state's quest for power and security. In their article analysing constructivism's progressive elaboration (2010), Nik Hynek and Andrea Teti insist on the fact that constructivists' theories have developed an approach to International Relations focused not only on the study of material reality but also on the representations of that reality, since constructivists argue that Truth is not discovered but created. Such an approach is useful since this research analyses the mutual misperceptions of Australian and French diplomats for the purpose of understanding how these representations have had a strong impact on the mutual relationship between the two countries. In the same vein, French philosopher René Girard argued that powers are primarily "mental powers": the ability "to inspire the dreams and desires of others", through vectors such as the cinema, the television or educational exchanges (Védrine 2001, pp. 2–3). The constructivist approach followed by this book comes from the belief, as Védrine explains, that diplomatic policies take into account: "national mentalities, history, zones of influence, established relations, military links, language, habits and cultures" (2001, p. 79). Such a position is crucial in this book's comprehension of Australian and French diplomacies at a global level.

At a lower level, in order to study the mutual perceptions that Australian and French diplomats have of their diplomacies, this book uses the framework of interpretive theories from political sciences. This corpus has been developed in the last decade and stresses the importance of representations in policy-making and debates. Interpretivists aim to unveil new political issues: the language, perceptions and symbols used by policy-makers in their decision-making processes. This approach's methodology is principally based on observations of the actors' representations. It focuses more on the political process than on its outcome. British political theorist Alan Finlayson clearly explains the basis of interpretive theory in 'From Belief to Argument: Interpretive Methodology and Rhetorical Political Analysis' (2007). Finlayson outlines the construction of his approach and asserts that "since politics involve the contest of ideas, beliefs and meanings, analysis should focus on arguments", using a "Rhetorical Political Analysis". Such analysis is central to this research, which examines the explanations that French and Australian actors have elaborated for their diplomacy in the last thirty years. The research questions investigate the mutual understanding, ambitions, and interests of Australian and French policy-makers, whether they have been politicians or government officials. This book thereby forges a clear analysis of the arguments developed by actors of Australian and French diplomacy to institute and then defend their intervention in foreign policies. The study of these arguments also enables the investigation of how French and Australian diplomats have communicated their actions and, through their arguments, which elements they have perceived as key issues. Political theorists frequently debate whether structures or agencies are more relevant to the comprehension of policy-making. Interpretivists take a position in favour of a shift from the study of political processes to a focus on political agents, their individual achievements, roles and understandings. The interpretive study of political traditions has been explained in depth by Mark Bevir and Roderick Rhodes in their article 'Interpretivism and the Analysis of Traditions and Practices' (2012), where they analyse the ambiguous relationship between policy-makers and political traditions. Moreover, interpretive theories have largely questioned the concept and construction of political tradition, a fruitful approach to this analysis of the diplomatic renewal between Canberra and Paris within their bilateral relationship. This research argues that the strategic partnership between Australia and France has been possible because policy-makers of both countries realised that, in order to face the extraordinary challenges of our current world, they needed to depart from their diplomatic traditions in order to look for new partners and forge new alliances.

Reconciling Political Science and History

This book has adopted this theoretical framework because it provides a pertinent support for analysing some key aspects of the research topic.

However, there are certain limitations to these intellectual approaches. Therefore, due to this study's multidisciplinary approach at the intersections of Political Science and History, it must also keep some distance from this theoretical framework. If theories of Political Science can be useful in order to understand diplomatic trends, an historical approach will help us avoid drawing any predictive conclusion on the future of the French–Australian bilateral relationship, since no theory can predict the future with intellectual honesty.

Therefore, this book acknowledges the following limits to its theoretical framework. The first involves the pioneering work of sociologist Saskia Sassen on globalisation processes. Sassen argues that most theorists of International Relations, by focusing so much on inter-state relations, do not always adapt their theories to a twenty-first century world characterised by an increasing diversity of actors. According to Sassen, such theories of International Relations do not sufficiently incorporate the growing actors and vectors of the expanding "domain of global politics". Her example regarding the way that transnational migrants are becoming increasingly important actors in global politics is striking and is clearly reflected in Australian and French political contexts at the moment. This is what Sassen gathers together within the concept of "denationalisation" inherent to globalisation: "the global, whether an institution, a process, a discursive practice, or an imaginary concept, both transcends the exclusive framing of national state, and also partly emerges and operates within that framing" (2011). This does not lead to the elimination of the national level but rather to its restructuring. The diversity of actors and vectors involved in Australian and French diplomacies has been of constant interest during the research process of this book and, except for Joseph Nye and his doctrine of "smart power", most political theories do not fully encompass the diversity of actors in International Relations. In fact, this book's corpus of primary sources reveals the involvement, or at least the attempted involvement, in foreign policy making, of a very large variety of actors, both operating at an infra-national level, such as regions, cities, churches, unions, universities and scholars, political activists and individuals from the civil society, or at a supra-national one involving many international institutions, companies and non-governmental organisations (NGOs). For this reason, this book investigates, empirically as well as theoretically, these actors and vectors of Australian and French diplomacies using, as explained above, interpretive theories dedicated in part to this increasing diversity of actors in policy decision-making.

Identifying a second limitation of International Relations theories, this book argues that such understandings of the world, by often claiming to be removed from the empirical aspects of their topic in order to build a logical theory, often marginalise extremely important elements of their objects of analysis. This opinion has been forged coming from an academic background in historical studies. A good example of this limitation can be found in Alexander Wendt's article 'Why a World State Is Inevitable' (2003). Wendt begins his argument, which explains the logical creation of a global government, by notifying the reader: "I am not concerned here with historical contingencies or timing. [...] Instead, I am concerned with the macro-structure of all pathways". Even if Wendt's ideal theory is extremely provocative, one must question the relevance of a theory which would have to exclude empirical elements, "historical contingencies", in order to be logical and accurate. Such an approach is hindered by a certain determinism, since it excludes the relevant facts that could undermine the theory in order to prove its accuracy. This criticism is as applicable to other International Relations theorists as it is to Wendt and other constructivists. This does not lead to a complete challenge to constructivist theories nor does it deny their value for this book. The development of any theory requires a certain distance from facts and events, because one can always find a historical element that might refute any given theory. However, it seems possible to think that many of these nearly ideal theories, despite the fact that they contain relevant and thought-provoking elements, have to be considered and adopted with caution since the foreign policies they analyse are conducted by actors, with their own individuality, logics and perceptions of the world, and through vectors which are socially constructed and thus continually evolving. The empirical dimension of the topic is consequently of fundamental importance, as demonstrated by post-modern historiographical studies since the middle of the twentieth century, notably under the influence of Michel Foucault and Jacques Derrida.

However, in his article "Metaphor in Science" (1979), Thomas Kuhn's analysis of physical and social realities enables research to overcome this opposition between theoretical and empirical realities. Kuhn argues that socially constructed worlds exist and co-exist with a real material world, without ontologically hindering it. Therefore, it is possible to study a topic both using empirical assessment of primary sources and secondary literature and, when relevant, through the lens of our theoretical framework. Moreover, the postmodern conclusion on the existence not of only one Truth but rather of several socially constructed truths reinforces the desire to compare the constructivist theoretical truth about the topic to the material truth constituted by primary and secondary sources. More precisely, according to theorist John Ruggie (1998), a "post-modernist constructivism" can exist because constructivist International Relations studies can be scientific, a point of view also defended by Jeffrey Checkel's "conventional" constructivism, which reconciles social sciences and constructivism (1998). This compatibility, which was largely contradictory to the idealist constructivism as expressed by Wendt, who now accepts it as a "thin" scientific social constructivism, is extremely important for this research since it legitimises the use of constructivist theories along with scientific and postmodern close readings of the sources. A new generation of constructivist authors, represented by Peter and Ernst Haas (2002) or Wesley Widmaier (2004), supports this idea, under the label of "practical constructivism" or "pragmatist constructivism".

Finally, this caution about theoretical approaches has been reinforced during the research process by the interviews and studies of actors' memoirs. Theories offer a reading of diplomatic actions when the actors themselves are cautious to refer to these theories and often do not want to see their actions labelled accordingly. It is even by referring to the Weberian understanding of "ethics" that Védrine resolves the debate between theory and empirical pragmatism, more precisely between realism and morals. Max Weber distinguishes two types of ethics, the 'ethic of conviction' and the 'ethic of responsibility', the need of moral values to guide political actions and the necessity to be pragmatic in calculating the effects of these policies. As Weber explains, political education must teach how to reconcile these two ethics in the decision-making process (Swedberg and Agevall 2005, p. 90).

This research is conducted equally following empirical and theoretical approaches. Postmodern constructivist theories provide the book with relevant readings of the topic's global issues, such as Joseph Nye's definition of smart power strategies, while interpretive theories frame the analysis of the actors' representations and arguments. However, these theories have some limitations that oblige the researcher to conduct his research not only with a theoretical framework but also by using empirical methods.

Methodology and Presentation of the Sources

Archives Analysis

The first methodological step of this research required a systematic analysis of archives. More than a year has been dedicated to the investigation of the following primary sources: archives, official statements, newspapers, other academic and journalistic commentary and surveys of public opinion. The research process began with the gathering of relevant data which has enabled this book to be constructed scientifically on an accurate and legitimate basis. This task has necessitated a review of a vast collection of archives with relevance to the research questions, both in France and in Australia. The complete lists of archives and primary sources studied or requested for the research is presented in Appendix. These archives provide a clear understanding of Australian and French policy-making processes. In fact, they constitute crucial resources for understanding the reality of Australian and French diplomacies, their ambitions, methods and achievements. The study of diplomatic archives is an essential task for capturing and comprehending the perceptions of France and Australia, along with their understanding and occasional support of each other's diplomatic actions on a regional and global scale.

This book is based on the analysis of more than a thousand documents in various French archives collections, from both the French National Archives (AN) and the Archives of the Quai d'Orsay (AD). Within the archives of the French Ministry of Foreign Affairs, documents related to Australia have been studied in the following collections:

- Central Office, Australia
- Permanent Mission of France to the United Nations, New York
- Permanent Mission of France to the United Nations, Geneva
- Permanent Mission of France to the Secretariat of the Pacific Community
- Permanent Mission of France to the Economic and Social Commission for Asia and the Pacific (ESCAP)
- Consulate of France Melbourne.

The French National Archives encompass many collections relevant to Australia's diplomacy and the French–Australian relationship. Archives of the Minister of French Overseas Territories have been studied in the following collections:

- Minister's cabinet, 1986–1988
- Minister's cabinet, 1988–1993
- Minister's cabinet, 1981–1995
- Minister's cabinet, 1997–2000
- Office of Political Affairs of the Ministry.

The French National Archives have also allowed access for this doctoral research to the archives of the French Prime Ministers related to Australia:

- Prime Minister's cabinet, 1988–1991
- Prime Minister's cabinet, 1991–1993
- Prime Minister's cabinet, 1992–1995
- Prime Minister's cabinet, 1995–1997
- Prime Minister's cabinet, 1997–2002.

Finally, former French Prime Minister Michel Rocard, whose engagement in the Pacific was significant, as this book demonstrates, allowed access to his personal archives for this doctoral research. These documents are located in the French National Archives and were produced when Michel Rocard was Prime Minister and later when he became a member of the European Parliament, where he was deeply involved in the EU's diplomacy with the Asia-Pacific region.

The Australian archives analysed for this research are curated by the National Archives of Australia (NAA) and are located in Canberra and in Melbourne. This book relies on the study of the following collections:

- Series M2391, Inward correspondence to Mr. Evans as Minister for Foreign Affairs and Trade, 1971–1989
- Series M3793, Papers relating to overseas visits, 1960–1988
- Series M3179, Papers relating to Mr. Evans' overseas visits, 1972–1999
- Series M3856, Overseas visits, background notes, letters of thanks, transcripts of speeches 1983–1991
- Series A9737, Correspondence, 1925–1992
- Series M3571, Foreign Affairs and Defence papers, 1983–1991

2 METHODOLOGICAL AND THEORETICAL FRAMEWORKS   35

- Series AWM260, Peacekeeping operation, miscellaneous records 1949–1988 (Australian War Memorial).

All these collections of archives have been extremely useful due to the wealth of information they encompass. Their relevance with respect to the topic comes primarily from the diversity of documents that have been studied for this book. In fact, the analysed documents are most frequently diplomatic cables, a various range of reports (sometimes very confidential), media releases, minutes, conversation transcripts and memoranda. These primary sources were mainly produced between 1985 and 1995. Due to the fact that Australian and French archives are unavailable for research purposes if they are less than twenty-five or twenty years old, the study of the post-1995 period has been based upon interviews, official sources and secondary sources.

This corpus of archives has been especially useful in order to understand particular aspects of the French–Australian relationship. It enables the reader to grasp how Australia and France tried to analyse how they were mutually advancing their interests and conducting their diplomacy, alternating between multilateralism and bilateralism. Paris and Canberra consistently studied the approach that the other country was trying to follow. This constitutes a very useful insight into their diplomatic methods. Therefore, these archives bring remarkable information about French and Australian involvement in several multilateral institutions, such as the ASEAN, the APEC, the PIF, the Secretariat of the Pacific Community (SPC) currently called the Pacific Community (PC), the Economic and Social Commission for Asia and the Pacific (ESCAP) and of course above all the United Nations (UN). Additionally, these sources highlight the strong competition existing between these institutions and how France and Australia tried to leverage them and the conflict between them for their own national interests.

The analysis of primary sources has also included official speeches and publications, for instance white papers and reports by French and Australian parliamentary foreign affairs committees (Commissions des Affaires étrangères 1995, 1997 and 2017). An extensive source of this information is the Australian, French and Pacific media archives. By examining these documents, this book has been able to determine whether Australian and French official statements, either oral or written, correspond to internal debates amongst policy-makers on their countries' interests. By using the same close reading methodology of the content and language of these documents as was applied to the archives, the reader can study how French and Australian actors explain their respective foreign policies.

Expert Interviews

The second step of the research has required fifteen interviews of some the main actors of the French–Australian bilateral relationship in the last ten years. More interviews have been conducted with anonymous policy-makers. These semi-structured interviews have been crucial to the book since access to archive collections is often restricted to documents produced more than twenty years ago. This methodological step has enabled the development of a clear vision of the actors' personal understandings, logics and decisions, in order to compare them to official statements and archival sources (Tables 2.1 and 2.2).

These crucial interviews have also enabled an understanding of French and Australian officials' mutual perceptions, as well as a comprehension of how policy-makers have made their decisions and on which information they based their actions. Interviewees have been asked questions regarding their country's foreign policy in general, the French–Australian bilateral relationship and their perception of their French/Australian counterparts.

Table 2.1 List of Australian interviewees

Interviewee	Position	Date and location
Mr. Gareth Evans AC QC	Former Australian Minister for Foreign Affairs	Melbourne, 13/04/16
Mr. Gary Quinlan AO	Former Australian Ambassador to the UN (2009–2015) and Deputy Secretary of DFAT	Melbourne, 17/04/15 and Melbourne, 12/09/16
Mr. Ric Wells	Former Australian Ambassador to France (2011–2014) and Deputy Secretary of DFAT	Canberra, 08/04/16
Mr. Stephen Brady AO CVO	Australian Ambassador to France (2014–)	Paris, 19/07/16 and Paris, 04/01/17
Mr. Daniel Sloper	First Assistant Secretary, Pacific Division, DFAT	Canberra, 31/03/17
Ms. Denise Fisher	Former Australian Consul-General to New Caledonia (2001–2004)	Canberra, 07/04/2016

2 METHODOLOGICAL AND THEORETICAL FRAMEWORKS 37

Table 2.2 List of French interviewees

Interviewee	Position	Date and location
Mr. Stéphane Romatet	Former French Ambassador to Australia (11–14) and Diplomatic Advisor to the PM	Paris, 21/06/16
Mr. Christian Lechervy	Permanent Secretary for Pacific Affairs, Representative to the PC and PREP	Paris, 22/12/16
Mr. Emmanuel Lenain	Director of Asia-Pacific Quai d'Orsay	Paris, 06/06/16
Mr. Cédric Prieto	Former Deputy Secretary at the French Embassy to Australia (2012–2016)	Canberra, 08/04/16
Ms. Myriam Boisbouvier-Wylie	Honorary Consul General of France in Victoria	Melbourne, 23/03/16
Mr. François Cotier	Director of Business France Australia	Melbourne, 27/04/16
Mr. Benoît Le Poittevin	Representative of Business France in Victoria	Melbourne, 27/04/16

FILLING A GAP IN THE RESEARCH ON THE FRENCH–AUSTRALIAN BILATERAL RELATIONSHIP

This book contributes to the field of International Relations by demonstrating how mutual empowerment is an innovative and effective tool for middle power diplomacies to strengthen their respective national interests in the current global context. The study of the evolution of the French–Australian relationship since the end of the Cold War testifies how two middle powers, one global and one regional, have found numerous shared interests and worked at adapting their strategies to strengthen their political, diplomatic and economic power, in particular by empowering each other in order to support their own ambitions.

Many scholars currently conducting research in International Relations tend to question the future of the global order created by the end of the Cold War. Are we witnessing a return to a multipolar world? Are multilateral institutions still useful and efficient or are current diplomatic policies deconstructing a multilateralism which would be in crisis? The interest over the future of the process of regionalisation takes part in this questioning, which remains vivid in every continent, from Europe to North and Central America and to the South Pacific. The book provides an example of strategic cooperation between two states aiming to secure their power in the context of redefinition of the global order. It demonstrates that France and Australia have increasingly engaged with each other, in particular since the creation of their Strategic Partnership in 2012, with the ambition of driving the ongoing regional integration of the South Pacific and to support their shared interests in the larger Indo-Pacific region.

Moreover, many specialists of International Relations challenge traditional and recent techniques of governance and the potential innovations that could be implemented to secure national interests. The definition of national interests themselves encompasses a large corpus of recent academic publications on foreign policy. After ten years of global economic crisis, which has reduced the amount of resources available to implement policies, which national interests should be prioritised? What have been the impacts of the global economic crisis on foreign policies? In addition, in a context of diversification of actors in International Relations, in particular with a larger involvement of multinational companies, the redefinition of the concept of national interest has become a key issue. The book contributes to the study of foreign policy-making by analysing how a global middle power diplomacy and a regional one have sought to modernise their diplomacy. They did so primarily by adapting the definition of their national interests, by engaging into a new partnership, the rapprochement of Canberra from Paris, and by developing new diplomatic tools, such as their economic diplomacy.

More broadly, as analysed previously, many researchers study the evolution of the concept of power, which has become a crucial topic of the academic literature on International Relations. These studies also question the concept of security, of its traditional components and of the rise of new threats created by new actors in International Relations. This leads researchers to study whether the new international order is characterised by the strengthening of the state or whether International Relations will be increasingly led independently of the state. This book argues that the development of a tangible French–Australian strategic partnership constitutes one of France and Australia's responses, by reinforcing the role and power of the state in conducting foreign policies in the Indo-Pacific region.

Finally, all these trends in the field of International Relations also pertain to a crucial question: what value can foreign policies bring to the world in the current global context? As this research demonstrates, French and Australian policy-makers are fully aware of the necessity for their countries to develop an innovative narrative on the regional and global value of their foreign policies, in order to address recurrent criticism of neo-colonialism. This effort aims to maintain their leadership in the Indo-Pacific region and, on a wider scale, to support their global strategy. Therefore, this book provides an analysis of how two middle power diplomacies collaborate to develop a new strategic narrative in order to legitimise their continuing regional leadership.

As it reflects the research questions framing this research, the relevant literature encompasses academic studies published in both English and French. However, it must be noted that French academic research pertaining to Australian diplomacy is characterised by its rarity. The same assessment can be made regarding Australian publications on French politics. In fact, such studies are noticeably limited, and consequently one of the core aims of this study has been to fill this lack of information in France and in Australia about both countries' diplomatic actions since the end of the Cold War, focusing especially on the processes that have led to the constitution of the current French–Australian partnership. Such a scarcity of studies related to the French–Australian relationship is not surprising, since the two countries have not historically been mutual key partners. Nonetheless, this topic has become more and more relevant due to the improvement of this relationship, Australia's significant diplomatic ambitions and France's current questioning of its power and strategic involvement in international relations.

However, this book is also based on a small number of available studies pertaining to Australia and France. Of the academic publications in French, Michel Bernard has written the only global history of Australia (1995). More importantly for this research, Xavier Pons (1988, 2000) and Fabrice Argounès have produced the few French diplomatic studies analysing Australia's diplomacy during the Cold War. Argounès' doctoral thesis (2011), analysing Australia's middle power through a realist lens, can be useful even though this book refutes its realist theoretical framework and argues that a constructivist approach is much more relevant for the understanding of Australia's foreign policy, especially in its dealings with France.[1] More recently, Martine Piquet has published through the University of Melbourne Press a small review describing French–Australian relations in the 1990s (2000). This work introduces some of the main issues structuring the relationship between the two countries but remains superficial due to its brevity, and furthermore her study ends in 2000.[2]

40   P. SOYEZ

In contrast, but logically, French scholars have authored more studies examining France's sovereignty over its territories in the Pacific and assessing French policies dealing with diplomatic issues in this part of the world. These studies have been extremely useful for the current research. Nathalie Mrgudovic and Sarah Mohamed-Gaillard are considered the key experts on this topic. With her engaging publication entitled *L'archipel de la puissance? La politique de la France dans le Pacifique Sud de 1946 à 1998* (2010b), Mohamed-Gaillard offers a unique insight into the logics and dynamics which have driven French policy-makers, diplomats and military officers in their actions in the South Pacific region. She also published an interesting but short journal article on French–Australian strategic relations in Oceania (2010a). In addition, Nathalie Mrgudovic has examined this question with her research gathered in *La France dans le Pacifique Sud: les enjeux de la puissance*. Isabelle Cordonnier's publication on French Pacific policies is also useful for this book (1995) such as Clémence Mallatrait's book on the relevance and importance of France presence in the South Pacific (2009). These analyses of France's strategies in the Pacific region partly refer to the French–Australian relationship, within their investigation of France's engagement with the main regional powers. However, none of them is dedicated solely to the French–Australian relationship. This is where this book fills an important gap. More recently, in December 2016, the Commission for Foreign Affairs of the French Senate issued a detailed inquiry on the current French–Australian strategic partnership, source of useful information for this research.[3]

A few Australian scholars have also dedicated very fruitful studies to France's presence in the Pacific. Denise Fisher's monograph *France in the South Pacific: Power and Politics* (2013) has been very useful for this research, including numerous articles on Pacific France and New Caledonia, where she was Australian Consul-General. Peter Brown, who, like Denise Fisher, has spent part of his career at the Australian National University (ANU) in Canberra, has authored a vast corpus pertaining to France in the Pacific, and to New Caledonia in particular. Even if most of Brown's publications belong more to French Studies than Political Science, this book relies upon some of his publications, for example his contribution on New Caledonia to Adler-Nissen and Pram's study of EU Overseas Countries and Territories (2013). In this last book, Holm and Poirine's chapters on French Polynesia have also been very useful (2013), along with Yoonah Choi's study of the impacts of European policies on the South Pacific through France's overseas territories (2007). David Chappell's article on the Noumea Accords has also provided a very interesting Australian point of view on the constitutional changes in New Caledonia and their regional repercussions (1999). In *Kanaky et/ou Nouvelle-Calédonie* (2005), Hamid Mokaddem offers the position of pro-independence Kanaks on this issue.[4] However, knowledge of France's diplomatic logic is still very limited in Australia and this book addresses this lack.

Many French studies have been dedicated to French nuclear testing in the Pacific and its consequences both on domestic politics as well as on French diplomacy. This part of the bibliography has been particularly valuable. After the last series of tests in 1995 imposed by President Chirac, the French National Assembly ordered a report on their effects on France's diplomatic relations with regional partners (1995). This document provides a unique insight into the information accessible to French policy-makers while also unveiling their anxiety about French–Australian relations. Because of its dominance in French foreign affairs, particularly immediately after the final nuclear testing, this issue has been the subject of numerous French academic publications. Although this book takes into account all the relevant articles listed in the bibliography, this study adopts the conclusions established in Pascal Boniface's accurate analyses of these events (1995). Moreover, Camille Grand (1997) and Dominique David (1995) have also illustrated this question accurately. In a more specific way, Grégory Derville (1996) has described the reactions provoked in Australia by the tests, whereas Marie-Thérèse and Bengt Danielsson have developed a global study about the topic (1993). A few studies in English exist about French nuclear testing. Alomes and Provis, in *French Worlds—Pacific Worlds, French Nuclear Testing in Australia's Backyard* (1998), gather ten contributing articles mainly by Australian scholars on this issue that poisoned French–Australian relations for decades.[5]

In order to put into perspective the Australian and French mutual understanding of their diplomacies and of their relationship, it has been important to analyse studies of French diplomacy as a whole. First of all, France, as a global middle power, claims to have its own model, different from any other world powers. This vision of its role based upon normative political theories, as well as this perception of the world and how countries should interact in this international order, are often identified as what French people call "*une certaine idée de la France*", "a certain idea of what

France is". Hubert Védrine, former French Foreign Minister between 1997 and 2002, who remains the main authority amongst French analysts of Paris's diplomacy, has clearly defined this vision in *France in an Age of Globalisation* (2001). More recently, Thierry de Montbrial and Thomas Gomart have assembled an extremely stimulating and fascinating book in which they asked almost twenty policy-makers and academics to address the question of France's diplomatic future (2017). In *Notre intérêt national, quelle politique étrangère pour la France?*, Gomart and de Montbrial assert that France needs to envision its diplomatic strategy less in terms of values and more in terms of interests. Their assessment of France's diplomatic ambitions has had a significant impact on this book. However, some excellent general studies exist, especially the one authored in 2017 by Pernille Rieker, who questions how France's *politique de grandeur* can still be relevant in the current international order.[6]

The corpus of publications in English about Australia's diplomacy in the last thirty years is obviously very large. Without claiming exhaustiveness, it is important to outline the main readings that have helped to structure this book. Geoffrey Blainey's "tyranny of distance" is a pertinent start to understanding the sensitive framework in which Australians are operating and their position in the world (1983). The idea of such "tyranny" has been updated and questioned by Allan Gyngell in *Fear of Abandonment* (2017), where Gyngell analyses Canberra's foreign policy since the end of World War II. In this inspiring analysis, Allan Gyngell demonstrates accurately how, since 1942, Australia's foreign policy has been driven by a fear of abandonment, a "rejection of isolation", urging Australia to engage with the world to secure its interests and values (2017, p. 363). This framework, further explained in the book, enables the research to focus on has been the manifest ambiguities presented by Australian foreign policies, which has led Philomena Murray, Alex Warleigh-Lack and Baogang He to claim that Australia can be characterised as an "awkward partner" (2014), rather than as a "middle power diplomacy", especially in regard to its regional partners. These academic and political debates have also been skilfully summarised and articulated regarding by Daniel Baldino, Andrew Carr and Anthony J Langlois in *Australian Foreign Policy, Controversies and Debates* (2014), a book which confronts opposing arguments on key issues of Australian politics and has been very fruitful to this research. The understanding of Australian policy-making actors, processes and tradition has also been developed in this book using Althaus, Bridgman and Davis's book

The Australian Policy Handbook (2013). Their study analyses deeply the national context in which Australian policy is made, the logics of its actors and institutions, its key issues and its methods of implementation.

Several global analyses of Australia's engagement in the international community since the end of the Cold War have provided an essential starting point for this dissertation. Stewart Firth has developed a remarkable synthesis of Australia's diplomatic engagement over the last decades (2011).[7] Gareth Evans's contribution to these global analyses of Australian foreign policies is also helpful, since his publication with Bruce Grant offers the understanding of someone who was one of Australia's main foreign policy-makers for many years (1995).[8] Equally, John Langmore and Philomena Murray's publications on Australian diplomacy present the insightful empirical approach of policy-makers, especially on the question of Australia's involvement in international governance. For example, Langmore evaluates Australia's diplomatic policies within the leading multilateral institution that is the United Nations, or Australia's positions in global economic and financial governance (2005, 2013). Philomena Murray's numerous contributions on EU–Australia relations enable one to understand the significant European dimension of the French–Australian relationship (Murray and Benvenuti 2014; Murray 2016). Derek McDougall has authored many excellent publications on Australian foreign policy. Singularly, he has elaborated a geographical approach in order to assess Australian diplomacy since the end of the Cold War. In fact, his main synthesis is divided into eight large regions of the world, where McDougall underlines Australia's engagement with these spaces (2009). Mark Beeson's contribution on Australia's foreign policy is crucial for comprehending the dynamic underlying these policies, and his arguments have been very fruitful for this book, especially *Navigating the New International Disorder, Australia in World Affairs, 2011–2015* (2017).[9] In his work, Greg Fry criticises Australia's diminishing involvement in the regional institutions of the Pacific, especially in the Forum of Pacific States (2015). According to Fry, Pacific States are no longer compelled to follow Australia's leading role in the region and now benefit from a wide variety of potential powers to protect them, especially China, whose involvement in the South Pacific is increasing. However, Australia, certain of its dominancy, has not realised that it is currently losing much of its influence in this region by reducing its participation in Pacific international organisations. Sandra Tarte's publications on regional involvement also provide fruitful reading (2004).

John Ravenhill's assessments of Australian foreign policies have been a crucial source for this book, not only because they accurately depict all aspects of Australia's diplomacy but they also provide the reader with precise data in order to form his own opinion (Ravenhill and Cotton 2007).[10] The alliance with the United States remains the main framework on which Australian security relies. Therefore, numerous studies have addressed the reasons and mutual interests of such a close partnership. However, many scholars, including Mark Beeson (2003), have started to criticise the American alliance, arguing that it serves American interests far more than Australia's, making the alliance deeply unequal. This book also studies the Australia-American alliance in a larger context, that of the United-States' new engagement in Asia, in order to evaluate what role Australia is playing in this renewed association. Jain Purnendra has studied the evolution of the partnership between Japan, the United-States and Australia and provides important reflection to consider for this work (2006). More globally, Craig Synder provides useful examinations of Australia's security interests and foreign policies (1998). Along these same lines, Jeffrey Richelson and Desmond Ball have investigated the intelligence partnership between Australia and the United States within the UKUSA Agreement. They develop a clear explanation of the mutual benefit for the two countries to share such a fundamental element of their security and provide the research with an accurate description of the global network (1985). Several monographs dedicated to the diplomatic leadership of the United States in the world provide fruitful descriptions of the American Power.

As this book demonstrates, policy-makers in Canberra increasingly assert that Australia's security, as well as economy, is involved as much with Asia as it is with America. Therefore, many scholars have examined the dynamics and realities of Australia's efforts to foster a closer relationship with its Asian partners. Michael Wesley presents one of the main references addressing this question in his book *The Howard Paradox* (2007). It seems that the academic world supports Australia's engagement with Asia much more than Australian politicians do, perhaps because policy-makers believe that Australia's public opinion would oppose a real diplomatic shift. John Ravenhill and Ian McAllister examine the assets and drawbacks of new partnerships with Asia and support this dynamic (1998), as does Hugh White in his very stimulating publications. White asserts for instance that Australia is now compelled by its strategic and economic interests to decide whether it will truly become closer to Asia. Australia's position between China and the United-States is no longer sustainable according to White (2010). These different positions on the potential deepening of Australia's strategic partnerships with Asian countries have been gathered by Richard Robinson, in the collection he has edited: *Pathways to Asia, the Politics of Engagement* (1996).

A different and interesting approach consists in studying the evolution of Australian foreign policy according to the ruling governments. Therefore, monographs dedicated to particular Australian governments must have a place in this literature review. For example, Andrew Carr and Chris Roberts have written the chapter dealing with foreign policies in a monograph about Kevin Rudd's government. Aulich and Evans (2010) also provide relevant questioning about Rudd's decisions regarding Australia as a "middle power diplomacy". The Howard years have been studied in several monographs, including the one edited by Robert Manne (2004), and Daniel Baldino has authored the chapter dedicated to foreign policies in Aulich and Wettenhall's publication about Howard's second and third governments (2005).[11]

Finally, the research leads to the questioning of Australia's changing identity, which is a challenging issue affected by Australia's ambiguous position between the West and Asia. David Walker has accurately described how Australia has built its nation through an anti-Asian logic (1999), a study also addressed by Paul Kelly's *End of Certainty* (1994). The investigation of Australia's fear of potential threats originating from Asia can be considered in regard to Joanna Bourke's theories around the notion of fear, both individual and collective. Bourke analyses the cultural construction of collective fears in our countries (2005). However, this book refers to Chengxin Pan (2002) in order to frame the questioning about the creation of a potential new Australian identity, which would incorporate the Asian components of Australia's society and therefore enable Australia to feel more part of a diverse Asian community. This modification of identity would then serve Australia's political, diplomatic and economic interests.

Conclusion

This study of the development of the French–Australian bilateral partnership is based on a methodology combining a close reading analysis of primary textual documents and expert interviews. These documents are understood through a theoretical lens encompassing "smart power", postmodern constructivism and interpretive theories. The textual and linguistic analysis of the relevant archives—ministerial reports, diplomatic cables, press reviews—has enabled an understanding of the techniques utilised by French and Australian diplomacies in dealing with their bilateral relationship, such as the main issues of their confrontations and partnerships. These documents provide useful information on the time period up to the middle to late-1990s. Political speeches and official publications from institutional actors are also helpful to this book. Expert interviews have been another extremely important stage of the methodology, because these meetings bring a unique approach to the logics of the bilateral relationship in the last 15 years and enable the comprehension of the mutual understanding that the actors of the relationship have developed through their experiences. These diverse sources, combined with a review of relevant literature, have enabled an analysis in depth, and with originality, of the most important issues concerning the evolutions of the French–Australian relationship, especially with respect to its economic component.

NOTES

1. Argounès has also published a broad introduction to Australia and its society (2006) and a limited article on Australia's strategy (2012). Both Pons and Argounès have also issued a number of interesting articles about the post-Cold War period. However, the main part of their work consists of studies of the evolution of Australian society during the Cold War or in the early 1990s. Although this book uses elements of their findings as a starting point, it develops a deeper and broader analysis of the topic, based on original French and Australian archives and interviews that to date no French scholar has studied or conducted.
2. As part of her social studies of former British Dominions, Piquet's main works have focused on Australia's ethnic diversity (2004) rather than on its diplomatic policies.
3. Another report issued by the French Senate contributes an internal political vision of France's economic involvement in the Pacific and of the regional strategies of Australia and New Zealand (1997).
4. Stephen Henningham is also very useful for this research, bringing a critical Australian perspective on France's diplomacy (1992) and more precisely, Australian governments' position regarding New Caledonia in the 1970s and 1980s (2017). With a similar way of addressing the topic, Robert Aldrich's work is also pertinent to this research (1994). Wayne MacCallum has also published articles on this question (1992), as has

2 METHODOLOGICAL AND THEORETICAL FRAMEWORKS 47

Nic Maclellan in numerous and accurate publications, very critical about French and Australian policies in the Pacific (Maclellan and Chesnaux 1998; Maclellan 2014a, b, 2015).

5. Complementary to Henningham's article on the topic (1996), Kim Richard Nossal and Carolynn Vivian have written a pertinent study about the testing (1997), in which they identify Australian criticism of French nuclear policy.

6. Frédéric Bozo's historical analysis of the discrepancy between France's global ambitions and its status of middle power has also been very useful (2012). Pascal Boniface (1998), who also founded the Institute of International and Strategic Relations, a reference think tank in France, has authored many studies on this French diplomatic tension, between the aim to remain a middle power with global reach and the ongoing idea of decline. This institute also produces an annual report on France's diplomatic activities in the previous year, which assembles very helpful information for fully understanding French diplomacy. Jean-François Eck's study of France's position in a globalised economy supplies another practical reading because Eck analyses the economic dimension of France's strategic choices (2006). Guillaume Le Quintrec has also published a short but beneficial general analysis of French diplomatic policies which enables us to have a broad understanding of diplomatic policies decided in Paris (1998).

7. This introduction remains a fundamental account for commencing a comprehensive study of the topic. Firth has authored numerous studies pertaining to Australian foreign policy and policy-makers that have been truly critical for unmasking the main issues that Australia has been facing in its international engagements, in regard to security, cooperation, economy or the participation of Australian diplomats in normative institutions such as the United Nations. His study on the regional aspect of Australia's migration policy is also valuable (2016).

8. Based on his personal experience and perspective, Evans accurately reveals the processes and methods of Australian foreign policy-making. Such a personal political vision on the topic can be compared to that of other former Ministers of Foreign Affairs, such as Alexander Downer's publications (2000, 2001, 2005), or scholars such as Michael Wesley and Tony Warren (2000). Therefore, Evans and Grant operate through an empirical approach to Australian foreign policies, invaluable for this research.

9. Beeson has also strongly criticised Australia's changing involvement in regional organisations and institutions in South-East Asia, which he describes as inconsistent and therefore not efficient enough to serve Australians interests (2008).

10. In their analysis *Trading on Alliance Security, Australia in the World Affairs 2001–2005* (2007), Ravenhill and Cotton frequently refer to

48   P. SOYEZ

surveys or empirical data, often adopting a quantitative approach. Thus, they represent a significant contribution to the literature for understanding either the logics followed by Australian policy-makers or the perception that Australians have of their country's diplomacy.

11. Two monographs have been fully dedicated to Australia's close engagement with the Unites States under the Howard governments. Robert Garran (2004) adopts a very critical point of view and reproaches Howard for having sacrificed Australia's diplomacy to the Bush administration's interests, for example during the intervention in Iraq in 2003. Former diplomat and specialist on the relationship between the United States and Australia, Alison Broinowski has the same critical vision of John Howard's foreign policy but tries to understand Howard's logic in his decision process (2003, 2007). Kim Beazley brings a clear insight into to foreign policy-making and processes under the Hawke government (2003).

REFERENCES

Aldrich, R 1994, *France and the South Pacific Since 1940*, Macmillan, London.

Alomes, S & Provis, M 1998, *French Worlds—Pacific Worlds, French Nuclear Testing in Australia's Backyard*, Two Rivers Press, Melbourne.

Althaus, C, Bridgman, P & Davis, G 2013, *The Australian Policy Handbook*, Allen & Unwin, Sydney.

Argounès, F 2006, *Géopolitique de l'Australie*, Complexe, Bruxelles.

Argounès, F 2011, 'L'Australie, entre puissance moyenne et puissance régionale : une analyse réaliste néoclassique', Thesis (Ph.D.), Université Bordeaux 4, Bordeaux, France.

Argounès, F 2012, 'L'Australie: la tentation de la puissance régionale', *Pouvoirs*, vol. 2, no. 141, pp. 103–116.

Baldino, D 2005, 'Australia and the World', in C Aulich & R Wettenhall (eds), *Howard's Second and Third Governments*, Australian National University Press, Canberra, pp. 189–207.

Baldino, D, Carr, A & Langlois, AJ 2014, *Australian Foreign Policy, Controversies and Debates*, Oxford University Press, Oxford.

Ball, D & Richelson, JT 1985, *The Ties That Bind*, Allen & Unwin, Sydney.

Beazley, K 2003, 'The Hawke Years: Foreign Affairs and Defence', in S Ryan & T Bramston (eds), *The Hawke Government, a Critical Retrospective*, Pluto Press, Melbourne, pp. 347–366.

Beeson, M 2003, 'Australia's Relationship with the United States: The Case for Greater Independence', *Australian Journal of Political Science*, vol. 38, no. 3, pp. 387–405.

Beeson, M 2008, *Institutions of the Asia-Pacific, ASEAN, APEC, and Beyond*, Routledge, London and New York.

Beeson, M & Hameiri, S 2017, *Navigating the New International Disorder, Australia in World Affairs, 2011–2015*, Oxford Press, Oxford.

Bernard, M 1995, *Histoire de l'Australie, de 1770 à nos jours, naissance d'une nation du Pacifique*, L'Harmattan, Paris.

Bevir, M & Rhodes, R 2012, 'Interpretivism and the Analysis of Traditions and Practices', *Critical Policy Studies*, vol. 6, no. 2, pp. 201–208.

Blainey, G 1983, *The Tyranny of Distance*, Sun Books, Sydney.

Boniface, P 1995, 'Dissuasion et non-prolifération : un équilibre difficile, nécessaire mais rompu', *Politique étrangère*, vol. 60, no. 3, pp. 707–721.

Boniface, P 1998, *La France est-elle encore une grande puissance?* Presses de Sciences Po, Paris.

Bourke, J 2005, *Fear, a cultural History*, Virago, London.

Bozo, F 2012, *La politique étrangère de la France depuis 1945*, Flammarion, Paris.

Broinowski, A 2003, *Howard's War*, Scribe, Melbourne.

Broinowski, A 2007, *Allied and Addicted*, Scribe, Melbourne.

Brown, P 2013, 'Negotiating Postcolonial Identities in the Shadow of the EU: New Caledonia', in R Adler-Nissen & UP Gad (eds), *European Integration and Postcolonial Sovereignty Games: The EU Overseas Countries and Territories*, Routledge, London, pp. 169–186.

Carr, A & Robert, C 2010, 'Foreign Policy', in C Aulich & M Evans (eds), *The Rudd Government*, Australian National University Press, Canberra, pp. 241–258.

Chappell, D 1999, 'The Noumea Accord: Decolonisation Without Independence in New Caledonia?', *Pacific Affairs*, vol. 72, no. 3, pp. 373–391.

Checkel, J 1998, 'The Constructivist Turns in International Relations Theory', *World Politics*, vol. 50, no. 2, pp. 324–348.

Choi, Y 2007, 'L'importance de l'Union européenne dans les territoires français du Pacifique', in *Pouvoir(s) et politique(s) en Océanie, actes du XIXe colloque CORAIL*, L'Harmattan, Paris, pp. 151–163.

Commissions des Affaires étrangères de l'Assemblée nationale 1995, *Rapport d'information sur les réactions internationales à la reprise par la France des essais nucléaires*, Assemblée nationale française, Paris.

Commissions des Affaires étrangères, de la Défense et des Forces armées du Senat français 1997, 'L'Australie et la Nouvelle-Zélande, têtes de pont de la présence française dans la région Asie-Pacifique?', *Rapport d'information no. 290*, Sénat français, Paris.

Commissions des Affaires étrangères du Sénat français 2017, 'Australie : le rôle de la France dans le nouveau monde', *Rapport d'information no. 222*, Sénat français, Paris.

Cordonnier, I 1995, *La France dans le Pacifique sud: approche géostratégique*, Publisud, Paris.

Danielsson, B & M-T 1993, *Mururoa, notre bombe coloniale: histoire de la colonisation nucléaire de la Polynésie française*, L'Harmattan, Paris.

David, D 1995, 'La France et le monde: inventaire après essais', *Études*, vol. 383, no. 6, pp. 581–590.

Davis Cross, MK 2011, 'Europe, a Smart Power?', *International Politics*, vol. 48, no. 6, pp. 691–706.

De Montbrial, T & Gomart, T 2017, *Notre intérêt national, quelle politique étrangère pour la France?* Odile Jacob, Paris.

Derville, G 1996, 'Quand la machine médiatique s'emballe', *Communication et langages*, vol. 109, no. 1, pp. 17–32.

Deutsch, K 1968, *The Analysis of International Relations*, Prentice Hall International, Englewood Cliffs.

Downer, A 2000, 'Australia's Global Agenda, Speech to French Institute of International Affairs', 31 January, viewed 1 August 2017, http://foreignminister.gov.au/speeches/2000/000131_aust_global_agenda.html.

Downer, A 2001, 'Australian Foreign Policy, a Liberal Perspective', *Australian Journal of International Affairs*, vol. 55, no. 3, pp. 337–341.

Downer, A 2005, 'Securing Australia's Interests: Australian Foreign Policy Priorities', *Australian Journal of International Affairs*, Canberra, vol. 59, no. 1, pp. 7–12.

Eck, J-F 2006, *La France dans la nouvelle économie mondiale*, Presses Universitaires de France, Paris.

Evans, G & Grant, B 1995, *Australia's Foreign Relations*, The University of Melbourne Press, Melbourne.

Finlayson, A 2007, 'From Belief to Argument: Interpretive Methodology and Rhetorical Political Analysis', *British Journal of Politic and International Relations*, vol. 9, no. 4, pp. 545–563.

Firth, S 2011, *Australia in International Politics*, Allen & Unwin, Sydney.

Fisher, D 2013, *France in the South Pacific: Power and Politics*, Australian National University Press, Canberra.

Fry, G 2015, 'Recapturing the Spirit of 1971: Toward a New Regional Political Settlement in the Pacific', *SSGM Discussion Paper*, vol. 3, Australian National University Press, Canberra, pp. 1–16.

Garran, R 2004, *True Believer, John Howard, George Bush & the American Alliance*, Allen & Unwin, Sydney.

Grand, C 1997, 'La diplomatie nucléaire du Président Chirac', *Relations internationales et stratégiques*, no. 25, pp. 157–169.

Gyngell, A 2017, *Fear of Abandonment*, Black Inc., Melbourne.

Haas, P & Haas, E 2002, 'Pragmatic Constructivism and the Study of International Institutions', *Millennium*, vol. 31, no. 3, pp. 573–602.

Henningham, S 1992, *France and the South Pacific: A Contemporary History*, Allen & Unwin, Sydney.

Henningham, S 1996, 'Testing Times: France's Underground Nuclear Tests and Its Relations with Asia-Pacific', *Modern and Contemporary France*, vol. 4, no. 1, pp. 81–92.

Henningham, S 2017, 'The Limits of Influence: Australia and the Future of New Caledonia, 1975 to 1988', *The Journal of Pacific History*, vol. 2, no. 4, pp. 482–500.

Holm, U 2013, 'French Concepts of State: Nation, *patrie*, and the Overseas', in R Adler-Nissen & UP Gad (eds), *European Integration and Postcolonial Sovereignty Games: The EU Overseas Countries and Territories*, Routledge, London, pp. 145–151.

Hynek, N & Teti, A 2010, 'Saving Identity from Postmodernism? The Normalisation of Constructivism in International Relations', *Contemporary Political Theory*, vol. 9, no. 2, pp. 171–199.

Kelly, P 1994, *The End of Certainty*, Allen & Unwin, Sydney.

Kuhn, T 1979, 'Metaphor in Science', in A Ortony (ed), *Metaphor and Thought*, Cambridge University Press, Cambridge, pp. 409–419.

Langmore, J 2005, *Dealing with America: The UN, the US and Australia*, University of New South Wales Press, Sydney.

Langmore, J 2013, 'Australia's Campaign for Security Council Membership', *Australian Journal of Political Science*, vol. 48, no. 1, pp. 101–111.

Le Quintrec, G 1998, *La France dans le monde depuis 1945*, Seuil, Paris.

Maclellan, N 2014a, 'François Hollande Says France Wants to Remain a Pacific Power: Is It Wishful Thinking?', *The Guardian*, 18 November, viewed 1 August 2017, https://www.theguardian.com/commentisfree/2014/nov/18/francois-hollande-says-france-wants-to-remain-a-pacific-power-is-it-wishful-thinking.

Maclellan, N 2014b, 'The Complicated Politics of a French Defence Treaty', *The Crickey*, 19 November, viewed August 2017, https://www.crikey.com.au/2014/11/19/the-complicated-politics-of-a-french-defence-treaty/.

Maclellan, N 2015, 'Transforming the Regional Architecture: New Players and Challenges for the Pacific Islands', *Asia Pacific Issues*, no. 118, pp. 1–8.

Maclellan, N & Chesnaux, J 1998, *La France dans le Pacifique, de Bougainville à Mururoa*, La Découverte, Paris.

Mallatrait, C 2009, *La France, puissance inattendue au XXIe siècle dans le Pacifique sud : éléments pour une approche géopolitique de l'Océanie*, L'Harmattan, Paris.

Manne, R 2004, *The Howard Years*, Black Inc. Agenda, Melbourne.

McAllister, I & Ravenhill, J 1998, 'Australian Attitudes Towards Closer Engagement with Asia', *The Pacific Review*, vol. 11, no. 1, pp. 119–141.

McCallum, W 1992, 'European Loyalist and Polynesian Political Dissent in New Caledonia: The Other Challenge to RPCR Orthodoxy', *Pacific Studies*, vol. 15, no. 3. pp. 39–40.

McDougall, D 2009, *Australian Foreign Relations, Entering the 21st Century*, Pearson, Sydney.

Mohamed-Gaillard, S 2010a, 'Les relations franco-australiennes en Océanie: représentations croisées de deux politiques régionales', *Outre-mers*, vol. 97, no. 366, pp. 123–133.

Mohamed-Gaillard, S 2010b, *L'archipel de la puissance? La politique de la France dans le Pacifique Sud de 1946 à 1998*, Peter Lang, Bruxelles.

Mokaddem, H 2005, *Kanaky et/ou Nouvelle-Calédonie*, Expressions, Marseille.

Murray, P 2016, 'EU–Australia Relations: A Strategic Partnership in All but Name', *Cambridge Review of International Affairs*, vol. 29, no. 1, pp. 171–191.

Murray, P & Benvenuti, A 2014, 'EU–Australia Relations at Fifty: Reassessing a Troubled Relationship', *Australian Journal of Politics and History*, vol. 60, no. 3, pp. 431–448.

Murray, P, Warleigh-Lack, A & He, B 2014, 'Awkward States and Regional Organisations: The United Kingdom and Australia Compared', *Comparative European Politics*, vol. 12, no. 3, pp. 279–300.

Nossal, KR & Vivian, C 1997, *A Brief Madness: Australia and the Resumption of French Nuclear Testing*, Australian National University Press, Canberra.

Nye, JS 2011, *The Future of Power*, Public Affairs, New York.

Pan, C 2002, 'A Case for Pragmatism and Self-Reflection in Australia's Asia Thinking and Engagement', *Australia in the Asian Century White Paper*, Department of Foreign Affairs and Trade, Canberra.

Piquet, M 2000, *Cold War in Warm Waters: Reflections on Australian and French Mutual Misunderstandings in the Pacific*, The University of Melbourne Press, Melbourne.

Piquet, M 2004, *Australie plurielle*, L'Harmattan, Paris.

Poirine, B 2013, 'Will the EU and the Euro Lead to More Sovereignty? French Polynesia', in R Adler-Nissen & UP Gad (eds), *European Integration and Postcolonial Sovereignty Games: The EU Overseas Countries and Territories*, Routledge, London, pp. 152–168.

Pons, X 1988, *Le géant du Pacifique*, Economic, Paris.

Pons, X 2000, *L'Australie, entre Occident et Orient*, La Documentation française, Paris.

Purnendra, J 2006, 'Japan-Australia Security Ties and the United States: The Evolution of the Trilateral Dialogue Process and Its Challenges', *Australian Journal of International Affairs*, vol. 60, no. 4, pp. 521–535.

Ravenhill, J & Cotton, J 2007, *Trading on Alliance Security, Australia in the World Affairs, 2001–2005*, Oxford Press, Oxford.

Robinson, R 1996, *Pathways to Asia, The Politics of Engagement*, Allen & Unwin, Sydney.

Ruggie, J 1998, 'What Makes the World Hang Together? Neo-utilitarianism and the Social Constructivist Challenge', *International Organization*, vol. 52, no. 4, pp. 855–885.

Sassen, S 2011, 'Sociology, Globalization, and the Re-shaping of the National', *Theory Talk #43*, 6 September, viewed 17 July 2017, http://www.theory-talks.org/2011/09/theory-talk-43.html.

Swedberg, R & Agevall, O 2005, *The Max Weber Dictionary*, Stanford University Press, Stanford.

Synder, CA 1998, 'Australia's Pursuit of Regional Security into the 21st Century', *Journal of Strategic Studies*, vol. 21, no. 4, pp. 1–17.

Tarte, S 2004, 'Regionalism and Changing Regional Order in the Pacific Islands', *Asia & the Pacific Policy Studies*, vol. 1, no. 2, pp. 312–324.

Védrine, H 2001, *France in an Age of Globalisation*, Brookings Institution Press, Washington.

Walker, D 1999, *Anxious Nation: Australia and the Rise of Asia 1850–1939*, The University of Queensland Press, Brisbane.

Wendt, A 1992, 'Anarchy Is What States Make of It: The Social Construction of Power Politics', *International Organization*, vol. 46, no. 2, pp. 391–425.

Wendt, A 1999, *Social Theory of International Politics*, Cambridge University Press, Cambridge.

Wendt, A 2003, 'Why a State World Is Inevitable', *European Journal of International Relations*, vol. 9, no. 4, pp. 491–542.

Wesley, M 2007, *The Howard Paradox, Australian Diplomacy in Asia, 1996–2006*, Australia Broadcast Corporation, Sydney.

Wesley, M & Warren, T 2000, 'Wild Colonial Ploys? Currents of Thought in Australian Foreign Policy', *Australian Journal of Political Science*, vol. 35, no. 1, pp. 9–18.

Wheeler, NJ 2013, 'Investigation Diplomatic Transformations', *International Affairs*, vol. 89, no. 2, pp. 477–496.

Wheeler, NJ & Booth, K 2008, *The Security Dilemma: Fear, Cooperation and Trust in World Politics*, Palgrave Macmillan, New York.

White, H 2010, 'Power Shift: Australia's Future Between Washington and Beijing', *Quaterly Essay*, vol. 39, pp. 1–74.

Widmaier, W 2004, 'Theory as a Factor and the Theorist as an Actor: The "Pragmatist Constructivist" Lessons of John Dewey and John Kenneth Galbraith', *International Studies Review*, vol. 6, no. 3, pp. 427–445.

Wilson, EJ 2008, 'Hard Power, Soft Power, Smart Power', *The Annals of the American Academic of Political and Social Sciences*, vol. 616, pp. 110–124.

Wolfers, A 1962, *Discord and Collaboration, Essays on International Politics*, The John Hopkins University Press, Baltimore.

CHAPTER 3

Economic Diplomacy, an Innovative Force of the French–Australian Relationship

Trade and investment have constituted, since the beginning of the French–Australian relationship, a core driving force of the political relationship between Paris and Canberra and of the people-to-people relationship between the two nations. Most importantly, when Australian and French policy-makers have cooperated to improve the French–Australian bilateral relationship despite decades of tensions and misunderstanding, economic interests have always been understood to be the most relevant aspect of this improvement and representative of both countries' soft power. Moreover, this study argues that, as a result of such issues, the intensification of the French–Australian relationship has acted as a leverage tool of modernisation for the two countries' own diplomatic strategies and practices. The importance placed by Canberra and Paris on the pursuit of economic interests illustrates the innovative impact of this partnership. In an effort to support their own countries' economies, French and Australian policy-makers and business stakeholders have had to modernise their understanding of what constitutes an economic diplomacy. Hence, both Ministries of Foreign Affairs have reformed their conception of actorship, of diplomatic goals, of decision-making processes and of institutional organisation.

This chapter critically analyses both Australia's and France's definitions and methods of implementation of the concept of economic diplomacy and the positive impact their economic diplomacy approaches have had on their bilateral relationship. It will also examine how

© The Author(s) 2019   55
P. Soyez, *Australia and France's Mutual Empowerment*,
Studies in Diplomacy and International Relations,
https://doi.org/10.1007/978-3-030-13449-5_3

56   P. SOYEZ

French–Australian trade and investment relations have been conceived, negotiated, framed and implemented, at the five levels of economic diplomacy: unilaterally, bilaterally, regionally, plurilaterally and multi-laterally (Bayne and Woolcock 2011, p. 8). Bayne and Woolcock consider that a diplomatic action is led plurilaterally within organisations comprised of a limited number of countries that are not from the same region, such as the G20 or the Organisation for Economic Co-operation and Development (OECD), and multilaterally with the involvement of most countries, like the World Trade Organisation (WTO). French and Australian policy-makers have used each of these levels of engagement for their own particular advantages. Furthermore, the current emphasis placed on foreign trade and investment in Australia and in France and which started for Paris under Nicolas Sarkozy's presidency, shows that policy-makers believe that a major element of growth lies in international trade in the context of globalisation, and that states must concentrate on fostering such economic interests.

This chapter commences by analysing how businesses and workers have been the primary actors in the intensification of the French–Australian bilateral relationship and have pushed their respective states to conduct institutional reforms in order to develop their economic diplomacies. Next, the analysis will consider the obstacles along with the solutions bilaterally implemented by Australia and France to strengthen their mutual trade and investment. This chapter will then demonstrate how the improvement of the French–Australian economic relationship has mainly been possible because Paris and Canberra found a solution to one of their major disputes: the liberalisation of agriculture trade. Finally, the relationship now benefits from a positive context originated from France's support for a free trade agreement (FTA) between Australia and the European Union (EU). This chapter examines both countries' real ambitions in this partnership.

The Economy: The Original Drive for the French–Australian Relationship

French and Australian economic actors have constituted, in the last decades, the primary pillars of their countries' bilateral relationship, for three reasons. Firstly, their mobility has led to the development of a significant French community in Australia and vice versa, which has forced Paris and Canberra to take a closer look at each other. Secondly, their economic interests have motivated French and Australian policy-makers to try and protect these commercial ties during political and strategic tensions. Finally, the promotion of French–Australian economic interests has informed the modernisation and structuring of both countries' economic diplomacies.

Economic Actors, Primary Stakeholders of the Improvement of the French–Australian Partnership

The significant improvement of the French–Australian relationship, from indifference and outright opposition to genuine trust and partnership, has been the positive outcome of the work of economic actors eager to develop trade relations between the two countries and who belong to two different categories: businessmen and young workers. In *The New Economic Diplomacy*, Bayne and Woolcock assert that business actors originally played a crucial role in implementing a diplomacy based on the economy. They outline the pioneering role of firms in developing new economic trade relations between countries: "In the past, business firms tended to comprise the most active interest group" (2011, p. 4). This has particularly been the case for the French–Australian relationship, which improved in the 2000s first for economic reasons, then due to political motivations. Rick Wells, former Australian ambassador to France and Deputy Secretary of the Department of Foreign Affairs and Trade (DFAT), accurately explains the improvement of the bilateral relationship by emphasising Australia's economic attractiveness: "France has always been very highly attuned to economic opportunities. The global financial crisis and the way that Australia emerged largely unscathed from that really made France realise that Australia was actually economically quite an interesting country where you could make money" (pers. inter., Canberra, 8 April 2016).

French diplomats confirm this commercial and financial motivation in fostering the French–Australian partnership. Stéphane Romatet, former French ambassador to Australia then Diplomacy Advisor to French Prime Minister Manuel Valls, explains that the mutual and ongoing hostile indifference between France and Australia fully disappeared at the end of the 1990s and in the early 2000s. He argues that this second phase in the bilateral relationship was characterised by France's progressive "discovery" of what Australia's realities, and vice versa (pers. inter.,

Paris, 21 June 2016). According to Romatet, economic actors drove this increased understanding to support their economic investments, without political considerations. For example, French companies were eager to benefit from Australia's considerable economic growth based on mineral resources and energy and that they became quite successful from the early 2000s. Consequently, in Australia, the French community became economically and culturally more visible and, in France, Australia's attractiveness rapidly increased to French students and young professionals, captivated by Australia's living conditions in a context of economic and political crisis in Europe.

Many actors in the French–Australian relationship comment on how important young French holiday-visa workers have been in forging a strong people-to-people relationship between the two countries. These young travellers have been attracted by Australia's highly efficient national branding, representing itself as a country of opportunities, young and dynamic, and where personal investment is highly rewarded. Myriam Boisbouvier-Wylie, Honorary Consul General of France in Melbourne since 2011, explains that an average of thirty thousand young French men and women a year come to Australia on a working-holiday visa, a very high number compared to other nationalities. In 2016 and 2017, this number decreased to twenty thousand but remains amongst the first three nationalities of working holiday visa holders (pers. inter., Melbourne, 23 March 2016). This growing flow has necessarily motivated the French Ministry of Foreign Affairs to have a closer look at Australia.[1] In 2016, as the former Australian ambassador to France Stephen Brady explains, Australia issued its 300,000th holiday-working visa to a French citizen, young French visa holders having been amongst the largest nationalities to benefit from this program (pers. inter., Paris, 19 July 2016). More importantly, the French business community has constituted a group of key actors in this bilateral relationship, with a more conscious aim of building up strong and long-lasting relations between France and Australia and with a genuine decisional impact.

Fully aware of this primary contribution from economic actors, French and Australian policy-makers have partly built their political cooperation on existing business relations. For example, on 20 June 2000, Australian Liberal Prime Minister John Howard addressed a letter to Lionel Jospin, then Socialist Prime Minister of France, thanking him for having organised Howard's visit to Paris. Howard explained how useful his meetings with his French counterpart had been, with particular emphasis on the economic component of the discussions. John Howard wrote that he was delighted to have had the opportunity to share the Prime Minister's views on the economic contexts of each other's countries, in order to foster the dynamic of economic cooperation between Australia and France. This could lead, Howard added, to a potential development of political cooperation. This letter demonstrates how economic relationships have been considered as leverage in order to develop, over time, political agreements (AN Pierrefitte, 20050038).

Between 2012 and 2017, the Hollande government increased France's economic ties with Australia to strengthen both countries' strategic partnership, as demonstrated by Australia's submarine contract with the French shipbuilding company Naval Group, which is analysed in Chapter 5. For example, in March 2016 the French government organised a visit to Australia of forty representatives from France's largest companies, as part of the French businesses confederation, the *Mouvement des Entreprises de France* (MEDEF—Movement of French Companies). Although such visits are quite common for French diplomacy, it was the first time that one of them was organised to Australia. From Canberra, Cédric Prieto, Deputy Secretary at the French Embassy between 2012 and 2016, described the MEDEF's visit as satisfactory. According to the diplomat, the visit's agenda was to demonstrate France's interest in Australia's economic potential by bringing representatives of leading French multinational corporations. French officials wanted to show that French investors see Australia as a country of future innovation and that French investment can support tangible projects in Australia. As a tool of nation branding, the visit was also intended to show Australian stakeholders France's most competitive technologies and savoir-faire in order to further link French and Australian markets and attract investment, despite potential impediments, such as cost and distance. For example, Myriam Boisbouvier-Wylie, who guided the French businesses in Melbourne, explains: "They had a meeting with several universities in Victoria to discuss how French tertiary institutions transform innovation into commercial products, which is something that France does well and Australia not so well" (pers. inter., Melbourne, 23 March 2016). The French diplomacy has continued this economic impetus toward Australia and has tried to organise new visits of a MEDEF delegation regularly. According to Frédéric Monlouis-Félicité, such visits also act as a diplomatic tool for bringing a country and its most important companies closer together, a link that globalisation has loosen by removing

60   P. SOYEZ

the notion of territory from multinational businesses (2017, p. 257). Developing a strong economic diplomacy also creates a manner of reasserting the nationality of major companies, for the sake of a nation's economic growth. In short, the trend, in France and in Australia, is to develop new partnerships between political and economic actors to support the national interest.

The visit of the MEDEF must be analysed as a significant manifestation of France's political support for its economic interests overseas, an economic diplomacy mostly renewed by former French Minister for Foreign Affairs Laurent Fabius, as the next section analyses. Moreover, this book argues that, in the current dialogue established between the two countries, France is more "proactive" than Australia regarding cooperation pertaining to the economy, innovation, infrastructure modernisation and creativity, a necessity for supporting a stagnating national economy. On the other hand, Australian diplomats focus more on security questions, such as nuclear proliferation. This reveals how economic interests are at the very heart of France's ambitions in Australia. Therefore, Australian and French diplomatic institutions, and primarily their ministries, are now fully devoted to supporting commerce and investment. However, according to Montlouis-Félicité, visits like the one of the MEDEF to Australia are not sufficient to implement an efficient economic diplomacy. The author calls for a redefinition of the national interest in which economic and political interest convergence, enabling companies to grow in foreign markets while enabling the state to expand its influence. From such point of view, diplomacies must incorporate businesses into their decision making-processes, not try to subjugate them (2017, pp. 265–267).

Reforming Australian Economic Diplomacy for More Efficient Public Institutions

The ongoing process of globalisation has led to an increased interconnection of national economies while at the same time increasing international competition for businesses. Governments must find in overseas markets a support for their national economies while also conducting policies reassuring their constituencies against the damages often caused by offshoring activities. Therefore, states are responsible for creating positive conditions for the success of their national economies overseas. More precisely, as Bayne and Woolcock explain (2011, p. 3) "the increase in economic interdependence over the last 60 years has put an end to such tidy distinction between what is domestic and what is international". Both authors emphasise the transformation of states' decision-making processes to increase the international efficiency of their national economic measures: "The advance of globalisation since the 1990s obliges economic diplomacy to go deep into domestic decision-making, so as to capture its international repercussions" (2011, p. 3).

French and Australian governments have reformed their diplomatic structures in order to support their international trade, which plays a crucial role in strengthening their national economies. Moreover, Australia and France have chosen specially to prioritise the concept of economic diplomacy within their diplomatic services and to test this concept on the French–Australian economic relationship, as this chapter demonstrates. Economic diplomacy comprises a vast concept that must be characterised by its aims. John S. Odell defines these objectives as "policies relating to production, movement or exchanges of goods, services, investments (including official development assistance), money, information and their regulation" (2000, p. 11), partly implemented by diplomatic administrations. Bayne and Woolcock explain how actors in economic diplomacies have to be "sensitive to market developments" (2011, p. 5). As this chapter illustrates, French and Australian institutional and business actors are constantly assessing their mutual markets in order to make their choices always more acute and efficient, especially in supporting their companies' investments and helping businesses get established in each other's markets. "This sets economic diplomacy apart from political diplomacy. [...] Markets can be endogenous to economic diplomacy, in that they form an integral part of the process" (2011, p. 5). Marie-Christine Kessler emphasises the public–private partnership that economic diplomacies develop: economic diplomacy can be defined by "the implementation, by a public authority, of commercial and financial policies, aimed at increasing its country's prosperity through the interests of its businesses, socio-professional groups and citizens" (1999, p. 247). Frédéric Monlouis-Félicité explains that economic diplomacies aim to reach three objectives: to support national businesses overseas, to attract foreign investments into the national territory and to adapt international economic regulations to a country's defensive and offensive economic interests (2017, p. 263). Guillaume Devin mentions the involvement of multinational firms in public commercial policies, a phenomenon illustrated by Australian and French economic diplomacies

(2002, pp. 223–225). The diplomatic effort implemented by the two countries to increase their mutual trade and investment presupposes that Paris and Canberra both support the multilateral management of economic globalisation. This chapter will further analyse how the respective decision-makers have disagreed on the trade regulations of the GATT, and also the WTO, regarding agricultural protectionism to support their own economic interests. However, the French and Australian governments have also worked to develop economic partnerships in response to the growing integration of economic activities worldwide. In order to reach their goals, Australian and French policy-makers have implemented all the tools usually used by economic diplomacies. "It embraces the whole spectrum of measures from informal negotiation and voluntary cooperation, through soft types of regulation (such as codes of conduct), to the creation and enforcement of binding rules" (Bayne and Woolcock 2011, p. 4).

Australia's public sector has been very innovative with respect to policy-making processes pertaining to economic diplomacy. In fact, according to Gary Quinlan, former Australian ambassador to the United Nations (UN) and now Deputy Secretary of DFAT, the formative development of Australia's modern diplomacy took place before the end of the Cold War, in 1987 when the Ministries for Trade and Foreign Affairs were merged to constitute the current DFAT (pers. inter., Melbourne, 17 April 2015). The Hawke and Keating governments reformed the administration in order to modernise Australia through its public institutions and to be well prepared to participate in modern globalisation. Both Labor governments positioned Australia as a liberalised market, cutting down import quotas and tariffs on most manufactured products, increasing tariffs cuts already implemented by Whitlam's Labor government in 1973. Australian diplomacy has been very efficient at supporting Australian trade and investment offshore while at the same time promoting the Australian market for foreign investments and commerce. DFAT has led active policies to support Australia's position in international trade and services, which are vital to Australia's economy.

Basing the analysis of this diplomatic innovation on an archival investigation encompassing hundreds of reports produced by Australian and French authorities, this book demonstrates that, when French and Australian Ministers for Foreign Affairs are on official visits, the subject of international trade has always been one of their priorities. For instance, a report produced by the French Ambassador to Australia

Bernard Follin on June 28th, 1985 to Roland Dumas, then Minister for Foreign Affairs, presents a detailed account of John Dawkins's visit to South East Asia as Australian Minister for Trade (AD La Courneuve, 2854). The French embassy emphasized Canberra's new effort to improve its economic relations in the region by explaining Australian decision-makers were then making a priority of the ASEAN economic market, where Australian companies had been outdistanced. Dawkins was sent to these countries in order to explain that Australia was not protectionist against their products and was determined to increase its trade with South East Asia. Between 1970 and 1980, Japan's imports from Australia had fallen by 37% and the ASEAN imported 30% less from Australia.[2] More broadly, Australian exports of products to Asia, mainly agricultural goods, natural resources and heavy equipment, had fallen from 6.4% in 1970 to 4% in 1983 (AD La Courneuve, 2854). Such commercial slowdown and its repercussions on Australia's economy created the incentive for developing an efficient and effective Asian economic diplomacy. A speech given by Bill Hayden, Minister for Foreign Affairs, in the House of Representatives on April 10th 1985 summarised this idea: "The bottom line for Australia is that, while the ASEAN countries will probably continue to offer expanding economic opportunities for non-ASEAN countries, we have no mortgage on these opportunities and will have to work hard to take advantage of them" (AD La Courneuve, 2854). In this citation, Bill Hayden explicitly legitimised the need for Australia to reform its diplomatic administration to give it all the necessary tools to support Australian exports to key foreign markets. This call for administrative reforms corresponds with Australia's commitment to participation in a globalised and liberal economy, based on international trade.

Ross Garnaut authored an influential report in 1989 entitled *Australia and the Northeast Asian Ascendancy*, commissioned by the Labor Government and officially realised by DFAT. The Garnaut report presented recommendations for reducing economic protectionism and, using free trade, reaching a deeper integration of Australia's economy into East Asian markets. Moreover, Garnaut believed that Australia's economy was too diversified and, therefore, not competitive enough in some key sectors. He recommended that Australia should adopt an "uninhibitedly internationally-oriented economic strategy"; a diplomatic administration dedicated to promoting free trade in Asia in order to facilitate Australian exports and increase East Asian investments in Australia.

Such a liberalised conception of Australia's economy has since been shared by both Labor and Liberal governments, although to different extent (Firth 2011, pp. 220–225). The creation of the APEC, a non-political organisation dedicated to economic policy, constituted the most visible action to support this economic focus, because members are not nations but rather economies. According to Gary Quinlan, this reform program, inspired by Australia's regional context, enjoyed a big success. From the 1990s, Asian-Pacific economic growth has been the main driver of the region's internal cohesion and its international integration into a globalised economy. This economic boom stimulated administrative reforms in many Asian-Pacific countries, especially Australia.

The creation of DFAT in 1987 was part of an extensive set of policies of the Hawke government, dedicated to supporting Australia's economy. At the beginning of the 1980s, Australia's economic performance was in a difficult position. The country reached a peak of male unemployment in 1983, with a rate of 9.9%, which was reduced to 5.4% in 1989. Moreover, between the 1950s and the early 1980s, Australia was ranked 19th out of 24 OECD countries for its per capita GDP growth rate. GDP per capita increased again from 1987, in parallel with the creation of DFAT[3] (Gruen and Grattan 1993, pp. 91–92). Therefore, especially as a country whose economy is deeply dependent on international trade, Australia had to reform its official structures in order to increase its economic performance pertaining to trade and investment. Australia's policies pursued outward-looking economic strategies and supported competitiveness and economic growth. Economic difficulties can bring institutional innovation (AD La Courneuve, 2864). In two and a half years, Australia's trade increased by 25% and economic growth rates improved. Australia benefitted from overall global economic prosperity (Gruen and Grattan 1993, p. 105). This new economic orientation for DFAT has remained a core policy for Australia's diplomacy since the 1980s, under both Labor and Liberal governments. It still constitutes a priority in the present. For instance, Quinlan elaborates on this focus on trade and investments by explaining that, under the Abbott government, every diplomatic post was asked to produce a plan for improving Australia's economic diplomacy in their respective country. Those plans were submitted to DFAT, which assessed them in order to determine how trade might be fostered but also to rank ambassadors on this dimension of their work as part of their performance reviews. Australian policy-makers have led an ongoing effort since the middle of the 1980s to reform their diplomacy to situate it at the service of Australian exports to key foreign markets. This early policy has constituted a model for their French counterparts, who have been urged to conduct the same institutional reforms to support France's stagnating economy since 2008.

An Economic Diplomacy à la française?

Since 2012, France has officially made trade and investment the two new major objectives of its diplomacy. This economic diplomacy, supported by Minister for Foreign Affairs Laurent Fabius, has partly renewed France's approach to public support for trade and foreign investment. François Cotier, Director of Business France in Australia, explains:

> Fabius has instituted [a policy] that the Ministry should have an economic objective in its guidelines. He asserted that there can't be any diplomacy that would not be economic, because any issue has an economic component. Diplomats have to use the economy in order to deepen France's influence in foreign countries. (pers. inter., Melbourne, 27 April 2015)

Before 2012, separate institutions were in charge of France's diplomacy, trade and investment. Commerce and investment were mainly overseen by the French Ministry for Economy, which had to accept, very reluctantly, the loss of authority on trade and investment to the French Ministry of Foreign Affairs, commonly called by its address, the "Quai d'Orsay" or the "Quai".[4] However, according to François Cotier, some diplomats were leading effective diplomatic activities for local French companies before 2012, although their business-focused engagement was the result of their personal interest in this issue, not because of potential directives from the Ministry (pers. inter., Melbourne, 27 April 2016). The Quai d'Orsay was traditionally responsible for strategic, political and cultural diplomacy. However, French policy-makers "realised that public support for companies and trade development is fully connected to the country's influence and foreign relations" as explains Emmanuel Lenain, former Director of the Asia-Pacific division of the Quai d'Orsay (pers. inter., Paris, 6 June 2016). Therefore, a decision was made to integrate both strategic and economic influences into the authority of French embassies. More precisely, every French embassy in the world was assigned representatives from various ministries, most of the time: Foreign Affairs, Economy, Defence, Education, and Culture.

Since 2012, even if the economic network of the Ministry of the Economy has been maintained in French embassies, it is now under the authority of the ambassador, and therefore of the Ministry of Foreign Affairs, which is now in charge of trade and investment. France, like many countries, followed the strategy that Australia had implemented quite early on.

However, this study does not claim the novelty of French official economic diplomacy. For instance, according to Ric Wells, this new French economic diplomacy was not a revolution:

> To tell the truth, I can remember when Laurent Fabius introduced this idea of economic diplomacy, there was a lot of publicity about it. I always thought that it did not pay appropriate recognition to the traditional very close integration between French policy and the pursuit of economic advantage. I think countries have traditionally admired the single-mindedness of the French government in pursuing openings for French businesses. (pers. inter., Canberra, 8 April 2016)

One anonymous interviewee from Canberra goes even further than Wells and asserts that Laurent Fabius' economic diplomacy was mainly a communication decision in order to be differentiated from his predecessors (pers. inter., Canberra, 2016). For example, Laurence Badel reveals interestingly that the Quai d'Orsay was already using the concept of "*diplomatie économique*" during World War I (2006, p. 173). More recently, Hubert Védrine gave a strong impulse to France's economic diplomacy at the end of the 1990s (Monlouis-Félicité 2017, p. 263). Badel reinforces this assertion by presenting a long-term study of the evolution of France's diplomacy and commercial objectives during the twentieth century. She points out three progressive trends that have led to France's current approach to economic diplomacy: the diversification of its actors, the increasing role of the multilateral approach and the new relationship between the state and businesses (2006, p. 169).

Before 2012, France had numerous public services dedicated to supporting France's trade overseas as well as foreign investment to France. In fact, French diplomatic and national archives both contain a large number of documents pertaining to France's official support for its business in Australia. This help even came directly from the Quai d'Orsay on many occasions. For example, during tensions pertaining to French nuclear testing, when French companies were facing public defamation from Australian media or institutions, public boycott or legal constraints in their activities, the Quai intervened to support French businesses by directly contacting Australian authorities to firmly request an end to such practices.[5] On the other hand, French diplomatic authorities have also tried to help Australian investors coming to France. More recently, French engagement in economic diplomacy has also come from the highest public representatives, as the 2015 submarine contract demonstrates (see Chapter 5).

Nonetheless, the last two French presidencies of Nicolas Sarkozy and François Hollande have substantially reformed the structures of France's diplomacy. The aim is now to find an answer to France's economic difficulties through institutional innovation. The global financial crisis has accelerated the need to reform France's diplomatic processes. French policy-makers were slow to recognise that economic diplomacy could be one of the possible solutions to try to restore France's economic growth. Since 2015, the French public agency "Business France" has been responsible for assisting French businesses in developing their activity in foreign countries. Business France also promotes France's image as a place to invest, and it supports foreign companies aiming to invest in France. This agency is under the triple authorities of the French Ministries of Foreign Affairs, Economy and Housing, even though, according to François Cotier, only the first two ministries are concretely involved with the organisation (pers. inter., Melbourne, 27 April 2016). Business France has, in Australia as in any other foreign country, three main objectives. The agency has been created to help French businesses in their activities in Australia; to support Australian investment in France and to promote France's economic image to Australian stakeholders. France also has a public agency supporting tourism to France, Atout France, which coordinates tourism's main actors to support France's image overseas. The same type of agency exists in Australia with "Tourism Australia". The importance of public support for tourism is crucial to both economies and, therefore, constitutes a key element of their economic diplomacy, with France being the largest tourist destination in the world.

Therefore, although Laurent Fabius did not invent the concept of economic diplomacy and although his predecessors were already conducting policies supporting French businesses overseas, Fabius still implemented decision-making institutions and processes created in order to improve French diplomatic efficiency in maximising economic interests overseas. This reform brought a solution to one of the main previous hindrances to France's economic diplomacy in the past, that Laurence Badel points out in her study: *The problem of the unity of France's economic action overseas* (2006, p. 170). Interestingly, it is a socialist government, even as moderate as the one of François Hollande, which has implemented such a policy-making process that greatly involves economic actors in France's diplomacy. The vision asserting that the state should remain the only actor with regard to economic policies is now outdated.

Has Australia Been a Model for France in the Creation of Its Economic Diplomacy?

Under the mandates of Presidents Sarkozy and Hollande, France benchmarked its public institutions against those implementing economic diplomacies within other G20 countries. The aim of this project was to learn from other diplomatic administrations how to efficiently reform the Ministry of Foreign Affairs in order to implement a stronger economic diplomacy, which has become one of France's main political priorities in a context of economic crisis.

Stéphane Romatet explains that he authored many reports on Australia's economic diplomacy while he was leading the French Embassy to Australia: "When Laurent Fabius was setting up his policy of economic diplomacy, I had informed the French Ministry of Foreign Affairs on how Australia has structured its own public organisation pertaining to this sector" (pers. inter., Melbourne, 21 June 2016). Romatet adds that he particularly stressed what he believed to be Australia's main areas where administrative support was the most efficient: economic diplomacy, tourism advertising and university promotion. He believes that Australia remains one of the leading countries regarding these three areas and that it benefits from a remarkably efficient public structure. Nonetheless, Romatet doubts that the Australian model was the only model directly shaping France's economic diplomacy. He believed that it was taken into account, with others, in forging the new Quai d'Orsay. For example, the creation in 2015 of Business France followed a benchmark research of many the same agencies in France's rival economies. François Cotier recalls that French policy-makers studied organisations such as Austrade, United Kingdom Trade & Investment, the Camera di Commercio Internazionale in Italy, the United States' Trade

Commission and Enterprise Ireland. French policy-makers wanted to have an agency dedicated to trade and investment, so that the embassy could focus on economic issues. This practice is now shared by most economies (pers. inter., Melbourne, 27 April 2015). Nonetheless, although Australia modernised its diplomatic administration very early, DFAT could not have been used as a complete model. Australia's DFAT had been weakened, until 2009, by more than a decade of budget cuts. The ministry still remains rather small compared to other G20 countries, with about half fewer diplomatic posts than the United States and France, the two biggest diplomatic networks in the world. Alex Oliver and Andrew Shearer have authored a very critical report for the Lowy Institute (2011, p. 7). According to these two authors, Australia's diplomatic service is still neglected and has not kept pace with Australia's strategic and economic ambitions.

However, this book demonstrates that the French Ministry of Foreign Affairs has used Australia as one of the countries in which to test its integrated economic diplomacy. According to Stéphane Romatet, Australia "represents many criteria necessary to constitute a test case. France must focus all its public means on [Canberra], because Australia is a very dynamic and mature market, with a very rapid economic growth and it constitutes a regional platform for businesses" (pers. inter., Paris, 21 June 2016). Romatet also explains this choice because of Australia's very "smooth" business environment, where investing is relatively easy. The Ministry has also incorporated new diplomats who were not previously from the institution. Cédric Prieto asserts categorically that former Minister Laurent Fabius purposely chose a new ambassador coming from the business world, Christophe Lecourtier, in order to implement France's economic diplomacy within the French–Australian bilateral relationship, amongst a few others (pers. inter., Canberra, 8 April 2016). Christophe Lecourtier had led the creation of Ubi France, France's former public agency in charge of supporting foreign trade, before its restructuring as Business France. Therefore, Lecourtier is very familiar with companies' needs when developing activities in foreign countries. François Cotier adds that Laurent Fabius gave a clear mandate to Lecourtier to set up France's economic diplomacy in Australia. Lecourtier's expertise on trade and investment is significant, and the fact that he was posted to Australia shows how French policy-makers intend to make their embassy in Canberra a leading institution in economic diplomacy. It also shows how France wants to strongly increase its trade relations with Australia. Implementing common practices or maintaining administrative differences, France and Australia have actively devoted their diplomatic effort to the bilateral improvement of their trade relations.

The Intensification of Trade Between France and Australia

One characteristic dominates the analysis of French–Australian trade: trade flows between the two countries have always been very uneven but their trend dramatically reversed between the 1980s and the 2010s. Although in 1986 French foreign policy-makers noted that France's trade balance with Australia was largely negative, in 2016, the situation is the exact opposite. This chapter analyses the reasons for this shift.

A Traditionally Uneven French–Australian Trade

In December 1986, France constituted Australia's 10th largest trade partner. French policy-makers noted that trade between Australia and France was undersized and called for a diplomatic effort to try to increase bilateral commercial relations. Therefore, the French Ministry for Foreign Affairs commissioned an internal assessment of trade between the two countries (AD La Courneuve, 2864).[6] In 1985, Australia represented only 0.5% of France's exports (4.2 billion francs). France was the source of 2% of Australia's imports, far behind Japan at 23%, the United States at 22%, the United Kingdom and West Germany at 7% each. These trade figures were not only very limited but also quite asymmetrical. In 1985, France's trade deficit with Australia was 1.3 billion francs. The Quai d'Orsay explained this deficit as being due to France's need for Australian commodities, especially wool for its textile industry, as well as coal and ore, but also due to the lack of French investment in Australia, even though diplomats stressed that France's "penetration of the Australian market" was constantly growing. In fact, commercial prospects seemed rather positive to them: between 1980 and 1985, France had tripled its exports to Australia, while France's imports from Australia doubled. While France and Australia were not, at the end of the Cold War, significant trading partners, French policy-makers were already planning to significantly increase these flows.

At the end of the 1980s, French policy-makers decided to focus their effort on two main economic sectors in order to increase French trade with Australia. Witnessing Australia's need to improve its communication infrastructures, France decided to support its communication and transport companies, along with high-technology industries (space, satellites and IT) and more broadly French industrial and engineering savoir-faire as a whole (AD La Courneuve, 2864). Trade relations between France and Australia progressively increased, for example by 8% between 1987 and 1988, notably with an increase of 15% in French exports to Australia (AD Nantes, 428PO/1/156). This trend has continued and, nowadays, French–Australian trade is still uneven but its balance is currently positive for France. The two countries are not mutual major economic partners, but French and Australian stakeholders believe there is strong potential for growth. Around 8000 French companies already export their products to Australia.[7] The following table shows how French–Australian trade is uneven, especially in merchandise (Table 3.1).

French–Australian trade mainly consists of merchandise, which has increased between 2016 and 2018. This trend is not significant over the long time as it fluctuates regularly. However, merchandise trade remains constantly uneven. Moreover, while two countries have started to trade fewer primary goods and more Elaborately Transformed Manufactures (ETM) since 2010, they still mainly trade primary goods (Table 3.2).

Table 3.1 French–Australian merchandise trade in December 2018

	Amount in 2018 in A$m	France's ranking in Australia	Australia's ranking in France	Main products exchanged	Progression since 2017 (%)
Australia's merchandise imports from France	5090	14th (1.7%) of Australia's imports	36th (0.5%) of France's exports	Pharmaceutical, alcoholic beverages, perfumes and cosmetics, aircraft, spacecraft	−2.7
Australia's merchandise exports to France	1554	22nd (0.5%) of Australia's exports	53rd (0.2%) of France's imports	Coal, aircraft, spacecraft, agriculture	26.1

(*Sources* DFAT-MAEE)

72   P. SOYEZ

Table 3.2   Type of merchandise traded by France and Australia

	Amount in 2018 in A$m	Amount in 2013 in A$m	Main exports
Australia's exports of primary goods to France	1000	720	Coal, oil-seeds, oleaginous fruits
Australia's exports of ETM to France	280	240	Aircraft and spacecraft parts, measuring and analysing instruments

(*Source* DFAT)

Table 3.3   French–Australian trade of services in 2018

	Amount in A$m in 2018	% of total services trade	France in Australia's services trade	Growth since 2017 (%)
Australia's imports of services from France	2326	2.5 of Aus service imports	14th in origin of services	12.4
Australia's exports of services to France	931	1.1 of Aus services exports	20th in destination of services	–5.7

(*Source* DFAT)

French–Australian trade is currently undergoing a slow restructuration, where goods are becoming less important but service flows are increasing. Activities pertaining to tourism have been the main services mutually exchanged by the two countries (Table 3.3).

If Australian policy-makers wish to see an increase in their trade relationships with France, this does not constitute a priority. In fact, even if the trade figures are heavily skewed on France's side, Australia's trade is being balanced on a global basis. Australian policy-makers do not worry about deficits or surpluses with individual countries which are not their major economic partners. This shows that Australia's trade with France, despite being significant, is not important enough to drive policy-makers in Canberra to set up strong measures to encourage Australian exports to France. These asymmetrical trade figures can be explained by Australian and French economic structures: Australia's economy is structured around a few crucial sectors, the sophisticated production agricultural products and mineral commodities. These products, especially agricultural goods, constitute a tangible part of France's production too. Therefore, France does not need to import them in massive quantities.

France's exports to Australia are also composed of a few specific sectors. The expertise of French companies is particularly valued in infrastructure engineering, utilities and transports. French companies benefit from their excellent international reputation. For instance, the French company Keolis, affiliated with France's public train company SNCF, operates most public transports in Australia, such as Melbourne trams, and buses in Adelaide, Perth and Brisbane. Keolis has 4000 employees in Australia. Cédric Prieto reinforces this vision of France's official marketing in support of the reputation of some elements of its economic sector. He explains that the French embassy in Canberra is fully committed to advocate for French industry's performance, especially with respect to the Naval Group contract. As Pietro explains, French officials try not to be seen as promoting only French wine, food and luxury brands, even though these elements are very important because, combined with WWI commemoration ceremonies, they support Australian tourism to France (pers. inter., Canberra, 8 April 2016).[8] Business France in Australia notices that French industrial products are more easily saleable in Australia than gastronomic and luxury products, a surprise considering that France is so closely associated with the luxury industry (F. Cotier, pers. inter., Melbourne, 27 April 2016). The French Embassy's motto is: "To bring France's added-value to Australia".

French diplomats are acutely aware of Australia's economic context and opportunities to efficiently promote French businesses. Both diplomatic and economic actors are determined to take an active part in Australia's economic transition towards innovative technologies and industries. France's main economic ambition in Australia has been to respond to Malcolm Turnbull's economic program, which was a program based on innovation. French policy-makers are wagering that, if Australia fully engages in innovation, creativity and new technology, French businesses can stand out from the crowd and expand their activities in Australia. This message is released not just to Australian diplomatic and economic stakeholders but also to French businesses in France eager to expand their activities overseas and to French citizens thinking of seeking work experience in a foreign context. "We tell them that Australia is looking at building smart cities, smart transport systems, information technologies. We explain that Australia wants to modernise its economy thanks to technologies facilitating interpersonal links and relations between institutions and citizens", says Prieto, who mentions Thales, defence companies and France's public rail company SNCF as targets of this promotion. François Cotier describes Business France's actions to assist French businesses willing to be part of Australia's innovative plan. In order to support Naval Group's bid for Australia's submarine contract, Business France organised a visit to Australia of twenty French companies working in sea and defence activities. The idea was to convince Australian policy-makers that, by choosing Naval Group, they would benefit from a vast ecosystem of innovative technologies from companies working in maritime and defence technologies that would develop a branch in Australia along with Naval Group. Business France's message was that France was not only delivering submarines but also its industrial savoir-faire, technology and innovation. In 2015, Business France also organised a broader visit of French actors in maritime innovation. This delegation visited Perth, Adelaide, Melbourne, Sydney and Brisbane (pers. inter., Melbourne, 27 April 2015). The message from the French embassy in Canberra is also aimed at French citizens already living in Australia. Cédric Prieto points out the role of French researchers in the Group of Eight Universities and explains that the Embassy supports their projects in environmental technologies, renewable energies, and intelligent transport systems, among others (pers. inter., Canberra, 8 April 2016). French officials want to maximise the presence of the large French community living and working in Australia, in order to involve them in strong trade relations between the two countries.

Overcoming Impediments to French–Australian Trade Relations

French economic and diplomatic actors point out difficulties hindering their activities in Australia. In the past, French–Australian trade relations were undersized because the two countries suffered from contentious political and diplomatic relations in the mid-1980s. France was displeased by Australia's condemnation of their nuclear testing program and by Canberra's support for the inclusion of New Caledonia on the UN list of colonised countries, especially in 1986, during the peak of the tensions, which are fully analysed in Chapter 6. Even though French officials decreed that no commercial retaliation measures should be taken against Australia in times of bilateral conflict, in order "not to be counterproductive for French companies" (AD La Courneuve, 2864), such significant and ongoing political tensions were not favourable to commercial relations, in that they created an atmosphere of mistrust between the two countries. Therefore, in 1986, Australian Prime Minister Bob Hawke had a meeting with the French ambassador to Australia to express his wish that French–Australian commercial relations should not be damaged by what he saw as only temporary political tensions. Hawke even asserted that Australia, which he compared to "an aircraft-carrier", wanted to work at increasing these flows of exchange by promoting his country's image as a favourable trade and investment platform for French business interested in the Pacific. French Prime Minister Jacques Chirac annotated the brief with this comment: "I am very open. I am very in favour of an improvement of our relationship, and even in favour of a meeting". Australia's Minister for Trade had visited Paris in June 1986 in order to reinforce trade relations between Australia and France in this complex context (AD La Courneuve, 2864). Moreover, France's asymmetrical trade with Australia indirectly protected French companies in Australia during peak times of tensions. On several occasions, a large segment of Australian public opinion, galvanised by unions and churches, urged the boycott of French goods to demonstrate its condemnation of French nuclear testing. However, former French ambassador to Australia Bernard Follin explained in a note to the Quai that on 13 September 1986, Australia's Foreign Minister Bill Hayden announced in a press conference that his government was opposed to these boycotts because, since Australia had a positive trade balance with France, Canberra would have more to lose in case of a retaliatory French boycott of Australian products.

Currently, one noticeable obstacle to French–Australian trade growth lies in Australians' informal protectionist behaviour when buying products. Myriam Boisbouvier-Wylie explains how it is often counterproductive to promote one's product as French in order to sell it in Australia. The French Honorary Consul in Melbourne, deeply involved in Victoria's business environment, asserts that many French companies do not wish to be known as French in Australia, but as Australian, so that Australians who only want to buy "proudly owned and made in Australia" products still buy what they sell.

> I believe that the way French companies make businesses in Australia has changed a lot in the last few years. In the past, French companies used

to come to Australia presenting themselves as French. They used to bring French employees to Australia. Nowadays, they mainly employ Australians and want to appear as local companies to be successful. (pers. inter., Melbourne, 23 March 2016)

In some very strategic economic sectors, such as defence, French companies don't want to advertise that they are French, because they do not want Australian politicians to demagogically dismiss their offers in order to present themselves to their electorate as the true champions of Australia. Boisbouvier-Wylie mentions the example of Thales, which does not want to appear too French because of the risk that the Australian public would criticise the fact that a foreign company produces Australia's military equipment. Therefore, two types of companies play the French card in their marketing. The first one is composed of the biggest French businesses, such as Air France, Peugeot, Renault or Michelin. Since these companies are directly associated to France, they may as well capitalise on it. The other group consists of businesses in sectors of food, luxury and cosmetics, where customers want to buy a French product. However, this phenomenon does not deeply hinder France's business in Australia, where, despite consumers' strong protectionism, French products globally benefit from Australians' Francophilia.

According to French and Australian diplomats, French businesses can also sometimes have to overcome a declinist vision of Europe in Australia. Since 2008, the significance of the crisis of the Euro Zone has reinforced, especially in countries like the USA and Australia, the idea that European economies are structurally declining and, consequently, might not present appropriate targets for investment. This negativity has the potential to discourage Australian businesses from looking for suppliers in Europe and reinforce their focus on the United States and Asia. Ric Wells refines this vision and explains that Australian businesses do not dismiss the EU as a whole, because they still highly regard the United Kingdom:

Getting Australian business to focus on Europe has always been a problem. There is nothing new about that and that is partly because of the still very strong business links between Australia and the United Kingdom. There is a huge amount of Australian investment in the UK. It just does not cross the channel very much. (pers. inter., Canberra, 8 April 2016)

The importance of Australia's trade with the United Kingdom is not surprising, since both countries share a language and a strong common history. They also share norms and common law jurisdictions. Therefore, it seems much easier for Australian businesses to trade with British partners than with partners from another European country, because of a lack of familiarity. Consequently, French companies face the challenge of convincing Australian businesses to cross the Channel and sell their products in France. François Cotier, who is directly involved in French–Australian trade and investment relations, tempers this vision. According to Cotier, the declinist vision of Europe hazily exists in Australia's public opinion, but Australian economic and political stakeholders have a very accurate understanding of European economies, of their strengths and weaknesses. For instance, Cotier gives the example of Australia's industrial actors and says that leaders of Australian industries are perfectly aware of France's industrial technology, for example in transport systems, electronic engineering or biotechnologies (pers. inter., Melbourne, 27 April 2016). Benoît LePoitevin, Business France's representative in Victoria, agrees that French start-ups benefit from a very positive image in Australia, especially in innovation and new technologies. Therefore, the fact that the Australian public may have a skewed vision of Europe is, realistically, not a big threat because what Australian stakeholders understand of France matters more. However, Cotiers acknowledges that, until recently, France had neglected its investment image overseas, for instance by not paying attention to international rankings of attractiveness, a situation that has changed with the modernisation of France's economic diplomacy (pers. inter., Melbourne, 27 April 2016). If France's economic image is not necessarily negative amongst Australian economic actors, neither has it reached its full potential.

French–Australian Cross-Investment Bilateral Policies: Making Investment Easier to Support Economic Growth

Increasing Mutual Foreign Investments

Like trade, investment flows between France and Australia are largely asymmetrical but Australian and French policy-makers have intended, since the early 2010s, to use the renewal of their political and strategic partnership in order to support more cross-investments between France and Australia.

French companies invest much more in Australia than do Australian investors in France. However, even though this cross-investment is limited, French investment in Australia has significantly increased. In 1986, Australia was the recipient of only 2% of France's foreign investment, which amounted to four billion francs. However, Australia constituted France's largest investment recipient in Asia, with French policy-makers locating Australia in Asia for this purpose. These investments were varied, in such areas as banking, insurance, mining, oil, gas and manufacturing, made by France's largest companies, such as the bank BNP, oil companies Elf Aquitaine and Total, and Pechiney in the metalworking industry (AD La Courneuve, 2864). This asymmetry has remained to the present day but has been transformed. In December 2017,[9] foreign direct investments (FDI), defined as the direct ownership of a business in one country by a foreign one, were higher from France to Australia and had increased since 2015. However, global investments flows, which are not limited to direct control of ownership and which also increased in 2015–2016 but since slightly decreased, followed the opposite trend[10] (Table 3.4).

Since the 2008 economic crisis, French and Australian policy-makers have strongly supported inward and outward investment as a major contributor to national growth. For example, the 30% rise of foreign investment to France between 2015 and 2016 was analysed by French policy-makers as a sign that the hardest times of the economic crisis were ending and that Paris could pretend to become as attractive as London and Berlin (Dancer 2017). Australian policy-makers are currently focusing on investment, because they see it as a major factor stimulating growth, as much as trade (S. Brady, pers. inter., Paris, 18 July 2016). More specifically, their focus is concentrated on investment in services, and the merging of Austrade with DFAT has been implemented

Table 3.4 French–Australian cross-investments in 2017

	France's FDI to Australia	Australia's FDI to France	France's global investment to Australia	Australia's global investment to France
FDI	A$6285 m	A$2432 m	–	–
Global investment	–	–	A$24,793 m	A$50,983 m

(*Source* DFAT)

to support this action. Investment policies follow various methods. Governments strive to promote their countries' images as high cost-effectiveness destinations. They also promote national companies and their products. Australian and French policy-makers cooperate to establish policies facilitating foreign investments. More precisely, Australian policy-makers focus more on encouraging inward than outward investment, because of how dependant Australia is on overseas capital.

Driving Forces and Obstacles to French–Australian Cross-Investments

Two main factors explain this investment asymmetry between France and Australia. Australian companies largely focus on investing primarily in the United States, then at the same level in Asia and in Europe, in particular in the case of London and Berlin, since the EU is Australia's second largest trading partner and its largest source of foreign investment. This can be explained by the fact that Australian companies are reluctant to invest in non-English-speaking countries. As is the case with trade, economic difficulties in the EU, even if they are lessening, could still potentially deter some Australian investors from focusing their activity in Europe with any confidence. France and Australia expect a significant increase of Australian investment in France due to Brexit. France aims to become Australia's main investment partner, alongside Germany, in the EU. François Cotier asserts that Australian companies have a good understanding of France's technologies and innovation, but argues that Australian investors know very little about the French economic market. Reciprocally, three obstacles limit French investments in Australia: distance from Europe, cost of an investment far away, and the small size of the Australian market.

The asymmetrical cross-investment between France and Australia can also partly result of France's image as a difficult place to invest. While this image is currently changing because of President Hollande's reform to reduce taxes on businesses, some firms have still described France as not necessarily investment-friendly. The health care company Ramsay's investment in France constitutes a significant example, because the company has recently criticised the French government for not supporting foreign investors. One of Australia's biggest investors in France, Ramsay invested more than a billion dollars in France between 2011 and 2014.[11] Ramsay's case highlights a recurrent problem for France's economy: the image of a country where it can be difficult to invest because of very strict regulations. This affects France's attractiveness to foreign investment in general, not only Australian. France's former ambassador to Australia explains that, when he was in Canberra, Australian stakeholders frequently pointed out difficulties with investing in France, pertaining to social regulations and tax systems. Romatet explains Ramsay's dissatisfaction with extremely strict French regulations in the health industry, which is more constraining than in Australia's less regulated environment. The diplomat wants to remain positive and assert that French stakeholders support Australian investors and look for ad hoc solutions (pers. inter., Paris, 21 June 2016). Former diplomatic tensions have no impact on French–Australian investment. Cotier explains that he has never heard from an Australian business actor any comment pertaining to the two countries' former tensions on nuclear testing and New Caledonia (pers. inter., Melbourne, 27 April 2016). In order to overcome these difficulties, French policy-makers in charge of France's economic diplomacy do not just promote the economic interests of their national market. They also point out how France can be an efficient conduit for investment in Europe, which represents a vast market of five hundred million consumers. Cédric Prieto confirms that the arguments used by France to persuade Australians to invest to France are partly based on France's strong integration into the European market. Interestingly, Prieto also explains that this European dimension can also be a drawback for France's interests because there is a fierce competition among European countries to attract foreign investment (pers. inter., Canberra, 8 April 2016).

In order to overcome these obstacles, Australian policy-makers focus on promoting Australia as one of the best destinations for foreign investment. There is an ongoing dialogue between the French and Australian actors of their economic diplomacies in order to improve cross-investment. Diplomats insist on the fact that "Australia offers a stable environment ideal for investment and business, a stable AAA financial system, a high rate of growth which gives solid returns on investments, a solid anchor to reach dynamic Asian markets". As with trade, French–Australian mutual investment is "solid", as described by Stephen Brady, because it encompasses industries that are likely to maintain their activities in the next few years. However, policy-makers believe that French–Australian cross investment is not achieving its potential (pers. inter., Canberra, 8 April 2016). Australian investment in France remains limited but several signs indicate the potential for improvement. ANZ reopened one of its branches in Paris in 2015. The bank had opened a first office in Paris in 1988, which was closed later for lack of investment.[12] ANZ does not only want to support Australian investment to France, it also intends to benefit from growing French investment in the Asia-Pacific region as well.[13]

Australia, an Inefficient Springboard for French Investment in Asia

Since the 1980s, the argument asserting that Australia provides a platform for European investment in Asia is frequently used in Canberra, and this book argues that Australian policy-makers promoting this idea are fully aware that their argument is misleading. Franco-Australian diplomatic engagement over recent years does not aim to strengthen the respective French and Australian economic positions in Asia, despite the marketing set up by Australia to attract foreign investment. The idea that Australia would be a suitable platform for foreign companies who want to develop their economic activities in Asian markets is based on two misconceptions. The first is that Australian geography, representing the gateway to Southeast Asia, allows quick and easy access to major Asian economic centres. Secondly, many Australian diplomats and economic stakeholders assert that their country, thanks to a multicultural society with large communities from Asia, allows foreign investors to employ Australian workers who have a very good knowledge of Asia and with networks in these markets. These arguments need to be refuted, as they have been widely criticised by the French and Australian policy-makers interviewed for this research, who point out that the two major Australian economic centres, Sydney and Melbourne, are no closer to the Chinese or Japanese centres than Paris. It is faster to travel to Beijing from Paris than from Melbourne. One of the DFAT senior officers interviewed for this research anonymously criticised this argument:

> We run the argument that Australia is a good economic springboard into Asia. I have run this argument myself quite vocally. There is some truth in it. Given the nature of the Australian population, you find in Australia skilled and competent people familiar with the languages and the ways of life of all the major Asian markets. [...] But you only have to walk down the streets of Paris to find the same advantages there. I don't want to overstate it. It is an asset that we have but we probably exaggerate it a bit. The reality is that some large European companies do choose to base

in Australia their Asian operations but not many. (pers. inter., Canberra, 2016)

This argument is not recent. Garth Evans asserts that, when he was Minister for Foreign Affairs, he had "always felt a bit unpersuaded of Australia as an investment destination because of our links to Asia", an argument "easy to exaggerate" (pers. inter., Melbourne, 13 April 2016). François Cotier, Director of Business France in Australia, goes further to completely reject this Australian economic marketing:

> It's ridiculous. Today, if you want to go to Asia, you go there directly without having to go by Australia. We would never use that as an argument to a French company to come here. [...] We understand that there are free trade agreements that simplify things, but there is no need to go to Australia to reach Asia. Yes, from Australia you can have opportunities in Asia, perhaps. But this does not justify coming to Australia. [...] It is a discourse that they all have, but that I do not believe. (pers. inter., Melbourne, 27 April 2016)

However, many documents from the French diplomatic archives illustrate that French policy-makers in the 1980s believed in this representation of Australia as a foot in Asia's door. Reports show that they have even presented the argument themselves to French business, before realising that this idea was actually a misconception (AD La Courneuve, 2851). Nowadays, according to Cédric Prieto, a French company willing to invest in Asia has more interest in doing so from France because, by trying to invest from Australia, it will be directly impacted by the concurrence of Australian companies willing to make the same investment (pers. inter., Canberra, 8 April 2016). The few potential benefits Australia brings in terms of investment in Asia are not so clear. For example, multiple FTAs signed by Australia with Asian countries, such as with South Korea in 2014, and with China and Japan in 2015, are not profitable enough to merit a detour to Asia that would require a positioning in Australia.[14] French companies with offices located in Australia for the Asia-Pacific region have realised that the country is a unique economic market whose integration into the Asian markets is not particularly deep. Such companies sometimes tend to move their headquarters to Singapore or Hong Kong. Conversely, it is interesting to move to Australia for a French company wishing to expand its business to countries of the Pacific. The considerable economic engagement of France and Australia in recent years has a mainly bilateral objective: to achieve a better interpenetration of the Australian and French markets.

Many political, cultural and economic obstacles have hindered French–Australian trade and investment relations, limiting their potential. To counteract this, French and Australian policy-makers have developed a positive discourse in order to convince economic stakeholders to invest in each other's countries for the purpose of mutual commerce and bilateral economic cooperation. Multilaterally, France and Australia are now promoting similar visions of the international regulation of a globalised economy. However, this alignment has been significantly difficult to achieve, since both countries have been opposed for decades on agricultural tariffs.

Overcoming Multilateral Economic Tensions Pertaining to Agricultural Protectionism

Bayne and Woolcock underline three major tensions which challenge and shape economic policies (2011, p. 11). The first is the constant tension between domestic and international pressures. In a globalised context, domestic economies are increasingly affected by other countries' economic policies, creating interdependence and/or competition. Agriculture constitutes a fundamental element of Australian and French societies, identities, industries and trade. Both countries are world leaders in agricultural exports. Therefore, pushed by strong domestic lobbies, French and Australian policy-makers have encountered strong opposition within multilateral institutions regarding their conception of agricultural policies and trade, between protection and liberalisation of the market. These have been much stronger in France than in Australia, though. This tension has hindered the French–Australian relationship for decades, and its resolution enabled the two countries to deepen their cooperation, not only economically, but also politically and strategically.

The Conflicting Trade Leadership of France and Australia: The Common Agricultural Policy Against the Cairns Group

At the end of the Cold War, French policy-makers noted that agricultural tensions were considered the main issue affecting the diplomatic

84   P. SOYEZ

and economic relationship between Australia and continental European countries (AD La Courneuve, 2852). Australian policy-makers, whether left-wing or right-wing, rarely supported absolute free trade, for internal political reasons in a country where unions are still quite influential. However, they were in favour of a liberalised economy enabling Australian businesses to conquer new markets all around the world. This economic vision has shaped Australian trade policies and supported Canberra's engagement with multilateral institutions (Firth 2011, pp. 224–225). For decades, the French–Australian relationship was hindered by the fact that Australian policy-makers strongly opposed what they saw as protectionist regulations from the EU.[15] The EU Common Agricultural Policy (CAP), which largely subsidises European farmers in order to maintain their income in a globalised agricultural sector, was the centre of this tension. On the one hand, France has been the main beneficiary of the CAP and is one of the world's biggest exporters of agro-industrial products. Therefore, French policy-makers have always been extremely eager to maintain a strong CAP, while Australian policy-makers and public opinion considered France to be their main European opponent regarding agricultural free trade (AD La Courneuve, 2864).

On the other hand, Australia, which also relies heavily on agricultural exports, took the leadership among countries defending a liberalisation of agricultural trade, as demonstrated by Linda Botterill (2003). This leadership was conducted multilaterally and also bilaterally. At a multilateral level, Canberra led its diplomatic actions at the GATT and then the WTO, through the Cairns Group of countries supporting the abrogation of European and American agricultural protectionism. The Cairns Group was created in 1986 and consisted of fourteen countries which defended agricultural free trade and were eager to find a common position before the 1986 GATT trade negotiation in Punta del Este. This group has united important food producers including Argentina, Brazil, Canada and New Zealand. In his inaugural speech in Cairns on 25 September 1986, Bob Hawke explained that its objective was:

> to seek for the exports of their agricultural industries the same regime of international trading rules as the majors have applied for decades to trade in industrial products. [...] The task before this group of fair traders is to develop tactics for maximising its influence in putting an end to the economic madness now pervading world agricultural trade. (AD La Courneuve, 2851)

Hawke accused the EU of giving about US$100 billion to its farmers, distorting the world agricultural market but also creating unemployment and poverty all around the world. He also accused the United States of threatening world freedom and peace by selling food supplies to the USSR.[16] Led by Australia, this group developed a common strategy to challenge European and American agricultural protectionism in multilateral negotiations at the GATT, then in the WTO. French diplomats admitted that the Cairns Group, even with a more moderate position than Australia had intended, constituted a diplomatic success for Canberra on the international stage (AD La Courneuve, 2851).

Australia has used several multilateral fora, such as the International Monetary Fund (IMF), to present itself as the voice of developing countries who have legitimately claimed that their agriculture was handicapped by European protectionism. At an IMF meeting in 1981, Australian diplomats used the argument that, by slowing down the agricultural modernisation of developing countries, European countries supporting the CAP were partly responsible for threatening global food security. French diplomats described this criticism as being hypocritical, saying that Australia had maintained its own tariff barriers but was focusing criticism on Europe in order to avoid being a target of developing countries' opposition (AD La Courneuve, 2855). French diplomats did, however, note that Hawke and Keating were less aggressive than Fraser in their attacks against the CAP. Hawke and Keating focused their criticism on Europe's price supports regarding meat, dairies, fruits and cereals (AD La Courneuve, 2864). This Australian multiple engagement led French foreign policy-makers to acknowledge that Australia had a leadership at the GATT on several macroeconomic issues, confirming the country's involvement in this multilateral organisation (AD La Courneuve, 2851). According to French diplomats, Canberra has been partly responsible for the introduction of the commodities trade issues at the GATT since 1982, particularly pertaining to ores and agriculture. Australia's general policy regarding international trade in commodities was, in 1985, presented by the Quai d'Orsay as the following:

> Australia supports a wider trade liberalisation, without rejecting a product by product approach [...]. Australia takes part in international efforts to stabilise the market, using products agreements, under the condition that such agreements remain fair and relevant to the trends of the international market.[17]

Along the same lines, Australia conducted bilateral negotiations to liberalise agricultural flows. For example, between the 16th and 26th of April 1986, Australian Prime Minister Bob Hawke visited Washington, London and then Brussels to negotiate regarding these questions. During his meetings, Hawke described the United States and the European Economic Community (EEC) as actors in a "war of subsidies" (AD La Courneuve, 2852). He outlined the economic crisis that the Australian agricultural sector was suffering from at the time and asked for guarantees for Australian agricultural goods entering these two markets. Hawke left the United States reassured of America's support for Australia's concerns, because President Reagan had declared that the United States' agricultural policies would consider the interests of their allies, and that Washington supported a progressive free trade negotiated by the GATT. Moreover, with the Andriessen Accord in 1985, European countries had accepted to renounce selling subsidised beef to Australia's traditional export markets in Asia (Murray 2013, p. 79). However, Hawke's achievements in Brussels in 1986 were less satisfactory regarding a long-term and vast agreement. While he had constructive meetings with some EEC leaders such as Jacques Delors, Hawke did not receive the guarantees on beef and dairy products that he requested (AD La Courneuve, 2852). In June 1986, the Australian Minister for Agriculture went to Paris to meet his French counterpart in order to discuss the economic situation of both countries' agricultures. John Kerin acknowledged that French farmers were in a "very delicate" situation but he also asserted that the Australian government considered France to be the strongest supporter of the CAP. These visits show how the settlement of agricultural disputes with the EU were a priority for Australian governments, using economic, social and even moral arguments.[18] They also show how virulent was French and Australian opposition on that topic, which considerably undermined the two countries' relationship and, more broadly, the EEC/EU–Australian relationship for decades. However, French policy-makers defended the CAP by quoting a 1986 report from the Australian Bureau of Agricultural Resources and Economics, which studied the farming industry, partly refuting the idea of an Australian farming crisis at the time. In fact, this report asserted that Australian policy-makers and media were wrong in generalising farmers' difficulties. According to this document, although Australian wheat, sugar and rice farmers were facing a crisis in the 1980s, "wool growers and beef producers [were] certainly not in crisis. Despite the picture portrayed by the lobby groups and the media, not many farmers are going bankrupt or being forced off the land", noting an increase of 15% in the value of farms in 1985 (AD La Courneuve, 2851). This document, translated into French, was used by policy-makers in Paris in order to support the CAP against Australian criticism.

Notwithstanding these tensions, some Australian policy-makers respected France's support for the CAP. Although both economies had opposite interests on that matter, this mutual acceptance of the importance of agriculture for both societies enabled policy-makers to try to find a solution to their conflict. For example, in a 1986 report to the Quai d'Orsay after his meeting with Bob Hawke, French ambassador to Australia Bernard Follin noted:

> After having listed all the well-known catalogue of Australian criticisms against the CAP, Mr. Hawke acknowledged that some of our concerns were legitimate, especially pertaining to the future of our farmers. Moreover, the Prime Minister described as promising [...] the non-aggressive dialogue established by the Australian Minister for Trade [and his French counterpart]. (AD La Courneuve, 2864)

On the other hand, the French embassy to Australia noted in 1985:

> Australia's dependence on international markets, currently depleted, have constrained Australian policy-makers to become interventionists, which is surprising for a mainly liberal economy and which goes against Australia's official positions in international fora. (AD La Courneuve, 2851)

French diplomats realised that the EEC needed to improve its relationship with Australia in order to support its agricultural exports. As the Quai d'Orsay explained in 1986: "Even though, obviously, we are competitors, we can learn to live together and even find areas for cooperation" (AD La Courneuve, 2851). The Quai believed that it was in both Australia's and France's interests to improve trade negotiations at the GATT in order to open the global market and to fight against protectionism, because the EEC was the world's primary agricultural importer.

The Settlement of the Conflict

In order to find solutions, Australian and French diplomats established, at the end of the 1980s, regular consultative committees on international trade. Moreover, both countries tried to develop scientific and research cooperation on agricultural studies. These projects remained limited and did not significantly improve the relationship. Nonetheless, they illustrated a conscious effort on both sides not to constrain the French–Australian relationship within the conflicting frame of multilateral trade negotiations. In 1986, France proposed the creation of joint ventures in the food industry in order to sell processed cereals, fruits, vegetables and dairies to Pacific countries. France also offered to share its farming IT technology with Australia (AD La Courneuve, 2851).

French Prime Minister Michel Rocard's official visit to Australia in 1989, the first such visit by a French Prime Minister, had the objective of discussing all conflicting issues with Bob Hawke in order to calm the tensions. The brief written by Rocard's Cabinet about a meeting between the two Prime Ministers unveils that macroeconomic regulation was the first topic they discussed (AN Pierrefitte, 19930409/3). Michel Rocard wanted to reassure Bob Hawke that France would commit to the agricultural agreement of the GATT Uruguay Round. He also explained to Hawke that, globally, France and Australia had a common understanding of world trade and shared interests in its regulation. Then, Rocard explained France's position regarding the CAP to the Australian Parliament's Trade and Foreign Affairs Committee. The French Prime Minister explained that the EEC would not reduce its subsidies until the United States would agree to do so, explaining that the European Community was giving US$26 million to its 12 million farmers, while Washington was giving US$30 million to its 2.2 million farmers. Rocard proposed that the US, the EEC and the Cairns Group ratify an international agreement at the GATT to significantly reduce all agricultural subsidies over a 10-year term, telling the Australian Committee that they had to be moderate and accept a long-term reduction, not an immediate one (AN Pierrefitte, 19930409/3). Ronald Reagan's progressive support to Bob Hawke enabled Australia to strongly tackle the CAP and the collaboration between the US and the Cairns Group isolated the EU. "Australia was instrumental in creating a political environment in which the EU appeared to be besieged" (Murray and Benvenuti 2014, p. 441). In 1992–1993, the EU accepted substantial reforms and subsidies reductions to its agriculture, enabling Australia to largely increase its food exports. The end of trade-related tensions between Australia and the EU, and France in particular, constituted a crucial step in the normalisation of the relationship between Paris and Canberra. Both countries now share relatively similar positions on multilateral economic agreements, as demonstrated by France's support for a FTA between Australia and the EU.

French–Australian Trade Relations and the Future EU–Australia Free-Trade Agreement

One of Australia's current strategic priorities is its diplomatic and economic rapprochement with the EU, as demonstrated by the Framework Agreement that both parties have signed on 7 August 2017.[19] In particular, Australian policy-makers are now committed to constructing a new FTA with one of their most important economic partners: the EU. France's support for such agreement demonstrates that, under the centre-left government of François Hollande and the current one of President Emmanuel Macron, the two countries have globally aligned their politics pertaining to multilateral trade regulations. This aspect constitutes a strong element of the French–Australian partnership.

Australia's Strong Support for FTAs

Since the 1980s, Australian diplomats have been championing bilateral or multilateral agreements in favour of Australian economic interests. This has represented a major change in Australia's diplomatic tradition (Firth 2011, p. 225). Over the last few years, Australian policy-makers have focused their activity on bilateral economic relations, by negotiating FTAs. The recent multiplication of such agreements between Australia and its Asian partners illustrates this focus. However, this choice does not mean that Australia is not engaged anymore in multilateral economic organisations. As it has proved by leading the Cairns Group, Australia's involvement in this organisation is not solely concentrated on agricultural issues, because the agricultural sector only represents 5% of Australia's exports, but also on services, industrial production and expertise on intellectual property. Australia is involved in UN and G20 negotiations as well in order to support its economy through international trade and investment by means of liberal legislation against countries that support more protectionist policies. Nonetheless, Australia's focus on FTAs shows how its leaders consider bilateral economic approaches to be the best available alternative when multilateral regulations are stymied.

90   P. SOYEZ

The establishment of an FTA with the EU has become one of Canberra's main diplomatic objectives. This aim dominates a significant part of DFAT's current resources. Australian and European policy-makers completed in 2017 a joint FTA scoping exercise, undertaken rapidly, in less than 18 months, which proves that all actors are fully committed to reach an agreement and official negotiations started in 2018. Moreover, a majority of EU policy-makers currently share Australia's support for such economic partnerships. The signing of the EU–Canada Comprehensive Economic Trade Agreement (CETA) in 2016 has demonstrated that, despite vivid debates over the protection of EU regulations within FTAs, such agreements can be reached. Wells also emphasizes Australia's determination to achieve this agreement by pointing out how the country needs European technologies for innovation (pers. inter., Canberra, 8 Avril 2016). Australian policy-makers want to have rapid negotiations with the EU in order to maximise the chance of having the agreement implemented (F. Cotier, pers. inter., Melbourne, 27 Avril 2016). Australia's determination to reach a FTA with the EU stems from the fact that the EU, as a whole, constitutes the world's main economy. The EU is Australia's second largest trade partner and its largest sources of foreign investment, a trend that has been maintained for more than two decades.[20] DFAT's latest trade figures illustrate how crucial economic relations with the EU are for Canberra. In 2017, Australia-EU two-way merchandise trade represented about A$68 billion and two-way service trade A$31.5 billion. For example, the EU imports primarily raw materials from Australia, such as coal, oil seeds, wine and ores and exports to Australia industrial products, mainly motor vehicles, medications and other pharmaceutical products. In 2017, Australia exported $A31.5 billion worth of goods and services to the EU, according to DFAT.[21] Moreover, Australia's economic growth is also supported by key FDI from EU member-states, worth A$1072.2 billion in 2016, the first origin of FDI to Australia. Nonetheless, according to Ravenhill and Cotton (2007), the asymmetrical trade relation with the EU explains why Australian policy-makers primarily made the choice to emphasize their relationship with Asian countries, where Australia has benefited from substantial trade surpluses. In fact, Australia was only the EU's 15th exports destination and 26th imports source in goods trade in 2016.[22] But now that Australia has negotiated multiple FTAs with its Asian economic partners, stakeholders in Canberra are determined to improve their economic relationship with EU member states thanks to this new FTA, and with the United Kingdom under a separate agreement.

The political and economic context in Europe has changed because of Brexit and Australian diplomats have feared that, with Brexit, the European Commission will put its FTA with Australia at the bottom of its list of priorities. However, as Stephen Brady stresses, despite Brexit, "there will still be a strong political push in Australia for an FTA with the EU– in fact it's an imperative" (pers. inter., Paris, 17 July 2016), an assertion now corroborated by the positive outcome of the joint scoping exercise in 2017. A year before, Julie Bishop had used her visit to Brussels for the launch of the EU–Australia leadership forum on 8 September 2016 to reassert Australia's desire for an FTA with the EU (G. Quinlan, pers. inter., Melbourne, 12 September 2016). Australia's former Minister for Trade Steve Ciobo also went to Brussels to support the initiative. In their joint declaration with Ciobo to the Trade and Foreign Affairs Committee of the European Parliament, Bishop asserted that Australia hopes:

> To further expand our partnership with a comprehensive Free Trade Agreement between our two economies. It will be incumbent upon us all as Members of Parliament to promote the benefits of Free Trade Agreements to our respective citizens. This too will be a partnership built on shared values, a partnership which develops our complementary economic strengths.[23]

Bishop and Ciobo also needed to reassure their European partners. Several EU policy-makers criticised Australia for supporting separate trade agreement negotiations with the United Kingdom while at the same time working with the EU on an FTA.[24] Australia has not hidden the fact that it also wants to start negotiations with the UK individually, but the Australian government will have to sequentially work at establishing its FTA with the EU, then with the UK. Philomena Murray and Margherita Matera assert that Australia would have made a mistake in concentrating its efforts on London rather than Brussels, even though Australia's trade with the EU is mainly concentrated in the UK (2016). The *Submission for the parliamentary inquiry into Australia's trade and investment relationship with the UK* (2017) made the recommendation to prioritise an agreement with the EU over one with the UK because of the EU's larger weight into Australia's economy, a policy currently implemented by Canberra. However, Australian and French foreign policy-makers understand that Brexit also constitutes an opportunity for a deepening of the French–Australian partnership on economic issues.

What Does France Intend to Achieve with an EU–Australia FTA?

French authorities support the negotiation of an FTA between Australia and the EU. However, their motivations must be questioned, because the economic benefits of an FTA for France remain unclear. French policy-makers and economic stakeholders disagree regarding the efficiency of such a trade and investment partnership. French diplomats close to the social-democrat government of François Hollande are genuinely optimistic about the economic consequences of the EU–Australian FTA. When asked if the French economy would really benefit from this economic agreement, Stéphane Romatet asserts that its consequences can only be positive, a belief also shared by Emmanuel Lenain at the Ministry for European and Foreign Affairs (pers. inter., Paris, 6 June 2016). Romatet sees in the FTA a tool that could further develop French–Australian trade and investments. More precisely, the diplomat explains that an FTA would reduce the barriers that French companies face when they choose to enter the Australian market, such as phytosanitary norms or access to government contracts, and vice versa. Romatet asserts that when he was French ambassador to Australia, French businesses supported this proposed FTA. Therefore, he dismisses the idea that France should not reduce the positive gap in its trade balance with Australia. He explains that supporting French imports from Australia is positive for France's economy because it implies an intensification of trade relations between the two countries, which should not have a negative impact on French exports to Australia. Romatet attests to France's political support for policies that would increase Australian investment to France: "If this FTA can help us, then we must fully support it". On the other hand, several French policy-makers have expressed their doubts about the possible positive outcomes of an FTA. For example, according to an anonymous French economic stakeholder in Australia, the support of the government of François Hollande for this EU–Australia FTA is economically counterproductive for France's interests:

> In substance, the European Union, and France in particular, do not have much to win from a free trade agreement with Australia. France's trade

balance is positive with Australia and it is uncertain that we would benefit in any way from such an agreement. Australia does not constitute a country where a free-trade agreement is a priority for French economy. Has France's support been requested by Australian actors, in a context of multiple Australian FTAs? This issue is much more political than economic. (pers. inter., Melbourne, 2016)

This French actor goes even further by explaining that Brussels should really balance defensive and offensive economic interests before changing European tariffs. According to him, free trade and market regulation are more theoretical issues than pragmatic economic policies, objectives in which many policy-makers believe without having always considered the economic outcomes. In fact, France has always been cautious of the modalities of the propositions of FTAs suggested by Australia. This mistrust is not recent and has been shared by other Pacific countries. In 1989, France and Japan both criticised Australia's economic vision of the Pacific's economic integration. France and Japan feared that Australian decision-makers intended to turn an integrated Pacific economy into "another group of Cairns" (AN Pierrefitte, 19980006/7). Tokyo then favoured a vision of the Pacific economy's integration less focused on regional issues but more open to globalisation, and where, therefore, countries like Japan, or France, would have a stronger say.[25] Thirty years later, the situation is quite the opposite and French policy-makers claim to fully share Australia's economic views on international trade.

French diplomats do not privilege multilateral economic agreements over bilateral ones. France has always combined bilateral, plurilateral and multilateral economic negotiations, a policy that recent governments have continued. As other countries including Australia have done, Paris has relied on bilateral agreements when multilateral ones seemed impossible to reach (Badel 2006, p. 175). The current crisis of the WTO and the difficulty of negotiating global trade agreements have persuaded French policy-makers, like their Australian counterparts, to currently emphasise bilateral negotiations.[26] However, demonstrations all around France in 2016 against CETA and TAFTA, and the popularity of protectionist candidates Marine Le Pen and Jean-Luc Mélenchon in the French presidential elections in 2017, show that a large segment of French public opinion views FTAs as economic postulates which rarely lead to economic growth, a perception also studied by Patrick Messerlin (2017, p. 278).[27]

On the Australian side, an anonymous source from DFAT summarised France's interest in pursuing an EU–Australia FTA: "It is not just about daily questions such as meat. It is about a psychological and deeper connection with the Asia-Pacific region" (pers. inter., Canberra, 2016). Consequently, France's official strong support for the negotiations between Canberra and Brussels is unusual and can also be explained by political and security agendas. This study argues that, while French diplomatic senior officials in charge of the French–Australian relationship appear to believe in the positive outcomes of the FTA, their support to this decision is also political. Accepting to support an EU–Australia FTA, which as explained previously, is a priority for Australia, can also be understood as a negotiation tool in order to benefit from Australia's support in the Indo-Pacific region and in the submarine contract negotiations. For example, while Gary Quinlan believes that FTAs often produce hidden advantages in cross-investments, he acknowledges that the economic benefits of the EU–Australia FTA could be slim for France. As Quinlan explains, Australia already has very low trade tariffs. An FTA would not significantly change Australian trade legislation in a way that would help French companies expand their business in Australia (pers. inter., Melbourne, 12 September 2016). Tariff advantages will be very limited. This is why France's main benefits from an EU–Australia FTA might be political and strategic, improving France's relationship with Australia and gaining support in the South Pacific. However, there is one economic sector for which France will have to strongly negotiate: agriculture.

A Resurgence of Tensions Between France and Australia About Agricultural Trade?

The FTA between the EU and Australia has the potential to increase Paris and Canberra's mutual engagement because France could become Australia's main partner in Europe in order to achieve this economic goal, alongside with Germany with which collaboration is not yet as advanced as with Paris (see in Chapter 5, p. 142). However, the potential clash between Australian and French agricultural interests, represented by strong agricultural lobbies in both countries and in other EU member states, could hinder this bilateral relationship. Cédric Priéto is clear: "We explain to our Australian counterparts that we also have strong agricultural interests. France has a longstanding agricultural tradition and this sector constitutes one of the most important ones of our economy. We won't sacrifice it on the altar of free trade" (pers. inter., Canberra, 8 Avril 2016).

Therefore, all stakeholders interviewed for this book foresee difficult and tense negotiations pertaining to tariffs for agricultural goods. Farming and food processing industries are still major components of both countries' economies and societies. Although the EU and Australia have settled their conflicts about the CAP as demonstrated previously in this chapter, the negotiations surrounding the EU–Australia FTA have the potential to reawaken these tensions. EU member states' main difficulty will be to obtain an agreement from Australian policy-makers to ease access to the Australian market for European agricultural goods. In order to reach this objective, France has two aims: to simplify quarantine procedures and health standards. However, Australian negotiators can be reluctant to reduce their protectionism by reforming the market for the sake of European products. On the other hand, according to French policy-makers interviewed for this book, French officials have tried to reassure their Australian counterparts about their determination to reach an agreement. French diplomats are fully aware that Australia's public opinion and politicians generally believe that France is not a reasonable partner in agricultural negotiations, for example with its strict policy of geographic designation of origins. However, Prieto asserts that this is a misperception and that France is willing to fully support the FTA despite the likely opposition from French farmers (pers. inter., Canberra, 8 April 2016). Knowing the significant influence of the agricultural lobby on French politics, such a statement would seem to demonstrate France's genuine commitment to the FTA. However, Brexit has increased Australia's concerns that agricultural interests might undermine FTA negotiations because London's withdrawal from the Union weakens supporters of trade liberalisation. Therefore, Australia believes that France could be its first partner in the EU to negotiate agricultural tariffs because countries like Spain or Portugal are also very eager to protect their agricultural interests. Without the UK in the negotiation, it's crucial for Australia to have France trying to find a middle way to accommodate its European partners.

In many respects, Brexit forces Australia to intensify its bilateral relationships with France and Germany. Regarding the CAP, Brexit positions France as Australia's principal partner for agricultural negotiations, and it is likely that Emmanuel Macron will pursue this dynamic. Brady emphasises the fact that Australia really needs France's support: "The most important outcome of Hollande's visit to Australia was his commitment to back the negotiation of an Australian Free Trade Agreement with the European Union. [...] The only way to make sure that the FTA will happen is to have direct political support from the top" (pers. inter., Paris, 19 July 2016). However, French support is not a certainty. Although French politicians and administration currently support the FTA, farming and food industry lobbies are traditionally very influential in French politics. They will be very likely to try to influence negotiators in order to maintain tariffs as protectionist as possible. Therefore, it is hard to know how politicians will respond to this pressure, depending on the political context in France in the future. The same analysis can be made for Australian politics, and an anonymous source from DFAT admitted that Australian policy-makers have no illusions concerning how agricultural lobbies, amongst other actors, will try to block the FTA. Nonetheless, both Australian and French diplomatic actors want to appear confident about the ability of both countries to conduct successful negotiations between the European institutions and Canberra. Since both countries are fully aware that negotiations will be difficult, it is unlikely that the negotiations will damage the French–Australian bilateral relationship.

CONCLUSION

Before being strengthened by a strategic and political partnership, the French–Australian bilateral relationship was primarily supported by the economic interests of its business communities. In fact, more than policy-makers, French and Australian economic actors have initiated the deepening of Paris and Canberra's relationship. Subsequently, French and Australian commercial ambitions have led the two countries to support their national economic interests in a foreign market by further involving public and private actors. Therefore, the French–Australian relationship has been a blueprint for the development of the economic diplomacies of Paris and Canberra. More precisely, policy-makers' desire to increase trade and investment in a market still mutually undervalued, whether France or Australia, has enabled the modernisation of Australian and French diplomatic practices and administrations, in order to support their national economic growth.

Nonetheless, French–Australian economic relations have not been free from conflict. Paris and Canberra have been in strong opposition for more than a decade on multilateral agreements pertaining to agricultural trade, France leading the CAP and Australia the Cairns Group. This antagonism has now partly disappeared, and the two countries share a common understanding and aspiration for the regulation of economic globalisation. This shift has mainly been made possible by the liberal economic policies of French presidents Nicolas Sarkozy and François Hollande, who have shown less aversion to FTAs. France's commitment to support the negotiations of the EU–Australia FTA constitutes a demonstration of France's engagement in its partnership with Canberra. Overall, Australian and French policy-makers have always conceived the pursuit of economic interests as a tool to maintain constructive relations despite strong political tensions. This has been particularly significant regarding one crucial and regular topic of dispute between the two countries: France's nuclear testing program in the South Pacific.

NOTES

1. In 2014, the French Ministry of Foreign Affairs estimated that around 75,000 French citizens were living in Australia. This number has likely increased since that time. http://www.diplomatie.gouv.fr/fr/services-aux-citoyens/preparer-son-expatriation/dossiers-pays-de-l-expatriation/australie/.
2. According to the same report, in 1983–1984, Australian exports to Japan had been 26.5%, to CEE 13.6%, to the US 10.9%, to ASEAN 8.8%, to South Korea 3.8%, to Taiwan 2.8%, to China 2.5% and to Hong Kong 2.5%.
3. Data are from the Australian Bureau of Statistics and published by the Reserve Bank of Australia http://www.rba.gov.au/statistics/frequency/occ-paper-8.html.
4. For a complete history of the tensions between French Ministries of Foreign Affairs and Economy for the authority on international economic negotiations, see Laurence Badel (2006, pp. 169–185).
5. See series AD La Courneuve, 2851 and AD Nantes, 428/1/156.
6. Report from the French Ministry of Foreign Affairs, 26 December 1986.
7. http://www.facci.com.au/fileadmin/template/australie/VIC/Publication/FACCI_-_Fiche_Australie.pdf.
8. According to Stephen Brady, one million Australians travel to France each year, which is considerable (pers. inter., Melbourne, 18 July 2016).

9. Investment figures from DFAT's website http://dfat.gov.au/trade/resources/Documents/fran.pdf.
10. http://www.facci.com.au/fileadmin/template/australie/VIC/Publication/FACCI_-_Fiche_Australie.pdf. According to the French-Australian Chamber of Commerce and Industry, almost 500 French companies have established a branch in Australia. This investment directly created more than 70,000 jobs in the country.
11. Ramsay's acquisition report http://www.ramsayhealth.com/~/media/Documents/RHC/Investor/Market_Briefings_02102014.ashx.
12. http://www.anz.com/australia/aboutanz/corporateinformation/history-ofanz/default.asp.
13. http://www.investmenteurope.net/regions/france/australian-bank-anz-opens-paris-office/.
14. Australian diplomacy has recently aimed at developing regional free-trade agreements, such as the TPP, or agreements with Singapore, Malaysia, Indonesia, China and South Korea. Australia is currently negotiating an economic cooperation agreement with India.
15. For a long-term study of EU–Australian relations at the WTO, see D Kenyon and J Kunkel (2005), "Australia and the European Union in the World Trade Organisation: Partners or Adversaries?", *Australian Journal of International Affairs*, vol. 59, no. 1, pp. 55–69.
16. French diplomats considered that Bob Hawke had been extremely confrontational in this speech, but that his position had not been shared by other countries, which, like Canada, called for a moderate dialogue with the US and the EEC. However, the Quai d'Orsay noted that Hawke did not single out France in his comments and that Australian officials had been very cordial by inviting a French representative to observe the meetings.
17. Brief on Australia and mineral resources written by Didier Lopinot, Economic and Trade Advisor to the French embassy to Australia, 30 December 1985.
18. For a detailed analysis of Australian and EU oppositions regarding agricultural trade, see P Murray and A Benvenuti 2014, "EU-Australia Relations at Fifty: Reassessing a Troubled Relationship", *Australian Journal of Politics and History*, vol. 60, no. 3, pp. 431–448.
19. This document aims to provide a tangible basis to increased collaboration between the EU and Australia in regard to "foreign and security policy, sustainable development, climate change, and economic and trade matters".
20. In *The National Interest in a Global Era, Australia in World Affairs 1996–2000*, James Cotton and John Ravenhill demonstrated that in 2000, the EU was already Australia's largest merchandise-trading partner.

3 ECONOMIC DIPLOMACY, AN INNOVATIVE FORCE ... 99

21. See detailed figures on DFAT's EU brief http://dfat.gov.au/geo/europe/european-union/Pages/european-union-brief.aspx.
22. See detailed figures on the EEAS' website https://eeas.europa.eu/headquarters/headquarters-homepage_en/9544/EU%20-%20Australia%20Relations%20factsheet.
23. http://foreignminister.gov.au/speeches/Pages/2016/jb_sp_160908.aspx?w=tb1CaGpkPX%2FlS0K%2Bg9ZKEg%3D%3D.
24. http://www.abc.net.au/news/2016-09-09/australia-uk-talks-a-dangerous-strategy:-european-politicians/7828276.
25. Japan's position was later modified when its former Prime Minister, Yukio Hatoyama, proposed in 2009 to enlarge ASEAN+3 meetings to encompass more countries, like Australia, and support regional free trade. This proposal was supported by Canberra, China, Wellington but not by the US (Clark and Pietsch 2012, p. 57).
26. For a complete history of France's economic focus on multilateral or bilateral negotiations, see L Badel (2006, pp. 169–185).
27. See an example of these demonstrations in *Le Monde* http://www.lemonde.fr/economie/article/2016/10/15/mobilisation-en-france-contre-l-accord-de-libre-echange-ceta-avec-le-canada_5014374_3234.html.

REFERENCES

Archives Nationales, Pierrefitte, France.

National Archives of Australia, Canberra, Australia.

Badel, L 2006, 'Pour une histoire de la diplomatie économique de la France', *Revue d'histoire du Vingtième siècle*, vol. 2, no. 90, pp. 169–185.

Bayne, N & Woolcock, S 2011, *New Economic Diplomacy, Decision-Making and Negotiation in International Economic Relations*, Ashgate, London.

Botterill, L 2003, *From Back Jack McEwen to the Cairns Group Reform in Australian Agricultural Policy*, Australian National University Center for European Studies, Canberra.

Clark, M & Pietsch, J 2012, 'Democratisation and Indonesia's Changing Perceptions of ASEAN and Its Alternatives', in D Novotny & C Portela (eds), *EU–ASEAN Relations in the 21st Century: Strategic Partnership in the Making*, Palgrave Macmillan, Basingstoke and New York, pp 45–61

Cotton, J & Ravenhill, J 2007, *The National Interest in a Global Era, Australia in World Affairs 2001–2005*, Oxford University Press, Oxford.

Dancer, M 2017, 'La France attire de plus en plus d'investissements étrangers', *La Croix*, 23 May, viewed 8 November 2017, https://www.la-croix.com/Economie/France/France-attire-dinvestissements-etrangers-2017-05-23-1200849374.

Devin, G 2002, 'Les diplomaties de la politique étrangère', in F Chatillon (ed), *Politique étrangère, nouveaux regards*, Presses de Sciences Po, Paris, pp. 223–225.

Firth, S 2011, *Australia in International Politics*, Allen & Unwin, Sydney.

Garnaut, R 1989, *Australia and the Northeast Asian Ascendancy*, Australian Government Publishing Service, Canberra.

Gruen, F & Grattan, M 1993, *Managing Government, Labor's Achievements and Failures*, Longman Cheshire, Melbourne.

Kenyon, D & Kunkel, J 2005, 'Australia and the European Union in the World Trade Organisation: Partners or Adversaries?', *Australian Journal of International Affairs*, vol. 59, no. 1, pp. 55–69.

Kessler, MC 1999, *La Politique étrangère de la France, Acteurs et processus*, Presses de Sciences Po, Paris.

Messerlin, P 2017, 'Politique commerciale et 'intérêt national'', in T de Montbrial & T Gomart (eds), *Notre intérêt national, quelle politique étrangère pour la France?* Odile Jacob, Paris, pp. 269–281.

Monlouis-Félicité, F 2017, 'Les grandes entreprises et la politique étrangère française', in T de Montbrial & T Gomart (eds), *Notre intérêt national, quelle politique étrangère pour la France?* Odile Jacob, Paris, pp. 255–268.

Murray, P 2013, 'Problems of Symmetry and Summitry in the EU–Australian Relationship', in S Lawson (ed), *Europe and the Asia-Pacific, Culture, Identity and Representations of Region*, Routledge, New York, pp. 66–85.

Murray, P & Benvenuti, A 2014, 'EU–Australia Relations at Fifty: Reassessing a Troubled Relationship', *Australian Journal of Politics and History*, vol. 60, no. 3, pp. 431–448.

Murray, P & Matera, M 2016, 'Brexit and Australia, the Way Forward', *Pursuit*, 2 July, viewed 17 July 2017, https://pursuit.unimelb.edu.au/articles/brexit-and-australia-the-way-forward.

Odell, JS 2000, *Negotiating the World Economy*, Cornell University Press, Ithaca.

Oliver, A & Shearer, A 2011, *Diplomatic Disrespair, Rebuilding Australia's International Policy Infrastructure*, Lowy Institute, Sydney, 2011.

Ravenhill, J & Cotton, J 2007, *Trading on Alliance Security, Australia in the World Affairs, 2001–2005*, Oxford Press, Oxford.

CHAPTER 4

Threatening Australia's Backyard? French–Australian Tensions on Nuclear Policies and Their Resolution

The biggest tension with France was obviously the nuclear testing program which came to an end in 1996 with the new Chirac government. That was a particularly difficult period for me because I was hugely criticised for not being tough enough with the French. The Rainbow Warrior and the nuclear testing was a constant remaining source of tension. (G. Evans, pers. inter., Melbourne, 13 April 2016)

France and Australia have progressively drawn closer in their strategic perceptions of world order and security, to an extent never before reached since the two World Wars. Such a partnership has been possible after three decades of economic and people-to-people ties, as analysed previously, but also by the improvement of their bilateral strategic dialogue, demonstrated by a gradually increasing military cooperation. This critical strategic engagement, analysed in depth in Chapter 5, was enabled by one prerequisite: the end of strong tensions between France and Australia regarding French nuclear testing in the South Pacific. As highlighted by the quotation above from Gareth Evans, former Australian Minister for Foreign Affairs, the French nuclear program in French Polynesia, conducted between 1966 and 1996, has been one of the major hindrances to the French–Australian bilateral relationship.

This chapter argues that the strength of French–Australian tensions pertaining to nuclear armament stems from the fact that nuclear issues have acted as two opposite tools of power for the two countries.

© The Author(s) 2019
P. Soyez, *Australia and France's Mutual Empowerment*,
Studies in Diplomacy and International Relations,
https://doi.org/10.1007/978-3-030-13449-5_4

101

102 P. SOYEZ

France has developed independent nuclear capacities to support its aim to remain a global power, while Australia has regularly used anti-nuclear campaigns as a topic of niche diplomacy to become a stronger middle power. Moreover, both countries' behaviours have exacerbated these tensions, France arrogantly refusing to discuss the issue with its Pacific neighbours and Australia conducting a duplicitous uranium diplomacy. The end of French nuclear testing in 1996 has removed the necessity for the two countries to directly oppose each other on this issue. In the current context of increasing threats from non-state actors, especially from terrorism, Australian and French policy-makers currently agree on the significance of nuclear threats to their countries' security due to uncontrolled nuclear proliferation. Nevertheless, the two countries still pursue opposing policies in order to deal with nuclear and security issues. Australia, on the one hand, regularly supports a nuclear-free world, depending on its governments' priorities. For example, Labor governments have often supported UN debates and actions against nuclear armament. However, Liberal governments have sometime withdrawn from such commitment to support their American ally and benefit from their extended nuclear deterrence, as Malcolm Turnbull did by refusing to allow the Australian mission to attend the September 2017 UN General Assembly (UNGA) sessions on nuclear disarmament, which led to the signature of a treaty banning nuclear weapons. France, on the other hand, has always strongly relied on deterrence with its independent nuclear armament since its development in the 1950s.

This chapter critically analyses the opposing foreign policies of France and Australia regarding nuclear issues and their consequences for their relationship. To begin, the study focusses on Australian actions against nuclear proliferation, especially on Canberra's awkward position concerning the Rarotonga Treaty. Next, this chapter examines the logic of the French nuclear testing program in the South Pacific and the tensions it induced in the region, especially with Australia.

Canberra's Multilateral Actions Against Nuclear Proliferation

There is a wide gap, to say the least, between 1950s-era Australia's hospitable welcome to British nuclear tests on its mainland, and its later angry condemnations of French tests thousands of miles from its shores. (Hymans 2000, p. 1)

Australia's position regarding nuclear armament has never remained constant. In fact, in the 1950s and 1960s, Canberra was an "active supporter of the development and spread of the bomb" but became, from the 1970s, a "world leader in the effort to rein it" (Hymans 2000, p. 1). Because of the fear of the growing Communist presence in Asia, Australian policy-makers, and Sir Robert Menzies in particular, toyed with the idea of acquiring nuclear weapons. The Prime Minister believed that developing Australia's nuclear deterrence was necessary in the case that Canberra's "great and powerful friends" would not come to defend its shores in front of a Communist attack. Therefore, Australia hosted British nuclear testing sites in Western Australia and South Australia, until 1963. In 1961, the Australian government considered a transfer of atomic weapons to Australia, so that Canberra could develop its own nuclear deterrence, but failed to reach an agreement on its modalities (Hymans 2000, p. 5). Menzies even considered, in 1965, the development of an independent Australian nuclear program without London's support. However, Australia progressively abandoned this idea and chose to support Washington's nuclear race in order to benefit from its deterrence. Moreover, in 1969, Australia signed a cooperation with France agreement on nuclear enrichment and, in 1971–1972, Canberra sent technicians to France to learn from French nuclear facilities how to enrich uranium for military purposes. However, the election of Whitlam's Labor Government in 1972 put an end to Australia's nuclear project and, as this chapter demonstrates, Australia started what Hymans describes as a "crusade against French Tests" (2000, p. 14). From the 1970s, Australian public opinion and politicians have manifested at least a certain resistance, or often a concrete opposition, to policies pertaining to nuclear energy and weapons (Falk et al. 2006, p. 845). The Australian rejection of the atom, and the global use thereof, can only be matched by the French belief in the importance of nuclear energy. Therefore, this opposition has reinforced French and Australian mutual misunderstanding and their dichotomist policies.

Foreign policy-makers in Canberra have developed international leverage tools and expertise for acting against proliferation of weapons of mass destruction, especially nuclear arsenals. More than just a moral and intellectual position, this approach has served Australian diplomacy by providing it with an essential topic of global security in relation to which Australia could appear influential. This dynamic, implemented repeatedly and in particular under Labor governments, has been part of Australia's niche diplomacy: developing an internationally acknowledged expertise on specific and crucial issues. In essence, global nuclear threats require multilateral solutions. This issue has enabled Australia, in addition to increasing its security, to adopt a specific diplomatic topic with global impact in order to function as an important diplomatic player in the international community. Australia's policy position on non-proliferation has led to its taking part in international fora, mainly the International Atomic Energy Agency (IAEA) and the UNGA. This has also led to strong disagreement between Australia and France on nuclear matters.

Australia's Activity at the IAEA Against Nuclear Proliferation

France and Australia have had, since the second half Cold War, opposing understandings of the use of nuclear armaments, Canberra regularly perceiving these arsenals as threats and Paris as safeguards of France's existence. Australian policy-makers have focused their diplomatic effort against nuclear energy within the IAEA, which became one of Canberra's most privileged strategic fora. This focus appears in a very interesting brief prepared for the Australian delegation to the 31st regular session of the IAEA General Conference, held in Vienna on September 21–25 1987 and attended by Bill Hayden as Minister for Foreign Affairs and Trade. This document provides a clear assessment of Australia's actions against nuclear proliferation at the beginning of the time period examined by this study. Australian diplomats sent to Vienna were given the objectives of fostering the institution's efficiency. For instance, Australian diplomats had to "work to minimise to the fullest extent possible the intrusion of divisible extraneous political issues", "uphold the IAEA's central role in international safeguards and the verification of non-proliferation commitments", for example by promoting "a prudent control of finances and urging prompt payment of financial support". Moreover, these diplomats were instructed to "underline Australia's commitment to the IAEA" (NAA M3793, 16). Australian policy-makers have been determined to support the institution as a means of strengthening indirectly their position on nuclear issues. Australia's involvement in the organisation has been tangible, Canberra constituting one of the eight originators of the institution's statutes, and being part of its Board of Governors since 1957. Australian diplomats have been consistently elected to key positions within the institution.[1]

Therefore, the IAEA has also created a significant focus for French–Australian diplomatic tensions. The Australian permanent mission to the IAEA has continuously aimed to promote non-proliferation and safeguard supports. In 1987, twelve decision-making positions of the institution were held by Australians officials, such as Director of the Standing Advisory Group on Safeguards Implementation. Australia's support for the IAEA can also be explained by the fact that the institution has been in charge of verifying "all peaceful nuclear activities in South East Asia and their peaceful use" (NAA M3793, 16). Australian policy-makers have perceived the IAEA as a means of protecting Australia's regional security since it controls nuclear activities in the territories of Australia's neighbours. The IAEA was even presented as "the most effective platform to pursue Australia's non-proliferation policy interests". Moreover, the brief added: "The IAEA safeguards system also provides the basic element for Australia's uranium export policies, to ensure that Australian origin of nuclear material remains in peaceful non-explosive use" (NAA M3793, 16). This demonstrates the fact that Australia's involvement in non-proliferation organisations was also a way for it to safeguard its uranium trade, a fundamental aspect of its diplomacy and commercial interests, which is discussed later on in this chapter.

More precisely, the IAEA Regional Co-operative Agreement (RCA) for Asia and the Pacific, which Canberra joined in 1977, has allowed Australia to assist its neighbours in their nuclear activities while also controlling the development of nuclear energy in its region. This agreement today consists of twenty-one states.[2] The RCA aims to support development and growth through research and infrastructures pertaining to nuclear issues. Most importantly, it provides another source of leverage for Australia to be part of multilateral programs in its region in various sectors such as medicine, industry, agriculture and nuclear science. It also enables foreign policy-makers in Canberra to monitor the nuclear activities of its neighbours. The IAEA is obviously a key forum for Australian diplomats to implement their non-proliferation policy. Within the organisation, and as a regional leader in nuclear technology, Australia has also conducted bilateral training programs with developing countries (AD Nantes, 37/146). Canberra's support for this organisation has fluctuated over the years. In 1985–1987, Australia's financial contribution to the IAEA was reduced because of "financial pressures". Without over-analysing this budget cut, it suggests that possibly during those years non-proliferation was not perceived as fundamental to Australia's diplomacy (NAA M3793, 16). Nonetheless, Canberra remains nowadays one of the main contributors to the organisation's budget.[3]

Canberra's significant involvement in the institution is also indirectly revealed by how French policy-makers have planned their reaction to Australian actions against nuclear energy at the IAEA. Interestingly, this opposition unveils the perceptions of a nuclear power—France—in regard to antinuclear policies. On 18 October 1985, the French ambassador to the UN in Geneva addressed a report to the French Minister of Foreign Affairs, describing the outcomes of the 29th General Meeting of the IAEA and how France should react to these decisions (AD Nantes, 37/103). The ambassador first reassured Paris and reported that even though New Zealand had mentioned the Rainbow Warrior sinking and called it an "act of terrorism", no other country had condemned France on that matter. However, the report noted that Australia, even if less virulent than New Zealand, again used the General Meeting of the IAEA to condemn French nuclear testing in the Pacific, supporting New Zealand's mention of their "consternation regarding France's obstinacy to maintain its nuclear testing policy in Moruroa atoll". Such statements have enabled Australian policy-makers to use the IAEA as leverage for regional leadership. For example, the report mentioned above noted that Australian diplomats used this forum to explain to their counterparts the content of the Rarotonga Treaty. In this document, the French ambassador stressed the fact that Australia and New Zealand were the only South Pacific countries represented at the conference, Fiji having decided not to send a representative this time. Therefore, according to French diplomats, Australia and New Zealand were the main spokespersons for their region's anti-nuclear policies before the international community. However, the virulence of the two countries differed. More precisely, New Zealand appeared in all the French archival documents as a leader in the anti-nuclear policy-making process, inspiring regional anti-nuclear agreements with Pacific Islander states, such as the Rarotonga Treaty. On the other hand, while French diplomats always believed that Australia was a supporter of Pacific anti-nuclear policies, decision-makers in Canberra appeared less committed to a total anti-nuclear position than their neighbouring states, because of Australia's strong interests shared with nuclear powers, especially the United States and the United Kingdom. With Australia's security relying on American support, Australia has never fully condemned nuclear armament in order not to challenge American deterrence, which can represent an indirect nuclear deterrence for Australia. Therefore, in this allocation of tasks, Australia emerged as the spokesman trying to coordinate the position of South Pacific anti-nuclear states with the diplomatic interests of global powers, and thereby strengthen its diplomatic weight regionally and globally.

Australian Diplomacy Against Nuclear Proliferation at the UN

Australia has also implemented its non-proliferation diplomacy within other multilateral institutions. The United Nations has provided the most efficient forum from which to advocate opposition to proliferation, while the IAEA was given priority for technical agreements and actions. Australian decision-makers tried to leverage each institution, depending on their capacities. Australia's sustained effort to increase international dialogue on nuclear weapons at the UN and its dedication to achieving a test ban treaty illustrates how foreign policy-makers often perceive international agreements as the most effective tool for securing their countries' regional interests. On such a critical and global issue, Australian diplomats have regularly believed that the UN presented the most efficient forum for forging policies against nuclear proliferation and especially against France's nuclear policies.

In 1983, the Australian mission to the UN submitted a resolution to fully ban nuclear testing around the world. The French Diplomatic Archives hold a draft of this resolution which was submitted by Australia to the United States, the United Kingdom and France, before being delivered to the ambassadors representing non-aligned countries. Australian diplomats, who had already proposed a resolution on that matter in 1982, were clearly leading international opposition to nuclear testing. Australia was then the foremost state to condemn countries, like France or China, which refused to be part of the UN working committee on nuclear testing. In this document, the Australian ambassador expressed his disappointment in regard to French support for nuclear testing. He asserted that such a position increased Australia's perception of France as a threat because of its nuclear activities (AD Nantes, 633). In 1984, in another diplomatic cable, New Zealand officials congratulated their Australian counterparts for taking the lead on this issue, while, as they asserted, Australia had just followed New Zealand in its 1975 proposed resolution (AD Nantes, 633). Another example illustrates this Australian support for international agreements on nuclear matters. In 1984, during the 38th UNGA, the USSR suggested a vote of the Assembly in order to assert that the Indian Ocean should become a nuclear-free zone, without waiting for the conclusions of the UN Committee dedicated to this issue. The US then threatened to withdraw from the Committee if the USSR did not respect the proper timeframe. In a brief preparing for Bill Hayden's visit to Europe in 1984, Australian diplomats asserted that Australia had to persuade the US to remain in the Committee in order to have the widest possible consensus on such an important security issue for Australia: "We consider it to be in Australia's interest that the Americans should remain in the Committee to demonstrate Western commitment to arms reduction" (NAA M3793; 23). Australian policy-makers were fully committed to securing efficient anti-proliferation negotiations in the interest of their security and to assert the role of Canberra on this issue.

Australia's next major attempt to lead an international condemnation against nuclear armament is found in the significant project of the Canberra Commission on the Elimination of Nuclear Weapons. Australian Labour Prime Minister Paul Keating initiated this Commission.[4] Progressively elaborated from the beginning of the 1990s, the Australian ambassador to the UN submitted in 1996 an official report on this issue. Officially, the aim of this Commission was to gather practical and convincing arguments that would lead, in a few steps, to the abandonment of all nuclear arsenals, as the report claims. With less naivety, the Commission intended to challenge the notion of nuclear deterrence by asserting that the solution to nuclear threat was not the possession of nuclear armament but the elimination of nuclear weapons themselves. The post-Cold War context was presented as an opportunity to remove threats associated with nuclear armament since opposition between the East and the West was over and yet the threat of nuclear proliferation among terrorist groups was an increasing reality. Several years of debates among decision-makers from all around the world were necessary to create this text. In order to demonstrate full credibility, the Canberra Commission gathered politicians, such as Gareth Evans and Michel Rocard, military officers such as General Lee Butler, who until 1994 was in charge of American strategic nuclear forces, and Field Marshal Lord Carver, the former Chief of the British Defence Staff. Members of the UN and of the IEAE were involved in the Commission too, including scientists like Nobel Prize winner Joseph Rotblat.[5] Australian diplomats proposed a precise plan to communicate and disseminate this text. This document was primarily aimed at heads of state and government when they would be gathered at a UNGA, but also at high public servants in Ministries for Foreign Affairs and Defence, at military schools, university research centres for defence and media companies (AN Pierrefitte, 680AP/94). The report was presented during the UN conference on disarmament in January 1996 but was not accepted by nuclear powers. Moreover, due to a change of government and the election of John Howard, Australia itself did not support the Canberra Commission anymore as it did not want to appear to challenge the United States' nuclear strategies. However, the Canberra Commission's Report is seen as a very influential step in the debates being forged by international leaders and policy-makers over a nuclear-free world, by presenting practical and convincing measures for ridding the world of nuclear weapons. Therefore, the Commission, which primarily aimed to increase Australia's security with a global disarmament, also strengthened Australia's leadership amongst countries positioning themselves against nuclear weapons. Acting in this niche diplomacy, Australian policy-makers have substantially participated in the international dialogue on nuclear armament and global security, supporting clear positions against nuclear proliferation.

Regarding this diplomatic objective, Australian diplomats and politicians have favoured multilateral organisations as fora for their struggle against nuclear proliferation, using each institution according to its advantages. They have also used these institutions to communicate their condemnation of French nuclear testing, Australia being a strong supporter of the Nuclear Test Ban Treaty, which was not ratified by France at the time. However, Australia's participation in the Rarotonga Treaty was more controversial and has revealed important contradictions in Australian diplomacy.

Australia's Ambiguity Regarding a Provision of the Rarotonga Treaty

In the second half of 1985, the South Pacific Countries ratified the South Pacific Nuclear Free Zone Treaty, prohibiting nuclear activities in a vast part of the Pacific Ocean. Australia was the instigator of the project, which increased Australia's security by reducing nuclear threats. However, Canberra's position regarding the Treaty's application unveils how Australian policy-makers have also used the question of nuclear security to support their leadership (AN Pierrefitte, 19950509/95). The ratification of the Rarotonga Treaty increased French–Australian tensions.

According to the Treaty, signatory countries renounced development of nuclear armaments. They also committed to support international tools against proliferation, such as the Non-Proliferation Treaty and the IAEA safeguards. Moreover, they renounced acceptance of nuclear explosives being stationed in their territory, and rejected nuclear testing on their land. Additionally, they refused any nuclear waste dumping in South Pacific waters. The Rarotonga Treaty was not coercive, however, and France continued its nuclear testing for another ten years. But the treaty did become a significant and tangible step in the recognition of the South Pacific's interests and particularities. Australia was one of the first countries to sign the Treaty during the South Pacific Forum on 6 August 1985. Protocols were approved in 1986, after long negotiations between the signatories regarding their severity.

Nevertheless, in order to defend its security through Washington's extended nuclear deterrence and, secondly, to strengthen its regional leadership by maintaining its commitments within ANZUS, Australia put pressure on other members of the Forum to accept the stipulation that signatories could still allow ships or aircraft to visit their territory while transporting nuclear armament. Australian diplomats had to really put their leadership into action in order to persuade their reluctant neighbourhood to accept this provision. In fact, some Pacific countries, such as Fiji, argued that allowing such ships and aircraft in the region, for Australia's sake, undermined the credibility of the Treaty. However, understanding that Australia would not ratify the agreement without this provision, Fiji accepted inclusion of the clause. In this respect, French policy-makers considered that Australia's position was at least ambiguous, if not hypocritical at times: presenting itself as a global spokesman against nuclear proliferation but then acting against its principles in order to avoid antagonising the American alliance and possibly endangering Australian national security.

Australia's largely successful ambiguity regarding nuclear armament comes from the dichotomy between its political interests and the satisfaction of its public opinion. The development of a virulent anti-nuclear dynamic amongst PICs, as well as amongst a significant part of the Australian electorate,[6] despite reinforcing Australia's security at first sight by protecting its region from nuclear threats, was actually questioning Canberra's global system of defence. In fact, the anti-nuclear movement in the South Pacific could have been interpreted as a threat to ANZUS by criticising American nuclear activities in the region, as New Zealand's position has shown. The assertion of a completely nuclear-free zone in the Pacific would have challenged the United States' global deterrence strategy and, therefore, potentially weakened the Western alliance in the region.

New Zealand was firmly opposed to Australia's stance on the Treaty in 1985–1986. With New Zealand deciding to refuse port visits by nuclear powered ships, even those from the US, "the United States position [was] that the New Zealand decision renders impracticable the discharge of their mutual obligations under ANZUS. The United States has ceased bilateral military cooperation with New Zealand, withdrawn from military exercises with New Zealand and cut back intelligence links with New Zealand" (NAA M3793, 54). This diplomatic tension was the source of strong anxiety among Australian politicians and diplomats, who were now caught between two traditional allies. Australia found itself torn between two opposite positions in regard to nuclear deterrence: the United States with its considerable nuclear armament and New Zealand supporting its prohibition. Since these were traditionally two of Australia's closest allies, by values and interests, Australian policy-makers could not adopt a definite position on the matter. Official statements were therefore quite ambiguous.

Australia's official position on America's decision was to assert that even if Australia disagreed with New Zealand, Australia believed that New Zealand had the right to make its own policy and that Washington's measure was counterproductive to the South Pacific's security. Therefore, Australian officials stated that Canberra would not withdraw from its military commitments with its neighbour, thereby ensuring that New Zealand would not be isolated from the Western community. However, many Australian leaders feared that ANZUS' credibility could be weakened and its deterrence effect lowered. Australian politicians felt the need to reassert that ANZUS was still maintained as a framework for South Pacific security and not replaced by any bilateral treaty. Moreover, since other Pacific states such as Japan supported and benefited from the Western alliance, Australian diplomats were obliged to reassure their allies that Australian–American military and intelligence links would still be maintained. Australian foreign policy-makers did not wish to lose their main security alliances in the Pacific, Washington and Tokyo, for the sake of the Rarotonga Treaty and anti-proliferation policies.

George P. Shultz, then US Secretary of State, reassured Bill Hayden on that matter during their meeting on July the 15th 1985: "Mr. Shultz opened his brief presentation by saying that [...] New Zealand had changed its status but remained a "friend". [...] The USA-New Zealand relationship would be adjusted but the USA saw no need to make any formal alteration to the ANZUS Treaty itself" (NAA M3793, 63).[7] However, "Mr Hayden agreed with Mr Shultz that handling of the problems arising from the New Zealand decision had proved to be a very painful experience". The tension between the US and New Zealand created a significant crisis for Australia, positioned as it was between two opposing key partners. Bill Hayden even explained to George Shultz that "New Zealanders were making an important contribution to security and stability in the South Pacific. On balance, they were probably more effective in the South Pacific than Australia: they were out there more often and had developed a knack of dealing with Pacific islanders". Therefore, Bill Hayden feared that Australia would be obliged to intervene in the South Pacific more often than in the past, which it had demonstrated a reluctance to do. This element is particularly interesting because Australia's diplomacy seemed, at this point, contradictory. Australia claimed to renew and increase its engagement in the South Pacific but Hayden explained privately to Shultz that "the current situation was obliging Australia to entertain new areas of responsibility" (NAA M3793, 63).

Australia sought to constrain New Zealand from becoming a virulent non-proliferation proselyte in the region, fearing that it might influence Pacific states to become even more active against American nuclear equipment, increasing their opposition to the Rarotonga Treaty in Vanuatu, Papua New Guinea, while also influencing Australian public opinion itself. In 1987, the Australian ambassador to the United Nations in Geneva warned his New Zealander counterpart during talks on disarmament that Australia had "concerns" about New Zealand's public position of exporting its nuclear policies to its neighbours (NAA M3793, 103). The report asserts that New Zealand's proselyting for its policy had been very disruptive in Australia, Japan, Vanuatu, Papua New Guinea and Sweden by influencing public opinions to lobby their governments for a ban on nuclear warships. DFAT public servants eventually stated that Australia's credibility had been undermined by New Zealand's decision (NAA M3793, 103). The report noted further that "New Zealand is less like us than we had assumed, [its] strategic view is not ours", highlighting the two countries' divergent approaches to regional security. The Rarotonga Treaty exposed the ambiguities of Australia's nuclear policies. This tension corresponds to Australian debates regarding security. Would Australia be more secure in a nuclear-free world or does Australia's security lie in Washington's indirect nuclear deterrence? Foreign policy-makers in Canberra did not want alliances and dynamics in Asia-Pacific to be modified because of the Nuclear Free Zone in the South Pacific. Consequently, it was crucial for Australia to be part of this Nuclear Free Zone movement in order to take charge of and protect its own security.

For this purpose, France played the role of a "scapegoat" and a "smokescreen" (Piquet 2000, p. 16), which became genuinely useful for Australia's regional assertion. In fact, the presence of a European power conducting nuclear testing enabled South Pacific countries to join together and put aside their divisions and tensions with Australia about the clauses of the Rarotonga Treaty. France had never been fully opposed to the idea of a denuclearised South Pacific, depending on the conditions. However, French policy-makers believed that, while Australia was the only regional power potentially able to develop a nuclear armament, such treaty was not necessary to tackle horizontal proliferation and, therefore, only aimed to attack the French nuclear testing program (Mohamed-Gaillard 2010, p. 349). France became seen as the power disrupting the construction of a nuclear-free zone in the Pacific, not Australia. Moreover, Australia tried to find multilateral leverages to reassert its attachment to a South Pacific Nuclear Free Zone. This book argues that Australian official narratives about France's presence in the South Pacific leveraged the tensions existing in New Caledonia and France's nuclear testing in order to increase Australia's regional leadership, as DFAT archives demonstrate. A 1987 report, in preparation for the South Pacific Heads of Mission Meeting, argues: "Policy opportunity: Australia will need to put more effort in maintaining the concept of regional consensus against [...] external pressure such as the French presence" (NAA M3793, 102). Another report from 1988, authored by the Quai d'Orsay, explained that opposition to France's nuclear activities used to increase whenever the diplomatic consensus in the South Pacific was wavering, as leverage to gather regional players against Paris (AN Pierrefitte, 19940509/95). France continued in this role as smokescreen until it changed its approach to management of this regional criticism. French foreign policy-makers and politicians realised that Paris needed to completely modify its approach to the problem. France could no longer assert that nuclear issues were only national matters. It had to accept regional dialogue regarding its nuclear testing program and improve integration with French territories in their regional environment. French stakeholders realised that, if they were successful in this attempt, it would be much harder to make France a scapegoat and a target of regional condemnation.

Such a tangible shift can be analysed through Joseph Nye's fourth step in the construction of smart power strategies: "Which forms of power behaviour are most likely to succeed?" (2011, p. 209). Given this antagonistic situation, France realised that its traditional approach of hard power assertion was counterproductive because it was reinforcing regional hostility. After having reassessed their strategy and objectives, French stakeholders came to the conclusion that the best way to maintain the nuclear program in French Polynesia was to work towards a regional recognition and integration, a soft power behaviour. As Nye explains, if hard power does not appear legitimate to other states, it can diminish a state's power by creating enemies (2011, p. 93). Hard power must be legitimate in order to be efficient. This book argues that France, after 1995, took into account that its nuclear testing program was hindering its nuclear deterrence legitimacy regionally, and therefore its power. Putting an end to the nuclear program in Moruroa enabled Paris to be accepted in the South Pacific, which, in the end, has reinforced France's hard power in the region.

AUSTRALIAN OPPOSITION TO FRANCE'S NUCLEAR TESTING PROGRAM

Developed under Charles de Gaulle's Presidency, the French nuclear program has, since its creation, constituted a crucial element of France's international power, both on symbolic and on practical levels. Nuclear deterrence has been part of France's *politique de grandeur* (policy of greatness), and, therefore, has been perceived as the main demonstration of its power. Moreover, it represents the core element of the country's military strategy and of its strike force. According to Nick Maclellan and Jean Chesnaux (1998, p. 78), France's nuclear power is also used to legitimise its seat as a permanent member of the United Nations Security Council. Australian policy-makers, between 1972 and 1996, were very critical of this French strategic postulate. This was the source of a deep mistrust between the two countries.

France's Nuclear Arsenal

For many reasons, the French state has no intention of withdrawing from its territories in the Atlantic, Indian, Pacific and Antarctic Oceans. The main one is intellectual and emotional: as the first article of the French Constitution asserts, the French Republic is "indivisible" which means that France cannot imagine disengage from its citizens and territories, even if they live thousands of kilometres from the mainland, as explained in more details in Chapter 6. From a defence point of view, French overseas territories play a key role in maintaining France's global power, and French Polynesia has constituted a fundamental component of this vision. After Algeria's independence in 1962, France transferred its nuclear testing facilities to Moruroa in French Polynesia, where it conducted its first atmospheric testing in 1966. All these territories have been part of France's demonstration of power with, for example, French Guyana hosting European Spaceport. However, French Polynesia has been the focus of this system because of its nuclear activities. For that reason, Australian attacks against French nuclear testing were considered in France as a threat against the French presence in the Pacific in general, and against its global security strategy. Régis Debray, former general secretary of the South Pacific Council, attached to the French Presidency, argued in 1986: "Denuclearising the Pacific would mean removing France".[8] One of the negative consequences of French nuclear testing is the fact that it deeply handicapped the French–Australian relationship, not only by creating direct conflict between the two countries, but also, and maybe mostly, by creating a long-lasting level of disagreement in French and Australian diplomatic mindsets which prevented any substantial agreement on other topics. Nuclear issues have complicated the shared history and memory between the two countries and limited their ability to move forward together. The PICs were also strongly opposed to French nuclear testing, but this contestation was not only led by institutional actors. Civil organisations such as political parties, unions and churches also led virulent condemnation of France's nuclear policies.

Condemnations were often lodged to international fora. The United Nations, and especially its General Assembly, was the first and most influential organisation to criticise France's positions, due to the large audience it could reach. South Pacific countries have also used many other institutions for this aim, such as the South Pacific Forum (now Pacific Islands Forum—PIF) or the Secretariat of the Pacific Community (now the Pacific Community—PC), where French diplomats were called upon to discuss these issues. However, when the PICs tried to raise their opposition to French testing at the World Health Organisation (WHO), France lodged a complaint to assert that this issue was not part of the WHO's prerogatives. French representatives to the organisation described it as unfair and offensive to use France's program of nuclear testing as a means of lowering France's credibility within the WHO. Moreover, French diplomats feared that they would have to justify France's nuclear policies in a new forum if Australia, New Zealand, Vanuatu and Papua New Guinea were to ask the WHO to take responsibility for this issue and commission a new report on the potential consequences of testing on the regional population. However, during a General Meeting on September 1989, the WHO decided not to get involved with the matter, agreeing with the French assertion that it was not part of its prerogatives (AD Nantes, 542). The organisation still issued strong statements against nuclear weapons later on. Australian decision-makers tried to use all the main multilateral institutions to force France to stop its testing. They also tried to use bilateral tools. Many sources testify that nuclear-related issues were part of the agenda scheduled for each Franco-Australian visit, whether in Paris, Canberra or Noumea. France's ongoing nuclear testing damaged France's regional reputation for many years afterward because this nuclear program was not only condemned by Pacific nations for its environmental impact, it was also perceived as a demonstration of France's continuous colonial strategy in the Pacific.

Three Important Steps in Australian–French Antagonism

France conducted nuclear tests in Moruroa between 1966 and 1996, leading to thirty years of tensions between Paris and Canberra. In *The Future of Power*, Joseph Nye asserts: "Military resources can implement four types of actions that are the modalities or currencies of military powers" (2011, p. 41). These actions encompass a large range of intervention: "(1) physically fight and destroy; (2) back up threats in coercive diplomacy; (3) promise protection, including peacekeeping; and (4) provide many forms of assistance". France's military presence in the South Pacific, based in New Caledonia and French Polynesia, aimed to enable France to implement these four types of actions, from nuclear armament to cooperation and aid to foreign countries.

However, the impact of nuclear testing on France's image in the Pacific induced a regional condemnation of its military presence until 1996.

Three events caused the exacerbation of this diplomatic conflict. The first key date of this opposition was the year 1973 when Australia caused France to be condemned by the International Court of Justice (ICJ) for its atmospheric nuclear testing. As explained previously, Gough Whitlam was elected Prime Minister in December 1972 and, for the first time after twenty-three years of opposition, Australia had a Labor government. Whitlam utterly modified Canberra's nuclear policy by ending it drastically to Australia's technological research and by becoming a leader in nuclear disarmament promotion. Therefore, on 9 May 1973, Australia and New Zealand requested that the ICJ take a position in regard to the disagreement between their governments and Paris, regarding the legality of atmospheric nuclear testing. The international organisation condemned France, which responded by refusing to recognise its jurisdiction for a few months. However, in 1974, France decided to fully recognise the ICJ again and to move its nuclear tests underground (Cot 1973, p. 253). At this point the opposition became fierce, especially between Australian public opinion and French interests. For instance, the Australian Postal Union decided not to deliver mail to the French embassy in Canberra nor to French Consulates in Melbourne, Sydney and Perth, for a period of two months. The French ambassador at the time wrote to the Minister of Foreign Affairs to complain about this issue, reminding the Department that stopping mail from and to an embassy was a direct violation of international law. The ambassador even ironically reminded the Minister that Elizabeth II had warranted the application of International Conventions in her territories and that, since she was still the Head of the Australian state, Australian citizens had to obey their Queen and deliver the mail. The French embassy also complained about the call to boycott a list of French companies made by the Australian Broadcasting Corporation (ABC) and the publication at the Australian National University (ANU) of flyers promoting violent actions against the French embassy and its diplomats in Canberra. The tone adopted by the French ambassador in these documents was very firm, asserting that the Australian government had a "duty" to support these requests and reproaching Australian officials vigorously for not being able to prevent illegal attacks against French interests (AD Nantes, 428PO/I/132).

The French bombing of the Greenpeace ship the *Rainbow Warrior* in Auckland harbour in 1985 and ratification of the Rarotonga Treaty a year later constituted the second period of increased tensions between France and Australia with regard to French nuclear testing. This intervention, associated with the violent situation then in New Caledonia (see Chapter 6), created a tangible crisis between France and its Pacific neighbours until 1988. In July 1985, the French secret services sank the Greenpeace ship that was headed for Moruroa to stop nuclear testing. This operation turned into a disaster because a photographer, who was also a member of Greenpeace, died in the attack. This, however, was not the first sabotage led by French secret services in the Pacific. According to Alexandre de Marenches, former head of the *Service de Documentation Extérieure et de Contre-Espionnage* (SDECE), a former French intelligence service, more than fifty successful operations of sabotage were conducted in the region between 1970 and 1981 (Maclellan and Chesnaux 1998, p. 92). However, the scandal created by the *Rainbow Warrior* bombing led to a very stringent and virulent condemnation of France's presence in the Pacific region with Paris being labelled a threat by Australian policy-makers. This condemnation came from public opinion, as testified by the thousands of letters of opprobrium received by French institutions in Australia. It was also orchestrated by the media, political parties, unions, churches, or any association with an opinion on the matter.

The national political context in Australia also explains this resurgence of tensions. During the Hawke governments, Australia's Labour Party felt torn between Australia's national interest of supporting the United States and Ronald Reagan's assertive nuclear policies. The United States had once again asserted its doctrine of peace through increased nuclear armament. Washington conducted an aggressive nuclear militarisation targeting the USSR, building a "credible American first strike capability" (Beazley 2003, p. 352). This aggravation of nuclear tensions between the United States and the USSR also affected Australian campaigns of criticism against nuclear deterrence. As shown by the French embassy to Australia's daily political reports to the Foreign Ministry in Paris, a part of Australian public and political elite opinion, particularly within the Labour Party, was reluctant to support Washington's military aggressiveness, denying America's claim that it was contributing to global security through deterrence. Australian policy-makers at the time supported arms-control initiatives, in the Australian region especially.

For example, in November 1983, the Hawke Cabinet presented a set of disarmament proposals, including the creation of a nuclear-free zone in the Pacific and a general ban on nuclear testing. "More generally, they committed Australia to promoting measures to reverse the nuclear arms race, [creating for example] an Ambassador for Disarmament" (Beazley 2003, p. 354). Consequently, France and its nuclear testing in the Pacific became the target of this condemnation, and opposition to France became fierce in public opinion. At the time, Australia authored many proposals for a comprehensive test ban. France was the main target of Australia's anti-nuclear diplomacy, since Australian policy-makers could not afford to criticise the United-States openly. According to Stewart Firth, Australia's opposition to French testing can mainly be explained by strategic reasons. As explained previously, the Hawke government was not fully opposed to nuclear armament, thinking that Australia was indirectly benefiting from the United States' nuclear protection through ANZUS. However, the Hawke government feared that French nuclear testing would substantially increase opposition to nuclear armament in Australian public opinion, which was already strongly against nuclear armament. Therefore, Australian diplomats and politicians feared that the majority of Australian opinion would become fully opposed to any nuclear activity in the region, as had happened in New Zealand, including from the United States, and would push for a full contestation of the ANZUS treaty. This would have completely disrupted Australia's system of alliances. Therefore, France's defence strategy was, according to the Hawke government, potentially clashing with Australia's own nuclear strategy (S. Firth, pers. inter., Canberra, 16 May 2016).

The third source of tension, the last nuclear testing, ordered by French president Jacques Chirac in 1995–1996, motivated important anti-French demonstrations in the South Pacific and in Australia. As Gareth Evans asserts: "The relationship went backwards rapidly after 1995. Before that, because relations had been improved and we were all getting along well with each other, the Matignon Accords were being handled. I obviously wanted the relationship on as even a level as possible. That was very difficult in the context of the test" (pers. inter., Melbourne, 13 April 2016). It is interesting to note that France's public opinion was largely opposed to the testing and that French politicians were divided on this decision. While foreign policies traditionally benefit from a large consensus in France, Chirac's decision split the political spectrum on this question. The majority of his opponents believed that, with this testing, France was sending the wrong signal to countries such as China, India and Pakistan who were seen as the main sources of nuclear instability. French public opinion also feared that France's diplomacy would be deeply discredited by Chirac's decision. However, even though South Pacific opinions were quite virulent against France, its diplomacy did not suffer from the testing. Gareth Evans summarises well this popular aggressiveness against France:

> The point I made publicly and which got me into trouble was by saying that it could have been worse. I was kicked around and we had to escalate our rhetoric. The main thing in my mind was that the French were, I thought, to be believed when they said it would be the final series; that they could do what they wanted to do after by computer simulations. I thought that was a big achievement. At the same time, they had committed to ratify the Comprehensive Test Ban Treaty. Even if we were all irritated by the French tests, it was the last thing we wanted to see happen, but it was not in itself, in my mind, the gigantic blow that could not be managed. That was basically Hawke's position, but the public opinion became so hysterical on that subject that we had to force ourselves to escalate the rhetoric and it made a difficult period. (pers. inter., Melbourne, 13 April 2016)

In fact, in 1995–1996, a significant part of the Australian public opinion responded violently against France in regard to the testing. The French Consulate in Perth was bombed and burnt down, French products were boycotted and media campaigns cultivated this animosity: "It was from our people that there was a very strong wave of opposition to this issue, which manifested itself in a very emotional way" says Denise Fisher, former Australian Consul to New Caledonia (pers. inter., Canberra, 7 April 2016).

However, in less than two years, France had fully abandoned its nuclear activities in the region. Its last nuclear test took place on 29 January 1996 and was aimed to be the last one before the digitalisation of such experiments. On 26 March 1996, France signed the Rarotonga Treaty, and the Comprehensive Nuclear-Test-Ban Treaty (CTBT) on 24 September 1996. In May 1998, the IAEA published a report asserting the innocuousness of the French testing and by July 1998, the testing site in Moruroa was fully dismantled (AN Pierrefitte, 20010326/22). In the light of Joseph Nye's theory (2011, p. 93), France had implemented a smart power strategy by putting an end to its nuclear testing program. French policy-makers understood that the testing, even if it demonstrated France's power of persuasion and deterrence, hindered its power of attraction by creating mistrust against France. By ending the nuclear tests, French policy-makers aimed to answer one of the five questions of a smart power strategy: "which forms of power behavior are most likely to succeed?" (Nye 2011, p. 209). Promising that France would not launch any more testing in the Pacific, decision-makers from Paris quickly succeeded in appeasing the opposition to their country on that matter. Strategically, opponents of French nuclear testing have in fact benefited diplomatically from this issue on two levels. Bringing opposition to nuclear activities to international institutions, especially the United Nations, has enabled countries like Australia, New Zealand and other Pacific States to identify a sensitive topic amongst the international community and take leadership on propositions related to it, as much as to collaborate for the region's security. Moreover, French archives demonstrate that the discourse against France and its nuclear activities has improved and facilitated regionalisation of the South Pacific around a common enemy. As Piquet explains, at the end of the Cold War, PICs wanted the international community to acknowledge their regional identity, interests and ability to lead their region, "as a catalysis element" (2000, p. 15). Therefore, Australian and New Zealander opposition to French nuclear testing appears to have been quite advantageous to these two countries in order to enable them to assert their leadership in the region. In 1995–1996, Australian opposition to French testing was driven by the Australian population and public opinion. Australian policy-makers did not condemn France strongly at first, but enough to satisfy their public opinion and neighbouring states and to legitimise Australia's leadership in the South Pacific, without hindering their relationship with Paris. It was only when they realised that a mild criticism of France's activities would only lead to tensions with the Australian electorate and with their regional partners that Australian politicians strengthened their discourse and reproaches.

France's Strategy to Legitimise Its Nuclear Testing Program

French politicians and diplomats have attempted to defend France's position on nuclear testing as being a national issue that should not involve any other state. As Martine Piquet summarises, a clear division between national and international arenas about nuclear testing is very hard to define (2000, p. 14). The French official discourse explaining that France did not have to justify such testing because it was only a question of national security, similar to the way in which tensions in New Caledonia were only seen as a national matter, failed to convince its Pacific neighbours. André Dumoulin and Christophe Wasinski, who have developed the most acute study of France's official discourse of legitimisation of its nuclear program, explain that it was both aimed at South Pacific countries but also, in France itself, at a significant part of the population which rejected the testing (2010, p. 79).

Fully aware of the regional criticism provoked by their nuclear activities in Polynesia, French policy-makers asked their embassies and consulates around the Pacific to gather press-reviews about the matter. The aim was to develop an accurate awareness of the different critiques against the testing in order to offer a relevant response to each and every argument. Therefore, the argument that arrogant French politicians did not even bother responding to critics is unfounded. On the contrary, archives from the highest institutions of the Republic, such as the Prime Minister's cabinet or the Minister of Foreign Affairs' cabinet, demonstrate that policy-makers at the highest level followed this issue closely, through many press reviews, reports pertaining to pro-testing argumentations and local scientific publications supporting French positions.[9] The discourse elaborated by French policy-makers in order to justify France's nuclear testing in the Pacific was threefold: strategic, moral and scientific. This discourse was primarily aimed at Australia in order to achieve regional appeasement in times of tensions.

First of all, French politicians tried to explain to their Australian counterparts that their two countries had opposing conceptions of how national security should be achieved and strengthened. This argument reveals quite well the constructivist vision of the world and of France's diplomacy in French policy-makers' logic. In fact, the argument that France and Australia failed to engage with security issues together because of their misunderstanding demonstrates that security, as with other issues of international relations, can be seen as primarily a social construction resulting from each country's history and intellectual tradition as much as its military means. Having an opposite conception of how national security should be conducted, France and Australia could not fully cooperate on this topic and the issue of nuclear weapons catalysed this conceptual tension. This first intellectual disagreement around the idea of security was both about the definition of the notion of security itself as well as the means to maintain it: independence and power in the French spirit, and protective alliance for the Australian mindset.

Australia has repeatedly reinforced its security within broader alliances and the cultivation of relations with a great power. Therefore, Australia's security has been conceived through the British alliance within the Empire and then by a close alliance with the United States, within ANZUS. Australia's security strategy requires protection by a foreign country. On the other hand, France's key concept regarding national security is independence. After the traumatic experiences of two world wars waged on its soil, France has led specific strategic, economic and energy policies in order to become as independent as possible. Decision-makers in Paris have refused to have State security be dependent on a great power's potential support. Following this point of view, France has had to present itself as a great middle power in order to maintain its national security. French presidents have repeatedly explained to international audiences this independent conception of national security. For instance, Socialist French President François Mitterrand insisted on the fact that:

> France ensures its own security through its national nuclear strike force, perceived as a tool in its dissuasive strategy [...]. This strategy, which protects France's independence in its decision-making, only makes sense if France's nuclear strike force is maintained to an effective level of dissuasion. [...] In a world where peace rests upon the balance of powers, a unilateral renouncement to its nuclear testing would challenge France's capacity to ensure its own security. (AD Nantes, 132)

Nuclear energy is crucial to this independent concept of security, which Joseph Nye would characterise as a "coercive diplomacy" (2011, p. 44). From the beginning, nuclear policies were a means for Charles de Gaulle to prove to the United States and the United Kingdom that World War II had not reduced France to being a second level power and that Paris' diplomacy would never be dictated by its former allies. According to many researchers, including Martine Piquet, France's nuclear assertion was a success (2000, p. 20). The drawback of this conception of security, however, is that it has deepened the gap between France and its allies in the South Pacific because French politicians and diplomats promulgated policies of security without significantly engaging with the other countries of the region, which were used to securing their security by alliances with great and powerful friends. By asserting at first that nuclear testing was only a French national issue, France did not try to convince its neighbours of the purpose of those actions and thereby created much regional resentment.

Second of all, and on a more ethical level, French diplomats regularly accused Australian politicians and public opinion of being somewhat biased in their criticism against Paris's nuclear program. The French government and its representatives were often frustrated at being the central target of Australian opposition to nuclear testing, when Australia had previously let the United Kingdom conduct nuclear testing on its own territory before attempting to develop its own nuclear program. More frequently, French diplomats expressed their surprise and irritation to see Australia only quietly condemn China's nuclear testing, when the nuclear site chosen by the Chinese government was closer to Australian shores than was French Polynesia. On that matter, on a few occasions and not without sarcasm, French diplomats even suggested that their Australian counterparts should find a solution to Canberra's opposition to London on nuclear testing wastes in Australia before considering French nuclear testing as a major issue. Australia and the United Kingdom have had tensions about the clean-up of former atomic tests sites in South Australia, at Emu Ridge and Maralinga, which have still not been fully resolved. For instance, in a 1985 diplomatic cable addressed by the French ambassador to the UN in New York to his Minister in Paris, the diplomat reported how the Australian Royal Commission had produced a report asking the United Kingdom to pay for the decontamination of its former nuclear sites. The cable quoted an editorial from *The Times* in London asserting that Australia could use its uranium exports to put pressure on the United Kingdom, which the French diplomat questioned, claiming that Australia was too faithful to London to risk hindering its special relationship with the United Kingdom (AD Nantes, 623). The French Ministry of Foreign Affairs even produced a report on those nuclear sites in Australia in preparation for using this information against Australia if necessary. The report assessed the tensions between families of Australian soldiers who had died because of the testing and the Australian and British governments. The Ministry even requested to DFAT to be allowed to visit the testing sites and to be informed of the level of remaining radioactivity (AD Nantes, 632).

Another ethical argument used by French officials to defend France's nuclear program was of a social nature. According to this narrative, the French state had the moral responsibility to develop all its territories economically, and nuclear activities were seen as an efficient platform to do so in French Polynesia. In a 1983 report, the Quai d'Orsay asked its embassies in Canberra and Wellington to provide Paris with the amount of funding spent by Australia and New Zealand in their former or current territories in the Pacific, such as the Cook Islands for New Zealand. The aim of this request was to show that France invested much more funding to develop French Polynesia than Australia and New Zealand did in their territories. In 1983, France's direct funding to French Polynesia was six billion francs a year, a considerable amount, in addition to all the normal public cost of the French administration in Polynesia. This funding financed infrastructures in the territory, such as airports or other transport systems. The French State built several large military-industrial facilities in this territory, such as Tahiti's airport, and Papeete's Department of Naval Construction and Weapons and the Geodetic Observatory of Tahiti for satellite monitoring. French Polynesia's infrastructures have been largely developed by and for military and nuclear activities (Maclellan and Chesnaux 1998, pp. 86, 89). Such considerable investments have been a direct consequence of the nuclear activities in French Polynesia, requiring a constant improvement of the archipelagos' infrastructures. Paris wanted to defend its nuclear testing by explaining that the population benefited substantially from these activities (AD Nantes, 632).

The third major argument used by French politicians and diplomats was scientific. The French nuclear testing program raised a legitimate strong regional concern about environmental and health issues. In response to this criticism, France produced international scientific reports that were trying to prove that the nuclear radiation was minimal in other regional countries, thousands of kilometres distant from Moruroa. Scientific arguments were the most effective type of discourses defending France's legitimacy in conducting these tests (AN Pierrefitte, 19940509/95). In 1983, France commissioned a report from an international group of experts and scientists from all countries that were part of the South Pacific Forum, and invited them to come and inspect the Moruroa site. This report, conducted by the New Zealander Atkinson, was very positive from France's perspective since it claimed that French testing did not significantly impact the regional environment. This report was used repeatedly by French officials to defend French nuclear activities. France claimed for instance that levels of radioactivity in the air and waters of French Polynesia were lower than levels in Australia, Japan or the United States. In order to legitimise its assertions, the French Ministry of Foreign Affairs ordered its attachés for nuclear affairs all around the Pacific to investigate and find the levels of radiation in the country where their embassy was located (AD Nantes, 632). Jacques Cousteau was allowed in 1988 to study Moruroa and was mostly reassuring on the radiation levels. However, Atkinson and Cousteau were preoccupied by the nuclear waste left under the lagoon, asserting that it would require hundreds of thousands of years to stop emitting radiation (AN Pierrefitte, 19940509/95). Laurence Monnoyer is, partly accurately, very critical of the use of scientific evidences in order to support strategic and political decisions, such as the nuclear testing. Monnoyer argues that policy-makers refer to scientific and technical expertise not to improve the political debate around a relevant issue but to close it by stopping any opponent to contest the policy and remove the debate from the public space (1997, p. 157). However, while French policy-makers have used, as demonstrated previously, scientific expertise to justify France's nuclear testing, this book argues that their intention was not to utterly shut the debate about the necessity for France to conduct the testing. They primarily aimed to contradict inaccurate information spread amongst the public opinion, in order to improve the debate.

Thus, many official narratives use primarily geographic arguments to demonstrate France's preoccupation with the impact of its testing. Moruroa had been chosen because of its distance from any large population centre. The testing site was located more than 1000 km from Tahiti and more than 4000 km from any other country, whilst American and Soviet testing were only a few hundred kilometres from Las Vegas and Novosibirsk. Moreover, Moruroa is located 4800 km from Auckland, 6600 km from Lima in Peru and 6800 km from Brisbane, making Australia in fact closer to China's nuclear testing in its own territory. These measurements were often brought to the attention of Australian diplomats in order to remind them that the potential risk was very low. It is interesting to notice that Gareth Evans, in his vain attempt to assuage Australian public opinion during the last testing in 1996, used the same argument:

There was no rational evidence of any implications for Australians in the escape of radioactive materials. It was 6000 km away. [...] In popular thinking, the Pacific test site waters were seen lapping the shores of Bondi, or the other side of New Zealand at worst, but this was ridiculous. (pers. inter., Melbourne, 13 April 2016)

The second type of scientific argument was about the testing process itself. The French Ministry of Defence frequently argued that France was conducting its testing following safer procedures than other nuclear powers, for instance by detonating the nuclear reaction twice as deep as that by the Americans in their testing (AD Nantes, 132). French policy-makers have quoted repeatedly, over more than a decade, a long article from Philip Baxter, President of the Australian Nuclear Energy Commission, where Baxter explains that if nothing had proved that French testing had had any impact on Australian health, neither had anything demonstrated the contrary. According to Baxter, French nuclear testing did not produce any more radiation than moving from Sydney to Canberra, where the nuclear radiation coming from the sun is greater because of the altitude.[10] Such scientific findings obviously must be questioned, especially when one can read, in a brief prepared in 1981 for the Minister of Defence: "No dangerous radioactivity has been observed in Moruroa" (AD Nantes, 132).

More recent reports, published since the end of the testing campaigns, have pointed out the opposite and that French government, consciously or not, underestimated or hid the tangible consequences of the testing on soldiers and civilians in Moruroa and in the archipelagos around. Such reports have proven that levels of radioactivity increased in French Polynesia in general due to the testing program. However, no report has indicated either environmental or health consequences in Australia. During his visit to French Polynesia and Wallis and Futuna, on 22 February 2016, Socialist French President François Hollande officially recognised the environmental impact of the testing on the archipelagos of the territory:

Without French Polynesia, France would have not been able to develop its nuclear armament and its deterrence strategy. [...] This gives France the ability to constitute a fully independent nation. [...] This contribution, through the nuclear testing, I want to solemnly acknowledge today. I acknowledge that French nuclear testing conducted between 1966 and 1996 has had an environmental impact, has provoked health consequences and also, paradoxically, had social consequences when the testing stopped.[11]

Hollande wanted to reform France's narrative in the South Pacific by removing mentions of nuclear testing from it. Therefore, the French President asserted that his visit aimed to put the nuclear era behind and that the French state would provide financial compensation for victims of nuclear radiation. In fact, since the 2010 law regarding these compensations, only around twenty cases have been accepted. Hollande claimed that the acceptance processes would be reformed to be more efficient, by clarifying, in the Enforcement Decree of the 2010 law, the definition of "risk" when the required safety measures had not been set up properly. The French state decided to ring-fence the "*dotation globale d'autonomie*," the budget transferred by the French state to the government of French Polynesia and often described as French reparation funds for nuclear testing. These funds should reach €90 million in 2017. Moreover, Hollande announced the funding of a new plan for Papeete's hospital. From an environmental point of view, Hollande asserted that Paris would pay for the complete cleaning of the Hao atoll and the installation of a surveillance office in the Moruroa and Fangataufa atolls. Additionally, the French President announced the creation of a research institute in Polynesia focusing on conducting historical studies of nuclear testing in order to maintain an accurate record of these thirty years. François Hollande's announcements received a positive response in French Polynesia, where the population expected a deeper support from the French state for victims of the testing, who were suffering from various forms of cancer. According to the newspaper *Le Monde*, Hollande could have hardly gone further in such recognition in his speech but a part of the local population still has doubts about the genuineness of his promises ("En Polynésie française", 2016). However, in October 2018, Polynesian independentist leader Oscar Temaru lodged a complaint for crimes against humanity against France to the International Criminal Court, as part of his strategy to promote the independence on French Polynesia.

French decision-makers have used all the available media and fora available to them to try to defuse and legitimise French nuclear testing in Polynesia. Many delegations of Australian politicians and scientists were received in Paris by the relevant institutions. Moreover, French diplomats have also persistently written to editors and Australian newspapers to explain France's diplomacy in response to condemnation in any article.[12]

Australia's Conciliatory Position Towards France

Australia's opposition to France's nuclear testing in French Polynesia has been significant, influential and recurrent for many decades. However, Australian decision-makers have also tried to remain accommodating with their French counterparts. French diplomats stressed that Australia maintained a conciliatory position between France and other South Pacific countries. New Zealand, Vanuatu and Papua New Guinea were the most virulent opponents to France's nuclear testing. During all their attempts to build official condemnation for the testing, especially during UNGAs, Australia tried to find a middle way that would pressure France to stop its activities without offending French officials. Australia's interests with France and Europe were too significant to risk them by aggressively condemning Paris, as demonstrated previously regarding the role of economic interests in times of strategic tensions. Australian diplomats also knew that attacking France on this matter would not result in Paris simply ceasing its nuclear testing. Australia's regional influence turned out to be a concrete asset that enabled France to avoid considerable condemnations for its nuclear testing program. For instance, in 1985, Australia tried vainly to enforce a conciliation between France, which had refused to stop its testing but had agreed to support a resolution against the dumping of nuclear waste in the sea, and PNG, Vanuatu and Tonga, which wanted the South Pacific Forum to draft a resolution against France.[13] Paris has globally benefited from the lack of consensus against its nuclear policies amongst Pacific countries, playing with the opposition between the United States–Australia on one hand, and PICs on the other.

Therefore, French foreign policy-makers were fully aware that Australia was the first country which had to be convinced of the necessity for France to continue its nuclear policy and that the potential contamination risks were supposedly minimal, in order to avoid aggressive regional condemnations. France's efforts to appease its Pacific neighbours and to justify its nuclear activities in Moruroa were always directed primarily toward Canberra, hoping that Australian diplomats would subsequently appease their regional partners. Except during the three main crises previously mentioned, France considered Australia as more of a partner in appeasing the region than as an opponent. For example, in a report previously mentioned, the French ambassador to the UN in Geneva explained to his Minister that France had avoided an IAEA censure against its nuclear testing because Australia had refrained from supporting

130 P. SOYEZ

such action (NAA M3793, 16). For that reason, France had only been strongly blamed for its testing when Australia went along with its neighbours' condemnation. From 1988, when France decided to change its diplomacy in the region from a distant attitude to one of engagement with its neighbours, Australia became "France's diplomatic priority" in the Pacific, because of its influence and because it was a leader in the region's security policies. Moreover, officials from the Quai also explained that a reconciliation with Australia eased multilateral relations as a whole in the Pacific because it enabled the United States and Japan to fully engage with both countries, without being obliged to support either Paris or Canberra (AN Pierrefitte, 19940509/51). Moreover, French and Australian policy-makers have not always been in opposition on this matter. For instance, during his visit to Paris in 1981, Bob Hawke made it known to the French Embassy to Australia that he wanted to mainly discuss three topics during his meeting with the French authorities. The nuclear question was one of them. But, specifically, Hawke had indicated that he wanted to talk about cooperation on peaceful uses of nuclear energy between the two countries, not about French testing in Moruroa (AD Nantes, 681). This cooperation encompassed elements such as the creation of mutual safeguards on uranium trade and enrichment, for instance. Gareth Evans slightly modified this idea of an Australian accommodation to the French position against Melanesian attacks:

> The Melanesians were always up to trying to be virulent and we were trying to accommodate and balance the situation. But I can't remember ever taking the view that the Melanesian position should be accommodated by taking a strong anti-French position. It was not what we wanted to do. We wanted to find a *modus vivendi* for the whole region where everybody had a place and let nature takes its course. [...] The Melanesians were always the most aggressive about it and it was something we wanted to balance out. (pers. inter., Melbourne, 13 April 2016)

However, this book suggests that Australia's conciliating influence could have been counterproductive. In fact, vehement PICs have, in the past, increased their animosity toward France when Paris was supported by Canberra, considering these temporary alliances as a collusion of middle powers. French diplomats have confirmed this process many times, questioning Australia's tangible influence over its neighbours. PICs have sometimes believed that Australia's conciliatory approach demonstrated more of an alliance between Western powers securing their global interests than Australia's will to bring peace in the South Pacific. Therefore, PICs regularly criticised Australia's ambiguous position on nuclear matters. While conducting a diplomacy aimed at reducing nuclear proliferation, Australia has been, for many decades, one of the main suppliers of uranium for nuclear powers. In fact, French diplomats even referred to Australia as leading a "uranium diplomacy".

Australia's Uranium as a Diplomatic Tool?

A 1987 DFAT report presented an accurate account of Australia's uranium policy at the beginning of the time period under review (NAA M3793, 16). At that time, Australia's uranium reserves were estimated at 462,000 tonnes of economically recoverable material (about 28% of the world's resources and supplying 14% of the world's needs) and 440,000 tonnes of higher cost uranium. The country's resources are considerable, with a production of about 6000 tonnes a year in the late 1980s and which has remained steady to this day. Australia was in 2013 the third largest producer of uranium in the world, after Kazakhstan and Canada, exporting more than 6700 tonnes of uranium for more than A$622 million, before a slight decrease in 2014–2015.[14] Australia has some of the largest uranium mines in the word, such as the Nabarlek and Ranger mines in Northern Territory and the Olympic Dam site in South Australia (NAA M3793, 16). Australian uranium exports must follow strict safeguards. Moreover, Australian nuclear policies have stated that Australian companies can only export this resource but not be part of its transformation for nuclear military purposes. Since the end of the 1980s, Australia has supplied uranium to nine countries: the United States, the United Kingdom, France, Belgium, Sweden, Finland, Germany, Japan and the Republic of Korea.

The report mentioned above presented a clear policy constructed with the intention of using the uranium trade as a leverage for ensuring global non-proliferation policies: "As a responsible supplier, we have the opportunity, and therefore the responsibility, to exercise a constructive influence towards the development of even more effective non-proliferation, nuclear safeguards and radioactive waste management practices" (NAA M3793, 16). The political benefit from uranium trade to Australian security and diplomacy is clear. By being a major player in uranium supply around the world, Australian policy-makers intended to impact non-proliferation policies in these export countries and in other countries as well. This was possible not simply by limiting supplies towards nuclear countries, as Australia was actually planning to increase its uranium exports, but rather by imposing draconian safeguards on the buyers. In fact, Australia has signed bilateral safeguard agreements with all its nuclear partners in order to limit proliferation, safeguards that are controlled by the IAEA. Australia has even funded a one million AUD program, led by the IAEA between 1980 and 1986, to sponsor research on the improvement of these international safeguards (NAA M3793, 16).

This vision of uranium trade as a tool to work against nuclear proliferation was not new in Australia. Malcolm Fraser had already stated, during his visit to London in 1978, that his country had "the duty to provide the world with energy resources using its uranium exports" and that, in this trade, Australia was asking for non-proliferation safeguards to be implemented in the countries to which it was supplying. Fraser's statement summarised clearly this first type of action implemented by Australia. Moreover, in the same speech, Fraser indirectly unmasked the way in which Australian diplomacy used uranium supplies to Europe to increase pressure for an agreement on agricultural trade in Brussels. Fraser explained that Australia was ready to guarantee to European countries access to its uranium and that, consequently, Canberra expected to be guaranteed access to European agricultural markets, out of reciprocity. Therefore, uranium supplies have been more than just a lever against non-proliferation (AD Nantes, 681). French–Australian relations also show how politicians and diplomats in Canberra have used uranium exports for diplomatic purposes. In 1983, in order to condemn French nuclear testing in the Pacific and foster international criticism against Paris, Australia decided to suspend all uranium shipments to France. This embargo was maintained for three years but eventually lifted on 19 August 1986, mainly because it proved to be completely inefficient. This move, in fact, had undermined Australia's trade and budget by closing an important market for Australian uranium without weakening France's nuclear policies, since Paris simply imported supplies from other producers (AN La Courneuve, 2842). However, when Canberra lifted the embargo, Australian politicians explained that it was not an approbation of France's nuclear policies in the South Pacific, since Australia had obtained from Paris a safeguard agreement that its uranium would not be used for testing or any military purpose. This example illustrates how Australia has used its uranium exports in order to influence nuclear countries' policies, but it shows as well the limitations of this approach.

Conclusion

Nuclear issues constituted a core element of tension in the Australian–French bilateral relationship until the end of the 1990s. On one hand, Australian governments tried to use regional condemnation on nuclear armament and testing in order to increase its leadership in the South Pacific, following the strategy of reaching visible results in diplomatic niche issues. On the other hand, France refused to question the importance of this nuclear testing program until computer simulation became fully reliable, because Paris linked this criticism to the condemnation of its presence in Pacific territories in general.

Tensions surrounding the French nuclear program in French Polynesia mainly mirrored how Australia and France had two very different perceptions and strategies regarding global security. In fact, two positions were facing each other in the South Pacific: the French one, basing global security on nuclear deterrence and conducting nuclear testing in order to maintain its strategic independence, and the Australian one, based on the reduction of nuclear armaments and full support of the American security order. The French testing and its strong condemnation in Australia represented the manifestation of this strategic opposition. However, the end of French nuclear testing in 1996 and France's support for non-proliferation, along with Australia's diplomatic ambition to assert its regional leadership, enabled the two countries to develop a tangible strategic dialogue to progressively become jointly responsible for the South Pacific's security. Although France stopped its nuclear testing program in 1996, the country's conception of its independence, security and strategy remained fully centred around its nuclear deterrence capacities. However, since this represented a significant element of divergence with Australia, French and Australian policy-makers have removed this opposition completely from their discourse in order to forge a tangible strategic alliance. The next chapter is dedicated to the analysis of the construction of the French–Australian strategic partnership.

Notes

1. For example, French Diplomatic Archives in Nantes hold a letter addressed by the Australian ambassador to the UN in Geneva to his French counterpart on October the 30th 1980 asking France to support the candidature of Dr. A. Wilson, from Australia, for the position of

Director General of the IAEA. Mr. Wilson did not win the election and no document enables us to know what was France's vote. However, in regard to the numerous documents where French diplomats feared that Australia could use the IAEA to criticise internationally France's nuclear policies, it is highly unlikely that Paris would have supported Wilson's candidature (AD Nantes, 37/146). Such candidacy reveals Australia's will to be a key player on this issue.

2. These countries were part of the agreement in 1987: Australia, Bangladesh, China, India, Indonesia, Japan, Korea, Malaysia, Pakistan, Philippines, Singapore, Sri Lanka, Thailand and Vietnam. By 2015, Cambodia, Fiji, Mongolia, Myanmar, Nepal, New Zealand and Palau had joined the agreement.

3. For more details, see http://austria.embassy.gov.au/files/vien/Australia-IAEA_Aug20.pdf.

4. The private archives of Former French Prime Minister Michel Rocard, who was part of this project, hold most of the documentation produced by the Commission, including its final report.

5. Paper by Mr. Gareth Evans: http://www.gevans.org/speeches/speech319.html.

6. During the 1980s, a strong opposition to nuclear activities arose amongst Australian public opinion. The Australian Nuclear Disarmament Party led that movement successfully and even won 500,000 votes and a seat at the Senate of Western Australia during the 1984 elections. https://labourhistorymelbourne.org/the-australian-nuclear-disarmament-movement/#_edn32.

7. Record of Australia-United States ministerial talks.

8. Interview in the French newspaper *Libération*, 14 February 1986, cited by Nick Maclellan and Jean Chesnaux (1998, p. 78).

9. Such press-reviews can be found for example in AD Nantes, « Représentation française à l'ONU – New York », file 632; AD Nantes, « Consulat de Melbourne 1854-1991 », file 132.

10. Article published in the *Sydney Morning Herald* on 17 May 1973 (AD Nantes, 632).

11. http://www.elysee.fr/videos/discours-devant-les-elus-de-polynesie-francaise/.

12. Several examples of official responses to newspaper editors or Australian delegations can be found in AD Nantes, « Consulat de Melbourne 1854-1991 », file 132.

13. This Australian management of the issue can be found in many archives, such as AD Nantes, « Représentation française à l'ONU – Genève », file 616. This 1985 meeting of the Secretariat of the Pacific Community, in Noumea, was a failure because of the inflexibility of Pacific Islander states

but also because France chose to implement a series of nuclear testing during the Forum itself, which was seen as a provocation.

14. See DFAT reports of Australia's uranium exports: http://dfat.gov.au/international-relations/security/asno/Pages/australian-safeguards-and-non-proliferation-office-asno.aspx.

REFERENCES

Archives Nationales, Pierrefitte, France.

National Archives of Australia, Canberra, Australia.

Beazley, K 2003, 'The Hawke Years: Foreign Affairs and Defence', in S Ryan & T Bramston (eds), *The Hawke Government, a Critical Retrospective*, Pluto Press, Melbourne, pp. 347–366.

Cot, JP 1973, 'Affaire des Essais nucléaires (Australie c. France et Nouvelle-Zélande c. France). Demandes en indication de mesures conservatoires. Ordonnances du 22 juin 1973', *Annuaire français de droit international*, vol. 19, pp. 252–271.

Dumoulin, A & Wasinski, C 2010, 'Justifier l'arme nucléaire. Le cas français pendant les années 1990', *Études internationals*, vol. 41, no. 1, pp. 79–96.

Falk, J, Green, J & Mudd, G 2006, 'Australia, Uranium and Nuclear Power', *International Journal of Environmental Studies*, Melbourne, vol. 63, no. 6, pp. 845–857.

Firth, S 2016, 'Australia's Detention Centre and the Erosion of Democracy in Nauru', *The Journal of Pacific History*, vol. 51, no. 3, pp. 286–300.

Hymans, JEC 2000, 'Isotopes and Identity: Australia and the Nuclear Weapons Option, 1949–1999', *The Nonproliferation Review*, vol. 7, no. 1, pp. 1–23.

Maclellan, N & Chesnaux, J 1998, *La France dans le Pacifique, de Bougainville à Mururoa*, La Découverte, Paris.

Mohamed-Gaillard, S 2010, *L'archipel de la puissance? La politique de la France dans le Pacifique Sud de 1946 à 1998*, P. Lang, Bruxelles.

Monnoyer, L 1997, 'La légitimation par la science: un défi pour la démocratie', *Hermès*, vol. 1, no. 21, pp. 157–169.

Nye, JS 2011, *The Future of Power*, Public Affairs, New York.

Piquet, M 2000, *Cold War in Warm Waters: Reflections on Australian and French Mutual Misunderstandings in the Pacific*, The University of Melbourne Press, Melbourne.

CHAPTER 5

Global Security as a Central Objective of the Bilateral Partnership

In his book *France in an Age of Globalisation*, Hubert Védrine, French Minister for Foreign Affairs between 1997 and 2002, assesses the main threats faced by the world in the early twenty first century (Védrine 2001). Védrine describes a world weakened by new uncertainties: tensions between unipolar and multipolar diplomatic contexts, and between deeper international regulations or more hierarchical or anarchical relations. Moreover, such uncertainties have been exacerbated by the lack of international agreement on managing the effects of globalisation. The development of "incontrollable transnational forces", due to the emergence of ultraliberal deregulations in the 1990s, has also been a source of a more individualist and consumerist world characterised by increasing social and political conflicts and where the gap between poor and wealthy populations is constantly increasing, as accurately presented by Thomas Piketty in *Capital* (2013). In addition to these tensions, the future of economically or diplomatically weak states is also more uncertain, and the global dynamic of cultural uniformity flattens out identities and ways of life, a process which populist discourses answer with threatening programs. These global uncertainties are demonstrated by significant international threats, such as terrorism or organised international crimes. However, according to Hubert Védrine, the proliferation of weapons of mass destruction, especially nuclear armaments, constitutes the world's current major danger (2001, pp. 12–13).

© The Author(s) 2019
P. Soyez, *Australia and France's Mutual Empowerment*,
Studies in Diplomacy and International Relations,
https://doi.org/10.1007/978-3-030-13449-5_5

137

Security issues represent one of the essential questions of relations amongst states. According to Buzan, Wæver and de Wilde, security should not be only conceived as the simple defence of national military interests. These three authors call for a wider definition and they consider that security constitutes the freedom from threats in five sectors: military, political, economic, environmental and societal. More precisely, the three authors explain that "the military sector is about relationships of forceful coercion; the political sector is about relationships of authority, governing status, and recognition". Economic security refers to trade, production and finance, and societal security pertains to collective identity. Lastly, "the environmental sector is about relationship between human activity and the planetary biosphere" (1998, p. 7). Moreover, security must be analysed at the local, national, regional and global levels (1998, p. 1). This chapter demonstrates that security has remained the most significant objective in the mutual engagement between Australia and France, engaged in all five sectors of the concept. Although opposing nuclear policies became the source of major French–Australian tensions, security has now become the main subject of cooperation between the two states, framed in 2012 within a Strategic Partnership and materialised recently by Australia's submarine contract which jointly engages Australian and French defence strategies for the next fifty years.

Moreover, post-modern constructivist theories and interpretive theories are relevant to this study of security issues. The relationship between Australia and France exemplifies the constructivist view on international security, because, in order to shift from considering the other as a threat to considering it as a partner for security, Australian and French foreign policy-makers not only had to change their perceptions of national interests, but also their mutual understandings. It was first and foremost by understanding their respective perceptions of security and then accommodating their approaches that French and Australian foreign policy-makers were able to foster cooperation on this issue. This chapter begins by analysing how the French–Australian partnership supports Australia's new conceptualisation of its regional environment. Then, it examines how both countries have used the protection of Antarctica as a leverage to foster their security cooperation. Finally, since the 2010s, Australia and France have considerably deepened their collaboration and forged an extremely tight security partnership, binding their strategies for the next few decades.

Three Levels of Bilateral Partnerships for the Indo–Pacific Region's Security

From the point of view of Australian policy-makers, the Australian–French bilateral relationship must be understood within the framework that Australia has constituted for its own security, at both global and regional levels. Australia has favoured multilateral approaches in its management of issues pertaining to global security, above all on weapons of mass destructions. On the other hand, decision-makers in Canberra have built their strategy of direct regional security by developing a network of bilateral, or sometimes tripartite, alliances. Like Australia, France's national security is based on both multilateral and bilateral partnerships, but not to the same extent as Australia. In fact, French diplomats seem to have more deeply embedded France's security strategy into international organisations protecting European security, alongside their own strong military forces and nuclear deterrence.

Australia's conception of its security has fluctuated between two approaches: forward defence—the idea that Australia cannot defend its vast territory and therefore needs to intervene outside of its region within alliances—and the idea of a continental defence within which Australia would not involve itself in foreign wars but rather focus on its immediate neighbourhood. According to Stewart Firth, "forward defence has been the more influential of the two doctrines" (2011, p. 136), as demonstrated by Australia's involvement in conflicts all around the world since World War I. However, Firth asserts that the increasing doubt in America's intervention in case of a potential attack on Australia's territory has led Australian policy-makers to consider continental defence as much as forward defence (2011, p. 136). Therefore, Australia's current security policy aims to accommodate these two approaches (Piquet 2000, p. 18). One of the reasons why Australia focuses increasingly on its regional security is that, despite its considerable reliance on ANZUS, Australian diplomats also regularly question the role of the United States in the Pacific more broadly. This question has become even more acute since Donald Trump's election to the White House in 2016. Julie Bishop's visit to Washington in February 2017 aimed to "build personal relationships between Canberra and the new administration" and to secure Australia's alliance with the United States, which Nick Bisley describes as a difficult task (2017). However, does "America First" means less American involvement with its allies?

How should Australia position itself facing increasingly tense relations between China and the United States?

This uncertainty has existed since the end of the 1980s. In a 1987 brief about Pacific powers, Australian diplomats drew an ambiguous portrait of American presence to the region. The report started by explaining that the USA devoted only a limited amount of its resources to the region, their aim being only to avoid any Soviet influence and maintain their military bases in Micronesia. Moreover, the report asserted that American foreign policy-makers only had a very limited expertise about the Pacific. This lack of regional knowledge can be problematic: "Subtleties and distinctions within the region have generally not been recognised" (NAA M3793, 102). This situation led Australia to feel a greater responsibility for the South Pacific's security. In order to develop its progressive network of bilateral alliances, Australian policy-makers have had to find suitable partnerships with countries it believed to be trustworthy. Following again a constructivist understanding of this process, Australia had to first construct partnerships with countries with which it had shared values, such as the United States. However, and more recently, Australian diplomats have felt the need to build dialogues with new regional partners from non-Anglo-Saxon cultures, in order to gain an understanding of each other's vision of regional security. This social and intellectual process appears to be a necessary stage in building new security partnerships, as the White Paper *Australia in the Asian Century* was already recommending in 2012. Countries such as Indonesia, Malaysia or Papua New Guinea have been the first targets of this renewal. Therefore, the transformation of French–Australian relations from the end of the 1980s to the present time perfectly illustrates Australia's engagement in this new regional dynamic and justifies the constructivist approach guiding this study.

In the post-Cold War context, Australian diplomats and politicians have had to reassess their regional relationships. Amongst the thousands of documents taken into consideration for this study, three Asian countries appear most frequently in regard to Australia's regional integration dynamic: Indonesia, Malaysia and Japan. Canberra's interest in deepening bilateral relations with these countries is different for each of them, because of their specificities but also because they represent, geographically, three diverse scales and modalities of regional integration.

The same strategic renewal has been engaged regarding the PICs. One has to keep in mind that Canberra's bilateral relations within its region take place and are constrained by the larger frame of Australia's alliance with Washington. As Firth points out, "no Australian government dares to craft a defence policy without first taking into account the likely reaction of the Pentagon in Washington" (2011, p. 156). However, Australian diplomats seem to have been successful in influencing the US in their vision of the region's security. The role Australia played in building a nuclear-free zone in the South Pacific without hindering American interests and positions has been very useful to Australia in gaining influence in Washington regarding South Pacific security. With this framework in place, Australian foreign policy-makers have been able to reinvent each individual relationship with their neighbours, particularly with France.

New Relationships with Indonesia and Malaysia for a Deeper Integration in South-East Asia

Indonesia has been considered by policy-makers in Canberra as a key component of Australia's security and defence policies. Based solely on Indonesia's position to the north of Australian shores, Jakarta must be considered a first-rank partner for both countries' security. Despite decades of ambivalent and changing relations since Canberra's support to Indonesian independence in the 1940s, Australia has, since the end of the Cold War and with the development of the region's cohesion, pushed towards an improvement and intensification of this crucial bilateral relation. The Australian–Indonesian diplomatic improvement addresses the need for Australia to develop programs of security cooperation in order to avoid regional instability or direct threats, such as terrorist activities, from its most important neighbour. However, Australian scholars and policy-makers have debated for decades on the depth of Australia's engagement with Indonesia.

During the 1980s, Australian and Indonesian relations were fragile—and they have remained so, as proved by the 2013 intelligence scandal about Australia's wiretapping of the Indonesian President. In 1985, in an assessment of the partnership produced by DFAT, defence relations between the two countries were "stable" but "less easy than with other ASEAN countries". In fact, the crises in Irian Jaya and, above all, in

East Timor were some of the crucial issues addressed by the briefs prepared by DFAT for Australian–Indonesian meetings. In a background brief established in December 1985 on Australia's bilateral relationship with Indonesia before the visit of the Indonesian Minister for Foreign Affairs to Canberra, DFAT officials insisted on the importance of finding a resolution to the conflict through the UN, gathering all the actors involved in this question, including Portugal as former colonial power. However, and more realistically, Australian officials from the DFAT Indonesian desk explained to Bill Hayden that tensions in East Timor might not be examined thoroughly enough by the UN since they were not an important consideration for most of its members (NAA M3793, 54). Bob Hawke's official statement asserting that Australia recognized Indonesian sovereignty over East Timor eased the relationship. The increasing number of mutual visits at the highest political levels demonstrated this improvement, with for example nine ministerial visits from Australia to Jakarta between March 1983 and December 1985 (NAA M3793, 55).

In 1985, defence partnerships between the two shores of the Timor Sea were mostly conducted within the frame of a Defence Cooperation Program, and negotiations over maritime boundaries were fruitful, despite a competition for petrol resources. In fact, "the development of pragmatic and constructive government-to-government relations, albeit with acceptance of differences and disagreements, has been the focus of Australian government policy towards Indonesia in recent years and this now appears to be bearing fruit" explained DFAT officials (NAA M3793, 55). Nevertheless, Australian diplomats have felt the need to go beyond this frame so they could deepen their relations with their Indonesian counterparts. Surveillance cooperation, combined exercises, senior military and military ship visits are seen as relevant tools for fostering this partnership. Moreover, Australian military units have trained their Indonesian counterparts in the Army, the Navy and the Air Force, in addition to conducting mapping campaigns together, engaging in joint maritime surveillance and providing technical assistance to Indonesia. Jakarta has asked Australia for its defence support, for example to provide experts to assess its military equipment (NAA M3793, 54).

A much deeper cooperation has been developed since then, with an improvement of the bilateral dialogue. This improvement of Indonesian–Australian relations occurred partly because of Jakarta's stronger engagement in international relations. Indonesia has been increasing its diplomacy at regional and global levels, and the deepening of its relations with Canberra has been part of that process. However, tensions pertaining to Australian intelligence in Indonesia, to mutual cattle exports and the execution of Australian prisoners in the past few years have revealed again the ease with which this relationship can be disturbed. According to Malcolm Cook, "the Australia-Indonesia relationship [is] the most complicated of Australia's relations with its neighbouring countries and the one most prone to public disagreement" (2014, p. 156). In fact, the Lowy Institute annual polling of Australian views of other countries between 2007 and 2012 shows that only 47% of Australians had a positive feeling towards Indonesia in 2007 and 54% in 2012, the lowest rate of all Australia's neighbours and diplomatic partners (Cook 2014, p. 156).[1] However, Rawdon Dalrymple asserts that Indonesia has always been a significant concern for Australia's diplomacy, which has never neglected this bilateral relationship (2014, p. 171). More broadly, Indonesia, as Australia's most important neighbour but also one of its main threats because of terrorism, has been the focus of Australia's commitment to regional security. Australia and Indonesia have deepened their relation even further during the first international visit of Australia's Prime Minister Scott Morrison in August 2018, when Joko Widodo and Morrison announced the success of their FTA negotiations, focussing on trade and tertiary education, and a future strategic partnership, then threatened by Australia's consideration to move its Israeli embassy to Jerusalem. Indonesia also called for a rapprochement of its intelligence agencies with Australia and the Five Eyes, a dynamic supported by Australia's Minister for Defence Christopher Pyne, in order to improve the international response against more than 60 terrorists groups in South East Asia pledging allegiance to ISIS. Unlike the French–Australian partnership, which aims to reinforce the Western alliance in the Indo-Pacific region, Australia's closer engagement with Indonesia aims to reduce potential threats coming directly from within parts of its partner and develop a new market for trade. The dynamic behind these engagements is, therefore, quite different.

The development of Australia's diplomatic relations with Malaysia has been influenced by a slightly different logic. Unlike Jakarta, from Canberra, Kuala Lumpur is not considered as a threat to Australia's security. On the other hand, with its fast-growing economy, its regional influence and most importantly its key role in the development of the

ASEAN community, which structures the region's integration, Malaysia has emerged as an important partner for Australia's participation as part of a diverse but integrated South East Asia, as much as Indonesia. Therefore, Malaysia does not occupy the same aspect of Australia's regional strategy as Indonesia. Kuala Lumpur constitutes a key element in Australia's diplomatic effort to build a closer engagement with the ASEAN, in order to fully benefit from the region's economic growth and to increase its cohesion for maintaining regional security.

Bill Hayden was advised, in a brief preparing for his visit to Malaysia in March 1985, to keep trying to improve security relations between Canberra and Kuala Lumpur (NAA M3793, 51). According to this background brief, Malaysia was at that time perceived as disinclined to be friendly with Western countries, including Australia. Hayden was thus told to continue to develop the bilateral relationship that Bob Hawke had started to build during his first visit to Malaysia in February 1984, followed by a return visit six months later. The report argued that deepening defence relations with Malaysia had to be part of a broader partnership involving Malaysia's economic development framework, since that was Kuala Lumpur's main objective (NAA M3793, 51). Security and defence were issues that were wrapped up in a general economic development. The report stressed how useful Malaysia was for Australian security. Malaysia, as a strong supporter of the non-aligned states, "wishes to see super power conflict removed from the region. It wishes to promote the concept of a Zone of Peace Freedom and Neutrality and [...] a Nuclear Weapons Free Zone". Therefore, even if Australia and Malaysia associated peace with different purposes, the victory of Western policies and the balance between the blocks, both diplomacies wanted to distance their region from the main zones of international tensions. For instance, both diplomacies have collaborated on arms control and non-proliferation policies, and "Malaysia's growing interest in the South Pacific is fully consistent with our interests".

Kuala Lumpur currently remains a significant partner for Canberra is the Asia-Pacific. Australia's engagement with Malaysia has been aimed primarily at being more integrated with South-East Asia by moving closer to a prominent member of ASEAN in order to get more involved with the regional political dialogue. This has been another of Australia's attempts to improve its security: trying to be more involved with South East Asia's political dialogue in order to influence it in regard to Australian security interests.

Asserting the United States' Role in Asia with Japan

On a larger scale, Australia's bilateral relationship with Japan emerges as fundamental for Australian decision-makers, but coming under a third modality, as archives reveal. Australian decision-makers perceive Australia's relationship with Japan less as a close and direct partnership such as that between Canberra and Jakarta, but more as a means of global surveillance and of achieving the Pacific's balance between international powers, in a trilateral alliance between Australia, Japan and the United States. From this point of view, Australia's security partnership with Japan is less frequently considered on a day-to-day basis than that with Indonesia, but it is more global, aiming at maintaining the Pacific as a whole as a secure region serving the interest of these three powers. Therefore, the Australian–Japanese alliance can be understood as a complementary dispositive to ANZUS.

Reports and briefs elaborated by DFAT for the purpose of deepening Canberra's relationship with Japan have been very frequent. According as much attention as it does to trade, Australia has been seeking to improve its regional security using close links with Japan. The 1980s saw an increasing Japanese interest and involvement in the South Pacific. Ministerial consultations were for instance regular, about once a year, between Japanese and Australian ministers, to assess common security issues in the Pacific, coordinate their development programs and improve peaceful relations amongst Pacific states (NAA M3793, 2). Australian diplomats wanted to share their expertise with their counterparts in Japan regarding the South Pacific and to encourage Tokyo to be more active in that region. But Japanese participation in Pacific security was not overt, according to Australian sources. In their brief about Australian regional security, Australian diplomats noted: "Japan's interest in providing aid to the region [is] constrained by Japan's awkwardness in dealing with existing South Pacific institutions, especially SPEC [and by] Japan's low opinion of the South Pacific states, as non-productive and difficult to deal with" (NAA M3793, 102). Therefore, the challenge for Australia was to influence foreign policy-makers in Tokyo to take a larger part in the promotion of this region of the Pacific's security. For example, documents demonstrate that Australia has tried to influence the Japanese to use their significant relationship with France to convince Paris to promote solutions in New Caledonia that would please Australia and other South Pacific states. Noting that France does not like to be told how to conduct its diplomacy and is willing to accept advice only from a limited number of allies that are not a threat to its independence, DFAT public servants believed that Japan was better positioned to influence France regarding New Caledonia than Australia. For example, the report raises the following question: "could the Japanese (possibly perceived by the French to be a moderate force after its recent abstention on the New Caledonia vote at the UN) put forward Australian and other South Pacific Forum countries' concerns including on New Caledonia, nuclear testing [...]?" However, Japanese politicians were supportive of Paris' policies in the territory. Therefore, Australian diplomats determined that their first task was to influence Japan on that matter, which proved to be totally in vain because Japan maintained its support to French policies in New Caledonia (NAA M3793, 102). However, Tokyo has since shown a much deeper engagement in Pacific security.

This was one reason why, in 2006, Australia supported Japan's candidature for a permanent seat on the UN Security Council. Moreover, in March 2007, Canberra and Tokyo signed the Japan–Australia Join Declaration on Security Cooperation in order to counteract China's regional diplomatic assertion. This was, as Firth points out, "the first such defence agreement reached by Japan with any country other than the United States since World War II" (2011, p. 71). This partnership was strengthened by the Trilateral Security Dialogue which brings together Tokyo, Washington and Canberra, and subsequently by the Australian–Japan Defence Security Agreement, signed in 2010 and implemented in 2013, which mirrors the US–Japan cross-servicing agreement of 2004 (Davison and Khan 2014, p. 141). More recently, Washington supported Japan at first as the supplier for Australia's new submarines, in order to reinforce the tripartite alliance in the Asia-Pacific region. The Japanese–Australian relationship for the security of the Asia-Pacific has tangible implications for France. Paris and Tokyo benefit from a positive relationship, especially in regard to the development and the security of the Pacific. Therefore, French policy-makers have praised the constructive engagement between Australia and Japan. Australia's alliance with Japan follows a logic close to the one supporting the French–Australian strategic partnership: maintaining a close relationship with an ally of the United States for the strategy of the Asia-Pacific region as a whole and as a counter-measure against China's diplomatic assertion in the region. Moreover, in its 2017 Foreign Policy White Paper, Australia also highlights its more recent but also significant partnerships with India and South Korea (DFAT 2017, Chapter 3). Insisting on Australia's bilateral link with Asia's three regional power increases the pressure Canberra intend to put on China to accept a ruled-based international order. Because of the situation in the South China Sea, Japanese Prime Minister Shinzo Abe asked Australia to join Tokyo in more military exercises. Both countries, which held 2 + 2 talks in October 2018, also attempted to convince India to increase its military cooperation with them and the United States, within the QUAD cooperation. This effort has been, so far, unsuccessful, India being reluctant to join alliances that would hinder its relationship with China. Japan and Australia agreed to deepen further their military cooperation during Shinzo Abe's visit to Darwin in November 2018.

A Particular Relationship with the South Pacific

Finally, this study also demonstrates Australia's dynamic engagement regarding security policies pertaining to Pacific Island Countries. This dynamic comes from the recognition by Australian foreign policy-makers of the necessity for them to stop assuming that PICs would automatically follow Western, and Australian, diplomatic interests. If, at the beginning of the 1990s, they noted that Australia had not "lost the PICs", Canberra must realise that it needs to be more careful about this. South Pacific states have developed their own vision of their region, of their interest and of the global international order. This maturity empowers them to follow their own interests, which are sometimes contrary to those of Australia. Consequently, Australian defence and security relationships with such partners had to be clarified at first, and then reshaped in order to be shared by all members of these renewed partnerships. The aim has been to develop a shared perception of the region between its actors and common objectives between Australia and its South Pacific allies, once their political powers have all become stable.

As a first step in this new relationship with the PICs, Australian policy makers felt the need to examine their partners' expectations of Australia. Canberra had to know when and where its leadership was desired so it could avoid disappointing these expectations and allowing the influences of external actors to grow in the South Pacific. Then Australia had to elaborate security policies using all the tools available to reach this goal, such as aid to development, "enhancing law enforcement/para-military forces for self-defence purposes" (NAA M3793, 102), common exercises and patrols, or military and security cooperation. In a more paternalistic way, Australian diplomats want to "encourage [the] PICs not to look abroad too often" (NAA M3793, 102) and underline the fact that they always feel the need to pay attention to the financial cost of these programs for their partners. The French–Australian strategic partnership is a contributing factor in Australia's strategy towards the PICs, because Australia considers France to be a significant ally in securing the fragile stability of many of these Pacific countries.

Some specialists in Australia's foreign policy debate about the extent to which the PICs benefit from Australia's regional engagement. For example, Jonathan Shultz identifies "three kinds of bullying" in Australia's policies toward the PICs (2014, p. 175). Firstly, Schultz claims that Australia implements a conflictual bullying in pursuing its own national interests over the ones of its Pacific partners, for example regarding climate change. He goes further and asserts that Australia demonstrates instrumental bullying in using the PICs to serve its global interests. Lastly, Canberra implements a punitive bullying by punishing the PICs when they oppose Australian policies. Therefore, Schultz considers that Australia has adopted a neo-colonialist attitude toward the South Pacific, using power asymmetry to force its leadership on the region. Joanne Wallis disagrees with this vision. According to her, while Canberra implemented neo-colonialist and bullying policies toward the PICs from 1980s to 2002, "Australia's approach since 2007 has shifted to one of 'partnership and engagement'". Wallis explains this change by the election of the Rudd government, which "sought to recalibrate Australia's relationship with the region" (2014, pp. 175, 187). For example, she asserts that this new Australian point of view on the PICs was demonstrated by the 2008 Port Moresby Declaration, and then by Canberra's bilateral development partnerships in order to achieve the United Nations Millennium Development Goals. This book positions itself between Schultz and Wallis's points of view. It considers that, as Chapter 7 will demonstrates, Australian and French Pacific policies combine a genuine interest for the development of the PICs with an effort to maintain their leadership over the region to serve their broader interests. These two ambitions are not necessarily contradictory.

The current French–Australian strategic partnership must be understood within this broader regional context, where South East Asian and South Pacific states have redefined their cooperation to adapt to the post-Cold War context. The constructive elaboration of this strong partnership has progressed through important stages. French–Australian cooperation for regional security through Antarctica's protection may not appear crucial at first sight. However, it is an interesting case study, because it constituted a fundamental element where Australian and French policy-makers worked conjointly towards a multilateral policy. Such cooperation enabled French and Australia diplomats to collaborate and work through their mutual misperceptions.

THE PROTECTION OF ANTARCTICA, THE FIRST EXAMPLE OF A SUCCESSFUL FRENCH–AUSTRALIAN LEADERSHIP FOR PACIFIC DIPLOMACY AND REGIONAL SECURITY

The security rapprochement operated by France and Australia since the 2000s has been possible because of past collaborations on a select areas of cooperation, including the peace process in Cambodia and the protection of Antarctica. In fact, one of the main early achievements of French–Australian collaboration for their countries' security was the involvement by the two countries in the determination of the status of Antarctica. France and Australia directed the diplomatic processes that led to an international agreement, signed in Madrid in June 1991, recognising Antarctica as an international natural reserve (AN Pierrefitte, 19970557/9). French and Australian decision-makers began their discussions on this issue at the end of the 1980s. In a brief written for Michel Rocard in order to prepare for his meeting with Bob Hawke in Australia in 1989, members of the cabinet of the French Prime Minister reminded him that the work produced by the international group of experts, organized by Canberra and Paris, on the protection of Antarctica had led to a draft agreement that was to be presented in Paris in October 1989. Bob Hawke wanted France to support Australia's determination to refuse the Convention of Wellington, a project enabling mineral prospecting in Antarctica despite its future status as a natural reserve. France had opposed this convention too since the onset of the negotiations. In Paris, France and Australia led the proposition for the transformation of this sixth continent into a natural reserve but decided together not to officially oppose the Convention of Wellington, nor to try to strong-arm the international community (AN Pierrefitte, 19930409/3). Eventually, France and Australia officially stated that they would refuse to sign this Convention, respectively on 20 April and 22 May 1989 (Puissochet 1991, p. 759).

In a letter addressed by Hawke to Rocard on 28 July 1989, the Australian Prime Minister detailed that the question of Antarctica had been the first and most explicit example of effective Australian–French leadership. In his letter, Hawke also assured Rocard that he was following this issue personally and closely in order to effect the desired outcomes. Moreover, the Australian Prime Minister reminded Rocard that François Mitterrand, French President at the time, was also opposed to the Convention of Wellington, and could use his influence in Europe to fully convince France's neighbours, especially Belgium and Mitterrand's close friend Helmut Kohl in Germany, as both Brussels and Bonn appeared inclined to support the French–Australian position. In order to support this diplomatic activity, Hawke finished his letter by explaining that he had appointed an Australian Ambassador for the Environment (AN Pierrefitte, 19930409/3). This diplomatic effort was successful. The French–Australian protocol draft was supported very quickly by Belgium, Italy and Greece. In 1990, Denmark and Sweden positioned themselves in favour of the French–Australian solution. Chile and Spain volunteered to host new negotiations. From the second half of 1990, the United States, previously a strong supporter of the Convention of Wellington, changed its position too. Therefore, during the meeting at Vina Del Mar in Chile in November–December 1990, France and Australia, supported by Belgium and Italy, presented their new draft of an international agreement banishing mineral prospecting from Antarctica.

Negotiations were quite fierce. Another brief sent by Rocard's cabinet to the Prime Minister on 16 June 1989 insists on the significant tensions between Canberra and Wellington on the Antarctica issue. The document explained how New Zealand had felt deeply betrayed by Australia when Hawke officially rejected the Convention of Wellington. In fact, New Zealand was suffering at the time from serious economic difficulties and was counting on revenues from mineral prospecting in Antarctica. In addition to the Australian–New Zealander tensions pertaining to ANZUS, French decisions-makers observed that France could take advantage of this rift between the two traditional partners in order to appear more respectable to Australia and to the PICs. Eventually, after several further weeks of negotiation, the French–Australian Protocol was signed in Madrid on 4 October 1991. The French co-leadership for the protection of the Antarctic environment created an interesting opportunity to demonstrate in the region that even though France had conducted nuclear testing in Mururoa, it was still concerned about the protection of ecologically important maritime or Antarctic ecosystems. According to diplomatic advisors of the French Prime Minister, Hawke was entirely pleased by France's support in regard to Antarctica, feeling that this partnership could be truly beneficial. Moreover, this brief described Australia as a global leader on environmental issues (AN Pierrefitte, 19930409/3).

During his visit to Paris in January 1991, Gareth Evans asked Michel Rocard to assure him that France would maintain its close engagement with Australia regarding Antarctica, which the French Prime Minister did. In order to testify tangibly of France's determination to work closely with Australia on that matter, Rocard even suggested making a joint visit to Antarctica in 1992 with Evans and possibly a member of the New Zealand government. However, according to the French Ministry for Foreign Affairs, Australia and New Zealand were not likely to achieve a tangible cooperation on that matter because Hobart and Christchurch were in competition to become the main city from which the project would be implemented. Ministerial briefs about Antarctica all praise the very high level of trust and partnership between Paris and Canberra (AN Pierrefitte, 19930409/4). The international status of Antarctica created an opportunity for France and Australia to test their ability to bring their diplomacy closer and provide co-leadership on an important issue. Ministerial archives both in France and Australia reveal that the transformation of Antarctica into a natural reserve was considered, at the beginning of the 1990s, as one of the most important achievements of this bilateral relationship.

The diplomatic effort regarding Antarctica set up by Australia and France was motivated by an obvious environmental incentive. However, the improvement of regional security was equally relevant to this policy-making process, for several reasons. The unexploited natural reserves located in Antarctica suggest that this sixth continent constitutes a potential new Eldorado for mining. Hydrocarbons and minerals have been found under these rocky lands and have been coveted by states and multinationals. This situation could have been the source of major international tensions, deeply hindering the security of a region where Australia and France have responsibilities and interests. Antarctica's status as an international natural reserve has reduced these potential conflicts by limiting Antarctica's economic interest. Moreover, by prohibiting mineral prospecting in Antarctica, the Protocol of Madrid had also frozen the presence of powers on this Southern continent. No new power can now make a settlement or conduct activities in Antarctica. This factor has obviously served French and Australian security purposes by securing the exclusion of any other powers from the South of their territories. The recognition of Antarctica as an internationally protected natural reserve secured the "non-militarisation" of this continent (Puissochet 1991, p. 756). Not only are international and regional powers not allowed to locate any military equipment on the sixth continent, but the protocol also stipulates that scientific research in Antarctica cannot have military purposes. This underscores the peaceful non-military status of this land and its waters. Antarctica provided a first step for Australian and French cooperation for regional stability. This partnership has since deepened to create a strong and trustworthy alliance between two countries which see themselves as conjointly responsible for the security of the South Pacific region. French–Australian cooperation regarding the protection of Antarctica has been implemented again in November 2017, when Paris and Canberra proposed to protect three areas of Antarctic waters, covering almost one million square kilometres, by classifying them as marine parks.

Common Enemies Create New Alliances? French–Australian Cooperation for Regional and Global Security

Regional and global security have constituted the main incentives for improving the strategic partnership between Australia and France. While both countries are obviously not each other's primary security allies, a very strong strategic dialogue is currently being deepened. European countries are third in Australia's list of diplomatic priorities, after the United States, then Canberra's close Asian relationships, and although Europe is important, it's not within the "inner circle" of Australia's diplomatic priorities. A similar hierarchy exists in Paris, where Europe remains the main focus, then the United States, then regions of the world such as Africa and the Middle East. This EU focus has even been reinforced with Emmanuel Macron's election to the French Presidency and plays significant role in the Australian–French rapprochement.

However, France has now become Australia's main security partner in continental Europe. Australia currently wishes to diversify and strengthen its links with continental European countries, especially with Germany and France. Canberra and Berlin, which have signed a declaration of intent on a strategic partnership, in 2012, have also established an Advisory Group in 2014 to enhance their relationship relating to five themes not clearly defined: business and investment, strategic dialogue, science and education, and culture and sports. However, according to Stephen Brady, referring to Australia's involvement in the last two world wars, the German–Australian relationship is much less emotional than the one between Paris and Canberra (pers. inter. 4 January 2017). As this chapter demonstrates, France constitutes Australia's main security partner on the continent because Paris remains the first military and diplomatic power in continental Europe and has territories in the Indo-Pacific region. "The fact is that at the moment, both Australia and France have something to offer to each other," says Wells, who also asserts that France and Australia have the same level of impetus in this rapprochement (pers. inter., Canberra, 8 April 2016).

Paris and Canberra intend to become smart powers regarding their security, through their mutual empowerment. Both France and Australia have fully embraced the doctrine that, as Joseph Nye explains, they "start asking questions about how the various tools of power can be combined into smart strategies for power *with* rather than merely *over* other nations" (2011, p. xvii). Both countries have put their tensions and their competition for regional leadership behind them. Their foreign policy-makers are fully aware that French and Australian national securities require mutual and integrated strategies. Moreover, the current elaboration of the French–Australian partnership mainly strives toward Wolfers' "milieu goal" (1962, pp. 73–77), mainly regionally but also globally. France and Australia have forged a considerable strategic partnership. The aim of this synergetic dynamic has not only been to accomplish specific outcomes, for instance against terrorism, but also to create a regional milieu in the South Pacific and in South East Asia that would support their common interests. At a global level, France and Australia are part of an international coalition against threats from non-state actors, which, by trying to create a more secure milieu, reinforces French and Australian powers as well. For example, Wells points out that "the single most important area of advantage for Australia is security and cooperation with France" (pers. inter., Canberra, 8 April 2016). This chapter illustrates how France and Australia are trying to implement "smart power" strategies through mutual empowerment framed by their strategic partnership since 2012.

Creating Trust Between Australian and French Policy Makers

The end of French nuclear testing, the Australian acknowledgement that France's presence in the South Pacific improved Australia's security (see Chapter 7) and the French–Australian collaboration on Antarctica, enabled Australian and French policy-makers to start developing a better understanding of each other's diplomacies and policies. In fact, these political and diplomatic shifts made it possible for decision-makers to focus on potential rapprochements on new security questions and the creation, albeit at an early stage, of a "we-feeling" according to Karl Deutsch's definition of the concept (1968).

Deutsch's approach to national identities is relevant for this aspect of the topic. He argued that states gather around 'plural security communities', alliances between several independent entities that share the same issues of security and believe that international agreements can peacefully resolve international conflicts. According to Deutsch, in order to build a plural security community, states require three key factors: the capacity to predict each other's position, an attitude of trust towards each other—the 'we-feeling'—and compatible fundamental values shared by their elites. National identities are a crucial component in the creation of such communities. The political and diplomatic contexts of Australia and France have enabled the realisation of these three requirements. France and Australia have always recognised that they share the same values—democracy, liberalism, freedom—and thus this was never a real issue. However, the mutual lack of trust was a problem. Reading Franco–Australian archives, the researcher quickly understands that Australian diplomats and politicians had little trust in their French counterparts and even expressed their mistrust explicitly in their reports. They often acknowledged for example that Australian decision-makers had to work on better relations with France but then finished their briefs by asserting the need to be cautious about French intentions since French people were regularly portrayed as untrustworthy (NAA M3793). This very pejorative vision of France was supported by France's nuclear testing, which was perceived as a sign of Paris's unreliability. On the other hand, French diplomats believed that Australia, because of its zeal to always demonstrate its sense of belonging to the Anglo-Saxon community, would necessarily side against French interests. For example, Australia's support for New Caledonia's independence movements was seen in Paris as an indicator of this ongoing Anglo-Saxon antagonism against France.

The positive resolution of these tensions enabled Paris and Canberra to be more transparent in their diplomatic intentions by building trust between the two countries. Therefore, decision-makers could mutually predict each other's intentions and start progressively to build this "we-feeling" connection on certain issues, especially in regard to South Pacific security. French–Australian cooperation improved mainly because of regular ministerial meetings at the end of the 1980s, enabling decision-makers to have a better understanding, and therefore trust, of each other. French and Australian Ministers met about ten times between 1988 and 1992 to engage direct discussions about conflictual issues between the two countries and find accommodating positions, for example regarding agricultural trade. Moreover, Gareth Evans sees in the "honest" and "friendly" relationship he and Bob Hawke established with Michel Rocard, French Prime Minister between 1988 and 1991, the first and most important factor that enabled the improvement of the bilateral relationship:

> I think that personal relationships were at the very heart of that. Michel Rocard was a very engaging character who formed a very good relationship with Bob Hawke, as did I with him actually, even as Foreign Minister. That was possibly the crucial single factor, the fact that Rocard was so open-minded, relaxed, and willing to approach issues in a refreshingly frank kind of way. It was very helpful. (pers. inter., Melbourne, 13 April 2016)

Since 2012, the frequency of the visits has increased dramatically and, according to Stephen Brady, Australian Ministers visited France 25 times and Australian senior officers 100 times in 2015. No country was visited more than France in 2015, not even the United States (pers. inter., Paris, 18 July 2016). More broadly, the improved mutual understanding between French and Australian political, diplomatic and economic elites has been a prerequisite for the improvement of the bilateral relationship, much more than in public opinion. The improvement of France's image in Australia was firstly operated within the business community. For example, when asked if France is still viewed with a critical British eye in Australia, François Cotier confirmed this is not the case for businesses, which are used to transcending those stereotypes (pers. inter., Melbourne, 27 April 2016). However, as shown recently when Australia announced that it would entrust France with its submarine contract, the traditional British contempt towards France can sometimes be detected in the general Australian perception. Traditionally a lot of Australian media coverage of Europe has come from London and the British press. That clearly had an effect on the way France and Europe are portrayed in the Australian media. France is singled out more than other European countries, (James 2016). However, this misperception now seems to have largely disappeared at the stakeholders' level. French diplomats also had to modify their understanding of Australia. Rick Wells points out one reason for this change:

> France, to the extent that it thought of Australia at all which was not very much, tended to regard Australia as just a shrill echo of the United States. That was then caught up in France's own rather complex and ambiguous relationship with the United States. Times have changed. French policy-makers and thinkers have a much less complicated and ambiguous view of the United States. That is partly a generational change. (pers. inter., Canberra, 8 April 2016)

Wells accurately refers to the fact that France's current foreign-policy practitioners, while maintaining this *certaine idée de la France* (a certain idea of what France is), of its independence, have a more acute understanding of the global evolution of the concept of power. They are aware that all the large European countries, although they still retain considerable assets and capacities for independent actions, do benefit from the protection of the United States, which has reduced France's disdain for Australia. However, the improvement of the relationship was also a consequence of the national political agendas of each interlocutor. In Australia, "the driving determination of the Hawke Government's foreign affairs, defence and trade was to create an environment which optimised Australia's capacity to sustain independent initiative and to use that to create a global and regional security and economic environment which enhanced Australia's security and prosperity" (Beazley 2003, p. 347). Australian policy-makers improved their relationship with

5 GLOBAL SECURITY AS A CENTRAL OBJECTIVE ... 157

France as part of this agenda for two reasons. At a global level, France was seen as one of the five main powers involved in most international issues. As a regional power, Australian policy-makers saw France as one of the major actors in the South Pacific, as a neighbouring state working for regional security. From Paris, interests in the South Pacific increased with Michel Rocard. As a new Socialist Prime Minister, Michel Rocard decided to change France's policy towards pro-independence tensions in New Caledonia and regarding nuclear testing. Rocard, who has been one of the few French politicians tangibly interested in the Pacific, renewed France's diplomatic approach towards the region. His government pursued radically new policies in New Caledonia, promoting compromise and negotiation, materialised by the Matignon Accords in 1988 (see Chapter 6). Moreover, with his government, France focused on improving its image in the region. Therefore, Rocard did not conduct nuclear testing and increased dialogue with Australia and other Pacific states, inviting them to engage further with French Pacific territories, with France being willing to interface with them more deeply in their region. French and Australian agendas converged on such national interests. Gareth Evans summarises these common interests:

> The issues Australia had to address included the role of the South Pacific Forum, keeping the region's coherence together, and dealing with the reality of the continuing French presence. It was important to get some kind of *modus operandi* in place where we understood each other and worked together. We did give quite a high priority to the South Pacific and to peace, stability and prosperity in this region. New Caledonia, which was reasonably close to our shores, had the potential for a bit of a spillover to the other Melanesian fragility areas. We had a particular responsibility for developing a good and working relationship with France. There was quite a lot of interaction. (pers. inter., Melbourne, 13 April 2016)

In June 1989, French Prime Minister Michel Rocard's official visit to Australia, on the invitation of Bob Hawke, constituted a very important step in this constructive dynamic. It was the first visit of a French Prime Minister to Australia. This visit followed the one of Bob Hawke to Paris a few months earlier, in June 1989. The invitation to Michel Rocard to visit Australia was a considerable and tangible sign sent from Australia to acknowledge the importance of France's role in the region. Although Rocard asserted that France would not put an end to its nuclear program, for example by visiting Moruroa like Mitterrand had in 1985, he mainly reassured Bob Hawke by showing that France wanted to fully commit to the region's security, balance and development. France's reconciliation with Australia was at the time France's main diplomatic objective in the region. Both governments intended to improve their relationship by putting aside the question of nuclear testing. France and Australia had to be able to strive together for a more secure South Pacific. Michel Rocard's visit was a success, and his interest in Australia did not diminish. He clarified France's objectives in regional security, brought transparency and began building trust in the region (AN Pierrefitte, 19940509/51).

At a ministerial level, Paul Keating and Gareth Evans went to Paris in March 1989 to meet Michel Rocard. They had already been to France in 1988 and would meet Rocard again in 1991. During the 1989 visit, Evans told his French counterpart, Roland Dumas, that his government would like to establish regular ministerial meetings between France and Australia to create an ongoing dialogue between the two countries on regional and global issues, such as Pacific policies and global trade regulations, in particular pertaining to agriculture. Dumas then promised Evans that he would try to come to Australia after his visit to Japan and Asia. Dumas even suggested that they should meet in person once a year, a proposition to which Evans could not commit. However, Evans travelled back to Paris in 1991. In a diplomatic cable dated 28 March 1989, an official from the Quai d'Orsay reported that, during his visit to Paris, Gareth Evans had constructive and courteous meetings with the Prime Minister and the Ministers for Foreign Affairs, Overseas French Territories and Commerce. Such a visit was fundamental because Evans explained Australia's position about France's presence in New Caledonia to French policy-makers, reassuring Paris about Canberra's support and presenting Australia as more of a partner in regional security than as an opponent. France on the other hand promised to be conciliatory with the Cairns Group on agricultural exportations (AN Pierrefitte, 19930409/4). Returning to Paris in January 1991, Gareth Evans even told his French counterpart that the DFAT considered France as its primary partner in continental Europe, especially when addressing security issues such as conflicts in Cambodia or Kuwait (AN Pierrefitte, 19930409/4). Gareth Evans and Michel Rocard built a relationship of trust and working together again on several occasions. For instance, they later worked together as part of the International Crisis Group in order to reflect on crisis management and lobby in their countries for diplomatic policies on responding to violent international crises (AN Pierrefitte, 680AP/40). Michel Rocard was also a member of the Canberra Commission on the Elimination of Nuclear Weapons, established by Gareth Evans and Paul Keating (see Chapter 4).

In a brief addressed to the French Prime Minister on 7 August 1989, the Department of the Cabinet of the Prime Minister asserted that, in order to develop security cooperation with Australia, France should try to align its actions in the Pacific closely with those of the United States and Japan. The report also explained that French diplomats had to be aware that Australia's desire to work with France on regional security issues came also from the fact that the ANZUS crisis with New Zealand and its economic difficulties had increased Australia's regional responsibilities. Therefore, Canberra, seeking not to be the only country responsible for the South Pacific's protection, sought new partners, such as France (AN Pierrefitte, 19940509/95). France played, indeed, a role in Australia's strategic agenda from the middle of the 1980's. Moreover, with the end of the Cold War, international relations in the West were characterised by a strong optimism around what was achievable in the UN Security Council and, more broadly, through multilateral organisations. Therefore, it was increasingly important for Australia to improve its relationship with France, which, as a global middle power and a permanent member of the Security Council, retained a significant level of influence. In addition, at the end of the Cold War, global and middle powers increasingly focused on achieving economic outcomes through new diplomatic strategies, as analysed in Chapter 3 in the case of Paris and Canberra. Therefore, Australian and French policy-makers also strove to improve their bilateral relationship in order to serve their economic and financial ambitions, as much as securing the South Pacific.

However, this rapprochement must not be exaggerated and French–Australian relations remain sometime distant. For example, according to Stéphane Romatet, the 1990s did not witness a meaningful deepening of bilateral cooperation, because both countries remained suspicious towards each other (pers. inter., Paris, 2016). France still considered Australia to be completely revolving in Washington's orbit, so that improving a bilateral relationship with Australia was not useful. The feeling that Australia, being opposed to French nuclear testing and to France's management of New Caledonian tensions, was opposed to France's presence in the Pacific, was still tangible in most French stakeholder's mind. Therefore, policy-makers in Paris did not strive to build a strong relationship with Australia, and vice versa. However, the end of the 1990s and the year 2000 saw a period of mutual discovery for France and Australia. The positive turn in the bilateral relationship effectively happened in the last few years, when both countries started to become increasingly motivated to build a strong relationship.

Recent French–Australian Strategic Dialogue

French–Australian cooperation for the security of the South Pacific is now framed within their Strategic Partnership, signed on 19 January 2012 and upgraded on 3 March 2017 with a Joint Statement of Enhanced Strategic Partnership. In 2012, Paris and Canberra agreed to a common declaration about their security cooperation in the South Pacific. Presented as the commemoration of the opening of the first French consulate in Australia in 1842, the partnership declaration begins by acknowledging that the two diplomatic administrations aim to promote democracy and human rights in the Indian and Pacific Oceans. The document then describes eleven sections of cooperation, which delimitation remains imprecise in order to allow for flexibility.

The 2017 joint statement of enhanced strategic partnership consolidates the mutual engagement made by Malcolm Turnbull and Emmanuel Macron during the former Australian Prime Minister's visit to Paris (Soyez 2017). It was designed to constitute a new tool to deepen French–Australian cooperation. It encompasses thirteen sections, mainly dedicated to both security and economic growth. However, as asserted previously in this chapter, defence and security issues remain the priorities. Politically, the 2017 declaration does not largely innovate when compared to the 2012 agreement. Both countries commit to implement annual meetings of their Ministers for Foreign Affairs, and, more broadly, to foster high-level bilateral exchanges between French and Australian parliamentarians, senior officials and diplomatic personnel in order to make their strategic dialogue more efficient. The intensification of this strategic dialogue is focussed on defence and security. While the document enumerates measures already mentioned in the 2012 partnership, such as implementing regular meetings between their Defence Ministries and 1.5 track dialogues, and joint exercises in the South Pacific, two significant elements have been added. Firstly, France and Australia declare that they are increasing the level of their intelligence cooperation, following their General Security Agreement. This decision illustrates a greater cooperation against terrorism, considered by both countries as their main current threat. Moreover, the document largely emphasises the consequences of the Australian submarine contract with Naval Group on the long-term military alliance between France and Australia, as this chapter will further analyse. While the 2017 declaration points out that French and Australian defence forces are engaged together in conflict zones all around the world, security and defence issues in the Indo-Pacific region remain a priority. This geographic area is frequently mentioned as the core space of the French–Australian cooperation because of both countries' multiple shared interests.

Secondly, the 2017 statement aims to foster French–Australian economic relations. Several tools are suggested to reach this goal. Firstly, France and Australia commit to organise a yearly economic forum gathering trade and finance stakeholders of their relationship. Most importantly, the declaration points out that France and Australia intend to use negotiations for the EU–Australia FTA as leverage to increase trade between the two countries. In order to expand trade flows, Paris and Canberra agree on concentrating their cooperation on energy and resources, transport and infrastructures and innovative technologies. Therefore, both countries assert that they will actively support a tangible cooperation in educational exchanges between French and Australian universities and research laboratories.

The significance of the 2017 Joint statement of enhanced strategic partnership lies in the very large number of concrete and tangible policies planned within thirteen different sectors of cooperation, at a much more detailed level than in the 2012 strategic partnership. Following five years of a fast and significant deepening of the French–Australian relationship, the 2017 statement offers a precise framework for a considerable spectrum of domains of collaboration. Politically, France and Australia agreed since 2012 to intensify their bilateral dialogue, at every administrative level. From the Head of State to the Ministers, Parliaments, high-ranked public servants, regions and cities, regular bilateral meetings are encouraged. François Hollande's state visit in 2014, the first from a President of the French Republic, underlines this will to coordinate policies with common interests. This visit was crucial for the bilateral relationship. Key Australian and French diplomats assert that it constituted a real trigger for further strategic dialogue. Before Hollande's visit to Australia, French official visits were limited.

According to Cédric Prieto, after the implementation of a strategic partnership in 2012, François Hollande's visit was the starting point of a newly deepened French–Australian relationship, open to many topics such as questions of economics and innovation or people-to-people cooperation (pers. inter., Canberra, 8 April 2016). From Australia's point of view, the fact that a French President visited Australia for the first time was of great importance and Hollande was warmly received. The importance of it was symbolic but symbolic demonstrations of cooperation enable two partners to enhance their 'we-feeling', as defined by Karl Deutsch. In May 2018, French President Emmanuel Macron visited Australia in order to strengthen the dynamic rapprochement of France and Australia's foreign policies.

Since the G20 meeting in Brisbane, Australian Prime Minister Tony Abbott visited France twice, in 2014 and 2015, along with former Minister for Foreign Affairs Julie Bishop. Minister for Defence Kevin Andrews met his French counterpart Jean-Yves Le Drian in Paris in April 2015, and Le Drian visited Canberra in March 2016. The aim of this visit was to strengthen the dynamic of strategic dialogue between France and Australia that François Hollande's visit had created. The first element on the French Minister for Defence's agenda was to support France's case for Australia's submarine contract, which he did very successfully. Le Drian also came to Canberra to enhance bilateral cooperation against terrorism, a crucial element of the French–Australian strategic partnership. In addition, the Australian Minister for Defence asked Le Drian to explain France's strategy towards North Korea and Russia as well as its security strategies in the Pacific and Indian Oceans. He also commented on France's diplomatic and economic ambitions in Indonesia and China, and on Paris's position on Chinese aggression in the South China Sea. French policy-makers intend to develop an efficient economic diplomacy toward these two Asian markets in order to support French exports, and to strengthen the strategic dialogue between the EU and Asian multilateral institutions. Le Drian's visits were considered by Cédric Pietro as tools to demonstrate that Australia and France have improved their cooperation. Pietro described the dialogue as very honest and fruitful (pers. inter., Canberra, 8 April 2016). Ric Wells provides the Australian point of view on this visit and confirms Pietro's description of its agenda. China was a central point of strategic discussion between diplomatic representatives:

We believe that France and other European countries have an important role to play in dealing with the rise of China, including on the South China Sea, where Australia is very concerned about the effects of Chinese behaviour on the international norms that underpin freedom of trade and freedom of navigation. We are often talking to France and the other Europeans about this issue and making the point that this is a global issue and one that certainly does affect Europe. More broadly, we will continue to value very much French expertise and views on what is happening in China. (pers. inter., Canberra, 8 April 2016)

The same is true for French foreign-policy makers, who value Australia's perception of Asia's regional dynamics and issues. Australian senior officials claim to have an accurate and, more importantly, quite integrated understanding of Asia. However, while countries like France, Germany and the United Kingdom benefit from an actual presence in Asia as substantial as Australia's and from larger trade relations, the difference is that, unlike France and other European countries, Australia has very much integrated its perspective on Asia. "We don't focus overwhelmingly on the commercial aspects, which I think it is fair to say that France and other Europeans do" explains Wells (pers. inter., Canberra, 8 April 2016). Australia combines this business interest with a strategic perspective, with their people-to-people links. Therefore, the Australian government and the Australian business community seem to have a sophisticated grasp of the dynamics playing in Asia, which is valued by France and other European countries. Australian policy-makers believe that they have quite interesting perspectives on Asia and that they can share this perspective with French policy-makers, academics, and businesses. Moreover, while French and Australian cooperation for the security of the Indian Ocean is still limited, that interest is growing fast in developing a more collaborative strategic dialogue, an area analysed further in Chapter 7. Moreover, since Le Drian's visit, Philippe Pereira, from the Direction of International Relations and Strategy of the French Department of Defence visited Canberra in April 2016. Additionally, French Prime Minister Manuel Valls visited Malcolm Turnbull in May 2016 to demonstrate France's commitment to its strategic partnership with Australia. Moreover, the respective departments within French and Australian Ministries for Foreign Affairs were asked to investigate all the themes and interests that could bring the two countries closer. More recently, in July 2017, Malcolm Turnbull visited France for two days to visit Australian submarines' construction sites and meet with Emmanuel Macron to maintain the strength of the French–Australian strategic partnership (Soyez 2017). In September 2018, Florence Parly, France's Minister for the Armed Forces, visited Australia for three days, inaugurating a French–Australian Defence Industries Symposium in Adelaide with her Australian counterpart Christopher Pyne.

Most of diplomats interviewed for this research have also underlined the importance of one strong area of cooperation: Australia's presence at the United Nations Security Council in 2013–2014, as one of the elected non-permanent members. During these two years, French and Australian delegations implemented weekly dialogues between their diplomatic representatives in New York in order to decide on common strategies for the Security Council (Gary Quinlan, pers. inter., Melbourne, 17 April 2015). Therefore, these two years have witnessed a strong increase and improvement of dialogue. Gary Quinlan, Australian ambassador to the United Nations and President of the Security Council during two one-month terms, September 2013 and November 2014, outlines this cooperation:

> Paris said it was really happy about Australia's role at the Security Council, very impressed because Australia was very active and took risks, which is unusual for a non-permanent member. During the time Australia was at the Security Council, we developed videoconferences every two months between the Quai in Paris and DFAT in Canberra. These meetings enabled the two countries to go over their diplomatic agenda and find common positions on international issues. We worked a lot together. These videoconferences were at the initiative of Paris, who wanted to maintain them after Australia's presence at the Security Council. I am not sure if Australia has maintained them. These two years have deepened the relationship between the two countries. (pers. inter., Melbourne, 17 April 2015)

France's main objective regarding Australia has been, in the last few years, to deeply reinforce its strategic dialogue with Canberra, which has been very successful. Australia's presence on the UN Security Council triggered this strategic cooperation. Although Australia was a non-permanent member of the Council, both countries cooperated on the world's most threatening issues. The fight against Islamist terrorism was the core threat in the Middle East and Africa. Australia's delegation to New York was particularly active on three issues: the war in

Syria, armament control and promoting a reform of the United Nations, especially against the P5's veto power at the Security Council, to open it to new powers. More precisely, one topic is cited by both Prieto and Quinlan to illustrate this important strategic dialogue: France's interventions in Mali and in the Central African Republic. At the request of both governments, France has led, since 2013, operations in these two African countries to fight against terrorism in Mali and to attempt to prevent civil war confrontations in Central Africa. Both operations have received the support of the Security Council. Australia played an important part in convincing the Security Council to fully support France's intervention. As Quinlan states: "Australia has supported France in Africa without any hesitation, while the United Kingdom and the United States had financial criticisms about the operations. Paris was surprised and appreciated Australia's support" (pers. inter., Melbourne, 17 April 2015). Cédric Prieto also confirmed this support:

> At our initiative, France and Australia built a common strategy on African issues, with France's operations in Mali and Central Africa. Australian diplomats were very cooperative and supported us tangibly in order to help us fund the two military operations. The French-Australian dialogue's quality on Sahel and the central region of Africa was considerable. (pers. inter., Canberra, 8 April 2016)

Australia has acknowledged the importance of France's military involvement in Africa in order to maintain security, as Minister for Foreign Affairs Bob Carr expressed in 2013 at the beginning of France's intervention in Mali (O'Malley 2013). Australia supports what France does in North Africa and the Sahel. Australian foreign policy-makers emphasise that France carries a very substantial burden in Africa, which Australia certainly acknowledges, as do others including the United States. For example, Wells points out correctly: "Although Australia's diplomatic presence in the Sahel and Francophone Africa is non-existent, we have a very big commercial presence there, with the expansion of investments from Australian mining companies. We are constantly aware of the security risks to those personnel. We know that France is probably the only Western country in that part of the world to whom we could turn for assistance" (pers. inter., Canberra, 8 April 2016).

The war in Syria was also a major topic of dialogue at the Security Council, within the bigger spectrum of security threats in the Middle East.

Australian diplomats were strongly engaged on the issue of refugees and humanitarian aid, especially about the creation of safety corridors towards Syria in order to supply international support for refugees and civilians still in Syria. The French and Australian delegations had a very constructive dialogue on these topics, such as regarding disarmament, with the treaty on small arms and light weapons initiated by Australia, and international sanctions, with Australia leading Security Council supervisory group discussions about sanctions against Iran, the Taliban and Al Qaeda. Terrorist and rogue states were also on the French–Australian agenda and the subject of dialogue. Globally, according to Quinlan, "Paris was really happy to see Australia take risks. This comes from the fact that Australia is traditionally bold, but it felt confident because of its close relationship with the United Kingdom and the United States". Australia will run again for the Security Council in 2029–2030 so that as the campaign for that gears up, the strength of the French–Australian partnership will be useful.

This French–Australian strategic dialogue continues on other stages now that Australia's term as an elected member of the Security Council has been completed. French and Australian foreign policy-makers meet annually in two track 1.5 dialogues, bringing together officials, think tanks and industrial companies. There are two main dialogues. One is organised by the Lowy Institute and the French Foundation for Strategic Research. Its organisation rotates between Sydney and Paris. The second track 1.5 dialogue is more focused on armament and is organised by the Australian Strategic Policy Institute in Canberra and French military consortiums such as Thales and Safran. The French government is part of both tracks, through the Centre of Strategic Analysis and Provision, an agency of the French Defence Department. This agency also conducts dialogues with the Australian Office of National Assessments.

France and Australia are deeply involved in this dialogue, hoping to reach a more efficient strategy for securing their interests. However, the diplomats don't necessarily have the same priorities. Australian diplomats, according to the French embassy, seek mostly a dialogue about non-proliferation, nuclear energy and nuclear armament and about the fight against terrorism, as key aspects of the bilateral relationship. France's expertise on these topics seems quite valued by DFAT. Australian diplomats seem to also look for France's strategy in Asia and its vision of the region, especially about China and France's diplomatic position regarding tensions in the South China Sea. On the other hand, France seems particularly interested in Australia's expertise in South East Asia and the Pacific. In regard to defence, both countries asserted their determination to work together in order to maintain peace in the Asia-Pacific region, because both countries are the main military powers in the South Pacific. The deepening of the French–Australian strategic dialogue is a significant demonstration of France and Australia's mutual empowerment because, in addition to their common interests, Paris and Canberra expects serve their own national interest because of their difference areas of expertise. French and Australian armies consult each other more often, within several frameworks such as the FRANZ, a crisis management partnership between Paris, Wellington and Canberra, dealing with aftermaths of natural disasters. This frame is fully analysed in Chapter 7. Both countries realise that there is quite a lot to be gained from cooperation in specific areas. Australian foreign policy-makers really wish to have a strong partnership with France for the region's security because New Zealand does not carry as strong a financial weight as France does. The acknowledgment on both countries' shared interests in tangible in Wells' comment:

> France and Australia have been one of the fairly small group of Western countries that has been willing to act decisively, including by the use of force, to achieve national objectives. There are not that many countries that are willing and capable of doing this. Obviously, France has far greater capabilities of doing it than Australia in this area but you have seen the development in both countries of a degree of almost admiration for the fact that both are willing and capable to act, with a degree of independence from the United States, on issues that affect them. (pers. inter., Canberra, 8 April 2016)

The progressive advancement of the French–Australian security partnership can be analysed through the lens of alliance theories (Snyder 1998). One of the benefits of Snyder's theories is his explanation of alliances' formation. Snyder correctly asserts that theories have studied in depth the fact that alliances can be created with regard to the benefits its members can expect after the conflict, but not enough in regard to the preparation for the conflict itself. He asserts that states partly build up alliances to find the strongest military powers to wage war or defend their security (Snyder 1998, p. 1). France and Australia have developed security partnerships not only to maintain peace and avoid regional tensions, but also to combine their military capacities in case of conflict and against terrorism. Snyder's theory of alliance management is also very useful. The author describes alliance management as the ability to control an alliance for the maximisation of the benefits one can gain from the alliance. This management can be at the same time unilateral and collaborative. It operates based on a bargain between members, a bargain between their common and competitive interests. Therefore, according to this theory, a player can manage an alliance by trying to always find benefits from it in order to overcome competitive interests with other members. The outcome of the bargain depends on three factors: the "dependence" of an actor on the alliance, the actor's "commitment" and the members' "comparative interests in the specific issue" (Snyder 1998, pp. 165–166).

The progressive transformation of the French–Australian relationship can be explained through this framework. The two countries have progressively focused on their common interests in security management and control over the South Pacific rather than on competitive interests related to regional leadership. Australian policy-makers have realised that pursuing a unilateral leadership over the South Pacific would be very expensive. They would therefore benefit from sharing the security management of the region with France in order to limit costs and responsibilities. France realised that Australia was not necessarily opposed to its presence in the Pacific and that it needed Australia's support to be accepted by its neighbours. The two countries' diplomacies have progressively turned from being antagonistic because of competitive interests to emphasizing common interests. However, the alliance remains limited to practical cooperation because the two countries can sometimes still be reluctant to fully commit to the partnership. This situation is what Snyder calls a "narrow bargaining range", when states cooperate on a limited number of issues, as opposed to a "broad bargaining range", which could characterise the ANZUS alliance (1998, p. 172). Australia has traditionally focused on the United Kingdom and the United States in terms of military cooperation, because of their shared doctrines, their shared interests, and quite often their shared equipment. However, the Australian defence force is increasingly aware of French expertise in some of these areas, including special forces, which is mutually the case. This shared knowledge was developed during common operations, in particular in Afghanistan and in the Pacific.

Intelligence Cooperation Against International Terrorism

The fight against terrorist organisations has been a common target bringing French and Australian decision-makers and security actors closer. The current strength of terrorist activities has reinforced this necessity. Terrorist threats are substantial in the Asia-Pacific region, especially in Indonesia, which has repeatedly been the theatre of attacks from the Bali bombings in 2002 to the terrorist actions in Jakarta in January 2016. To maintain global security, French and Australian soldiers also fought together against Daesh in Syria and Iraq. While France was the second largest contributor to this intervention, as the Australian ambassador to France Stephen Brady explained, Australia constituted the third. Four hundred Australian members of the RAAF have been engaged alongside the US Air Force, with eight aircraft involved. For instance, French aircraft, "Rafales", have used an Australian tanker aircraft for their missions over the Middle East. Moreover, three hundred Australians have been deployed in Iraq to train the local army, and dozens of Australian counsellors train Iraqi services in counter-terrorism. Australian and French intelligence agencies increased their levels of cooperation in 2015 as a result of the terrorist attacks in Paris and its region. Brady explained that counter-terrorism constitutes "one of the most important aspects of our bilateral relation".[2]

This synergy of intelligence was made official on 9 December 2016 when both countries signed a classified information sharing treaty. This agreement, in support of the delivery of the Future Submarine Program, aims to improve French–Australian security by establishing a shared classification of information and sharing responsibility in collecting information. The treaty, officially qualified as "a milestone in the development of the strategic partnership",[3] incorporates Australian and French attempts to set up smart power diplomacies. As Nye explains, "contextual intelligence, the ability to understand an evolving environment and capitalise on trends, will become a crucial skill in enabling leaders to convert power resources into successful strategies" (2011, p xvii). French and Australian stakeholders are dedicated to improving their security strategies and thereby gaining a better understanding of their environment by sharing expertise and intelligence resources. More precisely, France has a significant contribution to make to Australia's security, including in the campaign against Daesh in the Middle East but also in terms of broader cooperation in counter-terrorism and countering violent extremism. "That is a big Australian priority where we have a lot to gain from cooperation with France, including in having Europe in general tightening its security procedures" say Wells, who asserts that Australian policy-makers are very supportive of France's efforts to persuade the EU as a whole to adopt a Passenger Name Record system: "That is an important area for us where we want to cooperate with France" (pers. inter., Canberra, 8 April 2016). Australia has given a higher priority to partnerships with Europe regarding security and France has played a significant role in this rapprochement. According to Peter Jennings (2017), four reasons explain this recent focus on the EU to serve Australian security: the rise of China, Australia's engagement with NATO, Brexit, and Canberra's strategic partnership with France and its submarine contract with Naval Group. Both Australia and EU member states indent to work closely on counter-terrorism, counter-radicalisation strategies and cyber security. Both the EU and Australia have committed to develop their cooperation in the Framework Agreement signed on 7 August 2017 and fully operational since October 2018. Moreover, regarding intelligence cooperation with the EU, Australia has signed an Agreement on Operational and Strategic Cooperation with Europol in 2007 to increase police partnerships with EU member states. This cooperation is conducted through strategic dialogue at a political level about the developments on the ground in the Middle East, especially in Syria, Iraq, Afghanistan, Yemen and Pakistan. At an operational level, Canberra and Paris have direct cooperation missions between their intelligence agencies. They are governed by political dialogue but also develop themselves independently. These joint missions are concrete, combining French and Australian soldiers on the ground. Australians have had about one hundred and ten fighters in the Middle East, France about one thousand three hundred (C. Prieto, pers. inter., Canberra, 8 April 2016). France and Australia are not only using intelligence to fight against terrorism. Both countries share good practices on community deradicalisation, since Islamist groups conduct proselyting approaches within Muslim communities in both states.

Armament Contracts to Consolidate the Partnership

Finally, and more openly, French–Australian security cooperation has also been actively demonstrated by the provision of military equipment.

Australian Prime Ministers and Ministers for Defence have regularly chosen French companies to provide military equipment to the Australian Army, Navy and Air Force. France has been one of Australia's main armament suppliers, armament being one of France's biggest industrial sectors. With such French–Australian contracts, France not only delivers equipment but also shares its technology with Australia, which is equally important. Such a dynamic is part of French and Australian "smart power" diplomacy. As Nye explains, "On many transnational issues, empowering others can help us to accomplish our own goals. In this world, network and connectedness become important sources of relevant power" (Nye 2011, p. xvii). Armament contracts with Australia are seen in France as a tool to empower a very important and trustworthy ally in the Asia-Pacific region. This creates a lever to reinforce the Western alliance, between two countries sharing most of their regional interests, against potential threats.

Such technology transfers are not new. During his visit to France in 1989, Minister for Defence Beazley suggested to Edwige Avice, Minister Delegated for Foreign Affairs, that Australia had always been very satisfied with French military supplies, for example with radars, and that Australia would keep purchasing French surveillance systems. Moreover, French aircraft manufacturer Dassault sold to the Commonwealth of Australia five Falcon 900s in 1989, for 500 million francs. During this meeting, the two ministers agreed to set up unofficial meetings between the technology and innovation services of the French and Australian Ministries for Defence in order to assess how the two countries could intensify their military trade (AN Pierrefitte, 19930409/4). Recently, Thales, a major French supplier of military equipment, won an important contract on October 2015. The Commonwealth of Australia purchased AUD$1.3 billion worth of military vehicles, the Hawkei (a new fleet of 1100 vehicles and 1000 trailers). In order to be able to win such major contracts, Thales has opened three facilities in Australia, a manufacturing one in Bendigo and two support centres in Brisbane and Townsville. The company currently employs more than 3200 Australians.[4]

More importantly, on 26 April 2016, the Australian Federal government selected Naval Group, France's Defence Shipbuilding then called DCNS, to produce twelve new submarines for the Australian Navy. Naval Group was chosen over the Japanese Mitsubishi and the German Tyssen-Krupp. This order, estimated at around AUS$50 billion, is the biggest order ever made for the Australian Defence Forces.

The significance of this contract is considerable for the Australian–French partnership and for each country's own strategy. The French government has been very involved in the project. Knowing that, in 2013, Tony Abbott supported the Japanese offer, French Ministry for Defence Le Drian decided to organise a series of meetings with diplomats, strategists, senior officers and industrialists. Tony Abbott's departure in 2015 enabled the competition to become fully open to bids by European companies. Naval Group's campaign, supported by France, had been more secretive than the Japanese or the German ones. François Hollande and Jean-Yves Le Drian addressed their final letter to Malcolm Turnbull on 18 April 2016, a week before the result's announcement (Gallois and Taix 2016). The framing contract was signed in Canberra on 11 February 2019 by Australian Prime Minister Scott Morrison, French Minister for the Armed Forces Florence Parly and Australian Minister for Defence Christopher Pyne. The design contract was then signed on 5 March 2019.

French and Australian media have explained the political aspects of the selection of the French shipbuilding company. Naval Group was the only one which had a real plan to build the submarines in Australia, more precisely in Adelaide. The project is supposed to create 2900 jobs in South Australia. This prerequisite comes from the intention of the Australian Liberal government to show, before the Federal elections, that their policies are dedicated to job creation in innovative industrial fields. Thales had already delivered the latest version of the Collins submarine Platform Training Simulator in 2014, also providing Australian submarines with their sensors, sonar suites and communication masts. Moreover, the French company Naval Group has already delivered submarines to foreign armies, built in their own countries, such as India. They have an expertise in such contracts that Japan and Germany lack. Lastly, Naval Group also manufactures military technologies for the US Navy. Australia being very committed to the interoperability of its defence's equipment with the Americans, one can imagine that this also played a role in the decision-making. Washington is known to have followed the competition closely.

However, the decision of the Australian government to commission twelve submarines to Naval Group has raised controversy in Australia. Attacks have not come from the Labor opposition, which has remained globally silent about the tender, but mostly from specialists of International Relations and Defence in Australia. Criticisms have been made both regarding the need for the Australian Navy to acquire submarines and about the type of submarines commissioned. For instance, according to Hugh White and Michael Keating, Australia is dedicating too much of its public spending to twelve submarines and Canberra should make better use of this budget (Davies 2017). Providing an answer to this judgement is not an easy task. While Australia does not currently face imminent threats requiring A$b50 worth of submarines, it is difficult to know whether Australia can protect its regional security and support its leadership in the South Pacific in the future without providing the means to its ambitions. Andrew Davies asserts that the contract's problem does not lie in its cost, but in the fact that the first submarines will not be operational before 2035, which might be too late. Moreover, Davies also asserts that there are technological problems pertaining to the choice of Naval Group, because these twelve submarines necessitate to push "the boundaries of conventional submarine design" in order to increase their capability to their maximum (2017). In fact, following Australia's ambiguous relationship with nuclear energy, the Turnbull government chose to commission diesel-electric conventional submarines instead of nuclear-powered ones. Many critics condemned this decision for its cost-ineffectiveness, arguing that providing the Royal Australian Navy with conventional submarines would waste Australian public funding because the submarines' capability would be too limited to face Australia's unspecified future threats. The Australian government explained this decision by the lack of experience, infrastructures and personnel capable of operating nuclear submarines. However, nuclear-powered attack submarines are conceived to support a country's strategy of global deterrence, which has never been Australia's defence strategy. Therefore, commissioning such type of equipment would have not necessarily been relevant to Australia's context, Canberra having focussed on regional security, easily operated by diesel-electric submarines. Australia having never grounded its strategy on force projection, nuclear submarines appear irrelevant for Australia's ambitions. Moreover, while nuclear submarines are conceived for a global projection of a country's deterrence, conventional submarines are more suited for the protection of Australia's maritime borders and major ports (Ohff 2017).

This contract strengthens the French–Australian partnership. Such a military contract requires close technological cooperation between the two countries during the fabrication of the equipment and after the submarines' launch, for maintenance purposes. Therefore, the decision of the Australian government to commit to such a high level of military cooperation underlines vividly how its partnership with France has become a priority in Australia's management of strategic security in the South Pacific. The diplomatic and political efforts set up by the French state in order to support Naval Group's project has been explained by France's strategic re-engagement in the Asia-Pacific region (Le Corre and O'Hanlo 2016). French diplomatic services are currently concentrating their focus on Asia in order to balance the economic difficulty of the Eurozone, by being more invested in Asian growth and potential. France is also focused on securing its valuable Pacific resources. Thus, in its Defence White Paper published in 2013, France emphasises its engagement in the Pacific region in order to protect the sovereignty of its exclusive economic zone, the second largest in the world after the US. The same document insists on the importance of French overseas territories in France's strategy to remain a naval power, protecting its fishing and mineral resources. For this aspect, the White Paper refers to the French–Australian strategic partnership, presented as a key association for French power in the Pacific:

> In the Pacific Ocean, France fully takes responsibility for being a political and naval power in the region. She finalised a strategic partnership with Australia in 2012. This agreement underlines the increasing convergence of the two countries' interests on many regional and global issues, pertaining to the Pacific and the Indian Oceans. It underlines as well Pacific powers' support to France's presence in the Pacific, France being considered as a source of stability, able to supply immediate support, thanks to the means she has in its overseas territories. (French Defence White Paper, 2013, p. 59)

France intends to reinforce its presence in the Asia-Pacific region, based on its overseas territories but also on its traditional diplomatic links with some South-East Asian states. Moreover, in a context of increasing tensions in East Asia, particularly because of China's sometimes aggressive assertions, France wants to bolster its global strategy for security. This submarine contract is representative of this dynamic and was made fully official on 20 December 2016 by an Inter-Governmental Agreement (IGA). This IGA was signed in Canberra by PM Turnbull and Jean-Yves Le Drian and put a successful end to the negotiations for the contract.

CONCLUSION

Security has represented one of the core elements of the renewal of the French–Australian relationship since the end of the Cold War. As two of the main powers in the South Pacific region, Australia and France have in the past competed to impose their own defence and security agenda on the region. This competition was partly grounded on biased and inaccurate mutual perceptions and misperceptions. These misunderstandings can partly be interpreted as the consequence of the traditional opposition between Anglo-Saxon and French speaking worlds, each seeing the other as an unreliable competitor.

However, the end of the Cold War and the transformation of the Asia-Pacific region have obliged Australia and France to reposition themselves and redesign their strategic interests. Decision-makers from the two countries have been able to progressively construct partnerships pertaining to defence and security policies. From an Australian point of view, the improvement of Canberra's relation with Paris takes part in an Australian regional reengagement. In fact, in the post-Cold War context where Asia's position is growing fast, Australian decision-makers have felt the need to focus their diplomacy in the region. The deepening of bilateral relations has been a key instrument of this impetus, with Australia's neighbouring states, such as Indonesia and France. This agenda is shared by France, which has recently developed a more assertive foreign policy towards Asia and the Pacific. Australian and French agendas have converged into a genuine strategic alliance to find solutions to global threats, especially to terrorism. The French–Australian partnership has been manifested most recently through Australia's submarine contract with France, Canberra's biggest military contract ever.

This chapter also illustrates the relevance of the constructivist framework for the analysis of the French–Australian relationship. In order to overcome their tensions and start building a new partnership for regional security, Australian and French decision-makers and diplomats have begun to learn each other's identity and, therefore, cultural approach to security. They have found interests and issues on which the two countries could work together. They had to put aside their political traditions to understand their counterparts' way of thinking and perceiving the world and its interactions to then be able to communicate and cooperate, to

176   P. SOYEZ

slightly modify their perceptions of security and to enable them to coincide on some issues. This constructivist effort has been primarily implemented in the South Pacific, where Australian and French officials have learnt to accommodate their different understandings of political legitimacy.

NOTES

1. By comparison, according to this poll, 70% of Australians had a positive feeling towards Japan, 71% towards the United States and 85% towards New Zealand (Cook and Dalrymple 2014, p. 156).
2. Stephen Brady, interview in French 26 January 2016. https://theconversation.com/multiculturalisme-antiterrorisme-decheance-de-la-nationalite-ce-que-fait-laustralie-53614.
3. See the official statement. https://www.attorneygeneral.gov.au/Mediareleases/Pages/2016/FourthQuarter/Australia-and-france-sign-classified-information-sharing-treaty.aspx.
4. Thales website. https://www.thalesgroup.com/en/australia/press-release/australia-chooses-hawkei.

REFERENCES

Archives Nationales, Pierrefitte, France.

National Archives of Australia, Canberra, Australia.

Australian Department of Defence 2016, *Defence White Paper*, Australian Department of Defence, Canberra.

Australian Department of Foreign Affairs and Trade 2017, *Foreign Policy White Paper*, Australian Department of Foreign Affairs and Trade, Canberra.

Beazley, K 2003, 'The Hawke Years: Foreign Affairs and Defence', in *The Hawke Government, a Critical Retrospective*, Pluto Press, Melbourne, pp. 347–366.

Bizley, N 2017, 'Julie Bishop's Washington Mission: Find Out Who's Running the Show', *The Interpreter*, 22 February. Available at https://www.lowyinstitute.org/the-interpreter/julie-bishops-washington-mission-find-out-whos-running-show. Accessed 1 November 2017.

Buzan, B Wæver & de Wilde, J 1998, *Security, a New Framework for Analysis*, Lynne Riener, Boulders.

Cook, M & Dalrymple, R 2014, 'Relations with Indonesia', in *Australian Foreign Policy, Controversies and Debates*, Oxford University Press, Oxford, pp. 155–173.

Davies, A 2017, 'A Fall-Back Option for the Future Submarines?' *ASPI The Strategist*, 3 October. Available at https://www.aspistrategist.org.

au/a-fall-back-option-for-the-future-submarines/. Accessed 8 November 2017.

Davison, R & Khan, S 2014, 'ANZUS and the Rise of China', in *Australian Foreign Policy, Controversies and Debates*, Oxford University Press, Oxford, pp. 136–154.

Deutsch, K 1968, *The Analysis of International Relations*, Prentice Hall International, Englewood Cliffs.

Firth, S 2011, *Australia in International Politics*, Allen & Unwin, Sydney.

Gallois, D & Taix C 2016, Sous-marins vendus par DCNS à l'Australie: les coulisses d'un contrat 'historique', *Le Monde*, 26 April. Available at http://www.lemonde.fr/entreprises/article/2016/04/26/le-francais-dcns-remporte-un-megacontrat-de-sous-marins-a-34-milliards-d-euros-en-australie_4908510_1656994.html. Accessed 17 July 2017.

James, K 2016, 'The 'Arrogant French': Examination of a Cliché in Australia's Journalistic and Political Discourse', Presentation at the ISFAR colloquium, 6 December.

Jennings, P 2017, 'Australia-EU Cooperation on Security, Foreign Policy and Development', *Australian Outlook*, 5 June. Available at http://www.internationalaffairs.org.au/australianoutlook/australia-eu-security-cooperation/. Accessed 3 November 2017.

Le Corre, P & O'Hanlon M 2016, 'France's Pivot to Asia: It's More Than Just Submarines', *The National Interest*, 9 May. Available at http://nationalinterest.org/print/feature/frances-pivot-asia-its-more-just-submarines-16117. Accessed 17 July 2017.

Ministère français de la Défense 2013, *Livre Blanc, Défense et sécurité nationale*, Ministère français de la Défense, Paris.

Nye, JS 2011, *The Future of Power*, Public Affairs, New York.

O'Malley, N 2013, 'Mali Crisis Is Australian's Big UN Test, Says Envoy', *Sydney Morning Herald*, 16 January. Available at http://www.smh.com.au/world/mali-crisis-is-australias-big-un-test-says-envoy-20130115-2crlv.html. Accessed 3 November 2017.

Ohff, HJ 2017, 'Nuclear Versus Diesel-Electric: The Case for Conventional Submarines for the RAN', *ASPI The Strategist*, 11 July. Available at https://www.aspistrategist.org.au/nuclear-versus-diesel-electric-case-conventional-submarines-ran/. Accessed 8 November 2017.

Piketty, T 2013, *Le Capital au XXIe siècle*, Seuil, Paris.

Piquet, M 2000, *Cold War in Warm Waters: Reflections on Australian and French Mutual Misunderstandings in the Pacific*, The University of Melbourne Press, Melbourne.

Puissochet, JP 1991, 'Le Protocole au Traité sur l'Antarctique, relatif à la protection de l'environnement', *Annuaire français de droit international*, vol. 37, no. 1, pp. 755–773.

Schultz, J & Wallis, J 2014, 'Australia in the Pacific', in *Australian Foreign Policy, Controversies and Debates*, Oxford University Press, Oxford, pp. 174–192.

Soyez, P 2017, 'Macron and Turnbull Clarify Their Common Ambitions', *ASPI The Strategist*, 27 July. Available at https://www.aspistrategist.org.au/macron-turnbull-clarify-common-ambitions/. Accessed 30 July 2017.

Synder, CA 1998, 'Australia's Pursuit of Regional Security into the 21st Century', *Journal of Strategic Studies*, vol. 21, no. 4, pp. 1–17.

Védrine, H 2001, *France in an Age of Globalisation*, Brookings Institution Press, Washington.

Wolfers, A 1962, *Discord and Collaboration, Essays on International Politics*, John Hopkins University Press, Baltimore.

CHAPTER 6

New Caledonia, Cornerstone of an Ambiguous French–Australian Relationship

France, through New Caledonia, constitutes Australia's third-closest neighbour, and this French overseas community in the South Pacific has become a cornerstone of the French–Australian bilateral relationship. However, the legitimacy of the French sovereignty over New Caledonia, based on a conflicted colonial history, has been challenged both internally—by a strong pro-independence Kanak movement—and externally—by Oceanian public opinion, especially in Australia. In response, French policy-makers have conducted thirty years of institutional, political, economic and social reforms to provide the archipelago with the largest autonomy possible within the French republican frame. Nevertheless, New Caledonia's future cannot be understood as a Franco-French issue. This territorial conflict must be analysed within a broader and changing Pacific order. In fact, New Caledonia has increasingly become a strategic topic for all its neighbours in the pursuit of their own interests. The ongoing condemnation of France's presence in the region has partly come from Oceania's ideal of regional cohesion, solidarity and destiny, based on independence from former colonial powers. This drive obliged Australia to take a position against France in order to strengthen its own legitimacy. This chapter critically analyses the extent to which New Caledonia has proven to be, at the same time, the source of vivid tensions between Canberra and Paris and the mirror of their own strategic ambiguities.

Yet, New Caledonia currently represents one of the cornerstones of the strong cooperation that France and Australia have established for the

© The Author(s) 2019   179
P. Soyez, *Australia and France's Mutual Empowerment*,
Studies in Diplomacy and International Relations,
https://doi.org/10.1007/978-3-030-13449-5_6

stability of the South Pacific. This chapter examines the reasons for this positive shift and in particular question the opposition between French and Australian regional and global interests. Do France and Australia support French presence in New Caledonia for global rather than regional reasons? How has the 2018 referendum on New Caledonia's self-determination affected the French–Australian bilateral relationship and the two countries' attempts to exert leadership in the South Pacific? This chapter firstly examines France's controversial understanding and justification of its sovereignty over New Caledonia and the institutional solutions developed to solve the violent conflicts over the territory's sovereignty. Next, the analysis focusses on Australia's very ambiguous position regarding this issue, as a demonstration of the inconsistencies of its Pacific strategy in general and of own colonial memory. Moreover, how French and Australian policy-makers have disagreed on the sources of their past tensions pertaining to New Caledonia? In Paris, the conflict has been understood within a broader frame of competition for regional leadership between Australia and France, an idea refuted by Canberra. Finally, this chapter assesses the results of New Caledonia's referendum on the French–Australian partnership.

France's Sovereignty Over New Caledonia: From Brutal Imposition to Self-Determination

In 2014, over the 269.000 New Caledonians, Kanaks constituted New Caledonia's biggest community, representing 39.1% of the archipelago's population, followed by Europeans (27.1%) and other ethnic groups. This demographic census was made possible because of a modification of the French constitution, which traditionally forbids the collection of ethnic data, in order to modify the institutions of the archipelago. New Caledonia's institutional and political evolution since the beginning of the 1980s illustrates France's effort to rethink its own institutional model in response to internal and foreign condemnation, in addition to the difficulties of Paris' Oceanian strategy.

Before the Matignon-Oudinot Accords: Decades of Violence

Noumea is the capital of an archipelago with two names. Supporters of France's legitimacy over the territory call it New Caledonia, while citizens in favour of its independence call the archipelago Kanaky

(Mokaddem 2005, p. 25).[1] This dichotomy demonstrates two opposing visions of the concept of sovereignty, of the territory's future and of its relationship with Paris. One promotes more autonomy within the French Republic, the other full independence from it. In fact, there is in New Caledonia, much more than in French Polynesia, a strong political movement supporting independence. Three main political parties have represented this pro-independence aspiration, each promoting different means to achieve decolonisation and a different vision of an independent Caledonian society: the *Front de Libération nationale kanak et socialiste* (FLNKS—Kanak and Socialist National Liberation Front), the *Union calédonienne* (UC—Caledonian Union) and the *Parti de Libération kanak* (Palika—Kanak Liberation Party). A significant part of the Kanak population has for decades demanded New Caledonia's independence from France.[2] Jean-Marie Tjibaou, founder of the FLNKS and Kanaks' main leader,[3] explained accurately Kanaks' sense of belonging to the Pacific and not to France: "We belong here and nowhere else; you belong here but you also belong somewhere else" (Piquet 2000, p. 8). It is important to note that not all Kanaks support independence, much as not all "European" Caledonians advocate for France's sovereignty over the territory. Another significant portion of New Caledonians has lost interest in this crucial issue and considers that, independent or not, their life will not improve. New Caledonians in favour of more autonomy but with a continuing tie with France, called "loyalists", support several political parties, such as the *Rassemblement pour la Calédonie* (Rally for Caledonia), *Calédonie ensemble* (Caledonia together) and the local branch of the Republican party in New Caledonia. Until the end of the 1980s, France's response to violent protests against its sovereignty in New Caledonia was very strict and sometimes ferocious. In fact, the situation in the archipelago during the 1980s was close to tipping into a civil war, with dozens of political assassinations and other ongoing acts of violence committed all around New Caledonia (Angleviel 2015, p. 57).

The 1980s began with a significant deception of the independence movements, which led to a radicalisation of the conflict. François Mitterrand had promised, as part of his 1981 presidential campaign, to organise a referendum on self-determination in New Caledonia. However, once elected, this promise was not kept. Due to a lack of political agreement, a section of the pro-independence activists decided to quickly shift to violent actions against French institutions and their representatives in New Caledonia (Mohamed-Gaillard 2010, pp. 105–110).

Many instances of armed violence took place in the 1980s, finally reaching critical levels during the "ashes years" between 1984 and 1988. Faced with these brutal riots, the French state enacted strict policies to restore order, using the military together with an institutional reform in 1985 carried out by Prime Minister Laurent Fabius and the representative of the state in Noumea Edgard Pisani (Chappell 1999, p. 387). However, this political attempt did not restore peace to the territory, and the conflict was exacerbated until the tragedy of Ouvéa in April 1988, which is deeply ingrained in memories not just in New Caledonia but also in metropolitan France.[4] The massacre of six French soldiers and nineteen Kanak hostage-takers during this terrible event created a break in the conflict and was to lead all parties to negotiation. In fact, before Ouvéa, the conservative government led by French Prime Minister Jacques Chirac, heir of the Gaullist party, with his Minister for Overseas Territories Bernard Pons, instituted a policy dedicated to the assertion of French sovereignty over New Caledonia by reinforcing the state's authority and prerogative in the territory. France was still leading an imperial policy in its territories. French policy-makers did not want to imagine that the French identity could encompass a Pacific dimension and they were opposed to presenting France as such in the region.

France's strategy and policies in New Caledonia were aimed at serving the interests of metropolitan France in the context of the Cold War. From this perspective, the territory's future was a national matter, and certainly not a regional one, and for this reason the French state did not consider that it had to justify its sovereignty over New Caledonia to any other actor, either internally or externally. Therefore, French policy-makers' vision of the situation was clear: French territories in the Pacific had a strict French identity and Paris constituted their only interlocutor. They were to only serve France's global interests. Following this Eurocentric vision of New Caledonia's interactions, the Quai d'Orsay notified DFAT several times during the 1980s that France considered any debate at the United Nations about New Caledonia's status as an intrusion into French national affairs, in opposition to article 7 of the UN charter (AD Nantes, 10POI/1/513). Pacific Islands governments, supported by New Zealand and occasionally by Australia, relayed Kanaks' claim to full sovereignty over New Caledonia at the UN, using the argument that France, supporting the UN Charter, should implement its articles 73 and 74 and support the self-determination of its territories. Consequently, the regional integration of New Caledonia and French Polynesia was not on the agenda (Piquet 2000, p. 8). In the Pacific, just as in the Atlantic and Indian Oceans, France undermined the creation of regional links between its overseas territories and their neighbours. For example, French policy-makers feared that the regional integration of Paris' territories in the Caribbean Sea would lead to a strong American influence over Martinique and Guadeloupe. Regarding New Caledonia, French-policy makers feared that Australia would use its regional leadership to gain a neo-colonial influence and undermine French interests in its territory.

Since the 1950s, and still to the present time, French and Australian opposing views regarding the future of New Caledonia is a result of different understandings of their imperial history. French policy-makers and diplomats have constantly denied to any foreign country the right to question France's sovereignty over its territories. This strong tension with Canberra comes from the fact that France and Australia have a completely opposing vision of decolonisation. On the one hand, a large part of Australian public opinion perceives New Caledonia as constituting a colony and that France has, morally, no legitimacy in maintaining its power over the archipelago. On the other hand, French policy-makers believe that New Caledonia is no more of a colony than is Australia, because Australia has never been decolonised and still conducts questionable policies targeting its indigenous population. In fact, according to this French point of view, Australia has kept most of its British and colonial institutions, and its head of state remains the British monarch. Moreover, French policy-makers explain that during the decolonisation process of the 1950s, some former colonial territories chose, by referendum, to remain part of France but with a large degree of autonomy. Therefore, French policy-makers considered that Australia was stepping beyond its area of competence and authority in claiming that France should leave New Caledonia. The dispute was sometimes fierce, and French policy-makers have often argued that Australia is one of the very few countries which cannot give lessons on colonial matters: "One of [France's] favourite retorts was to say that Australians had themselves been zealous supporters of British imperialism in the past; that they have not refrained from casting covetous glances at neighbouring islands; and that on their own territory, their treatment of the indigenous population had hardly been a model of democratic benevolence" (Piquet 2000, p. 7).[5] Therefore, there has been a genuine conflict between the two countries about the legitimacy of their presence in the region. On numerous occasions, French diplomats have repeated this metropolitan opinion by asserting that Australians were no less colonisers than French people, and that they maintained their colonial society through disgraceful policies towards Aboriginal Australians, so that Australians' opinion on France's presence in New Caledonia was not relevant.

Moreover, the French perspective on this matter has also been that Australian public opinion was vigorous in its criticism of France's presence in the region because of traditional and on-going Francophobia amongst British nations, a Francophobia analysed by Klem James (2016). France's assessment was clear. The United States has maintained its sovereignty over territories in the Pacific institutionally comparable to French ones, Hawaii excluded. In fact, the Commonwealth of the Northern Marianas has a US Commonwealth status and the Marshall Islands, the Republic of Palau and the Federated States of Micronesia have signed "Compacts of Free Association" with the United States. Moreover, Niue, the Cook Islands and Tokelau are freely associated with New Zealand, and the Christmas Islands, Cocos Islands, Coral Sea Islands, Heard and McDonald, Lord Howe, Macquarie and Norfolk Islands have the status of Australian territories. However, Australian public opinion never condemned Washington's, Wellington's and obviously Canberra's sovereignty over these archipelagos (Chappell 1999, p. 387). Consequently, according to French policy-makers, Australia's public opinion which vigorously attacked France's presence in the South Pacific was partly based on racism. The French ambassador to the Pacific Christian Lechervy explains this conflicting understanding of legitimacy, which still frequently resurfaces in French–Australian relations. In fact, tensions pertaining to France's presence in New Caledonia "are still on the table because they are linked to our relationship with our colonial history. This topic is at the very heart of Australia's political identity and diplomacy. The way France and Australia build their influence is not neutral" (C. Lechervy, pers. inter., Paris, 22 December 2016). The vast majority of conflicts between France and Australia have come from mutual misperceptions which are then used in order to defend one's own legitimacy. Lechervy goes even further and asserts that French policy-makers have always been shocked by "the absolute ignorance of many politicians, academics and public servants in Australia about French Pacific territories, about their institutional complexity and evolutions" (pers. inter., Paris, 22 December 2016). Lechervy's assessment has been corroborated during this research since not many Australian policy-makers have a clear understanding of what France's *Outre-mer* is. However, the contrary is also true, and French officials' knowledge of Australia could sometimes stand to be updated.

However, French policy-makers have progressively realised that their attitude on this issue was counterproductive, because, by refusing to explain their policies and strategies for New Caledonia, they were not responding to the growing regional opposition to their presence. France's position was perceived regionally as arrogant by refusing dialogue and not being inclined to appease the situation. French policy-makers before Michel Rocard did not understand that they needed to appear open to regional discussion to calm their Pacific neighbours, even without accepting any criticism of France's sovereignty. "The main flaw of the French 'Republican' model is that [...] all it managed to do in the case of the Pacific was to isolate France's territories from the rest of the region, within a Franco-French context, and with little room for relationships with the island nations geographically and culturally close to them" (Piquet 2000, p. 13). France made a mistake when asserting that New Caledonia's troubles were only a French matter. It would seem more accurate to say that France did not want to understand because of a conservative vision of its *politique de grandeur* (politic of greatness). Therefore, when French policy-makers came to the realisation that Paris could not afford anymore to behave with the same assertiveness as the one of De Gaulle, France chose to progressively increase its dialogue with Australia on New Caledonia to explain its position and appease the tensions.

Two Decades of Institutional Innovation to Strengthen France's Presence in New Caledonia

From 1988 to 1991, the French government under Prime Minister Michel Rocard initiated a complete shift in France's policy in New Caledonia and in the South Pacific in general. With this new political agenda, France managed to gain the support of Australia in asserting its reformed New Caledonian and Pacific strategies. Michel Rocard, who had an accurate understanding of France's *Outre-mer* and of the South Pacific in general, developed a genuine dialogue with Kanak pro-independence leader Jean-Marie Tjibaou (FLNKS) and loyalist leader Jacques Lafleur (RPCR), enabling all the parties involved to negotiate. Less than three weeks after the Ouvéa tragedy and the presidential elections in France in May 1988, the new Prime Minister Michel Rocard established a mission of dialogue in order to bring pro-independence and loyalist leaders to the negotiation table (Angleviel 2015, p. 210). This mission was a success, and the new government fully committed to finding a solution to the tensions in the archipelago. This policy led to the Matignon-Oudinot Accords, signed in June and August 1988. This agreement between all parties (the state, independence and loyalist movements) enabled a large level of autonomy, an economic readjustment between communities and, more importantly, planned a referendum within ten years (Mokaddem 2005, p. 12). The referendum was postponed by another ten years on 5 May 1998 by the Noumea Accords, signed under the Jospin government. These two agreements revitalised the relationships of France's overseas territories in their region. Rocard shifted France's strategy and committed to the regional integration of these territories, for example by granting 5.5 million Pacific francs to the New Caledonian government in Noumea in order to create its own funding for the South Pacific Commission. The Quai d'Orsay was convinced that New Caledonia could deepen its relationships with its neighbours and demonstrate its solidarity on shared issues (AD Nantes, 27POI/142). Australian policy-makers, who believed that France was, finally, trying to contribute to a *modus vivendi* in the region, valued this French conciliatory position, as Gareth Evans remembers: "The French wanted a harmonious cooperation relationship in the South Pacific and they saw that Australia was quite important in that respect" (pers. inter., Melbourne, 13 April 2016). Moreover, France's clarification of its position in New Caledonia enabled Australian policy-makers to clarify their own ambiguous support for Kanak independence movements.

AUSTRALIA'S AMBIGUOUS STRATEGY REGARDING KANAK PRO-INDEPENDENCE MOVEMENTS

France and Australia developed significant disagreement over Australia's ambiguous position pertaining to pro-independence movements in New Caledonia, to the extent that the territory's future became one of the three key tensions between Paris and Canberra, along with France's nuclear testing program (Chapter 4) and international agricultural trade (Chapter 3). Archival study reveals how embarrassed Australian policy-makers were by this issue and how their strategy varied depending on their interlocutor, an inconsistency that weakened France's trust in Australia.

A first distinction must be made between Australia's official statements regarding New Caledonia's independence and Australian policy-makers' personal opinions and policies. The dichotomy is obvious. Officially, Australia's strategy was to try to remain neutral regarding the opposition between the French state and the Kanak pro-independence movements, not to appear as betraying South Pacific countries but keeping a functioning relationship with France as a representative of global power. Gareth Evans, in commenting on the official position of the Australian government, claims that Australian policy-makers did not favour any particular outcome: "If the domestic sentiments were to move towards independence, that would have been totally fine by us and consistent with the larger decolonisation movement. We would have been very comfortable with that but we were not in the business of actively promoting it. It was important to get some kind of modus operandi in place" (pers. inter., Melbourne, 13 April 2016). However, according to the former Minister for Foreign Affairs, Australia supported France after the Matignon-Oudinot Accords when France decided to engage in the path toward self-determination. However, this neutral position represented a shift in Australian political discourse, which took place in 1988 and 1989. At an individual level, Australian politicians' positioning regarding New Caledonia also significantly varied following their political affiliation. Members of the Labor party tended to be more inclined to support Kanaks' demands and concerns from other Pacific Islands states. However, Liberals focused more on protecting the regional interests of the Western alliance and, therefore, their relationship with Paris.

New Caledonia as a Threat to Australia's Security?

In October 1986, Australia's Foreign Minister Bill Hayden told his French counterpart Jean-Bernard Raimond that Australia had "the desire to see New Caledonia join the community of independent South Pacific countries as soon as is realistically possible" (NAA Canberra, M3797/18). This non-official statement, far from being neutral, can be explained by the fact that Australian policy-makers considered New Caledonia's instability a threat to the security of the South Pacific in general, and to Australia in particular. In particular, Australian politicians were not opposed in principle to France's presence in New Caledonia, but they thought that New Caledonia's political instability was quite dangerous for Australia's security. Canberra was afraid that the tensions

188   P. SOYEZ

between Kanaks and the French state would worsen and become very violent, as the mid-1980s proved to be, and that this conflict could possibly disrupt the whole region's stability. In fact, in the 1980s, in the context of the Cold War, some Kanak pro-independence leaders developed links with the USSR, which was eager to increase its presence in the Pacific, a region traditionally under American influence. Moscow's bet was that, by helping pro-independence movements in New Caledonia or in other countries of the Pacific, these territories could be used to serve communist interests. Australia was obviously very concerned by the increasing Soviet presence in its region. Moreover, Kanak pro-independence leaders developed links with Kaddafi's Libya, which was financing terrorism worldwide. A few Kanak activists even travelled to Libya for terrorism training in 1984 and 1987 (NAA Canberra, M3793/54). In fact, during the 1980s, Tripoli gained a certain influence in the South Pacific, especially in Vanuatu and Irian Jaya, which Australia and France perceived as a direct threat to the region's stability. For instance, in 1987, Libya invited representatives from New Caledonia, Vanuatu, Indonesia, the Solomon Islands and Aboriginal Australian communities to Tripoli for a conference, before supporting, in the same year, the coup in Fiji (Mrgudovic 2008, p. 346). Debate exists over whether Kaddafi's strategy was to develop genuine connections with the region or to put pressure on France because of Paris's support for Chad against Libya. Whatever Kaddafi's motivation was, some Australian stakeholders were tempted to support these pro-independence movements, thinking that if New Caledonia became independent with Australia's support, it would be, in a way, in debt to Australia and would not need to turn either to Moscow or to Tripoli for assistance.

The end of the 1980s corresponds with a stronger Australian engagement in the South Pacific. When appointed Minister for Foreign Affairs, Gareth Evans explained to the press that his first diplomatic travels would be dedicated to visiting Pacific states, in order to improve regional cooperation (AN Pierrefitte, 19930409/4). For example, Evans decided to open a new Australian embassy in the Federated States of Micronesia in 1988, a policy which had several aims. By opening this embassy, Canberra showed its support for the Federation's claim to statehood. It also enabled Australia to demonstrate the fact that Australian policy-makers regarded the South Pacific as a priority, after several years of neglect, in order to reinforce its regional influence, especially within the Pacific Islands Forum. In a 1988 letter, South Pacific Consultancies wrote to

Gareth Evans: "Your readiness to visit these small countries is seen by them as the most important testament of Australian intent to assist them […] and to take them seriously" (NAA Canberra, M3793/45). In a diplomatic context where Pacific stability became a priority for Australia, New Caledonia's civil conflict was perceived as a significant threat by Australian policy-makers. Moreover, the Labor government was inclined to genuinely listen to the understanding that Pacific Islands states had of their region's development. However, this lead to a certain ambiguity.

Different Political Discourses for Different Interlocutors

The deep ambiguity of Australia's strategy regarding New Caledonia comes from the fact that Australian policy-makers changed their political discourses on this issue depending on their interlocutors. Until the 1988 Accords, during dialogue meetings of regional partners, Australia officially supported Kanak independent movements. Australian policy-makers did not want to appear as a hindrance in the decolonisation process of the South Pacific. This position was accurately described in a 1987 report from DFAT on the PIF ministerial meeting organised in Auckland on 3–4 March 1987 (NAA Canberra, M3793/13). Australia's position was three-fold. First of all, Australia wished "to see New Caledonia join the community of independent South Pacific countries as soon as is realistically possible" as Hayden had told Raimond a year before. Thus, before the new context of the Matignon-Oudinot Accords, Australia presented itself to Pacific islands states as being in favour of an independent New Caledonia. Secondly, the report asserted that Australia desired "to see a multi-racial independence which recognises the rights of the indigenous people as well as safeguarding the rights of other long-term residents". Thirdly, Australia wanted to "maintain a constructive dialogue with all parties involved in the New Caledonian issue, including the French Government". In this document, Australian policy-makers explained that their policy regarding New Caledonia was based on the will of a majority of Kanaks to become independent, but also on the pressure from other Pacific states and lastly on the fact that France represented a source of "concern" for Australia. Canberra also explained to its neighbours that PIF member states had to avoid any action or word that France could use to protest against regional involvement in the conflict. However, Australian policy-makers admitted that their position on the future of New Caledonia could be "ambivalent", supporting independence but seeking to maintain France's "goodwill": "It would be inconsistent with our general approach to demand that independence must be the outcome of the referendum" (NAA Canberra, M3793/13). Therefore, Australia chose not to officially recognise any Kanak pro-independence leader as a representative of New Caledonia. More broadly, in their dialogue with Pacific states, Australian officials did not want to seem too forgiving of France, which would have hindered its regional credibility (NAA Canberra, M3793/238).

Australian policy-makers were often followers rather than leaders on that topic: they reacted to the emotions of Australian public opinion, or to their neighbours' pressure, more than they acted independently. Australia's position towards France tended to become more harshly critical when member states of the Pacific Island Forum strengthened their criticism. The reason was that Canberra did not want to appear to be supporting Western powers against Pacific interests in its region. A 1987 meeting brief between Gareth Evans and his Indonesian counterpart illustrates this analysis. In that document, DFAT expressed its opposition to New Caledonia's inclusion on the list of non-self-governing countries, because this was seen as counterproductive to the effort to bring about a shift in French policies. Australian diplomats explained that France's support for Australia at the UN was a global strategic priority. However, the document asserted that DFAT faced "strong pressure" from the Forum, which Australia could not ignore to protect its regional leadership. Therefore, in this brief, DFAT advised Gareth Evans to ask his Indonesian counterpart for his assessment of the situation to find if there was another regional leader supporting a conciliatory approach, so Australia would not appear to be the only one (NAA Canberra, M3793/54). This example shows how the position of Australian politicians regarding New Caledonia fluctuated depending on Canberra's strategic priorities. If the Australian government focused on its global interests, Canberra's condemnation of France's policies in New Caledonia would soften in order to maintain a constructive relationship with Paris on global issues. When Canberra prioritised its regional leadership, the Australian government tended to follow its Pacific neighbours' strong criticism of France.

New Caledonia's inclusion on the UN list of non-self-governing territories particularly illustrated this ambivalent strategy. On many occasions during the 1980s, French policy-makers asked the Australian government to lobby against New Caledonia's listing. Australia had supported

France on that matter against its neighbours until 1987, when violent tensions in New Caledonia enabled the Pacific states to put a stronger pressure on Canberra against Paris (AD Nantes, 10POI/1). Regional pressure explained Australia's vote in favour of the inclusion of New Caledonia on the list in 1987. Australian policy-makers explained their decision by asserting that it was "a means of ensuring that the territory's progress towards self-government and independence [was] regularly reviewed by the United Nations" (NAA Canberra, M3793/13). Nonetheless, pressures from Australian and Pacific public opinion motivated this decision, which made French policy-makers furious. A letter from Jacques Chirac, then Prime Minister, to his Minister for Foreign Affairs, shows that Chirac asked him to be firm with Australia. The French government sent an order to all its embassies around the world to officially condemn Australia's decision and to point out Australia's dreadful policies against indigenous Australians in their own country. Then, Chirac ordered France's embassy at the UN to lobby against any Australian candidature for an executive position within the institution. Lastly, and more significantly, Chirac decided to expel the Australian Consul from Noumea, a decision described as "cynical" by DFAT (NAA Canberra, M3793/104). Therefore, France reproached Australia strongly for its position as follower and not as leader, which Paris understood as a sign of weakness in leadership. According to French diplomats, Australia was so eager to appear as the leader of the South Pacific that it felt it had to placate the region more than focusing on its global interests. Therefore, in 1987, from French officials' eyes, the true leadership of the Pacific was in the Forum, not in Canberra.

Similarly, the difficulty of Australian policy-makers in articulating a clear position regarding New Caledonia is also revealed in their public speeches addressed to the Australian public. Archives from the French Consulate in Melbourne reveal that a significant part of Australian public opinion was supportive of Kanak pro-independence movements, especially the unions, because of their global support for decolonisation processes. Hence, during the 1980s, Australian public opinion pushed the government to strongly condemn France's policies in New Caledonia. This proved to be difficult for Australian politicians who, as analysed previously, had to focus at least in part on their global interests and thus needed to remain ambivalent towards France. During his visit to Noumea in September 1988, Gareth Evans said to the Australian press that he supported Kanak leaders from the FLNKS in their battle to reach independence and that, in order to do so, Australia would offer to fund aid programs to New Caledonia: "I support the aspiration of the people represented by the FLNKS to autonomy and independence". Evans then described New Caledonia as an under-developed country. During the same press conference, the Minister explained that Australia wanted to increase its relationship with the FLNKS and New Caledonia in general, by increasing mobility, development programs, tourism and trade, especially mining, between the Canberra and Noumea. French politicians and officials were strongly critical of this press conference and were shocked that the Australian Minister for Foreign Affairs presented New Caledonia as a "state". French diplomats bitterly claimed that Evans ignored what was being negotiated in Noumea (AN Pierrefitte, 19930409/4).[6] However, such public statements must be understood as the Australian government's attempt to satisfy Australian public opinion by showing that Australia was supporting the Kanaks against the French state.

Debates were fierce at the UN over France's policies in New Caledonia. There were on one side countries in opposition to France, mostly in the Pacific, Africa and Latin America, which regularly condemned either France's management of the crisis or Paris's sovereignty over the archipelago in general, and on the other side countries that supported France's narrative and policies to legitimise its presence in this part of the world. These debates, mostly led at the UNGA or the UN Committee of 24 (UN Special Committee on decolonisation[7]) demonstrate the significant effort of the Pacific states to raise awareness on New Caledonia's violent tensions and to assemble a majority of countries eager to condemn a French-ruled New Caledonia. They also enabled this researcher to understand France's diplomatic efforts to counteract this ongoing condemnation, either by trying to legitimise its sovereignty or by lobbying within the UN. For example, France's claims were supported by its traditional allies, such as London. Paris also obtained unexpected support, such as from Cuba. Havana explained that withdrawing France's colonialism from Noumea would only lead to New Caledonia's domination by Australian neo-colonialism. Debates were particularly tense during the UNGA in order to push the Committee of 24 to make a decision regarding the inclusion of the archipelago on the list of non-self-governing territories, such as in 1986 when the Pacific countries' campaign was successful. Such debates are still currently significant, for instance when French Polynesia was added to the UN list in 2013, a decision which deeply displeased France. Pacific states continue to monitor the situation in French Pacific territories, while the UN Committee listens, every year, to the requests of pro and anti-independence New Caledonians.[8]

Yet, Australia's condemnation of French Pacific policies lessened when addressing the issue with its Western allies, since Canberra did not want to appear as weakening the Western alliance in the Pacific. For instance, this was the case in the United Kingdom–Australia dialogue. Despite political disagreements between London and Paris during the 1980s, the United Kingdom and France strongly supported each other when their sovereignty over overseas territories was challenged. For example, French President François Mitterrand immediately offered his quick support to Prime Minister Margaret Thatcher during the Falkland Islands war. Both old imperial powers shared the same understanding of the inviolability of their sovereignty over their territories. Australian policy-makers were fully aware of this connection. This is why, in October 1987, when the British Minister of State for Foreign and Commonwealth Affairs visited Canberra, Bill Hayden was advised by DFAT to be very cautious in presenting Australia's position regarding tensions in New Caledonia. Bill Hayden explained to his British counterpart that Australia had no intention of denying France's legitimate presence in the South Pacific through its sovereign territories, a presence described as positive politically, economically, strategically and culturally. However, Hayden urged Britain, apparently in vain, to shift from abstention to action and publicly condemn France's policies in New Caledonia and Mororuoa. He stressed the idea that French policies in the South Pacific were hindering the Western alliance and, therefore, indirectly, London's interests. Hayden went further and explained that, since Australia had supported the United Kingdom during the Falkland Islands war, Canberra expected London's support for Australia's position regarding New Caledonia (NAA Canberra, M3793/104). This document attests that Australia's discourse and assessment on New Caledonia was quite different when addressed to a global ally or to Pacific islands states. Bill Hayden had used the same tone and arguments with the United States when requesting their support, in vain as well. During a meeting in Washington in 1985, Hayden's American counterpart George Schultz indicated to him that he "thought it was necessary to support the French in their efforts in New Caledonia and that [...] all have interest in seeing the situation handled in a way which ensured a continuing French involvement".

Interestingly, Hayden then explained to Schultz that he agreed with the American position (NAA Canberra, M3793/63). Therefore, Australian diplomacy was unsuccessful when looking for support in London and Washington against French policies in New Caledonia. Australia was, again, torn between its regional and global alliances.

Paris's assessment of Australia's involvement in the Caledonian conflict was ambiguous as well. As seen previously, France officially expressed strong resentment against Australia's position when Canberra supported Kanak claims, but French officials would temper their discontent as soon as Australia softened its criticism. In fact, France also acknowledged that, at numerous times, Australia was trying to find a conciliatory position between France and the Melanesian countries, which were the nations most eager to refute France's legitimacy in New Caledonia. Therefore, as France did regarding its nuclear testing program, the Quai d'Orsay focused its pedagogical effort on Australia so that Canberra might then appease its neighbours' condemnation. For example, Gareth Evan explains that "the Melanesians were always the most aggressive about it and it was something we wanted to balance out" (pers. inter., Melbourne, 13 April 2016). Therefore, even if it seems really difficult to ascertain precisely to what extent Australia did support the Kanaks' movements, it seems clear that the Australian government was torn in two directions. On the one hand, in order to maintain its support from the unions as well as regionally, the Australian government supported the Kanaks' claims by multiple means, for example by turning a blind eye on funding transfers to New Caledonia. On the other hand, Australia gave a high priority to maintaining peace in the South Pacific, in order to secure its stability and prosperity. In this context, Australian diplomacy tried to encourage the Pacific states to coexist and avoid a spill over of tensions in Melanesia, especially in New Caledonia, which is geographically closest to Australian shores.

An interesting example illustrates this Australian diplomacy of compromise quite well (NAA Canberra, M3793/13). During the years of strong opposition between France and the Pacific states, in 1986 and 1987, Paris tempered its relationship with Canberra. Australian policymakers were determined to restore constructive dialogue with France, about many global issues. However, in order to maintain their leadership in the South Pacific, they did not want to appear as pro-France in the eyes of the PIF member states. Therefore, in 1987, Australian policymakers established the following strategy with the support of France's ambassador to Australia. They decided that an efficient way to improve their relationship with Paris would be to encourage the Forum to send a representative to Paris to meet with Prime Minister Jacques Chirac and to seek clarification on French policies. Canberra did not wish to be the one suggesting the idea at the Forum and therefore decided that it would try and persuade the Chair of the Forum to suggest the idea himself. Australia's attempt to remain close to France while appearing to be sympathetic to the Pacific states' anti-French position is clearly revealed. Australia always maintained frequent interactions with France in order to make sure that, despite occasional tensions, the two countries could sustain a good and working relationship on global issues. This was extremely important for Australia, which understood the necessity of being able to collaborate with France on global issues, but less relevant for countries like Fiji or Vanuatu. These events took place at the end of or right after the Cold War. In this context, countries optimistically believed that changes were achievable in the Security Council and through cooperative international behaviour elsewhere, on all ranges of policy issues. Australian policy-makers understood that, therefore, it was a mistake to give up on global cooperation with a P5 member over regional issues in Melanesia. This argument is supported by Denise Fisher's view on Australia's accommodating position: "My understanding, having been a diplomat at that time, is that the official role of the Australian government, within the Pacific Island Forum, within regional discussion, was actually one of restraining the Pacific countries in their opposition to France, largely because of our own relationship with the United States and Britain. We understood the broader strategic issues" (pers. inter., Canberra, 7 April 2016).

Australian Active Support for Kanak Independence?

Australia's practical support for Kanak leaders is hard to accurately analyse, because French and Australian sources are unclear regarding this important question. Nonetheless, based on archives in Canberra and Paris, Kanak leaders received direct support from Australia on several occasions, not just politically but also financially. The question is to know whether this support was official, from the government, or if it came from civil society. Denise Fisher, former Australian Consul to New Caledonia, explains that a dichotomy exists between Australian public opinion and the Australian government. She asserts that civil society developed and conducted Australia's support for Kanak leaders, through unions, churches and other associations. However, she claims that the Australian government itself did not provide any support:

> The water is muddied even further by the fact that many of the Australians who were in connection with Kanaks independent movements were people like the Teachers' Federation, the unions. We had a Labor government at the time and it was very closely linked to the unions. (pers. inter., Canberra, 7 April 2016)

However, a very important document, held by the French National Archives, contradicts Australian policy-makers' position regarding this official support and illustrates a direct support from an Australian policy-maker to the Kanaks (AN Pierrefitte, 19980589/9). On 21 January 1987, the Cabinet of the French Minister for Defence issued a report to the Ministry of Overseas Territories about Australian support to the Kanaks. This report explained that French intelligence had discovered that Mr. John Dauth, Australian Consul to New Caledonia, had organised a secret meeting in the bush with leaders of the pro-independence movement. Dauth and the Australian public servants present with him did not inform the French state's representative that this meeting was organised, where Dauth especially met with Jean-Marie Tjibaou, main leader of the pro-independence movement, and the Moindou brothers, two radical leaders who were charged with the murder of French officials at the time of the meeting. The report also explained that intelligence had demonstrated the Australian Consul was financing Kanak associations to indirectly finance the FLNKS, which, according to the report, was a common type of support from Australian representatives in Noumea. The document asserted that France had complained to Australian officials several times about Dauth's activities and that Australian ambassador to France Peter Curtis had also contacted John Dauth to advise him to be more careful. Therefore, the report concluded by saying that the French government had decided to expel the Australian Consul from New Caledonia and not to replace him for several months. This document is important because it illustrates accurately how, despite Australian policy-makers' official discourse, France was aware that Australian officials had directly helped the FLNKS. Moreover, Australian support to Kanaks also came directly from Canberra. In a DFAT transcript of the meeting between Bill Hayden and his American counterpart George Schultz in Canberra in July 1985, one can read: "Kanak leaders were received at Ministerial level when they visited Australia, and the FLNKS was also opening an information office in Australia" (NAA Canberra, M3793/63). More broadly, French policymakers were convinced that the Australian Labor government was backing up pro-independence movements. The French government believed that unions could not support the Kanaks without the tacit agreement of the Labor government, which was turning a blind eye to the situation.

Australia's position regarding New Caledonia damaged the potential trust that could have existed between French and Australian policymakers, because French authorities understood Canberra's support to Kanaks, even if it was limited, as a manifestation of Australia's effort to evict France from the South Pacific, a fear which seems unfounded. As Romatet explains, "About the New Caledonian issues, Paris had the perception that, combined with Canberra's opposition to the nuclear testing program, Australia was a hostile country to France's interests in the region" (pers. inter., Paris, 21 June 2016). French policy-makers believed, like Jacques Chirac in 1986, that Australia sometimes was a hindrance in their attempts to stabilise the situation in New Caledonia. "This Pacific dispute, added to the fact that Australia was considered too close to the United States, made France believe that there was nothing to build with Australia" concludes Romatet (pers. inter., Paris, 21 June 2016).

Denise Fisher provides the Australian point of view on this particular tension. She asserts that Australia had a better understanding of the situation in New Caledonia than France because "we looked at French territories as diplomats and we could see, and still now, analyse and make recommendations to our governments. We saw what was happening before the French did" (pers. inter., Canberra, 7 April 2016). This claim is questionable because France, as the local power, had also a broad and accurate look at the situation, through all its institutions, as ministerial archives indicate. However, Fisher goes further and claims that: "The French were not listening and saw [Australia] as part of the problem, because we were pointing it out. We were pursuing Australia's interest by seeing what was going on". Her interpretation of this conflict is interesting because it illustrates Australia's understanding of the situation in New Caledonia in the 1980s and how it was different from French policy-makers' assessment of the crisis.

198   P. SOYEZ

Our analysis was that the Kanaks wanted independence, the French were mishandling the decolonisation process and the rest of the Pacific was opposed to France. There was a problem. But France was saying that we were the problem. That was the clearest case of misperceptions. At that time, French policy-makers wanted to send Australia's ambassador to France back home, but the Quai d'Orsay refused in order to protect the relationship with Australia. (Denise Fisher, pers. inter., Canberra, 7 April 2016)

Australia's Strategic Shift Regarding New Caledonia from 1989

In 1989, one year after Evans' strident declaration in Noumea against France's presence in New Caledonia and in the context of the Rocard government's negotiations with Kanak and loyalist leaders, Australia's position shifted significantly. This modification followed Michel Rocard's management of the Matignon-Oudinot Accord. During his visit to France in April 1989, Gareth Evans made a significantly different declaration to his French counterpart. After having asked numerous questions to Roland Dumas in order to have a more accurate understanding of the situation in New Caledonia, Evans assured the French Minister for Foreign Affairs that Australia did not favour independence over autonomy. He asserted as well that Canberra had no intention of interfering in the negotiations being held between the French state and the Kanaks. Gareth Evans claimed that the only diplomatic aim that Australia was seeking was to maintain a harmonious regional environment. Therefore, Evans told Roland Dumas, in private, the opposite to what he had publicly asserted the year before to placate Australian public opinion. Roland Dumas responded by reminding Evans that since New Caledonia still was a French territory, Australia's diplomatic actions regarding Noumea had to be made with the Quai d'Orsay and not with local parties. Then, the two men discussed the core element of conflict between France and Australia: New Caledonia's inclusion on the list of non-self-governing territories. Evans told Dumas that he hoped that France would not try to block all debates about New Caledonia at the United Nations. In his attempt to reassure French policy-makers, the Australian Foreign Minister also asserted that Australia would not vote again in favour of Noumea's inclusion on the list, and that Canberra would try to influence its neighbours accordingly. Roland Dumas pretended, quite questionably, that France had no intention of influencing any Pacific territories about New Caledonia and added that France would leave them free to discuss the matter. This assertion seems dubious since France did try to use its influence within the United Nation in order to gain support for its policies in New Caledonia. Therefore, the two ministers tried to find a middle ground and to give the meeting a positive outcome. Gareth Evans stated again that Australia was not opposed to France's presence in the South Pacific as long as it "was constructive and respectful" (AN Pierrefitte, 19930409/4).

A COMPETITION FOR REGIONAL LEADERSHIP?

French–Australian tensions in New Caledonia must be understood within the broader diplomatic context of the South Pacific in the 1980s and 1990s. In fact, archives and interviews demonstrate that French policy-makers believed that Australia's strong opposition to France's policies in New Caledonia came from the competition for leadership between Canberra and Paris over the South Pacific. According to the proponents of this opinion, Australia questioned France's legitimacy in New Caledonia in order to reduce France's influence in Oceania and thereby allow Australia to maintain an unchallenged leadership. Australian policy-makers completely refute this theory. The Australians do not believe that France and Australia have ever competed for leading Western influence over the South Pacific. In fact, Australian policy-makers have always been certain of their regional leadership, even though it is regularly criticised by the PICs.

French policy-makers have had a different assessment of the South Pacific's balance of power. They have claimed that there was a competition between Paris and Canberra for regional leadership and that this rivalry was channelled through the opposition between the Pacific Islands Forum and the South Pacific Commission, now called Pacific Commission. Since its creation in 1971, the Forum, of which France is not part, has acted as the most important political regional institution in the South Pacific and a very efficient tool for Australian influence over its neighbours. The PIF has also been the main political frame where PICs have condemned French policies in the region. In fact, France's presence in the South Pacific has been used as a target in order to forge a stronger regional connection. However, PICs have very rarely condemned France unilaterally (Mrgudovic 2008, p. 42). On the other hand, the SPC, partly founded by France, has constituted the main regional institution for development and technical cooperation and was used by Paris as an instrument to gain acceptance in the region. Naturally, Australia has relied on the PIF while France has relied on the SPC. Many documents in the French diplomatic archives demonstrate that France genuinely believed that a strong competition between the two regional institutions existed and that France, in order to maintain its presence in the region, had to always convince its partners of the necessity to support the SPC for regional development. Therefore, French diplomats seemed to have rejoiced from any tension within the Forum and used these opportunities to reinforce the SPC's multilateral role during these conflicts. In 1986, when Australia reduced its financial support to the SPC by 65% officially because of economic difficulties, within broader cuts in its aid budget, France saw in this withdrawal the perfect occasion to push its own diplomatic interests in the region through the SCP, because Paris had regularly accused Canberra of purposely weakening the institution. Paris decided to make up for the deficit in the Australian funding in order to maintain all the projects led by the organisation and thus become the main financial supporter of the SPC. Moreover, when, in 1987 during the coup in Fiji, the PIF was unable to develop one common answer to the crisis, French policy-makers analysed this failure as a positive context to support the SPC's influence (AD Nantes, 27POI/1/141–142). France resented Australia's indirect attempts to weaken the SPC for many years.

Furthermore, at the end of the 1980s, several Pacific Islands Countries, such as Papua New Guinea, Vanuatu and the Solomon Islands, supported the idea of a single regional organisation, based on the PIF but with authority for technical cooperation as well. These countries believed that the SPC was a colonial institution, conducting neo-colonial policies. Other Pacific countries, mainly in Polynesia, disapproved of the idea because they believed that the suppression of the SPC would reduce French, British and American aid to the region. Australia, which still had interests in the SPC, supported the idea of a single organisation but left the initiative on this matter to the PICs. Canberra's ambiguous position, officially in favour of a single organisation but not actively promoting it, reinforced France's suspicions regarding Australia's lack of support for its presence in the Pacific. French policy-makers believed that Canberra was reinforcing its regional leadership by supporting an initiative launched by the Pacific states and partly aimed against France, since Paris would likely be excluded from any single multilateral institution (AD Nantes, 27POI/142). In 1988, the Quai explained Australia's ambiguity by the fact that DFAT was divided between senior officials in Canberra, who were opposed to a single Pacific organisation, and Australian diplomats posted in the region, who supported this project (AD Nantes, 27POI/167). Conversely, Australian archives show that Australian policy-makers conceived their ambiguous support as a way of not being involved and choosing a strategy dependent on the stronger party (NAA Canberra, M3793/238). In fact, Australia's official position was that Canberra would "follow the wishes of island countries" and reports show that Australia was fully aware that France's presence in the South Pacific would be weakened by this institutional reform (NAA Canberra, M3793/13).

In the midst of this competition, the United States acted as a mediator. In 1988, Washington indicated to the Western powers involved in the region that they did not intend to support one organisation against the other. The US criticised the Forum, which they perceived as a tribunal where Pacific Island states expressed their grievances against Western power. Therefore, they considered the Forum as a weakening force against the Western Alliance and lobbied against a single Pacific regional institution, from which they might be excluded, like France and the United Kingdom. Washington supported the idea of a stronger partnership between Western nations of the Pacific in order to control the region more completely. Australian policy-makers responded to their American counterparts that the Melanesian countries wanted to control one of the Pacific organisations and that Western countries had to accept that goal. Australian diplomacy worked at maintaining the dynamic of a regional consensus around its interests and perceived France's Pacific policies as an external threat to this consensus. In 1987, DFAT authored a report dedicated to forging a strategy which would enable Australia to reinforce its regional influence. In this report, France was depicted as a country which considered itself as a major and influential player in the region. The report asserted that France was conducting a cheque-book diplomacy to encourage Pacific states to accept its influence, especially Fiji, Tonga and Western Samoa. Australian diplomats explained that: "to exert direct influence on the French Government is notoriously difficult and not infrequently counter-productive". Consequently, they recommended that Australia look for new means to counter France's influence, especially by asking Japan to act as a mediator between Paris and Canberra. The report's section on France concluded: "French approach is hard-nosed and [...] opportunistic, should we try to compete?" (NAA Canberra, M3793/102). The existence of the report itself illustrates that French policy-makers were not fully mistaken when they felt that France and Australia were competing for leadership. Australian policy-makers even recommended that DFAT carefully assess whether the increasing Japanese interest in the region, which they supported within the frame of the Washington-Tokyo-Canberra cooperation, challenged Australia's leadership. However, the document wanted to be reassuring by asserting that Australia had maintained its influence over the United States on issues pertaining to the South Pacific.

When asked to comment on this former rivalry for leadership, many Australian politicians and diplomats, all convinced of Australia's unique leadership in the region, assert that Paris and Canberra have never competed in asserting their superiority in the Pacific. For instance, Ric Wells describes France's view as a misperception by French diplomats, which still exists to a certain extent currently. The diplomat explains that France put a lot of emphasis on the SPC because the organisation is partly based in New Caledonia, and obviously, because France is a member of it and not of the Forum. "On that basis, France does have a tendency to see the South Pacific through the eyes of the SPC" says Wells (pers. inter., Canberra, 8 April 2016). On the other hand, even if Australia considers the SPC as an important regional institution, it only constitutes a forum of technical cooperation and technical capacity-building. Ric Wells draws this conclusion:

> Not unnaturally France is always concerned to ensure that due credit is given to the importance of the SPC. We understand that and we factor that into our thinking. From Australia's point of view, France's role in the South Pacific is very important. We want France to stay. We understand the factors that drive France in the South Pacific are not the same factors that drive us. (pers. inter., Canberra, 8 April 2016)

Denise Fisher denies this existence of such competition as well but admits that she found that perception still existed in New Caledonia when she was Australian Consul in Noumea (pers. inter., Canberra, 7 April 2016). Moreover, in order to prove that Australia did not see a leadership competition, Denise Fisher asserts that Canberra has welcomed the increasing regional involvement of other partners. For example, she also mentions that Australian policy-makers supported Japan when Tokyo initiated a series of bi-multilateral meetings between Japan and the entire Forum, called PALM discussions. Several interpretations can explain this French and Australian difference in the perception of their leadership roles. According to Evans, French policy-makers believed that Australia wanted to reduce France's influence in the region because they knew that their presence in the region was illegitimate. This book rejects this interpretation, firstly because French policy-makers have never thought that France's presence in the South Pacific was illegitimate, but also because Australian policy-makers do not question the consequences of their own colonial history on Australia's regional diplomacy. France's concrete perception of a strong competition of regional leadership with Australia might also stem from a certain complex of superiority, leading French officials to see themselves as a global power with a strong, and overestimated, influence in the Pacific. This vision has changed, and French diplomats are modestly aware of France's current position in the region. However, even if some policy-makers in Paris believed that Australia wanted to expel France from the Pacific, this had never been on the agenda in Canberra. While there was the perception of a certain rivalry between the two countries, Australian governments never worked at rejecting France out of the region (Mohamed-Gaillard 2010, p. 368).

This rivalry seems to mostly belong to the past. Only a few French policy-makers assert that there is currently a certain competition of leadership in the region. More precisely, Cédric Prieto believes that France is aware that although Australia supports France's presence in the region, Australian policy-makers intend to maintain the supremacy of their leadership against foreign competition. Prieto says: "In the Pacific, our relationship is a bit ambiguous because Australians want to assert their leadership in the region that they conceive as their backyard. They don't want to compete on their ocean" (pers. inter., Canberra, 8 April 2016). However, if a limited rivalry can occur on some aspects, it seems that the competition for influence between France and Australia does no longer exist. France and Australia have now mostly aligned their strategies in the Pacific to support their joint interests, as demonstrated in 2012 by their joint declaration of strategic partnership, which has been enhanced and strengthened since March 2017. As explained by Daniel Sloper, First Assistant Secretary at DFAT's Pacific Division: "France is not a regional competitor to Australia. It could be one, but that would require withdrawing capacities elsewhere in the world which would not serve France's global interests. The Pacific is important for France but it's not its first priority" (pers. inter., Canberra, 31 March 2017).

This strategic alignment, fully analysed in Chapter 7, can also be explained because Australia's regional leadership has been challenged by some PICs, especially Fiji and PNG. These countries have diversified their partnerships, for instance with Asian powers such as China. Engaging more on the international arena has enabled some Pacific nations to question Australia's influence in order to forge their own, a reality sometimes overlooked by Australian politicians and diplomats (Wallis 2017). Fiji's regional assertion constitutes one of the most convincing examples of the fragility of Australia's leadership. Moreover, Fiji's successful effort to promote the Pacific Islands Development Forum (PIDF), from which Australia and New Zealand are excluded, has understandably weakened Australia as a respected regional organisation (Firth 2011). In Auckland in 2014, Fijian Interim Prime Minister Bainimarama even explained that he did not consider that Australia was part of the South Pacific, explaining that Australia's lack of environmental policies was the sign that Canberra was not part of the region.[9] Moreover, the difficulty with which the Pacific trade agreement PACER Plus has been negotiated demonstrated that PICs are increasingly more assertive in defence of their own interests, against the ones of Australia if necessary. In fact, it took eight years for Australia and New Zealand to negotiate this commercial agreement with twelve Pacific countries who wanted to balance free trade with more development programs. The agreement was signed in Tonga in June 2017.[10] Besides, Australia's regional image and relationships have been significantly damaged by its immigration policy in Nauru (Firth 2016) and in Manus Island, in PNG (Wallis and Dalsgaard 2016). Therefore, the competition for regional leadership between France and Australia has tangibly decreased because Australian policy-makers are increasingly aware of the non-Western challenges to its influence. A stronger partnership with France could help Australia to reinforce its leading role in the South Pacific. However, New Caledonia's institutional future remains central to the development and deepening of the French–Australian relationship.

Outcomes of New Caledonia's 2018 Referendum

France's presence in the South Pacific was questioned in November 2018, when a referendum on greater autonomy or independence was hold in New Caledonia. This consultation had the potential to have significant consequences on the future of France's three territories in the

Pacific, and, therefore, on France's global strategy and power. In the 1998 Noumea Accords, the French government and the leaders of loyalist and pro-independence movements agreed that New Caledonians would vote on a referendum of auto-determination within twenty years. This extremely contentious referendum was hold at the end of this period, on 4 November 2018. 56.4% of voters to remain part of the French Republic, while 43.6% expressed their desire to become independent, a higher figured that polls expected before the vote. None of the parties engaged in this process agreed on the fundamental understanding of the concepts of "sovereignty" and "legitimacy" (Mokaddem 2005, p. 25). The referendum's electorate had been agreed on in November 2017 in a context described by all parties as very constructive. "Do you want New Caledonia to accede full sovereignty and become independent?": this question, defined after tough negotiations, satisfied pro-independence leaders, who wanted to mention the prospect of "full sovereignty" to motivate their electorate. On the other hand, "loyalists" leaders wanted the word "independence" to be part of the question, in order to make voters understand the serious implications of the referendum on New Caledonian-French ties.

This book does not aim to provide an opinion on the result of the referendum, as it argues that only the people of New Caledonia can legitimately express such an opinion. In fact, while every population must be able to express its rightful desire to be sovereign over its territory and access that right, the ethnical diversity of New Caledonia must remain a key factor and the French state's very large contribution to the development of New Caledonia is also undeniable. One vision argues that, more than firstly deciding between a French and an independent New Caledonia, efforts should be primarily made to finish the decolonisation of any political, economic, judicial and social institution in New Caledonia and to empower the young generation of Kanaks within the current New Caledonian system. In fact, an independent New Caledonia, but with the same institutions and with the same European and Kanak elite in power would not necessarily offer a more positive prospect to young generations, especially without France's crucial financial support to the territory. However, this chapter solely analyses the role played by the referendum in New Caledonia in the French–Australian bilateral relationship.

France's message to Australian policy-makers was that "the situation is under control" (C. Prieto, pers. inter., Canberra, 8 April 2016).

206 P. SOYEZ

Representatives of the French State praised Paris' management of the situation since 1998. For instance, Cédric Prieto explains:

> The political process in New Caledonia, which has been rather innovative, has enabled a peaceful transition in the territories, by opposition to what happened in many Pacific states, such as in Bougainville. Australian policy-makers seem to follow and understand accurately the issues pertaining to the referendum. They globally remain hopeful about its outcomes and they think that the political process is well and exemplarily directed. (pers. inter., Canberra, 8 April 2016)

French policy-makers have made a significant informational effort in order to explain France's policies in New Caledonia clearly and accurately. For example, when Manuel Valls visited Canberra in May 2016, a part of his discussion with Malcolm Turnbull was dedicated to New Caledonia. The former French Prime Minister described to his Australian counterpart how Paris is planning the next few years around the referendum. Australian stakeholders support France's policies in the archipelago. They recognise that France's position toward Kanaks' aspiration has dramatically changed and that Paris has conducted an appropriate democratic process. "We are far more relaxed than we would have been twenty years ago because the way that the situation is going does seem to be quite benign" explains Wells, for example (pers. inter., Canberra, 8 April 2016). Therefore, New Caledonia is not the source of a strong concern in Canberra anymore. Australian policy-makers are more worried about potential regional disruption from the situation in Bougainville and its referendum on independence from Papua New Guinea in 2020. New Caledonia's referendum had little impact on the French–Australian relationship. Potential tensions surrounding the referendum, which could constitute a cloud in the future of the Australian–French relationship, did not happen and the vote went smoothly. $ Stéphane Romatet is categorically insists that Australian policy-makers would like a *status quo* after the referendum, a French presence negotiated against a few institutional evolutions bringing a little more autonomy to local powers (pers. inter., Paris, 21 June 2016).

Nonetheless, according to Ric Wells, the future of New Caledonia "is something that Australia very much wants France to get right. Although we don't talk a lot about it, that is something which is always there in the relationship" (pers. inter., Canberra, 8 April 2016). Wells goes even further and explains: "if it all went wrong, then that would be a big problem for both Australia and France, but it is not going to go wrong because of France". Australian diplomats seem to be cautious about how the process will be managed in such a way that the Kanaks do not feel disenfranchised, which would create greater division. The French government is aware of Australia's attention to its management of the situation. Australia is very careful to closely watch France's management of the referendum because the archipelago is in an uncertain period. For example, Romatet explains that "states don't like uncertainty and I think that Australia would like to see the period of uncertainty end as soon as possible" (pers. inter., Paris, 21 June 2016). Denise Fisher expresses a less optimistic assessment of the situation and describes Australia's attitude toward this issue as "complacent" (pers. inter., Canberra, 7 April 2016). According to her, there is a risk that, in case of tensions during the second referendum, a large part of Australian public opinion will support the pro-independence Kanaks and will push the Australian government, as in the past, to strengthen its position against France, which could hinder the French–Australian partnership.

Daniel Sloper contradicts Fisher's assertion: "Regarding New Caledonia's referendum, there was certainly some people in the public in Australia with natural sympathy for the Kanak movement but I am not so sure it would lead in a change of government position" (31 March 2017). Nevertheless, the risk of a confrontation remains low.

Therefore, Australian policy-makers do not want New Caledonia to become independent, for all the strategic, security and economic reasons explained in this chapter. Australia's interest is that France should remain, institutionally, the sovereign power over the archipelago. They were pleased to see the not to independence will this election. Anonymously, many Australian diplomats express a clear hope that New Caledonia will not become independent, since Canberra fully supports France's presence in the South Pacific (pers. inter., 2016). Some even explain that Australia hopes that France would keep its military base in Noumea even in case of an independence of the archipelago. Stéphane Romatet describes Australia's support for France's presence in New Caledonia as a realist foreign policy: "Australia's nightmare would be to see New Caledonia evolve like Fiji or Vanuatu, which means either with a non-democratic regime, or with collapsing society and economy. Maintaining France's presence in New Caledonia is the best guarantee" (pers. inter., Paris, 21 June 2016). Canberra is convinced that French control over New Caledonia enables the two countries to bring their Pacific strategies closer, as the next chapter analyses.

Conclusion

French–Australian tensions and cooperation pertaining to New Caledonia constitute an extremely interesting case study because the archipelago has played the role of a mirror of their bilateral relationship. The study of the archipelago's relevance in the bilateral relationship spotlights many conflicts between Paris and Canberra, pertaining to political legitimacy, colonial memory and regional understanding. This critical analysis also illustrates France and Australia's different approach to global security in general since the end of the Cold War. Nonetheless, the fact that Noumea is now located at the very heart of the French–Australian strategic partnership also demonstrates the extent to which the two countries have worked together in order to support their shared interests. In fact, France and Australia are now engaged in a deep security partnership in Oceania, demonstrated by numerous and regular joint actions and exercises. This significant alliance has been possible due to the strategic convergence supported by French and Australian policy-makers, a process enabled by the end of the French nuclear testing program and the improvement of the situation in New Caledonia since 1988. The next chapter demonstrates how this strategic partnership illustrates the French and Australian focus on their respective and shared global interests, using leadership in the South Pacific to improve international security.

Notes

1. This book chooses to use New Caledonia because this name remains the official one of the territory.
2. The official results of the census are available on the INSEE website: https://www.insee.fr/fr/statistiques/1560282.
3. Tjibaou remained the main figure of the pro-independence movement until his assassination with Yiewene Yiewene by Djubelly Wéa in 1989 in Ouvéa. Wéa, a Kanak in favour of a radical independence, murdered Tjibaou for having signed the Matignon-Oudinot Accords and for not having supported the Kanaks responsible for the Ouvéa hostage-taking.
4. On 22 April 1988, 27 French soldiers, *gendarmes*, were taken hostage in Ouvéa by a group of local pro-independence Kanaks, eager to influence the presidential election of May 1988. Six French soldiers were killed by the Kanaks. France's response was extremely brutal as well: 19 Kanaks were killed when the French army tried to free the soldiers from the caves

6 NEW CALEDONIA, CORNERSTONE OF AN AMBIGUOUS FRENCH ... 209

where they were being held as prisoners. French President Emmanuel Macron has attended in May 2018 the commemorations of the 30th anniversary of the events in order to appease local tensions between pro-independence supporters and "loyalists".

5. French diplomats refer to Australia's colonisation of Papua New Guinea and its overseas possessions of the Christmas Islands, Norfolk Islands, Cocos Islands.

6. The text of the press conference is provided by a note from the Minister for Foreign Affairs' Cabinet, dated from 22 September 1988.

7. The Committee gathers: Antigua & Barbuda, Bolivia, Chile, China, Congo, Cuba, Dominica, Ecuador, Ethiopia, Fiji, Grenada, India, Indonesia, Iran, Iraq, Ivory Coast, Mali, Nicaragua, Papua New Guinea, the Russian Federation, Saint Kitts and Nevis, Saint Lucia, Saint Vincent and the Grenadines, Sierra Leone, Syria, Timor-Leste, Tunisia, United Republic of Tanzania and Venezuela.

8. See latest UN report on French Pacific territories (2016): https://www.un.org/press/en/2016/gacol3299.doc.htm.

9. See a report on Bainimarama's speech: http://www.abc.net.au/news/2014-08-11/an-fiji-pm-bainimarama-pledges-to-accept-election-result-during/5662368.

10. The PACER Plus agreement gathers Australia, the Cook Islands, the Federated States of Micronesia, Kiribati, Nauru, New Zealand, Niue, Palau, the Republic of the Marshall Islands, Samoa, the Solomon Islands, Tonga, Tuvalu and Vanuatu.

References

Archives Nationales, Pierrefitte, France.

National Archives of Australia, Canberra, Australia.

Angleviel, F 2015, *Un drame de la colonisation, Ouvéa, Nouvelle-Calédonie, mai 1988*, Vendémiaire, Paris.

Chappell, D 1999, 'The Noumea Accord: Decolonisation Without Independence in New Caledonia?' *Pacific Affairs*, vol. 72, no. 3, pp. 373–391.

Firth, S 2011, *Australia in International Politics*, Allen & Unwin, Sydney.

Firth, S 2016, 'Australia's Detention Centre and the Erosion of Democracy in Nauru', *The Journal of Pacific History*, vol. 51, no. 3, pp. 286–300.

James, K 2016, 'The "Arrogant French": Examination of a cliché in Australia's Journalistic and Political Discourse', Presentation at the ISFAR colloquium, 6 December.

Mohamed-Gaillard, S 2010, *L'archipel de la puissance? La politique de la France dans le Pacifique Sud de 1946 à 1998*, P. Lang, Bruxelles.

Mokaddem, H 2005, *Kanaky et/ou Nouvelle-Calédonie*, Expressions, Marseille.

Mrgudovic, N 2008, *La France dans le Pacifique sud: les enjeux de la puissance*, L'Harmattan, Paris.

Piquet, M 2000, *Cold War in Warm Waters: Reflections on Australian and French Mutual Misunderstandings in the Pacific*, The University of Melbourne Press, Melbourne.

Wallis, J 2017, 'Crowded and Complex: The Changing Geopolitics of the South Pacific', *ASPI The Strategist*, 24 April. Available at https://www.aspistrategist.org.au/crowded-complex-changing-geopolitics-south-pacific/. Accessed 17 July 2017.

Wallis, J & Dalsgaard, S 2016, Money, Manipulation and Misunderstanding on Manus Island. *The Journal of Pacific History*, vol. 51, no. 3, pp. 301–329.

CHAPTER 7

An Appeased Neighbourhood: French–Australian Cooperation in the South Pacific Region

As the leading power in the South Pacific, Australia has developed a regional strategy that is inextricably tied to its asymmetrical relationship with its neighbors. Australia is one of the wealthiest and most developed countries in the world, whereas the South Pacific consists of island states with limited natural and administrative resources, often fragile economies and regular political instability. For example, in 2018, the United Nations Development Program (UNDP 2018) ranked Australia 3rd out of 189 countries regarding the HDI, while Vanuatu was ranked 138th, Solomon Islands 152nd and PNG 153rd. This social, economic, cultural and political gap, by contrast, has reinforced Australia's position of leadership in the region, but at the same time confirming its perception of responsibility and duty towards its neighbors. Moreover, the strategy of Australian diplomats in the South Pacific is also governed by the fact that Canberra is designated as the main representative of the Western alliance in the region. This leadership is considered to be further strengthened by the ANZUS treaty, even if it provides little guarantee to Australia's security in practical terms. Therefore, in the global context, Australia's leadership in the South Pacific represents a crucial asset to enable Canberra to achieve diplomatic status as a middle power.

France, despite ongoing regional contestation regarding its nuclear testing or its New Caledonian policies, will nevertheless continue to remain a Pacific country until the majority of its overseas population decides to break its institutional links with the metropole. France's

© The Author(s) 2019
P. Soyez, *Australia and France's Mutual Empowerment*,
Studies in Diplomacy and International Relations,
https://doi.org/10.1007/978-3-030-13449-5_7

211

historical sovereignty over Pacific archipelagos has obliged its policy-makers to elaborate a strategy for this region which remains crucial to the country's diplomacy, as described in Chapter 6. In fact, half a million French citizens live in France's three overseas communities in the Pacific: New Caledonia, French Polynesia and Wallis and Futuna. Thanks to these vast archipelagos, France has sovereignty over the second largest exclusive economic zone in the world, after the United States and ahead of Australia. Overseas territories play a key role in France's global strategy, enabling the country to deploy its armed forces all around the globe. They also provide platforms for France's defence strategy, which is based on deterrence, as the French nuclear testing sites have demonstrated in the past.[1] The important role of these territories with respect to Paris's diplomacy has induced complex and unique ties between France and its *Outre-mer*. Each archipelago has a unique political status, with various levels of autonomy from Paris, and a different level of regional integration. Therefore, France's diplomacy in the South Pacific is characterized by its complexity. It combines French metropolitan objectives with the strategic interests of the increasingly autonomous French territories. However, as French policy-makers acknowledge, France must build a new strategic narrative combining its different identities in the South Pacific: being at the same time a Melanesian, Polynesian, Oceanian, Republican and European state.

This chapter critically analyses the logics and interests which have enabled Australia and France to become significant partners for the security and development of the South Pacific, while at the same time reinforcing their own leadership positions and reducing their regional "awkwardness". This study also examines the regional contestations of this strategic partnership and the numerous levels of cooperation established by French and Australian policy-makers to convince the region to accept their influence. The analysis will first of all focus on France's strategy for strengthening its presence in the South Pacific and second of all on how Australia's regional interests have increasingly converged with French ones. Then, this chapter will present a critical assessment of the political and diplomatic benefits from French–Australian academic and military cooperation in the South Pacific. It will also analyse France and Australia's strategies framing their aid to development programs in the region. Finally, this chapter will demonstrate how the French–Australian cooperation in the South Pacific is now used as a model by Paris and Canberra in order to strengthen their partnership in the Indian Ocean.

France's Pacific Ambitions: To Normalise and Reinforce Its Presence in the Region

Despite tensions pertaining to New Caledonia, the French nuclear testing program and the perception of a competition for regional influence, France has not always had a conflicting relationship with the two other leading powers of the South Pacific, Australia and New Zealand. In fact, the three countries' understanding of their prominent role in the region has not always been diametrically opposed. However, as a rule, Australian, French and New Zealander Pacific strategies have not matched. During his official visit to France in 1988, Russell Marshall, Minister of Foreign Affairs of New Zealand, attributed these recurring regional tensions to France's lack of genuine interest in the South Pacific. Marshall asserted that his country and Australia had multicultural societies which had enabled them to experience a deep connection with their region, while considering themselves to be, at the same time, firmly part of the Western alliance. This statement confirms the opinion of many Australian and New Zealander officials regarding their role in the South Pacific. More importantly, it also shows a certain lack of intellectual questioning about Canberra's and Wellington's vision of their region because it is doubtful that their multicultural societies actually have a genuine impact on their diplomatic care for their neighbours, especially in the light of Australia's migratory policies. Marshall challenged his French counterpart to understand that although Australia and New Zealand are fully committed to the Western international order, the latter "was composed of several compartments and that the one in which we live [the Pacific] has a different vision of its security than Europe". Moreover, Marshall asserted that New Zealand welcomed France's presence in the region as long as it was willing to take into account the region's specificities and not view the Pacific only through a European lens, as demonstrated by the Rainbow Warrior crisis. France needed indeed to fully grasp this diversity, which French policy-makers have now fully integrated, thirty years after this meeting. However, his French counterpart at the time Roland Dumas answered that he understood Marshall's point of view but that, in a context of Cold War, "the South Pacific region could not be put apart". Dumas meant that Australia and New Zealand needed to show more solidarity with the leaders of the Western alliance and their interests, including France. For example, he asserted that, for that reason, France could not support the Rarotonga treaty (AD Nantes, 27POI/167).

Nonetheless, France's policy regarding the Pacific shifted dramatically after 1986. French policy-makers, especially the Prime Minister at the time, Jacques Chirac, came to the realisation that France needed to put an end to its regional isolation in order to maintain its sovereignty over its territories. Then, after 1988, French Prime Minister Michel Rocard, who was known in France for his genuine passion and sound knowledge of Pacific cultures, implemented France's new strategy and diplomacy in the South Pacific. His government gave France a reformed vision of its role in the region, in collaboration with Australia, thanks to a rapid improvement of the French–Australian bilateral relationship (Mrgudovic 2008, p. 41). French policy-makers have sought to better understand the South Pacific and improve France's image and integration in Oceania in the last two decades. In order to do so, they have developed a narrative, partly genuine, asserting that France values the South Pacific and that Paris wants to be fully supportive of its sustainable future and is ready to take responsibility for this goal. They have particularly sought Australia's support in order to promulgate this narrative. Therefore, France and Australia no longer hold opposing strategic understandings of the South Pacific, since French policy-makers have forged, in the last decade, a clearer ambition for the South Pacific, while at the same time Australia's global interests have led Canberra to engage more with Paris.

Improving France's Image in the South Pacific: The Need for a New Narrative

Leading a smart power strategy requires the development of an efficient narrative. In fact, Nye asserts that "the ability to get the outcomes we want will rest upon a new narrative of smart power" (2011, p. xvii). French policy-makers are engaged in a process of re-conceptualisation of France's presence in the South Pacific. In order to keep normalising—understood as gaining in legitimacy—and, therefore, strengthening its integration in the region, France needs to clarify its strategic and political narrative in order to accurately convince the Pacific states of its role, interests and ambitions in a changing region. Currently, France's image in the South Pacific is two-fold. Although Paris is partly respected for its engagement in the region's development and its lobby for increasing EU aid policies and humanitarian assistance, memories of past tensions are still vivid. Prejudices are still strong, reinforced by language barriers and the national identities of countries which have gained their independence recently against European powers (C. Lechervy, pers. inter., Paris, 22 December 2016). Older generations, who were actively involved in these independence movements, sometimes despise the link that French territories maintain with Paris and have nursed a vivid memory of France's violent repression of contestations in the past. Therefore, French diplomats must work at improving France's image if Paris wishes to be fully and permanently accepted in the region. Moreover, French policymakers have been increasingly aware of the importance of building a structuring narrative by comparing their diplomatic practices to the relative success of the narratives forged by India, with its Acting East Policy, by China and the maritime silk road, and by Australia with its concept of the Indo-Pacific region. Internally, New Caledonia's referendum on independence, hold on 4 November 2018, also pushed France to clarify its institutional presence in the region through a new narrative which aims to legitimise France's sovereignty over its Pacific communities.

Pacific Islanders' perceptions of France's presence in the Pacific and of the French–Australian strategic partnership are ambiguous. Officially, their leaders often praise Paris's current regional improvement. For example, Vanuatu's Prime Minister Charlot Salwai declared in September 2016 that his country's relationship with France was constructive, that Vanuatu has been a strong supporter of the regional integration of the French Pacific territories and that it benefited from France's neighborhood presence, despite some particular disagreements which don't damage the relationship itself (Toa 2017). The logic is the same, as Nic Maclellan explains, for PNG, which had been a long supporter of the FLNKS in New Caledonia, but which now supports France's increased presence in the region in order to develop business and tourism links with France. However, Maclellan asserts that PICs are still concerned "about France's objectives", especially Nauru and Tuvalu. These two countries, explains Maclellan, had obtained in 2013 the relisting of French Polynesia on the UN list of non-independent territories (2016). This political disagreement between members of the Forum shows that some Pacific islanders consider the strategies of France and Australia in the Pacific as the continuation of non-Pacific colonial powers in the region's future, when others see it as a chance for development. According to Daniel Sloper, "France is both seen as a distant colonial country but also, through its territories, very much as a participant in the region because many Pacific countries cannot address the challenges they face on their own. [...] It is important for France not to be seen as a country outside the region pursuing its own interest" (pers. inter., 31 March 2017). However, the Australian diplomat does not seem concerned about the criticism raised by some of the PICs. In fact, Sloper claims that:

> Regarding Australia, many see us as a genuine partner. There are obviously tensions on certain issues, but I think that this is a healthy indicator showing that we can survive these tensions and progress in a constructive way. Some countries would see us as a donor of last resort, but there is also an appreciation that we are trying to work with them to address key issues that they face. (pers. inter., 31 March 2017)

More precisely, according to Sloper, one must distinguish the PICs vision of Australia's regional engagement when expressed bilaterally and multilaterally. For example, he explains that while multilaterally, Fiji's Prime Minister asserts that he does not see a role for Australia and New Zealand in some of the regional bodies in order to serve his own strategy, Fiji maintains a very productive relationship with Canberra bilaterally. However, Daniel Sloper's comment must be put into question as it hides the increasing disagreement between the PICs and Australia, in particular regarding trade policies, Australia's significant cuts in its aid programs—by a third of its 2012 level—and Canberra's harsh policies regarding asylum seekers which contrary to the requirements of the Refugee Convention. Canberra has also failed to take significant account of the voice of the PICs regarding the existential threat that climate change has for such island countries and so has failed to represent their strong concerns, as demonstrated during the 2018 Pacific Islands Forum where Australia's lack of concrete action to reach the Paris agreement emissions target was heavily criticised. This weakens Australia's regional leadership, most obviously while Australia remains the world's largest coal exporter. According to Jonathan Schultz, Australia's South Pacific policies can be described as neo-colonialist, because one can identify "three kinds of bullying" in Australia's policies toward the PICs (2014, p. 175). Firstly, Schultz claims that Australia implements a conflictual bullying in pursuing its own national interests over those of its Pacific partners, for example regarding climate change. He goes further and asserts that Australia demonstrates instrumental bullying in using the PICs to serve its global interests. Lastly, Canberra implements a punitive bullying by punishing the PICs when they oppose Australian policies.

Therefore, Schultz considers that Australia has adopted a neo-colonialist attitude toward the South Pacific, using power asymmetry to force its leadership on the region.

This book argues that Australia's ambiguous and regularly dismissive links with the South Pacific can be explained because of Australia's problematic relationship with its own colonial history. Many academic studies have demonstrated the lack of in-depth questioning of Australia's colonial past within public opinion, for instance the idea that Australia had been colonised by the British and not Australians, despite the fact that Australia is still currently ruled by British and colonial institutions. Facing Australia's history would completely challenge not only Australia's identity as a supposably very successful multi-cultural society, which can be questioned when regarding the situation of many indigenous communities, but also Australia's law and political system. Australia's denial of its colonial history has been denounced by many scholars such as Australian historian W.E.H. Stanner in 1968, who created the concept of the "great Australian silence". This important breakthrough in Australian historiography has been recently developed by numerous historians, especially Henry Reynolds in his book *Why Weren't We Told?* (1999) and James Boyce in *1835 The Founding of Melbourne and the Conquest of Australia* (2011). Such historical studies have been crucial to deconstruct and contradict a traditional historiography which denied Australia's colonial past. For example, while Geoffrey Blainey's theory of distance is important to understand Australia's foreign policy (1983), Blainey also denied Australia's genocidal policies against its indigenous population (Beasley 2014), as did Keith Windshuttle's dubious book *The Fabrication of Aboriginal History: Van Diemen's Land 1803–1847*. Henry Reynolds has proven how the majority of Australians still live with a distorted and idealised version of the past, the vision of a more peaceful settlement than it was. For example, Reynolds demonstrates that the choice of the word "settler" has been used for its positive and uncontested connotation, instead of "coloniser" or "colonist" which would refer to a more violent process. Many Australian senior policy-makers interviewed for this research denied the consequences of Australia's active colonisation of its land and of archipelagos around it. One interviewee, a former Australian diplomat now teaching in a renowned Australian university, even asserted to us that Australia "had never colonized anyone" (Canberra, April 2016).

France's colonial history, all around the world and including in the Pacific, was as serious as Britain's. This book does not aim to draw any comparison between the impacts of French and British/Australian colonisation nor does it aim to defend one country against another. However, debates around colonisation and decolonisation, their consequences on France's identity and population, are by far more significant and frequent in France than in Australia (Bandel et al. 2005).[2] This is mainly explained because a large part of the French population and immigration is the consequence of its colonial history and that, in New Caledonia, Kanak still constitute the largest community, when indigenous Australian now represent three percent of Australia's population.[3] Therefore, having faced their colonial history more comprehensively, French policy-makers have realised the need to invent a new strategic narrative in the Pacific, in order to address accusations of neo-colonialism by the PICs. On the other hand, Australian diplomats, as demonstrated by this research and as noticeable in Canberra's 2017 *White Paper on Foreign Policy*, still believe that Australia's narrative in the South Pacific does not require updating. This has impacted Australia's ambiguous commitment to the South Pacific and increased the PICs' discontent with Canberra. Lastly, as this thesis has demonstrated, while France has been a significant colonising power in the Indo-Pacific, Paris was regularly used as a scapegoat by Australian policy-makers, eager to hide Australia's own colonial identity by pointing out France's history.

In order to respond to such criticism against former colonial powers, France's new narrative needs to take into account the forces and dynamics that cross the South Pacific, integrated into a larger Indo-Asia-Pacific area. French policy-makers are considering four different regional trends in their attempt to restore France's narrative (C. Lechervy, pers. inter., Paris, 22 December 2016). First of all, the South Pacific is currently attempting to incorporate itself in the rest of the world. This diplomatic process started in 1997 with the creation of the PALM Summits, gathering Japan and the Pacific Island states together. This dynamic is now mainly institutionalised by various South Pacific+1 summits which have enabled Oceania to increase its official dialogue globally. Such summits exist with South Korea, China, Taiwan, India, Morocco, Turkey, Cuba, the UEA and France, thanks to the France-Océanie summits. In 2015, within the frame of the COP 21, French President François Hollande invited more than 20 heads of state from the Pacific to the fourth *Sommet France-Océanie*, demonstrating how Paris understands this South Pacific desire for engagement with the international community. Second of all, PICs are increasing their diplomatic capacities worldwide. In addition to the South Pacific+1 summits, their governments also take part, individuality, in ad hoc coalitions, such as the Non-Aligned Movement or the Alliance of Small Island States. This dynamic has expanded following the elaboration of a climate change diplomacy, a crucial issue for Pacific countries. Such gatherings enable Pacific states to explain their own situation to the international community. France needs to understand each state's individual capacity to shape its own regional policy and interests, and such coalitions can be useful for this purpose.

Furthermore, while the South Pacific integrates itself with the rest of the world using multilateral meetings with a third country, the region is also contracting with respect to sub-regional areas. These smaller entities, sometimes based on uncertain imagined communities,[4] have been institutionalised. For example, several institutions intend to represent Micronesia, such as the *Micronesian Presidents' Summit* or the *Micronesian Chief Executives Summit*. The same dynamic exists in Melanesia, which is the most institutionalised part of the South Pacific with the Melanesian Spearhead Group. The South Pacific is characterised by a tendency to gather into three anthropological and cultural sub-regions, Melanesia, Micronesia and Polynesia, each demonstrating a certain insular spirit. These sub-regions can also be even subdivided, such as the current diplomatic negotiations between New Caledonia, Vanuatu and the Solomon Islands. Lechervy goes further and asserts that this Oceania-only dynamic targets France and Australia, but also to a lesser extent New Zealand, for example with the creation of the Pacific Islands Development Forum which excludes Canberra, Wellington and Paris.

Through a fourth and final regional dynamic, some Western powers reaffirm their sovereignty over specific territories directly administered from the centre of the state. France and the United States possess islands in the Pacific which have no political autonomy, being directly administrated from Paris and Washington. These islands, where there is no population, represent significant strategic interests. For example, Moruroa and Fangataufa atolls have been separated from the French Polynesian community and are directly administrated from Paris. For security reasons, the French government forbids access to these islands where former French nuclear testing was conducted, in order to protect France's nuclear secrets and visitors from the effects of radiation. For different reasons but following the same logic, France strongly asserts its sovereignty over Clipperton Island against Mexican claims. Therefore, whatever the institutional future of New Caledonia and French Polynesia will be, France will remain engaged in the South Pacific. Policy-makers in Paris consider that they have a special responsibility to defend France's interests over these islands. A similar policy is conducted by the United States: the Bush administration decided for example to directly administer from Washington its islands without population. Therefore, France will continue to define itself as a global and Pacific power and will keep being seen by its neighbors as a singular actor, "in and out" of the region.

Consequently, forging France's new narrative in the South Pacific by taking into account the four prerequisites presented above constitutes a difficult task. France must forge a strategy encompassing the fact that Paris is at times excluded from regional cooperation, sometimes included and valued, but always involved through its Pacific territories. If no one questions the role that New Caledonia and French Polynesia should play in their sub-regions, where they represent wealthy and influential actors, the role of metropolitan France is more up for debate. To satisfy this question, French policy-makers are currently implementing a very interesting shift in France's strategy in the South Pacific. French interests being too diverse in Oceania, France is abandoning the idea of a single Pacific diplomacy in favour of two separate ones: (1) a French diplomacy in Melanesia executed jointly from Paris and Noumea, and (2) a French diplomacy in Polynesia, established jointly from Paris and Papeete. Wallis and Futuna will fluctuate between the two to benefit from its immediate neighbourhood. Australian diplomats do not share this strategy because they don't believe that Canberra needs to fundamentally modify its regional engagement. For example, Daniel Sloper explains: "We engage with each region directly [...] but we don't pursue sub-regional strategies" (pers. inter., Canberra, 31 March 2017).

In order to improve France's image in the region and fully normalise its presence, French policy-makers also intend to remove any reference to the nuclear testing program from France's new Pacific narrative. Since the end of the 1990s, France has focused its narrative on its capacity to bring foreign aid and development support to its Pacific neighbours, for example after the large destructions in Vanuatu due to cyclone Pam in 2015. However, according to Christian Lechervy, in a context of the multiplication of powers involved in the region, this justification of France's role and influence is no longer sufficient (pers. inter., Paris,

22 December 2016). France's image has been improved due to its civilian-military presence but now needs to be amplified through new ambitions. France's new approach is to progressively incorporate into its discourse Australia's concept of an Indo-Pacific region. In fact, France also has joint interests in the Pacific and the Indian Oceans. Both countries cooperate to support their ambitions in this vast zone. Therefore, accepting the concept of an Indo-Pacific region could enable France to forge a new Pacific narrative which also serves its bilateral relationships with Indonesia, Malaysia, Singapore and Thailand. On the other hand, Australian policy-makers are less concerned about Canberra's narrative to legitimise its Pacific strategies. None of the interviewees believe that Australia should transform its narrative. For instance, according to Daniel Sloper, Australians would only "need to have a broader discussion about the way we characterise our engagement in the region. We need to look at what brings us together and why cooperation delivers outcomes, nationally and regionally". The diplomat demonstrates Australia's strong, and partly wrong, confidence in its regional leadership, despite ongoing criticism from the PICs against Canberra's regional engagement: "We are comfortable where we sit but that is not to say we could not do more" (pers. inter., Canberra, 31 March 2017).

The South Pacific, *l'Océanie*, is a major component of the global ambitions of France's power. French policy-makers are convinced that France's presence in its three Pacific overseas communities supports the role and vision that Paris accords itself, its *grandeur* and influence. France has an ambitious vision of its influence in the world, based on its military strength, its seat at the UN Security Council and its important role in the European Union. More importantly, although France is fully aware that it has now become a high middle power, French policy-makers still believe that France's role is global. Therefore, French policy-makers believe that Paris' global diplomacy has to reach every continent, including Oceania in the Pacific. Consequently, Australia constitutes one of the obvious components of this power deployment in this part of the world and France's appropriation of the concept of Indo-Pacific strengthens this ambition (S Romatet, pers. inter., Paris, 21 June 2016).

Moreover, beside the construction of a large strategic narrative, French policy-makers have also pursued direct actions of nation branding, even against regional criticism. Keith Dinnie defines nation branding as "the unique multidimensional blend of elements that provide the nation with culturally grounded differentiation and relevance for all of its target audiences" and believes that states are dedicating increasing amounts of resources to the development of such policies (2016, pp. 4–5). France has had to develop nation branding policies in the South Pacific in order to be accepted by its neighbours there. In fact, many documents in the French diplomatic archives confirm that some states consider France to be still acting as a colonial power in the region and that French policy-makers have been fully aware of this critical context (AD Nantes, 11POI/616). A combination of multilateral meetings, official dialogues, festivals and development programs has enabled French policy-makers to meet with leaders of the various Pacific states in order to explain to them how France's strategy in the Pacific has been revised and renewed and, therefore, to improve Paris's image in the region considerably.

In order to demonstrate their commitment to the Indo-Pacific region and to improve France's image, French policy-makers have also increasingly travelled to this part of the world. As previously mentioned, François Hollande was the first French President to visit not only Australia, but the Philippines and Futuna as well. No President had visited Wallis since 1979. Prime Minister Jean-Marc Ayrault was the first French Prime Minister to visit Manilla and subsequently Manuel Valls, as Prime Minister, visited Wellington, where no French head of government had visited since 1991. French parliamentarians have also been increasingly engaged with the region, and not just because of the French–Australian submarine contract. For example, in December 2016, the President of the French Senate officially received the visit of his Fijian counterpart. French parliamentarian diplomacy plays a significant role in France's engagement in the Indo-Pacific region. French Prime Minister Edouard Philippe visited New Caledonia in December 2017 and November 2018 in order to assert that the French state is fully committed to secure a peaceful referendum.

In improving Paris' image, French policy-makers have also used the fact that PICs have been obliged, from the 1990s until recently, to lower their global ambitions and focus on their shorter-term interests. In fact, a series of natural disasters, political coups or development issues has regularly weakened these countries, forcing them to rely more on foreign support with regard to national matters. Therefore, France, because of its development aid programs, its economic strength and its global diplomatic network, is increasingly considered as a potential asset for the region.

National and territorial promoters of France's Pacific policy have worked together to recast France's approach to the South Pacific and to ameliorate their relationships, from Paris, Noumea and Papeete, with Pacific neighbours. Australia's support for these policies, corresponding to Canberra's strategy and interests in maintaining its leadership, has been crucial for the success of France's ambitions. France, along with its territories, has engaged in two main approaches in order to be regionally perceived as a guarantor of stability and as no longer a source of disruption: improving its image while at the same time increasing the regional integration of its territories.

Integrating French Pacific Territories into Their Region

The regional integration of the South Pacific is understood in this book according to Penelope Mathew and Tristan Harley's approach to the concept of regionalisation (2016, p. 26). It consists of the aim to build stronger regional coherence by combining first a political wave of creation of supra-national institutions, like the Pacific Islands Forum, and subsequently a recent agenda of opening economies to regional partners. For decades, France thwarted any process that could lead to the regional integration of its territories. This policy was mainly implemented, between the end of the 1970s and the early 2000s, by France's ongoing refusal to allow its overseas territories to become members of regional organisations, such as the Pacific Community (PC). French policy-makers were fully aware of the political benefit from regional cooperation. Their aim, however, was that only France should benefit from these inclusive processes, and not either New Caledonia nor French Polynesia, avoiding any nation-branding by the territories themselves. Any attempt from Australia to integrate New Caledonia and French Polynesia into regional fora was perceived in the Quai d'Orsay as an indirect manoeuvre from Canberra to weaken French influence (AD Nantes, 27POI/1/79). French policy-makers' assessment of this dynamic is now largely reversed, and France's second diplomatic priority in the South Pacific has consisted of deepening the regional integration of its overseas communities so that they can develop efficient working relationships with their neighbours. Such policy aims at normalising France's presence in the region by enabling Paris to represent itself as a Pacific nation too. Therefore, to reach this goal, France has developed an increasingly important "territorial diplomacy" to its archipelagos in the Pacific.

French territories, in this new approach by the metropolitan government, are now encouraged by the French state to develop their own diplomatic agency, under the supervision of Paris, in order to improve trans-border cooperation with their neighbours. This institutional revolution started in metropolitan France as part of European integration policies but has now been extended to overseas territories which have developed their own diplomatic administration. This administrative process has been enabled by the constitutional laws of New Caledonia and French Polynesia. In 2016, the Letchimy law reinforced this dynamic by enabling French overseas territories to sign international agreements with a greater degree of autonomy, Paris only ensuring that such agreements would not countermand France's unity and law. Institutionally and legally, the competencies of both local and national actors have been clarified. Local actors currently are able to use all the authority that their territories have received from the state, which, according to Christian Lechervy, was not the case previously (C. Lechervy, pers. inter., Paris, 22 December 2016). This territorialisation of diplomatic responsibility aims at gaining economic and political efficiency for regional cooperation. New Caledonia now has its own *Service de la Coopération régionale et des Relations extérieures* (SCRRE—Department of Regional Cooperation and Foreign Relations), whose size is comparable to the Ministries of Foreign Affairs of other Pacific Island states.[5]

In France's *Outre-mer*, territorial diplomacy is primarily implemented through the regional integration of the territories. For example, the New Caledonian SCRRE will open, in January 2019, five independent posts: in Vanuatu, Australia, PNG and Fiji in addition to the one already opened in New Zealand. The SCRRE also has an office in Paris, in charge of relations with European institutions. Therefore, France's territorial diplomacy is expanding, especially in the South Pacific. New Caledonia has developed its own bilateral agreements, with New Zealand for instance, and trilateral cooperation with France and Vanuatu. The practical applications of this territorial diplomacy are flexible and relate mainly to economic but also to political and cultural collaborations. The French state strongly supports the development of this territorial diplomacy and aims to implement this strategy even if territories need financial assistance in order to achieve their goals. Metropolitan policy-makers are also watchful to make sure that territorial diplomacies do not weaken France's global ambitions by making them too diverse and less clear. Therefore, the challenge for policy-makers in Paris remains the following: to support the expansion of territorial diplomacies while building a coherent global French narrative throughout the South Pacific. The challenge for France is also to maintain a strategic efficiency while developing a two-fold diplomacy, which constitutes a highly difficult task. French policy-makers in Paris are also prepared to clamp down on these territorial diplomacies if New Caledonia and French Polynesia make decisions that could possibly counteract metropolitan interests. In fact, the French state will not accept any local decision relating to global international issues that would clash with its own strategy. "France's voice can only be one regarding issues negotiated at the UN Security Council" (C Lechervy, pers. inter., Paris, 22 December 2016). For instance, France carefully monitors the FLNKS's activities within the Melanesian Spearhead Group and the Non-Aligned Movement. Therefore, while the current relations between France's metropolitan and territorial diplomacies are serene, French policy-makers are aware that, in the future, they might have to oppose certain contradictory local initiatives.

As Nathalie Mrgudovic explains, French policy-makers' attempt to support this integration process has to be primarily analysed by means of political speeches. In fact, for decades, political discourses have asserted the unity and single identity of the French territories, in the metropole and around the world, in order to reinforce the link between Paris and the *Outre-mer*. This concept, forged for the French colonial empire but based on the French Revolution ideal of national equality, asserts the theory of the indivisibility of the national territory, in Europe and overseas, in parallel to local cultures (Holm 2013, p. 145). Then, realising that France's presence in the South Pacific was linked to its integration in the region, French politicians began a complete transformation of their political discourse. Mrgudovic's quote from former French President Jacques Chirac during his speech in Tahiti in 28 July 2003 illustrates this shift very well. Chirac claimed at the time that "As a member of the vast Pacific family thanks to its territories, France naturally shares the [region's] same concerns" (Mrgudovic 2008, p. 37). This statement takes on even greater significance considering that Jacques Chirac was the leader of the Gaullist movement and followed De Gaulle's and Mitterrand's conception of France's foreign policy, its ideal of unity and *grandeur*. Therefore, this shows how French stakeholders have, over time, become more comfortable in recognising the individuality of French overseas territories within the French Republic.

First in discourses and then manifested in actions, France has implemented, in the last two decades, significant new policies enabling the integration of French Pacific territories into regional multilateral organisations (Brown 2013, pp. 173–174). France's diplomatic ambition to strengthen its presence in the Pacific by developing regional links from New Caledonia and French Polynesia started at the end of the 1990s. For example, a note written in 1997 by the Cabinet of the French Minister for Overseas Territories to the Minister presents instructions to be given to the French ambassador to the Secretariat of the South Pacific. The document emphasised the efforts that France had to expend in order to maintain and reinforce Vanuatu's French speaking and Francophile components. According to the brief, the development of economic relations between Vanuatu and New Caledonia presented one of the tools to use for this objective (AN Pierrefitte, 20010326/5). Vanuatu has played an important role in France's strategy to be accepted for its Pacific presence. After a difficult decolonisation period, Vanuatu became for a time one of the strongest opponents of French sovereignty over its Pacific territories. Policy briefs held by the NAA, authored by DFAT to prepare Australian Ministers for Foreign Affairs for their visits to the South Pacific, show how Vanuatu was eager to pursue virulent condemnation of France in international organisations, such as the UN or the FIP (NAA Canberra, M3793/9/92/97). For instance, Vanuatu lobbied for New Caledonia's re-inclusion on the list of non-self-governing territories in 1986. France punished Vanuatu by reducing its assistance by ten million francs in 1986 and by fifteen million in 1987. Moreover, France singled out Vanuatu as a "villain" because of its flirtation with Libya (NAA Canberra, M3793/9). During the same period, Australia's relationship with Vanuatu was tense for the same reason. Bill Hayden officially visited Port Vila in June 1988 in order to restore links with Australia (NAA Canberra, M3793/92 and 97). This explains why French policy-makers have focussed the increasing New Caledonian territorial diplomacy to facilitate engagement with Vanuatu.

France has developed many cultural diplomatic tools for integrating its territories with their neighbourhoods. For instance, the support that France has supplied to the *Festival des Arts du Pacifique*, the Festival of Pacific Arts, emphasises this strategy. Australia's support for the festival has followed the same logic, along with its use of sports competitions, on which Australia frequently relies to strengthen its regional links (NAA Canberra, M3793/162). This dynamic also prevails for New Caledonia's participation in the Melanesian Arts Festival. Moreover, in 2011, French President Nicolas Sarkozy attended the 14th Pacific Games, hosted in Noumea. The creation of the New Caledonian University in Noumea has also been conceived as a way, through student exchanges—mainly to Australia—to improve France's image in the region (NAA Canberra, M3793/162).

This process of regional integration has been the most visible and significant step in the creation of a territorial diplomacy. New Caledonia, member since 2016 of the Pacific Committee of the World Health Organisation and of the International Organisation of La Francophonie, is likely to soon join the International Labour Organisation and is an associate member of UNESCO since October 2017. However, the most significant achievement of this territorial diplomacy was the active French lobby implemented from Paris in order that New Caledonia and French Polynesia become full members of the Pacific Islands Forum, which they became in September 2016 during the 47th PIF meeting in Micronesia. In fact, until then, if the Forum had not actually denied the fact that French Pacific territories were part of the region, still the organisation had refused to give them membership because of their lack of sovereignty. However, according to Daniel Sloper, this decision also demonstrates the difference that PICs establish between France and its territories, a vision that can nuance the depth of Paris's regional integration (pers. inter., Canberra, 31 March 2017). Since the Forum represents the main regional institution, French policies had aimed at this integration from the start of their new Pacific strategy. For instance, already in 1989 and following the Matignon-Oudinot Agreements, France obtained permission for the FIP to integrate Paris into its new post-Forum dialogues. In 2005, the FIP had launched a *Pacific Plan* in order to clarify its ambitions for the future. This plan described the increasing connection with French and American Pacific territories as a tool to strengthen the development of the members of the Forum. The plan did not question the restriction of membership in the Forum to independent states only, but it enabled a renewed questioning on how the organisation should interact with French territories, which became observers at the Forum in 1999 for New Caledonia and 2004 for French Polynesia (Mrgudovic 2008, pp. 355, 363).

This integration of French territories in the Pacific does not only result from dynamics originated in Paris/Noumea/Papeete to the region. This process has also been possible thanks to an inclusive approach from the region towards France. In fact, as in other regions, Pacific multilateral institutions have suffered from a certain level of crisis. These organisations, especially the Forum, have been heavily criticised internally and externally for their lack of efficiency when dealing with major issues such as political coups, natural disasters or ongoing economic problems. Therefore, because of the discontent regarding regional institutions, the role of middle and global powers in supporting the region has gained much more importance. This logic has been relevant for Western powers such as the United States, France, the United Kingdom, the European Union, and is now the same for increasing powers in the Pacific: China, Taiwan, Japan, Russia, amongst others, as addressed further on in this chapter. France's economic and diplomatic capacities have been welcomed where multilateral institutions have been described as unable to maintain and support the region's stability and development.

Maintaining its presence and strategy in the South Pacific comes with a significant financial cost for France. For instance, in 2010, the cost of maintaining all its overseas territories represented seven billion euros of the state budget (Crouzet 2009), including New Caledonia of more than one billion euros a year, without taking into account some of the FANC budget (Brown 2013, p. 177). More precisely, in 2011, the French state allocated €1,234,184,954 to public services in New Caledonia, which also received more than 51 million euros from the EU between 2004 and 2011. The following figures were published by the High Commission of the French Republic to New Caledonia and do not include military expenditures (Steinmetz 2014, pp. 55, 60) (Table 7.1).

France's policies in the South Pacific, in support of its global power, must be successful in order to be economically justifiable. During a decade of economic difficulties, the need to transfer billions of euros to the Pacific has been sometimes challenged. Policy-makers do not directly need to demonstrate to the public that this investment is justifiable because the strong attachment of the French to the *Outre-mer* is deeper than concerns about its cost. However, the French public opinion regularly concerned regarding the fragile economy these territories, which pushes governments to develop policies to tackle poverty in these islands—plans which have all partly failed in the last decades. The problem is acute because French overseas territories remain heavily dependent on the mainland in Europe with regard to investment and infrastructures. This dependence and lack of autonomy are the direct

7 AN APPEASED NEIGHBOURHOOD: FRENCH–AUSTRALIAN COOPERATION ...   229

Table 7.1 New Caledonia in the French state's budget in 2011

Nature of expenses	Amount (€)	% of the total budget allocated to New Caledonia
Salaries and pensions	797,961,444	64.65
Intervention expenses	236,445,448	19.16
Operating expenses	163,860,134	13.28
Investment expenses	24,387,297	1.97
Operators' expenses	6,740,008	0.55
Others	4,790,623	0.39
Total	1,234,184,954	100

consequences of forty years of policies, between the 1950s and the 1980s, when France prevented any form of regional integration of its territories in order to keep them firmly attached to Paris. Consequently, economic enterprises in New Caledonia, Wallis and Futuna, French Polynesia and their regions have not yet reached their potential. Their GDP per capita is very high; New Caledonia's equals the average GDP per capita of EU members, creating a large economic gap between Noumea and most of its neighbours. Internally, the cost of living in the *Outre-mer* is extremely high, and economic inequalities are striking, which increases social tensions, as shown by the sizable demonstrations in French Guyana in May 2017.

Therefore, French policy-makers have increasingly focused on developing economic relations between their Pacific territories and the neighbouring states. In New Caledonia, France supports Noumea's regional trade, tourism and the establishment of Pacific customs cooperation. The aim is to make New Caledonia more autonomous economically in order to reduce the burden on the French budget, without making it too strategically and diplomatically independent (C. Prieto, pers. inter., Canberra, 8 April 2016). The key actor in this New Caledonian economic integration is the Agency for the Economic Development of New Caledonia (ADECAL). This agency is jointly directed by the French state, the government of New Caledonia and the local provincial governments of the archipelago. ADECAL guides public policies devoted to the improvement of New Caledonian economy. It has published an investment guide in 2014 and it regularly works with Business France in Australia in order to support French Pacific companies considering investment in their neighbourhood. New Caledonian businesses primarily engage in trade and investment with Australia, where Business France has helped several businesses to settle, especially in the agri-food industry. Next New Caledonian and French Polynesian companies look towards New Zealand and Papua New Guinea, then to Asia, especially Japan, before thinking of global investments (F. Cotier, pers. inter., Melbourne, 27 April 2016). However, interestingly, Cotier explains that French companies from mainland Europe rarely consider investing in French Pacific territories, because these markets are too small to legitimise the investment. In the Pacific, French companies focus on Papua New Guinea because of its large the population. France's involvement in the South Pacific is complex, combining both national and territorial interests. Based on the conception of a new strategic narrative, an enhanced regional integration of French Pacific territories and intensified policies of nation branding, France's mission in the Pacific would be nearly impossible without the strong support of its closest ally in the Southern hemisphere: Australia.

Australia's Support for France's Presence in the Pacific: A Convergence of Interests

While France and Australia may occasionally have separate diplomatic approaches, for instance regarding the focus to give to the PC, they increasingly follow the same regional understanding. More broadly, this alignment of French and Australian strategies is also based on the fact that Australia has fully acknowledged that it shares more values with France than it does with many other countries in the South Pacific. This understanding is not new. In a 1987 briefing for the Australian representative to the South Pacific Heads of Mission Meeting in Canberra, DFAT officials recommended that Australia had to fully accept that it did not share significant values with the PICs. Advisors explained that, by accepting this fact, Australia would be able to free itself from the Forum's pressure and conduct its own strategy. They added that Canberra had to look for "common interests with these states instead of trying to share values" (NAA Canberra, M3793/102), a conception currently promoted also in France (de Montbrial 2017, p. 15). Therefore, Australian policy-makers have progressively accepted the fact that France and New Zealand were the main South Pacific states with the same fundamental values as Australia. This rapprochement between Australia, New Zealand and France partly explains the growth of disagreement between the PICs and Canberra previously mentioned.

Australia and France's support to the PICs is not only aimed to support their middle power strategies. Some Australian and French ministers, such as Gareth Evans and Michel Rocard, and a significant number of senior public servants in both countries—maybe more in Australia due to geographic proximity—are also moved by an authentic attention and consideration to the PICS, their populations, societies and cultures. However, this genuine concern of and for the development of the PICs goes along with the pursuit of Australia's interests as middle power, both motivations often existing together without necessarily opposing each other. As Firth explains, "as preached to the developing world by an aid donor such as Australia, good governance also means adopting market-oriented policies, embracing free trade and permitting the free flow of foreign investment, and is a way of extending globalisation and economic integration", consequences which support Australia's regional leadership (2011, pp. 294–295). This chapter concentrates on these interests and how they have enabled Australia's rapprochement with France.

Australia's Strategic Interests in the Region Are Increasingly Compatible with French Ones

More than for any other nation, the South Pacific countries represents crucial interests related to power and security for Australian policy-makers, and these issues are a regular source of concern. The stability of the South Pacific constitutes one of Canberra's priorities and engages a significant part of Australian policy-makers' diplomatic action. Australia benefits from a strong regional leadership and intends to maintain it. However, Australia's Pacific strategy also proves to be ambiguous, as Australia belongs to both the South Pacific and to the Western alliance. As Firth explains, Australia and New Zealand, more than any other countries, have had to lead, bilaterally and multilaterally, South Pacific strategies due mainly to their geography. In the last two decades, Australian policy-makers have developed an increased interest in the Pacific region, economically and strategically. In fact, Firth argues that Australia cannot afford to ignore its neighbors' affairs in order "to create a beneficial strategic and economic environment for each other" (2011, p. 181).

In particular, Canberra's current Pacific strategy corresponds to the concept of an "arc of instability" around Australia's Northern and Eastern shores, which emerged in the 1990s (McDougall 2009, p. 204). This designation underlines that Australia is surrounded by multiple nations which, from time to time, can demonstrate significant political, economic and social differences as well as weaknesses. Therefore, one of Australia's first priorities has been to strengthen its neighbors' stability. For example, Daniel Sloper insists on the fact that "Australia's interest is to strengthen the region's resilience in terms of security" (pers. inter., Canberra, 31 March 2017). First and foremost, as the wealthiest country in the region, Australia's interest lies in supporting the PICs so they do not become havens for terrorist activities, in a region that Firth describes as "turbulent" (2011, p. 182). This strategy fully corresponds to Arnold Wolfers' "milieu goals", whereby Australia is using its asymmetrical relationship with Pacific Islands states in order to shape conditions beyond its shores so its neighborhood serves and protects its interests from potential threats. Michael O'Keefe goes further and asserts that, since the 2000s, "Australia is the regional hegemon in the South Pacific, and this new regional interventionism can be seen as an attempt to maintain this position", using multilateral institutions and cooperation (2007, pp. 140, 144).

Australia's numerous interventions in the South Pacific, for example in the Solomon Islands, East Timor, and Bougainville, also confirm that Australian policy-makers believe in an Australian responsibility towards the South Pacific, a region questionably considered by many in Canberra as their "backyard". This vision can be criticised for its neocolonial overtones, arguing that the Pacific would naturally depend on Australia's protection. This dismissive vision of the Pacific serves Australia's power. All Australian interviewees for this research have mentioned Canberra's ongoing sense of responsibility towards its neighbors. For instance, Gareth Evans asserted this idea as early in the 1990s: "The South Pacific is also the part of the world where we are thought to exercise most influence", a statement that Evans mostly explains because of Australia's history, wealth and aid programs (1995, p. 173). Moreover, Canberra has led multiple missions of state-building in its region, an action defined by Stewart Firth as the construction of the institutions of modern government in fragile states (2011, p. 182). By doing so, Australia has intended to maintain, and even strengthen, its regional leadership, which reinforces Canberra's influence at a global level. The multilateral dimension and legitimacy gained by Australia from its intervention in the Solomon Islands, endorsed by the PIF, underlines Canberra's aim to see its influence over the region acknowledged by its neighbors (Gyngell and Wesley 2007, p. 228). Regional leadership has a global political impact. Australia's position as the main representative of the Western alliance in the South Pacific supports its global diplomatic ambitions. The logic is the same for France.

However, as recognized by Gareth Evans in his assessment of Australia's regional strategy (1995, p. 174), Australia's care not to offend the PICs and not appear too often as a "deputy sheriff" can be counterproductive. Here lies the ambiguity of Australia's relationship with the South Pacific that Derek McDougall also points to in his study of Australian diplomacy (2009, p. 220). When Australian policy-makers try to secure their regional leadership by appeasing Pacific Island states and following their lead, as they did regarding New Caledonia's inclusion on the UN list of non-sovereign territories, it creates uncertainty regarding the strength of Australia's leadership. Australia's colonial history and its Western-driven strategy have sometimes weakened Canberra's influence in the South Pacific; the ways in which Australia has conducted Pacific multilateral institution's policies have at times led Australia's Pacific neighbours to criticize Canberra's legitimacy. Therefore, one of Australian policy-makers' priorities has been to continuously represent their country as a fully vested member of the South Pacific community (SPC) in order to remain influential, and not be viewed as the heirs of a non-regional power. As explained previously, Australian politicians have also tried to appease an Australian public opinion eager to condemn colonial practices overseas, in order to avoid tackling the ongoing Australian colonial treatment of Aboriginal communities. France has played a significant part in Australia's assertion of leadership in the South Pacific, especially within the South Pacific Forum, which was organised in 1971 explicitly against France and the US, positioning Australia as the most developed country of the organisation (Morgan 2014, p. 137). Until the end of the 1990s, France was considered the common enemy, and Australia presented itself as the mediator between France and the nations of the Pacific. Nowadays, because of the new Pacific context, Australia relies on France to help strengthen its regional influence.

Australia does not wish to carry the burden of regional security and development alone. Hence France, the second major Western actor in the region, has become increasingly useful for Australia. Australian policy-makers no longer consider France's presence in the South Pacific a threat to its security because they do not view France as a simply neo-colonial entity. On the contrary, they believe that French sovereignty over its overseas communities constitutes an asset to Australian security, especially because, as Denise Fisher explains with either pragmatism or disdain depending on one's point of view, "The Pacific is a very difficult region to deal with: it's isolated, it's remote, bureaucracies are tiny. We need to be working as together as we can on this" (pers. inter., Canberra, 7 April 2016). The 2016 Defence White Paper argues that Australia intends to lead the region's security thanks to her relationship with New Zealand, the United States, France and Japan (Australian Department of Defence 2016, p. 56). More precisely, the document further asserts that Australia and France "are strong partners in the Pacific where France maintains important capabilities and we also work closely together to support the security of our respective Southern Ocean territories" (Australian Department of Defence 2016, p. 138). This shift in Australia's reliance on France for support of its security came about in the early 2000s. It has also been possible because France has improved its relationship with the United States. Under the presidencies of Nicolas Sarkozy and François Hollande, Paris, like Canberra, has welcomed a stronger involvement of the US in global security, especially in the Pacific. To achieve this mutual engagement, Australian and French policy-makers have analysed their shared interests and sought solutions to protect them in an uncertain international context. However, Daniel Sloper explains that Australia would like to do more in the region and to have more continuity in its engagement:

> Australia thinks that it is important for France to extend beyond a military and assistance role to one of a greater engagement economically and for people to people relations. Australia wants France to widen and demonstrate its regional engagement to the broader region. It is in France's interest to engage more in the region. (pers. inter., 31 March 2017)

Indo-Pacific Threats to Australia's Security and Regional Leadership

The chapter dedicated to the Pacific in Canberra's 2016 Defence White Paper begins with the following assessment: "Geography, shared history, business and interpersonal links tie Australia's interests closely to stability and prosperity in our immediate neighbourhood" (Australian

Department of Defence 2016, p. 54). The document then lists Australia's priorities to influence and maintain regional security, especially strengthening Canberra's relationship with PNG, establishing a defence architecture within South Pacific multilateral organisations, and insuring that the region benefits from Asia's economic growth without being destabilised by its actors. Finally, according to what Australian policy-makers say, the region's security will also be strengthened by mechanisms of conflict prevention in the South Pacific where tensions are frequent and can only increase with climate change. Australia perceives two types threats to its traditional security in the region: immediate ones, such as terrorism in Indonesia and political tensions in Papua New Guinea; and strategic threats with the increasingly disruptive presence of China in the Pacific.

The future of Papua New Guinea is a significant concern to Australia, even though it does not challenge its strategy as a whole. Though Australian policy-makers do not consider that Papua New Guinea is a failed state, they have assessed that, in the last ten years, the situation on the ground has deteriorated in terms of poor governance, health issues and the level of social violence and corruption. Therefore, Australia is concerned about the future of the country and the destabilisation it could induce throughout the region. Another immediate threat to the region's security that concerns Australian diplomats pertains to the consequences of climate change for Pacific states. Australian senior public servants believe that it will be Canberra's responsibility to organise the regional response to this critical issue, for example by agreeing to relocate these populations in Australia: "We have plans to help them sustain themselves but we have to be prepared to welcome them" concludes Quinlan. The diplomat goes further and explains that these immediate threats reinforce Australia's leadership within its neighbourhood but also give Canberra the responsibility for overall management (pers. inter., Melbourne, 12 September 2016).

Strategically, one of the central driving forces in the deepening of the French–Australian bilateral relationship in the Indo-Pacific region stems from the diplomatic rise in Asian powers, in particular China. The current improvement in their strategic partnership can be seen as an attempt to protect their shared interests in security and the economy by asserting the Western alliance in the Indo-Pacific region. By doing so, France and Australia are maintaining a suitable regional environment for their strategic and economic interests, a "milieu goal" according to Arnold Wolfers. The French–Australian strategic partnership, recently reinforced by Australia's contract with the French shipbuilding firm Naval Group for their submarines, has been conceived as a leverage tool to maintain a suitable milieu for Australian and French interests in the Indo-Pacific region, partly in response to the assertion of Asian powers.

French and Australian diplomats acknowledge that Asian countries present a set of vast opportunities in terms of strategic cooperation and economic activity. However, the current French–Australian strategic partnership was constructed because Asian ambitions also present cause for concern. Indeed, the global restructuring of power has seen the diplomatic as well as economic affirmation of some Asian powers, first and foremost China. Australia and France seek to foster, rather than hinder, the diplomatic emergence of these Asian powers so that they do not undermine the South Pacific order, which up to now has been primarily sustained by Western countries. Australian and French policy-makers also fear that a greater engagement of China in the South Pacific will focus the tensions between Beijing and Washington on this part of the world (C. Lechervy, pers. inter., Paris, 22 December 2016). Arnold Wolfers explains that "Nations have been advised to act on the principle of collective security [...] in order to help create a milieu in which threats to national possessions will cease to arise" (1962, p. 76). In particular, according to policy-makers in Canberra and Paris, China's diplomatic and military assertion is natural but also destabilising for the Indo-Pacific region and for international order at large. These two specific situations, considered as a potential threat, have led French and Australian policy-makers to increase their cooperation in response to tensions in the South China Sea and China's increasing presence in the South Pacific.

China is seeking to assert its political power, and the South China Sea has become the playing field for these claims. This maritime area has been the subject of territorial disputes among riparian States for decades, particularly between China, the Philippines and Vietnam. These disputes therefore place Beijing in opposition to a number of states that are Asian allies of the United States and thus indirectly of Australia. Since 2008, Beijing has used interpretative limits of the United Nations Convention on the Law of the Sea[6] to claim archipelagos and extend its exclusive economic zone, more precisely to the Paracel Islands, the Spratly Islands and the Scarborough Shoal. Tensions have run particularly high since 2014 when China became involved in the construction of artificial islands on the reef it had taken over in the Spratly Islands (Medcalf and Townshend 2016). On 12 July 2016, The Hague Court of International

Arbitration issued an unfavourable judgement against China with regard to its various maritime disputes with the Philippines; a decision immediately challenged by Beijing (Thibault and Philip 2016), which currently works on a charm offensive in Southeast Asia.

Australian and French policy-makers share a mutual understanding of this issue. First of all, France and Australia are well aware that they cannot hinder Chinese diplomatic ambitions. Such an inclination could even be considered to be counterproductive. Indeed, Paris and Canberra perceive China as a major partner with whom they must cooperate because of the important political, diplomatic and economic potential of an agreement with Chinese power. However, Beijing's claims in the South China Sea are perceived as a threat by Australian and French policy-makers because they call into question the standards of international law, which is the guarantor of global stability. Emmanuel Lenain confirms that France and Australia are working together to ensure that "the transition takes place through stability and the rule of law. For us, this condition is necessary for the region and the world to remain as peaceful as possible" (pers. inter., Paris, 6 June 2016). For this diplomat, the two countries should pressure China to respect the main freedoms enshrined in international conventions and which underpin the South Pacific's stability. Above all, they are concerned with the freedom of maritime and air traffic that China is challenging in the South China Sea by seeking to extend its territorial waters (Regaud 2016, p. 8).

This goal is paramount as each party has significant interests. First of all, the commercial stakes are very high. The South China Sea is a maritime space with one of the most dense amounts of traffic, and this is which plays host to maritime connections to most major Chinese, Taiwanese, Japanese, and Korean ports, among others. These flows then head to the Strait of Malacca and then on to India and Europe, and to Australia in the South. Thus, half of the trade traffic heading towards Europe crosses this sea. As the Australian economy is highly dependent on international maritime trade, the freedom of trade flows is essential for its economic growth. Additionally, the South China Sea contains fishery resources, although these are already overexploited, as well as reserves of gas and oil. The issue concerns not only the economy, but also strategy and security. Maintaining freedom of movement is a priority.

In order to affirm this important point of international law and protect the trade flows, major powers, such the United States and France, regularly have their military fleets patrol the South China Sea.

Australia welcomes French military presence in the region and the two countries have increased their patrols in 2018. Closer strategic and operational relations with France mean that Australian policy-makers would like to see a serious French presence in the Indo-Pacific, together with the continued presence of the United States, and an increasing Japanese presence. This corresponds to a logic of power balance in which France has become a significant player. During a visit to Singapore in June 2016, France's Minister for Defence at the time Jean-Yves Le Drian strongly expressed France's determination to influence China to respect international law and conventions in the Asia-Pacific.[7] Christian Lechervy provides France's assessment of this new regional context: "We are currently witnessing the development of maritime relations between Asia (North and South) and the South Pacific", through many examples, such as Indonesia's elaboration of a political discourse about its Melanesian identity, Vietnam's opening of a consular post in New Caledonia in 2016 or the creation by East Timor of a genuine Pacific diplomacy (pers. inter., Paris, 22 December 2016). "Slowly, from a political and institutional point of view, Asia incorporates in the Pacific" asserts Lechervy. This Asian engagement in the Pacific is demonstrated by aid programs from Asian powers, now that Japan, China and Taiwan constitute some of the most generous contributors to South Pacific countries and institutions. Since the end of the Cold War, China and other Asian states have increased their connection with Pacific states, which have welcomed the involvement and aid from new donors. Beijing joined the post-Forum in 1989, Taiwan in 1993, followed by many other Asian countries (Mrgudovic 2008, p. 358). Today, China is investing heavily in the Pacific. It has built up very ambitious development aid programs that support its diplomatic ambitions in the region. The Chinese-led Asian Infrastructure Investment Bank, launched in 2014, is one of China's main mechanisms for these ambitions. Therefore, the Pacific states now have more choice in their diplomatic partnerships. Thus, as Nic Maclellan analyses, more and more elites from Pacific countries are being trained and educated in Asia—be it China, India or Indonesia (Maclellan 2015, p. 5). Therefore, multilateral institutions such as the Forum will have to prepare themselves to welcome new Asian members. Additionally, Asian powers are increasingly engaging with the South Pacific from a commercial point of view. This shift is clear with the French Pacific territories, Singapore currently constituting Wallis and Futuna's second largest trade partner for example (Institut d'Emission d'Outre-Mer 2008, p. 36). Even though this does not lead to pushing Western powers away from the South Pacific, the region is now developing new partnerships and France and Australia need to take this context into account to maintain their regional leadership. In January 2018, the Australian Minister for International Development and the Pacific Concetta Fierravanti-Wells strongly criticised China's increasing presence in the region, position officially disapproved by Minister for Foreign Affairs Julie Bishop. This debate demonstrates Australian policy-makers increasing concern regarding this issue. In its last Defence White Paper, published in 2013, France emphasised the importance of its engagement in the Pacific region and insisted on the importance of French overseas territories in France's strategy to remain a naval power, and to protect its fishing and mineral resources. On this issue, the White Paper referred to the French–Australian strategic partnership, presented as a key association for French power in the Pacific, corresponding to Wolfers' definition of "milieu" goals:

> In the Pacific Ocean, France fully takes responsibility for being a political and naval power. France finalised a strategic partnership with Australia in 2012. This agreement underlines the increasing convergence of the two countries' interests on many regional and global issues, pertaining to the Pacific and the Indian Oceans. It underlines as well Pacific powers' support to France's presence in the Pacific, France being considered as a source of stability, able to supply immediate support, thanks to the means she has in its overseas territories.[8]

This strategy for the South Pacific is shared by Australian policy-makers. From an Australian point of view, the alliance with France is to be protected, faced with an increasingly volatile Chinese presence. Australia originally supported this increasing Asian involvement in the region, as Julia Bishop asserted again in January 2017 during a meeting with her American counterpart.[9] This process has been perceived as a legitimation and support for its Asia-Pacific narrative and Canberra's rapprochement with the ASEAN. However, the Franco-Australian partnership aims to act in response to maintain Western leadership in the region. The presence of the French Armed Forces in New Caledonia and their significant involvement and capacity for action is reassuring to Australians. Romatet confirms that Australians "see it as a factor for stability, faced with aggressive and unsettling rise of China, whilst also

240 P. SOYEZ

faced with Russia's grip, another aggressive presence in the region [...] Australia saw this environment as purely Australian, now France is very well considered" (pers. inter., Paris, 21 June 2016). A further factor in the Australian–French partnership is that France can act as a relay for European institutions to maintain a strong EU commitment to the funding of development programs in the South Pacific.

France's Support for South Pacific Interests Within the EU

Australia and France use their foreign aid for development programs to maintain stability in the South Pacific and thereby secure their regional interests, since Pacific nations' economies are often characterised by their relative weaknesses. PICs are heavily dependent on foreign aid and, consequently, on the influence of the major donors to the Pacific. This has led the Australian diplomats to claim in a 1986 report: "We are a superpower in the region" (NAA Canberra, M3793/162), a position which has often and increasingly caused discontent against Australia. Canberra's aim has been to finance these countries' development, partly out of a genuine concern for Pacific nations, but also in order to receive support for its broader national interests, through regional security, economic opportunities or votes at the United Nations. French policy-makers have followed the same mixed motivations. Australia devotes most of its limited foreign aid to the Asia-Pacific region, demonstrating how much Australia prioritises strategically its close neighbourhood, despite budget cuts. The website of AusAid, DFAT's development and aid agency, clearly claims that foreign aid "reflect[s] Australia's national interests".[10]

However, Australia's recent and official commitment to the Indo-Pacific region must be questioned. In his introduction to Australia's 2017 *Foreign Policy White Paper*, PM Malcolm Turnbull asserts that: "This Foreign Policy White Paper shows Australia to be focused on our region, determined to realise a secure, open and prosperous Indo-Pacific" (DFAT). Moreover, the same document explains the tools selected by Australia to implement its future reengagement in the Indo-Pacific region. Australian policy-makers claim that Canberra will work at the Pacific's economic prosperity, by promoting free-trade within a PACER Plus agreement and labour mobility to increase the skills level in the PICs. However, since these Pacific workers will be trained in rural and regional Australia in professions in shortage in Australia, such rural communities will be the primary beneficiaries of this policy.

Therefore, these two economic engagements clearly aim to benefit Australia more than the PICs. However, the White Paper also explains that Australia will also allow more Pacific Islander students to come and benefit from Australia's education thanks to more scholarships. Canberra also promises to commit to the region's security with New Zealand and France. Finally, in order to reduce contestation from the PICs, the Australian government asserts that it will increasingly fund research on how to tackle the effects of climate change in the Pacific. The Indo-Pacific focus presented by the 2017 White Paper aims to bring an answer to PICs criticism against Australia. However, one can question Canberra's dedication to development programs when looking at Australia's recent slashing of its financial commitment to its aid budget.

Australia's strategic use of aid has a cost, and the Abbott and Turnbull governments have demonstrated their lack of interest by reducing it, especially to please the most conservative Australian voters. In fact, Australia's aid budget has been slashed by a third since 2011, when it was amounting to A$4.170 billion, around 0.35% of its GNI (Firth 2011, pp. 285–290). In 2016, Australia only devoted 0.25% of its GNI to development assistance, representing US$3.02 billion, far from the UN target of 0.7%. Australia's was the 17th most generous donor in terms of % of GNI, 12th in terms of volume. Australia's aid program has even fallen to 0.22% for the period 2017/2018.[11] In 2016, France devoted 0.35% of its GNI to development assistance, representing USD 9.5 billion. Paris was the 5th most generous donor in terms of volume and the 12th donor regarding % of GNI.[12] While both countries could be more generous, Australia has chosen to reduce its aid budget despite its strong and continuing economic growth, while France has increased again its aid since 2014 even though its economy was still stagnating after years of economic crisis. However, the significant reduction of Australia's generosity has not deeply impacted its regional leadership because Canberra has largely spared the South Pacific from those cuts. Tony Abbott and Malcom Turnbull's aid policies demonstrated that the development programs were not a diplomatic priority in Australia's budget, but also that the South Pacific remained of first importance. For this reason, Australian policy-makers intend to rely increasingly on the financial support of other regional powers, above all France and the EU. Australia has tried to involve more international agencies and foreign players in Pacific aid programs, such as the World Bank or the European Union. Sharing the same interest, France has lobbied within

EU institutions to make sure that the Pacific would fully benefit from the community's foreign aid, although trade still remains limited. Consequently, compared to Australia, France's role in the region takes greater importance.

With Australia, France is one of the main contributors to development in the South Pacific. This aid is provided through four main types of policies: (1) French direct financial support to its territories; (2) France's foreign aid programs to Pacific states; (3) direct contribution from French overseas territories to their neighbours; and (4) France's contributions to European foreign aid programs in the Pacific. Being the only sovereign state in the Pacific that is also a member of the EU, France naturally supports development funding for the Pacific within the European Union. Australian policy-makers are fully aware of this, which partly explains Canberra's support for France's presence in the region. Already in 1987, Australia was explaining to ASEAN members that, despite issues in French Polynesia and New Caledonia, France's presence in the Pacific had positive aspects, especially France's support "for funds for EEC development assistance under the Lome Agreement" (NAA Canberra, M3793/9). Several documents from the French diplomatic archives also demonstrate that Australian policy-makers called for stronger European funding for development projects in the Pacific, through France's connections in Brussels (AD Nantes, 27POI/167). More recently, the 2017 Australian *Foreign Policy White Paper* asserted that "A strong European Union remains vital to Australia's interests and will be an increasingly important partner in protecting and promoting a ruled-based international order. [...] We will further strengthen bilateral relationships with key EU member states, especially France and Germany" (DFAT 2017, Chapter 6).

EU contributions to the South Pacific are crucial to the region's development. Between 1975 and 2006, through the Lomé and subsequently the Cotonou agreements, the European Union contributed €194 million to development projects in the Pacific. During the same period, the EU provided more than €2 billion of direct bilateral aid to the region (Mrgudovic 2008, p. 370). In his study of the European Development Fund in New Caledonia, Peter Brown has analysed the tools and realisation of Europeans aid to the French territory (Brown 2013, p. 178). Brown describes "European soft power" in the Pacific and this thesis argues that France and Australia, fully aware of this European component, have partly forged their partnership around it.

Ambassador Christian Lechervy asserts that, during the negotiations for the renewal of the Lomé Agreement by 2020, the fact that France remains a strong Pacific power will significantly strengthen Europe's development programs for the region. France conducts the same kind of lobby in order to maintain international aid funding to African countries, since Paris carries most of the responsibility for securing vast regions of the African continent (Védrine 2001, p. 86). This European financial and technical support is crucial for the development of the Pacific, and France has remained a solid intermediary between Oceania and Europe. French policy-makers have regularly reminded their counterparts in the Pacific of that role, which is perceived as a tool for French leadership in the South Pacific as well as in Brussels. This Australian appreciation for France's role within European institutions representing Pacific countries is greatly emphasised nowadays. This European contribution to the region also reflects that the EU intends to strengthen its position in the Indo-Pacific region, in terms of traditional and non-traditional security, and trade and investment.[13] In fact, the EU is trying to articulate new policies in order to renew its engagement with the region (Murray 2016, p. 172). Australia has supported this impetus so far, but only as long as it reinforces Australia's leadership. Australian policy-makers don't want the introduction of the EU as a significant actor in the Indo-Pacific to disrupt the regional order that Canberra has tried to build up. (Quinlan, pers. inter., 12 September 2016). The diplomat explains that DFAT supports a strong European involvement in the Asia-Pacific region but institutionally, at the limit of the already-existing engagement: EU membership to the ASEAN Regional Forum, which is a security forum but more of an operational one, and the ADMM+, the ASEAN Defence Ministries' Meeting. This process is also part of the EU–Australia aid delegated agreement, which enables the two signatories to provide aid to development programs on each other's behalf, as happened in Fiji and South Sudan in 2014.[14]

However, Australia's reliance on European funding to share the cost of foreign aid in the Pacific has been framed since 2014 in the EU-Australian delegated development programs, the first between the EU and a non-European donor, and reinforced the 2016 Framework Agreement. These delegations of funding aim to deliver aid more effectively. This EU-Australian rapprochement constitutes one of the reasons explaining Canberra's support for the regional integration of French territories. As explained previously, France strengthened its presence in the South Pacific during the 47th Pacific Islands Forum in 2016 because New Caledonia and French Polynesia at that time became full members of the organisation.[15] Australia has actively supported this double integration,[16] and DFAT has also supported this full membership, seeing this as a positive decision for Australia. According to Stephen Brady, Australian policy-makers have conducted a "nimble diplomacy" constituting "France's strongest support" on that matter: "Australia's support for France was decisive lobbying for New Caledonia's inclusion in the PIF. France had lobbied for French territory integration and Australia's nimble diplomacy ensured success at the last PIF leaders meeting" (pers. inter., Paris, 4 January 2017). Australia has defended the French territories' determination to become full members of the Forum for two reasons.[17] Supporting France's goals in the region strengthens the strategic partnership between the two countries, a high level of political and diplomatic cooperation manifested by Australia's recent submarine contract with the French public shipbuilder company Naval Group. Also, supporting South Pacific regionalism is a means for Australian and French policy-makers to ensure that France remains part of this inclusive dynamic, which will enable Paris to influence the maintaining of significant European aid programs in the South Pacific. Consequently, Canberra wishes to see France remain in New Caledonia after the upcoming referendum on independence.

France is not the only actor promoting the idea that its Oceanian territories constitute a bridge between the South Pacific and the European Union. This argument has been used for more than a decade by the French Pacific territories themselves, in order to convince their neighbours to integrate them more deeply into regional organisations. For instance, during his visit to New Zealand in July 2005, pro-independence President of French Polynesia Oscar Temaru asserted that his territory wanted to gain full membership to the Forum rapidly so Papeete "could fully play its role of intermediary between the Pacific and Europe" (Mrgudovic 2008, p. 366). In Strasbourg, New Caledonian deputy at the European Parliament Maurice Ponga is the Vice-Chair of the EU's Development Program and strongly supports Pacific interests. Peter Brown has analysed how New Caledonian leaders intend to act as European "bridgeheads" in the South Pacific (Brown 2013, pp. 178–179). In fact, the European dimension of French territorial diplomacy has now become absolutely crucial in the regional participation of New Caledonia and French Polynesia.

7 AN APPEASED NEIGHBOURHOOD: FRENCH–AUSTRALIAN COOPERATION ... 245

This factor will oblige France, in the long term, to oversee the dispersing of European funds for foreign aid by reassessing which political actor is best suited to lead aid programs. Should the EU transfer funds to Paris, which would then send them to French Pacific territories before being allocated to their regional cooperatives, or should these funds be sent directly from Brussels to Noumea's and Papeete's administrations? Moreover, according to Lechervy, "Philippe Germain was the first to suggest organising a meeting in New Caledonia between EU and Pacific representatives, not the French state, although Paris supports this dynamic" (pers. inter., Paris, 22 December 2016). Australian policy-makers intend to benefit economically from France's support for the emancipation of its territories, especially for their mining industries.

Australia's Commercial Interests in French Pacific Territories

Since the very end of the 1990s and the normalisation of the French–Australian relationship, French governments have worked to develop the economic relationship between Australia and France's Pacific territories, mainly with New Caledonia. France had been reluctant to encourage such commercial and financial ties for decades, seeing in Australia's investments in its territories a tool to influence and separate them from Paris. This antagonistic attitude has changed, and decision-makers in Paris now support these economic developments. They believe that, by fostering New Caledonia's trade, they will give the archipelago fewer reasons to vote for its independence. The economic dimension of the French Pacific territories' regional integration is as important as the political one (E. Lenain, pers. inter., Paris, 6 June 2016). Lenain explains that the Quai d'Orsay "wishes to develop trade relations and flows of students and workers" between New Caledonia and its neighbours. The impetus is concrete both in France and Australia so that former political tensions between Paris and Canberra have been put aside in order to foster these business relations (François Cotier, pers. inter., Canberra, 27 April 2016).

Such inclusive trade dynamics come from the French territories as well. A significant revolution is currently taking place regarding French territories' international trade. Political actors in these territories now realise that they must go and look for economic growth in a broad Pacific, encompassing Asia, the United States, Japan, Australia and New Zealand.

For instance, many Caledonian stakeholders travel to Asia to negotiate nickel contracts and boost the attractiveness of their territory. New Caledonia looks towards the West, French Polynesia towards the North and Wallis and Futuna towards its Pacific neighbours. For more than two decades, Australia has demonstrated its commitment to develop trade and investment with New Caledonia. Australia has mainly imported ores and seafood from the French territory. In 1997, the Commonwealth was the second largest economic partner of New Caledonia, representing 12% of its imports. Moreover, at the end of 1996, France and Queensland signed an agreement to develop trade between Brisbane and Noumea (AN Pierrefitte, 20010326/6). At a federal level, Alexander Downer visited New Caledonia in 1996, 1999 and 2004 as Minister for Foreign Affairs and Trade, in order to support Australian investments in the island (Mrgudovic 2008, p. 375). In 2002, Australia and New Caledonia signed an economic and trade agreement for the same purpose. In 2003, Australian merchandise exports to New Caledonia reached A\$209 million and increased to A\$311 million in 2014 (mainly coal and civil engineering equipment). Australia imported A\$202 million of merchandises in 2014 from Noumea. Australia now is New Caledonia's third largest economic partner, behind France and China. Ore trade is at the core of this dynamic. New Caledonia operates some of the largest nickel mines in the world. A major part of these exports goes to Australia, now with the support of French authorities, which use the French Australian Chamber of Commerce and Industry for this purpose. In 2014, two-way investment reached A\$424 million, mainly coming from New Caledonia to Australia (\$374 million).[18] More recently, at the end of 2016, the President of New Caledonia Philippe Germain led a delegation to Canberra where he reminded Australian policy-makers of the economic potential of his archipelago. He was not the first Caledonian stakeholder to lead such a visit. Australian–French Polynesian trade and investment are much more limited. However, Australia has also demonstrated its economic interest regarding French Polynesia, and conversely, Polynesian stakeholders work at increasing their exports to Australia, such as pearls. Papeete has led numerous marketing operations to Australia, either in Canberra or Paris, and Air Tahiti Nui has now direct flights to Melbourne, Sydney and Brisbane.

Practical Cooperation in the Pacific: Increasing the Ability of Australian and French Actors to Work Together

France and Australia are two of the main contributors to security, aid and development projects in the South Pacific. Such project cooperation has enabled Australia and France to make their strategies in the South Pacific more visible. Development programs have primarily enabled French and Australian policy-makers to improve their mutual bilateral cooperation. French–Australian cooperation is often criticised on the basis that, by engaging deeply with France, Australia might be seen to favour its global interests over its regional ones (Maclellan 2016). This book argues that this criticism is not convincing because the alleged opposition between global and regional interests is largely imagined. In fact, on many levels, the improvement of the bilateral French–Australian partnership does not only serve these two powers' leaderships, but also the common interests of the region as a whole. However, first and foremost, this cooperation has enabled France and Australia to build up common working practices.

The Primary Importance of Academic and Scientific Cooperation

In order to create a "we-feeling", as theorised by Karl Deutsch (1968), French and Australian policy-makers have primarily favoured the development of scientific cooperation. These projects, at first ad hoc but then extended to long-term research collaboration, have enabled France and Australia to overcome their diplomatic tensions by maintaining a less political link between the two countries. Therefore, French–Australian scientific cooperation has constituted the cement of the current strategic partnership between Paris and Canberra. French and Australian policy-makers have always relied on their scientific cooperation to bring the two countries closer and tackle trust issues between them. Both countries have also relied on their scientific and technical support for Pacific states to strengthen their regional leadership. These two dynamics, one French–Australian and the other from France and Australia to the Pacific region, have been conducted simultaneously.

In 1986–1987, when France decided to refuse any future official visit between Australia and France, scientific cooperation proved to be one of the few areas, along with trade, where the two countries were still benefiting from positive collaborations. Scientific and technological joint programs maintained a certain level of dialogue between Paris and Canberra with the perception that the bilateral relationship could produce positive outcomes. For example, in 1988, Australian policy-makers supported Paris' scientific agreement project with Australia based on the following arguments: "While on ice during the freeze, [the agreement] has been the subject of continued discussions at official levels and officials on both sides are proceeding with planning on the assumption that it will be put in place at some time in the future" (NAA Canberra, M3793/99). Other Australian reports show as well that cultural relations were not impacted by the political tensions between France and Australian at the end of the Cold War. Both DFAT and the Quai d'Orsay have since taken constant care to protect cultural and scientific cooperation from political and strategic conflicts. On 24 July 1989, Prime Minister Bob Hawke wrote to Gareth Evans to inform him that, during his visit to Paris, he and Michel Rocard had agreed to intensify scientific cooperation in order to improve the French–Australian relationship (NAA Canberra, M3793/46). The two Prime Ministers agreed on the formation of an Australia–France Working Group to pursue common interests on the Environment. This group recruited official and scientific experts, who, as requested by Hawke and Rocard, cooperated primarily on several issues of sustainability such as the greenhouse effect and the pollution of the Antarctic environment. This example illustrates clearly the link between scientific and diplomatic cooperation. This dynamic has been maintained until today, as demonstrated by the emphasis stressed by French and Australian policy-makers on the scientific and industrial cooperation induced by Australia's submarine contract. This scientific cooperation accompanied an emphasis on the increase and improvement of the French–Australian cultural relationship, through education, language and exhibitions. Student exchanges between the two countries are now extremely frequent, supported by the presence and development of French-speaking schools in Australian states' capitals, and the creation of Cotutelle Ph.D. programs in every tertiary discipline. These demonstrate the vivacity of academic links between the two countries.

For some decades, policy-makers in Canberra and Paris have also chosen to implement their scientific collaboration, technical assistance at the service of development programs in the South Pacific. They have done so, as seen previously, out of genuine concern for the region, to reinforce their regional leadership, but also to give their officials an opportunity to develop the practice of working together. By doing so, they have implemented their soft power in the South Pacific. Joseph Nye defines a country's soft power as "three basic resources: its culture (in places where it is attractive to others), its political values (when it lives up to them at home and abroad), and its foreign policies (when others see them as legitimate and having moral authority" (2011, p. 84). Moreover, Nye adds that "the fact that creating soft power through public diplomacy is often difficult does not mean that it is unimportant" (2011, p. 101). Australian and French support to the South Pacific has encompassed various domains, such as health and technical assistance in farming and fishing practices, amongst many others, in order to bolster both countries' moral authority and, therefore, soft power. This concept of soft power "will enhance the probability of other elites adopting policies that allow us to achieve our preferred outcomes" (Nye 2011, p. 101). The SPC, which became the PC in 1997, has constituted an efficient tool for this purpose. France has emphasised the responsibility of the institution in applying the Lomé agreement to the region and in leading regional technical cooperation (AD Nantes, 27POI/142). At the end of the 1980s, France's financial and technical aid to the Pacific was part of its Funds for Cultural and Technical Cooperation for the Pacific, which enabled France, for instance, to finance SPC summits in small Pacific countries. However, while the SPC has constituted a support for French interests via political dialogue, the institution has also been a forum of contestation of France. For instance, after *les évènements* in 1986, PNG decided to boycott the SPC for two years, considering that the institution only represented a forum for France's interests (AD Nantes, 27POI/142).

France funds scientific and technical projects through bilateral cooperation, for example with Vanuatu, and multilaterally, through the PC. The origin of this aid has been transferred from Paris to Noumea mainly, but also to Papeete and Wallis and Futuna. For example, since 2002, New Caledonia and Vanuatu have been linked by a cooperative agreement directing New Caledonia's financial and technical support to Vanuatu. France's scientific and technical support in the Pacific is, consequently, more and more territorial. In 2004, regarding members' contribution to their organisation, metropolitan France constituted the PC's third largest donor, after Australia and New Zealand. Combined with its Pacific territories, France's contribution to technical assistance was almost as high as New Zealand's, around €3.4 million, but still far behind Australia's at €5.8 million (Mrgudovic 2008, pp. 328–329). Nowadays, New Caledonia is the PC's largest donor within its members. Another tool of France's technical assistance to the region, France's Pacific Fund was created in 1987. This fund contributed to financing specific scientific and technical projects in the South Pacific, including French–Australian projects. In 2016, France allocated €1.38 million to support twelve projects relating to health, education, environment, infrastructures and culture.[19] Significantly, the direction of the Pacific Fund rotates every two years between the Presidents of New Caledonia and French Polynesia. Therefore, this institution has also enabled French Pacific territories to increase their technical cooperation with their regional partners.

Nonetheless, French–Australian scientific cooperation has regularly been undermined in one particular domain: the protection of the environment and the fight against climate change. In fact, as demonstrated by France's deep involvement in reaching a strong agreement during the COP 21 in Paris, French policy-makers have tended recently to appear as a credible and, sometimes successfully, influential environmental diplomacy, as demonstrated in June 2017 by President Macron after Donald Trump's decision to withdraw the US from the Paris agreement. This environmental focus aims at enabling Paris to strengthen its diplomatic influence pertaining to an increasingly crucial issue. In the South Pacific, a region of the world with unique ecological diversity but also supremely vulnerable to human activities, the fact that France intends to lead regional environmental projects improves its image and strengthens its presence. Therefore, French policy-makers in the South Pacific frequently advertise France's support for regional cooperation and projects regarding the protection of the environment. France's support for environmental programs in the region can also be analysed as an effort to tackle its image as a polluter due to its nuclear testing. In 2008, about half the French–Australian projects of scientific cooperation pertained to the environment (Mrgudovic 2008, p. 318). France has set up ongoing research programs and training to study the conservation of fishing resources, a crucial issue for Pacific states (AD Nantes, 11POI/616). However, Canberra has been regularly criticised severely, especially by French policy-makers, for its weak commitment regarding environmental policies (Morgan 2017).

Joint Military Actions and Regional Leadership

In order to support their common strategic interests in the region, France and Australia have developed regular military cooperation over the last two decades. These manifestations of hard power, combined with their soft power, represent the implementation of Australian and French smart power strategy in the South Pacific. These joint operations serve a number of purposes, with different leverage tools for the region's stability: direct military surveillance along with technical assistance to the PICs. These operations mainly include maritime patrols to secure trade routes and fish resources, and aid programs following natural disasters. Therefore, they combine traditional and non-traditional security objectives. French and Australian joint operations have not only been beneficial thanks to their outcome. With regular military joint exercises in the Pacific, programs of military cooperation have been conceived by Australian and French policy-makers as preliminary regional steps to foster the development of a collaborative culture and tradition between French and Australian forces for intervention at a global scale. Such joint exercises and operations have been of use as tools to reduce French–Australian mutual misperceptions both by policy-makers and by members of the military.

French and Australian military forces mainly cooperate in the South Pacific during FRANZ operations. Initiated in 1992, the FRANZ cooperation assembles Australian, French, and New Zealander troops for aid and development programs after natural disasters or any humanitarian crisis. France is militarily present in New Caledonia through les Forces Armées de la Nouvelle-Calédonie (FANC—New Caledonia Armed Forces), with 1663 staff members, belonging to the Army, the Navy and the Air Force. The FANC benefits from modern equipment, as any other French military unit. More broadly, France has 8000 soldiers in the Indian and Pacific oceans, who protect its territories and interests as well as those of its allies.[20] The 2016 Australian Defence White Paper emphasises the importance of the FRANZ Arrangement, where "Australian and French defence forces [have] worked alongside each other to provide life-saving humanitarian assistance" (Australian Department of Defence 2016, p. 138). The FRANZ cooperation has been deployed almost every year after cyclone destructions, and its last significant operation was conducted in 2016 in Fiji after the tropical cyclone Winston which partly destroyed the archipelago. The FRANZ arrangement also increasingly organises joint operations through which Australia, France and New Zealand protect Pacific Island Countries' EEZ from illegal fishing. In fact, many countries in the South Pacific don't have the means to protect their maritime resources from fishing boats, mainly coming from Asia where sea resources have been overexploited. This is a crucial problem because South Pacific countries largely benefit from the fishing licences they sell in their waters. This constitutes a critical issue for the West Pacific, a central element of France's environmental diplomacy to protect biodiversity, offering as an example the arrival of Vietnamese fishing boats in New Caledonian waters in order to fish species that have now disappeared from the overexploited South China Sea (C. Lechervy, pers. inter., Paris, 22 December 2016). Joint air and sea patrols are now common. French frigates come to Australia once or twice a year to conduct such operations and exercises, and also to participate in the Tasmanex exercises, which have assembled forces from Australia, France and New Zealand since 2001. Australian and French forces also train together in the Pacific during "Southern Cross" exercises. Initiated by France, these exercises are regularly located in Northern New Caledonia and enable French, Australian and Pacific States forces to train together and thereby improve their collaboration. The French–Australian strategic meeting held in Noumea in March 2017 aimed also to increase bilateral cooperation.[21]

Australia and France mutually value their highly trained military force in the South Pacific. Australian policy-makers express their satisfaction at being able to share the military cost of securing their area of the Pacific with France, Australia's only substantial military partner in the South Pacific. This military cooperation also demonstrates a very strong symbolism, assuring the rest of the world of Australia's support for France's presence in the South Pacific. During John Howard's visit to Paris in 2000, the Prime Minister expressed very clearly to French President Jacques Chirac and his Prime Minister Lionel Jospin that Australia wanted France to remain in the Pacific, that Australia recognised France as a Pacific power and that France's contribution to the region's stability was essential. Gary Quinlan explains that he suggested to John Howard that he make it the first point of the meeting in order to put an end to any potential misunderstanding. Therefore, in order to demonstrate this desire to collaborate closely with France, John Howard invited the aircraft carrier *Charles de Gaulle* to come and be part of joint exercises with the Australian Navy (G. Quinlan, pers. inter., Melbourne, 12 September 2016). Although the *Charles de Gaulle* never came to

Australia, this example illustrates the political symbolism of joint exercises. More importantly, regular military cooperation in the South Pacific has enabled French and Australian forces to understand each other better and improve their interoperability, assets that Paris and Canberra have used to further their global interests during military interventions in the Middle East.

However, Australia's support for French military presence in the South Pacific has limits. Although Canberra supports France's regional military presence, Australian policy-makers have refused France's offer to support Australian-led peace keeping interventions in the South Pacific, in order to fully maintain their prime leadership against a potential French competition. For example, when asked if, in case of a necessary peacekeeping operation in Bougainville, Australia would ask France to accept the role of regional ally and be part of the intervention, Gary Quinlan says that it would be very unlikely: "There can be a strategic cooperation but nothing beyond that" (pers. inter., Melbourne, 12 September 2016). France's military interventions in Asia-Pacific have been limited. FANC participated in the INTERFET UN force which gathered seven thousand Blue Helmets under Australian command during the conflict in East Timor. However, at the start of the RAMSI mission in the Solomon Islands, France offered to participate to the intervention but Australia rejected this offer. Officially, this refusal was motivated by the idea that the intervention of a global power could intensify the conflict. It may also be possible that Australian policy-makers believed that fully operating with France would hinder Australia's regional leadership, by increasing the South Pacific's perception of Australia as a continuing foreign European nation exercising a neo-colonial influence. Nonetheless, the extensive French–Australian military cooperation in the South Pacific has inspired the two countries to also collaborate in the Indian Ocean, where France and Australia are keen to defend their shared interests against the rise of new disruptive actors.

The Future of the French–Australian Strategic Partnership in the Pacific: A Pattern of Cooperation for the Indian Ocean

As with French–Australian relations in the South Pacific, Australian and French connections in the Indian Ocean have shifted since the 1980s. In 1986, Bill Hayden discussed the matter with his French counterpart

Jean-Bernard Raimond during the 41st UNGA in New York. Raimond explained that France was irritated by Australia's increasing involvement in the Indian Ocean at the time. French policy-makers suspected that Australia's presence would encourage island states of the Indian Ocean to take a closer and unwelcome interest in French South Pacific policies. Therefore, Hayden defended Australia's strategy and reassured Raimond that Australia's Indian Ocean policies were conducted in the context of Canberra's legitimate interests as an Indian Ocean littoral state and not on the basis of any opposition to the French presence (NAA Canberra, M3793/18). Paris and Canberra have extended their cooperation to the Indian Ocean where both countries have worked together since 2003 at protecting their ZEE around their territories (Mrgudovic 2008, pp. 306, 311).

On the contrary, Australia and France currently consider each other as partners in maintaining the region's security. Their cooperation established in the South Pacific has been used as a pattern to be applied in the Indian Ocean, where France and Australia are developing their dialogue to enhance their shared interests. While French–Australian cooperation remains limited in this region, much less than the one in the Pacific, it is likely to become more frequent in the next few years. In fact, both countries have increased their focus in this region, for security and economic purposes, and intend to use in the Indian Ocean the same diplomatic tools that they have used in the South Pacific in order to build their partnership. France constitutes a power in the Indian Ocean mainly thanks to two territories, La Réunion and Mayotte islands, where more than one million French citizens live. France also maintains its sovereignty over several unpopulated archipelagos, which provide it with a vast economic exclusive zone and multiple bases for research.[22] The strategic importance of these archipelagos is very significant because they enable France to deploy its navy and armed forces in Africa and South Asia, as it does in the Pacific. Paris also enjoys close relationships with three states that have belonged to the French colonial empire: Madagascar, Djibouti— where Paris has a military base—and the Comoros. Moreover, more than half of the European Union's imports travel through the Indian Ocean. Therefore, it is vital for Paris to secure its interests in the Indian Ocean against various threats, such as piracy or the assertion of new states, like China. The region represents increasing interests as well for Australia, which is one of the largest and most influential states of the Indian Ocean.

Australian policy-makers are increasingly aware of France's desire to develop its presence in the Indian Ocean. Australia, France and India are building their trilateral cooperation through joint navy exercises and strategic dialogues, especially the International Solar Alliance. Moreover, France wants to become a full member of the Indian Ocean Rim Association (IORA) (C Prieto, pers. inter., Canberra, 8 April 2016). This institution is a relatively informal association comprising most riparian states of the Indian Ocean. The IORA has partners for its cooperation dialogue, such as France, the United Kingdom, the United States, Japan and China. The Quai d'Orsay intends to become a full participant in the organisation in order to be more influential in regional agenda and policies, especially the ones pertaining to international cooperation against trafficking, pirates, and maritime security. The second aspect of France's ambitions for its membership of the IORA deals with the blue economy, France wanting to improve regional cooperation on sustainable fishing and energy resources.

The Indian Ocean has only recently been on the agenda of Australian–French strategic meetings. Although both Australia and France are fully aware that they constitute Indian Ocean powers, and although the region is not at the heart of their dialogue, both France and Australia increasingly value the importance of each other's work in the region. Therefore, France aims at increasing its military presence in this region and empowering its partners, Australia and, to a second extent, India. According to Gary Quinlan, French policy-makers intend to deploy half of their next generation of nuclear submarines in the Indian Ocean. In fact, France will start studies for the renewal of its nuclear arsenal in 2017. The construction of this third generation of submarines is due to commence in 2019, with a first delivery in 2035. France also supports the building of an Indian maritime reach and naval capacity, such as Australia has. On 23 September 2016, the Indian government signed a contract with French aircraft company Dassault for 36 fighter jets "Rafales" for €8 billion. Such aircrafts have the capacity to carry nuclear armament as well. The recent submarine contract between French shipbuilding company Naval Group and Australia must be understood in this same logic of the empowerment of the three regional allies (Soyez 2016).

Conclusion

> The two Governments reassert the importance of their cooperation in the Pacific and Indian Ocean regions, where they both have an interest in promoting peace, security, stability and prosperity, and support the growing integration of French territories into their regional environment. (French–Australia Joint Statement of Enhanced Strategic Partnership 2017)

The joint statement by France and Australia outlining their enhanced strategic partnership, signed in Melbourne on 3rd March 2017, clearly officialises twenty years of increasing bilateral cooperation in the South Pacific. It constitutes a milestone in defining a long process of regional cooperation between Canberra and Paris and aims at reducing their regional "awkwardness". The South Pacific region, where both Australia and France are sovereign powers, has played a crucial role in the strategic renewal and mutual empowerment carried out by Canberra and Paris, transforming a suspicious competition into a strong cooperation. Based on important scientific collaboration, used as a continuous link despite political turmoils, French and Australian policy-makers have progressively reassessed their shared interests in the South Pacific in order to merge them and to implement a tangible military partnership for the region's security. This strategic process has enabled the two Western powers to align their leadership in the face of new regional actors, especially China, whose increasing presence in Oceania is perceived in Canberra and Paris as natural but also threatening.

The concrete collaboration of France and Australia in the South Pacific has also generated positive outcomes for both countries' global ambitions. However, in a context of significant aid cuts from Australia, this bilateral partnership has been ambiguously received by the PICs, as Pacific Island nations remain cautious about what they consider as a potential neo-colonialist rapprochement. Australia's relatively recent support for France's presence in the South Pacific and for the regional integration of its territories has strengthened France's power by legitimising its influence in this part of the world, while Paris is currently engaged in the redefinition of its diplomatic narrative in Oceania. This strategic and institutional renewal goes along with an increasing acceptance of administrative and identity-related differentiation between France and its Pacific territories, as demonstrated by New Caledonia's referendum in 2018. Moreover, by enhancing regular cooperation in the South Pacific, France and Australia have improved their ability to lead joint military actions, reinforcing their cooperation within the Western alliance against global threats to their security, such as the fight against terrorism. Finally, Australia has also sought this mutual empowerment because its last two Liberal governments have reduced Canberra's aid to the Pacific and have intended to share the cost of development programs with other powers. Therefore, France's presence in the region has been increasingly profitable for Australia.

Notes

1. For more information on France's global security strategy, see Chapter 4.
2. Many scholars have analysed the impacts of colonial history on French identity, such as Benjamin Stora, most important historian on the Algerian War and on its consequences on French society and identity, and Catherine Coquery-Vidrovitch in "Colonisation, racism et roman national en France" (2011).
3. See figures from the Australian Bureau of Statistics' last census http://www.abs.gov.au/ausstats/abs@.nsf/mf/3238.0.55.001.
4. See Benedict Anderson (1983) for the concept of imagined communities.
5. More information on the SCRRE can be found on its website https://cooperation-regionale.gouv.nc/.
6. Established in 1982 and entered into force in 1994, the United Nations Convention on the Law of the Sea constitutes the international legal framework for maritime disputes. The Convention aims to balance States economic and strategic interests, especially by settling disputes around exclusive economic zones. Moreover, it guarantees passage rights for vessels and aircraft. It is noteworthy that the US has not ratified UNCLOS.
7. http://discours.vie-publique.fr/notices/163001891.html.
8. French *Defence White Paper*, Paris, 2013, p. 59.
9. http://foreignminister.gov.au/speeches/Pages/2017/jb_sp_170126.aspx.
10. http://dfat.gov.au/aid/Pages/australias-aid-program.aspx.
11. See figure on the Lowy website https://www.lowyinstitute.org/issues/australian-foreign-aid.
12. See more detailed figures on the OECD website http://www2.compareyourcountry.org/oda?cr=oecd&lg=en.
13. See for instance Frederica Mogherini's speech at the IISS Shangri-La Dialogue 2015 https://eeas.europa.eu/headquarters/headquarters-homepage/6254/speech-high-representativevice-president-federica-mogherini-iiss-shangri-la-dialogue-2015_en.
14. See first agreement http://foreignminister.gov.au/releases/Pages/2014/jb_mr_140417.aspx?w=tb1CaGpkPX%2FlS0K%2Bg9ZKEg%3D%3D.

258   P. SOYEZ

15. The full version of the media release can be found here http://www.forumsec.org/resources/uploads/embeds/file/2016-communique-working-19-09-2016.pdf.
16. See the media release on the Ministry of Overseas Territories http://www.outre-mer.gouv.fr/?le-processus-d-integration-de-la-nouvelle-caledonie-et-la-polynesie.html.
17. Press release on the Presidency of French Polynesia's website http://www.presidence.pf/index.php/pr-presidence/3055-la-polynesie-francaise-devient-membre-a-part-entiere-du-forum.
18. Source DFAT http://dfat.gov.au/geo/new-caledonia/Pages/new-caledonia-country-brief.aspx.
19. http://www.diplomatie.gouv.fr/fr/dossiers-pays/oceanie/la-france-et-l-oceanie/le-fonds-pacifique/article/le-fonds-pacifique.
20. http://www.forcesarmees.nc/index.php/presentation/les-moyens.
21. http://www.forcesarmees.nc/index.php/articles/acualites/193-defense-maritime-du-territoire-renforcement-de-la-cooperation-entre-les-fanc-et-l-australie.
22. France's vivid tension with Mauritius in order to maintain full sovereignty over the Trimelin island demonstrates France's dedication to protect its overseas territories.

REFERENCES

Archives Nationales, Pierrefitte, France.

National Archives of Australia, Canberra, Australia.

Anderson, B 1983, *Imagined Communities*, Verso, London.

Australian Department of Defence 2016, *Defence White Paper*, Australian Department of Defence, Canberra.

Australian Department of Foreign Affairs and Trade 2016, 'Wallis and Futuna Country Brief', viewed 17th July 2017, http://dfat.gov.au/geo/wallis-futuna/Pages/wallis-and-futuna-country-brief.aspx.

Australian Department of Foreign Affairs and Trade 2017, *Foreign Policy White Paper*, Australian Department of Foreign Affairs and Trade, Canberra.

Bandel, N, Blanchard, P & Lemaire, S 2005, *La Fracture coloniale: la société française au prisme de l'héritage colonial*, La Découverte, Paris.

Beasley, C 2014, 'The Breaking of the "Great Australian Silence": How and Why the Writing of Indigenous Australian History Has Changed Over the Last 40 Years', *The ANU Undergraduate Research Journal*, vol. 5, Australian National University Press, Canberra.

Blainey, G 1983, *The Tyranny of Distance*, Sun Books, Sydney.

Boyce, J 2011, *1835 the Founding of Melbourne and the Conquest of Australia*, Black Inc., Carlton.

Brown, P 2013, 'Negotiating Postcolonial Identities in the Shadow of the EU: New Caledonia', in R Adler-Nissen & UP Gad (eds), *European Integration and Postcolonial Sovereignty Games: The EU Overseas Countries and Territories*, Routledge, London, pp. 169–186.

Coquery-Vidrovitch, C 2011, 'Colonisation, racisme et roman national en France', *Canadian Journal of African Studies*, vol. 45, no. 1, pp. 17–44.

Crouzet, C 2009, 'L'outre-mer coûte près de sept milliards à l'État', Le Figaro, 11 February, viewed 17 July 2017, http://www.lefigaro.fr/economie/2009/02/11/04001-20090211ARTFIG00602-l-outre-mer-coute-pres-de-sept-milliards-a-l-etat-.php.

De Montbrial, T & Gomart, T 2017, *Notre intérêt national, quelle politique étrangère pour la France?* Odile Jacob, Paris.

Deutsch, K 1968, *The Analysis of International Relations*, Prentice Hall International, Englewood Cliffs.

Dinnie, K 2016, *Nation Branding, Concepts, Issues, Practice*, Routledge, London.

Evans, G & Grant, B 1995, *Australia's Foreign Relations*, The University of Melbourne Press, Melbourne.

Firth, S 2011, *Australia in International Politics*, Allen & Unwin, Sydney.

Gyngell, A & Wesley, M 2007, *Making Australian Foreign Policy*, Cambridge University Press, Cambridge.

Holm, U 2013, 'French Concepts of State: Nation, *patrie*, and the Overseas', in R Adler-Nissen & UP Gad (eds), *European Integration and Postcolonial Sovereignty Games: The EU Overseas Countries and Territories*, Routledge, London, pp. 145–151.

Institut d'Emission d'Outre-Mer 2008, *Wallis et Futuna en 2007*, Institut d'Emission d'Outre-Mer, Paris.

Maclellan, N 2015, 'Transforming the Regional Architecture: New Players and Challenges for the Pacific Islands', *Asia Pacific Issues*, no. 118, pp. 1–8.

Maclellan, N 2016, 'France and the Forum', *Inside Story*, 13 October, viewed 17 July 2017, http://insidestory.org.au/france-and-the-forum.

Mathew, P & Harley, T 2016, *Refugees, Regionalism and Responsibility*, Edward Elgar, Cheltenham.

McDougall, D 2009, *Australian Foreign Relations, Entering the 21st Century*, Pearson, Sydney.

Medcalf, R & Townshend, A 2016, 'Shifting Water: China's New Passive Assertiveness in Asian Maritime Security', *Lowy Institute Reports*, 29 April, viewed 17 July 2017, https://www.lowyinstitute.org/publications/shifting-waters-china-s-new-passive-assertiveness-asian-maritime-security.

Morgan, W 2014, 'Regional Trade Negotiations and the Construction of Policy Choice in the Pacific Islands Forum (1994–2004)', Thesis (Ph.D.), The University of Melbourne, Melbourne, Australia.

Morgan, W 2017, 'Coal Comfort: Pacific Islands on Collision Course with Australia Over Emissions', *The Conversation*, 1 March, viewed 17 July 2017,

260 P. SOYEZ

https://theconversation.com/coal-comfort-pacific-islands-on-collision-course-with-australia-over-emissions-73662.

Mrgudovic, N 2008, *La France dans le Pacifique sud: les enjeux de la puissance*, L'Harmattan, Paris.

Murray, P 2016, 'EU-Australia Relations: A Strategic Partnership in All but Name', *Cambridge Review of International Affairs*, vol. 29, no. 1, pp. 171–191.

Nye, JS 2011, *The Future of Power*, Public Affairs, New York.

O'Keefe, M 2007, 'Australia and the Fragile States in the Pacific', in J Ravenhill & J Cotton (eds), *Trading on Alliance Security, Australia in World Affairs 2001–2005*, Oxford University Press, Melbourne, 2007, pp 131–149.

Pacific Islands Forum 2016, 'Forum Communiqué', 10 September, viewed 17 July 2017, http://www.forumsec.org/resources/uploads/embeds/file/2016-communique-working-19-09-2016.pdf.

Regaud, N 2016, *France and Security in the Asia-Pacific, from the End of the First Indochina Conflict to Today*, ASPI Strategic Insights, Canberra.

Reynolds, H 1999, *Why Weren't We Told?* Penguin Books Australia, Ringwood.

Schultz, J & Wallis, J 2014, 'Australia in the Pacific', in D Baldino, A Carr, & AJ Langlois (eds), *Australian Foreign Policy, Controversies and Debates*, Oxford University Press, Oxford, pp. 174–192.

Soyez, P 2016, 'French–Indian Relations Take Off', *ASPI The Strategist*, 28 October, viewed 17 July 2017, https://www.aspistrategist.org.au/french-indian-relations-take-off/.

Stanner, WEH 1968, *The Boyer Lectures 1968—After the Dreaming*, Australian Broadcasting Commission, Sydney.

Steinmetz, L 2014, 'L'État, l'Union européenne, la Nouvelle-Calédonie: leur représentation réciproque', in I Amiot & Y Tommasini (eds), *L'éducation civique en Nouvelle-Calédonie*, SCÉRÉN—Vice Rectorat de la Nouvelle-Calédonie, Nouméa, pp. 53–66.

Thibault, H & Philip, B 2016, 'Mer de Chine: les Philippines attendent que la Chine lui rende ses bancs de sable', Le Monde, 11 July, viewed 17th July 2017, http://www.lemonde.fr/asie-pacifique/article/2016/07/11/mer-de-chine-arbitrage-attendu-sur-le-conflit-entre-pekin-et-manille_4967793_3216.html.

Toa, E 2017, 'Bilateral Approach for Issues with Maritime Borders', *Vanuatu Independent*, 17 September, viewed 17 July, https://vanuatuindependent.com/2016/09/17/bilateral-approach-for-issues-with-maritime-borders/.

United Nations Development Program 2018, *Human Development Report*, United Nations, New York.

Védrine, H 2001, *France in an Age of Globalisation*, Brookings Institution Press, Washington.

Wolfers, A 1962, *Discord and Collaboration, Essays on International Politics*, The John Hopkins University Press, Baltimore.

CHAPTER 8

Conclusion

France and Australia are two middle powers, one global and one regional, engaged in a process of mutual empowerment to strengthen their respective national interests and face the traditional and non-traditional threats of the current global order. This book analyses the actors, mechanisms and outcomes relevant to the transformation of the French–Australian bilateral relationship between 1985, a moment of strong tensions between both countries because of France's Pacific policies, and the present time when Paris and Canberra are closer than they have ever been since World War I. This study mainly demonstrates that the construction of the French–Australian genuine strategic partnership has been conceived by Australian and French policy-makers as a process of mutual empowerment. Canberra and Paris have increasingly and mutually supported each other in order to modernise their own diplomacies, thanks to a new alliance and new practises, and to answer together new regional and global challenges. This bilateral rapprochement takes parts into a larger questioning in International Relations pertaining to the redefinition of the notion of national interest. As this book also demonstrates, this progressive empowerment has been possible because of the settlement of three main conflicts between France and Australia pertaining to, primarily, the Common Agricultural Policy (CAP), then French nuclear testing as well as Australia's opposition to French policies in New Caledonia. However, this study demonstrates that the progressive rapprochement between France and Australia has primarily been possible

© The Author(s) 2019   261
P. Soyez, *Australia and France's Mutual Empowerment*,
Studies in Diplomacy and International Relations,
https://doi.org/10.1007/978-3-030-13449-5_8

because French and Australian policy-makers have instituted numerous opportunities for dialogue and cooperation in order to overcome their ongoing misperceptions and misunderstandings. This dialogue has enabled their strategic positions to evolve and to align their approach to regional and world challenges. Therefore, this book on the development of the French–Australian bilateral partnership has been informed by combining a close reading analysis of primary textual archives and expert interviews with a theoretical lens encompassing "smart power" doctrine with postmodern constructivism and interpretive theories. This study of the transformation of the Australian–French bilateral relationship demonstrates the limitations of the realist approach to middle powers diplomatic strategies. This book shows that the development of the French–Australian Strategic Partnership is a positive evolution; more complex than a "diplomatic transformation" as defined by Nicholas J. Wheeler: "a process in which two adversaries go through a series of steps of de-escalation which progressively reduce the role that the threat or the use of force plays in their relationship" (2013, p. 479). The complex logics driving this evolution are explored here.

The deep rapprochement that Paris and Canberra have implemented at a fast pace since 2012 should not be limited to a rationalist and conjunctural security strategy in the Indo-Pacific region. This study has revealed the importance of the current security, diplomatic and economic shifts in the Indo-Pacific region, in particular in the South Pacific. Paris and Canberra's mutual empowerment does not constitute simply the least dangerous strategy to reach security for both powers, nor does not only mitigate past tensions between France and Australia, whether they pertained to international trade regulation, nuclear strategy or sovereignty. The recent French–Australian mutual empowerment has necessitated a global reconceptualisation of France and Australia's presence, role and identity in the Indo-Pacific, encompassing the vast diversity of French and Australian actors of their Pacific presence. These actors, increasingly interconnected, pursue different interests. Therefore, French and Australian policy makers have had to develop new political and identity narratives encompassing all these dimensions in order to reassert together their country's legitimacy and role in the region. This long, complex and ongoing intellectual process goes much further than a realist, short term diplomatic move in order to reduce a potential threat. This diplomatic shift has been difficult to implement individually and in cooperation, firstly because of the sources of tension analysed in this book but also because of the profound misunderstanding affecting French and Australian policy-makers' judgement.

The strategic, intellectual, identity-related, legitimising and mutual empowerment implemented by Paris and Canberra must be analysed through the smart power doctrine because of its englobing dimension. This process is firstly based on increasingly diverse French and Australian communities in the Indo-Pacific region, smartly interconnected between themselves but also within a globalised public opinion. Smart power goes further than a realist approach to states' strategies because it requires an innovative and inclusive reconceptualization of the state's identity, legitimacy, objectives, social components and tools, as demonstrated by France's institutional process in New Caledonia. A French–Australian smart mutual empowerment capitalises on the social dynamics and interactions of the French and Australian communities in the Indo-Pacific.

Consequently, this book goes further than Booth and Wheeler's concept of the security dilemma sensibility (2008) because it does not limit itself to security strategies; it extends the study of the transformation of conflict into cooperation to include identity, in all its components. In fact, this study starts following Wheeler's definition of the diplomatic transformation and of its three stages. It also acknowledges Wheeler's useful studies of the importance of the interpersonal level in trust-building between states (2013). While Wheeler claims that trust can exist between policy-makers but not communities (who would simply 'cooperate') (2013, p. 480), this book proves the contrary. While highlighting that interpersonal links between French and Australian policy-makers have played a crucial role in improving the bilateral relationship by enabling these leaders to walk away from their mutual misconceptions, this book argues that this empathy "at the highest level" was only possible because of the primary improvement of the French–Australian people-to-people relationships. These inter-community relationships opened the way and forced officials to empathise. In summary, the renewal of the French–Australian bilateral relationship has gone beyond a "de-escalation" from conflicts as described by Wheeler, to an inclusive, smart and mutual empowerment.

When building "smart powers" strategies in order to face traditional and non-traditional threats, both countries have understood that the development of an efficient economic diplomacy was part of a broader diplomatic objective of influence. Therefore, the French–Australian bilateral relationship has primarily been supported by the economic interests of its business communities, which foreign policies increasingly encompass. In fact, the notion of national interest is being redefined and broaden to incorporate new objectives and new actors. French–Australian economic relations have been strongly impacted, for decades, by opposition from Paris and Canberra to multilateral agreements pertaining to agricultural trade, France leading the CAP and Australia the Cairns Group. This antagonism has currently been significantly alleviated, and the two countries now share a common understanding and aspiration for the regulation of economic globalisation. Therefore, both countries are increasingly engaged in a logic of mutual economic empowerment for their own national benefit. France's commitment to support the negotiations of the EU–Australia FTA constitutes a demonstration of France's engagement in its partnership with Australia. Indirectly, the French–Australian relationship has created a conducive atmosphere for the development of economic diplomacies between Paris and Canberra. The desire of policy-makers to increase trade and investment in a market still mutually undervalued, either France or Australia, has enabled the modernisation of Australian and French diplomatic practices and administrations, which has supported reciprocally their national economic growth. Australian and French policy-makers have conceived the pursuit of economic interests as a means of maintaining constructive relations despite strong political tensions. This has been particularly useful during significant tensions pertaining to France's nuclear testing program in the South Pacific.

French–Australian cooperation is now framed within an ambitious, vast and well-designed strategic partnership, enhanced in March 2017. This document enables both diplomacies to commit and engage with each other in a very large number of issues: security, policy-making, strategy, economic, aid, research, culture and education. In order to develop this strategic partnership and to protect their shared security interests, Australian and French foreign policy-makers have attempted to limit their disagreements regarding France's nuclear program in French Polynesia. Nuclear issues constituted a core element of tensions in the Australian–French bilateral relationship until the end of the 1990s. This issue has highlighted Australia's and France's conflicting strategies regarding global security. Australia and France had two opposing positions in the South Pacific: the French approach, basing global security on nuclear deterrence and the need to conduct nuclear testing in order to maintain its strategic independence, and the Australian approach, based

8 CONCLUSION   265

on the reduction of nuclear armament and full support of the American security order. Moreover, this book illustrates that such strong antagonism can also be best understood in light of Canberra and Paris's different ambitions for their own power. Australian governments tried to use regional condemnation of nuclear armament and testing in order to increase Australia's leadership in the South Pacific, following this strategy to bring about visible results in a diplomatic niche issue. On the other hand, France refused to question the importance of their nuclear testing program until computer simulation became fully reliable, because Paris linked this criticism to the condemnation of its presence in Pacific territories in general, and thus to its *politique de grandeur*. However, French and Australian policy-makers are currently fully aware that the protection of their shared interests pertaining to global security is dependent on their mutual empowerment. Therefore, French and Australian policy-makers have completely removed this opposition from their discourse in order to forge their tangible strategic alliance, as part of their "smart power strategy".

Australia and France increasingly share the same traditional and non-traditional threats to their security due to the current context affecting the concept of power, a power transition among states, like the diplomatic rise of China, and a power diffusion to non-state actors, such as terrorist groups (Nye 2011, p. xv). Therefore, global security has become one of the core elements of the renewal of the French–Australian relationship since the end of the Cold War. In order to overcome their tensions and start building a new partnership for regional security, Australian and French decision-makers and diplomats have had to learn to understand and respect each other's cultural approach to security, a strategy that this book analyses according to constructive theories, such as Deutsch's theory of security communities. Then, they have found interests and issues on which the two countries could work together. They had to set aside their own political traditions in order to understand their counterparts' way of thinking and perceiving the world. Australian and French agendas have converged into a strategic alliance for finding solutions to very diverse threats, especially terrorism. This partnership has been demonstrated most recently through Australia's submarine contract with France, Canberra's biggest military contract to date. Such rapprochement enabled France and Australia to modify their representations of security and to agree on certain key issues, thereby reducing their regional "awkwardness". As noted in chapter I, according to Murray, Warleigh-Lack and He, "awkwardness refers to an uncomfortable state of affairs in which one party strives to participate in a region but lacks full belonging and commitment to the goal of the latter" (2014, p. 280). This definition illuminates the Australian and French regional engagement because the two countries share regional strategies, both desiring to secure their global interests within the Western Alliance and their partnerships with their neighbours. While both focuses are not necessarily opposed, they do not always match either, especially because the PICs have their own agendas regarding the defence of South Pacific interests.

From an Australian perspective, the improvement of Canberra's relation with Paris takes also part into Australia's reengagement in the Indo-Pacific region. In fact, in the post-Cold War context where Asia's diplomatic influence is growing fast, Australian policy-makers have felt the need to focus and increase their diplomacy in the Pacific region. The deepening of bilateral relations with Australia's neighbouring states as well as with France has been a key instrument of this impetus. This agenda is shared by France, which has recently developed a more assertive foreign policy towards Asia and the Pacific as part of its global objective of developing a confident strategy for furthering its national interest. This bilateral engagement must also be understood in the broader context of the EU's increasing strategic and economic focus on the Asia-Pacific region, since France is Brussels' main relay in the South Pacific. The rapprochement of France and Australia in their South Pacific strategy is a key component of their approach of mutual empowerment. Based on important scientific collaboration, which was a continuous source of engagement despite years of political turmoil, French and Australian policy-makers have progressively reassessed their shared interests in the South Pacific in order to merge them and to implement a tangible military partnership for the region's security. The South Pacific region, where both Australia and France are sovereign powers, has played a crucial role in the strategic renewal and mutual engagement implemented by Canberra and Paris, transforming a suspicious competition into a strong cooperation. This strategic process has enabled these two Western powers to align their leadership in the face of new regional actors, especially China as a disruptive and increasingly aggressive presence. However, both countries must imperatively take into account their increasing unpopularity in the region, in particular for Australia which significantly cut its aid budget since the Abbott government.

Moreover, this book also demonstrates how Australia's significant denial of its colonial history impacts its strategy with the PICs. To forge their "smart power" Pacific engagement and strategic narrative, both Paris and Canberra must commit to their other regional partners if they want to maintain their national interests in the Pacific.

This constructivist effort toward shared security has been primarily implemented in the South Pacific, where Australian and French officials have learnt to accommodate their different understandings of political legitimacy especially with regard to France's policies in New Caledonia. In fact, French–Australian tensions and cooperation pertaining to New Caledonia constitute an extremely interesting case study because the New Caledonia archipelago has played the role of a mirror for the bilateral relationship. New Caledonia has symbolised many of the conflicts between Paris and Canberra pertaining to political legitimacy, colonial memory and regional understanding. Nonetheless, the fact that New Caledonia is currently located at the very heart of the French–Australian strategic partnership also demonstrates the extent to which the two countries seek to empower each other in order to support their shared interests. In fact, this book also demonstrates that Australian foreign-policy makers support France's diplomatic innovations in hopes that France will maintain a presence and influence in New Caledonia after its 2018 referendum on independence.

The French–Australian bilateral relationship has begun to produce positive and constructive outcomes for the two countries. While the negotiations of the EU-Australia FTA could possibly hinder this dialogue, this topic should have the potential to deeply affect the forward-looking cooperation established between Paris and Canberra. For instance, in France, Emmanuel Macron's victory during the presidential elections provides confidence that France will strongly maintain its global engagement and the modernisation of its diplomatic strategies and narratives. The success of French and Australian mutual empowerment has led French and Australian foreign policy-makers to predict deeper collaborations in the future on new topics and in new spaces, for instance in the Indian Ocean. Their cooperation will further enliven the concept of the Indo-Pacific region, which they both support as part of their continuing effort to renew their diplomatic narrative.

The improvement of the French–Australian bilateral relationship and their mutual empowerment serves as an instructive example of the positive outcome that can result when middle power diplomacies show a willingness to innovate and develop trans-regional partnerships while facing an increasingly unstable international order. The current context of International Relations is characterised by the redefinition of power and of what national interests encompass. The growing French–Australia partnership offers an original answer from two middle powers to implement smart power strategies and reinforce their diplomatic narratives, their means of action, their protection from threats and, finally, their regional and global influence.

REFERENCES

Murray, P, Warleigh-Lack, A & He, B 2014, 'Awkward States and regional Organisations: The United Kingdom and Australia compared', *Comparative European Politics*, vol. 12, no. 3, pp. 279–300.

Nye, JS 2011, *The future of Power*, Public Affairs, New York.

Wheeler, NJ 2013, 'Investigation Diplomatic Transformations', *International Affairs*, vol. 89, no. 2, pp. 477–496.

Appendix—List of Archives

Colour code:
Request access granted, archives analysed
Request access denied

French Ministry of Foreign Affairs—Archives La Courneuve

Serie E—Political Division—Asia-Pacific 1980–1986

International Organisations:

Box	Documents number	Title	Dates
2602	2.1.2	Denuclearisation in South Pacific	1980/1986
2603	2.1.2	Rarotonga Treaty	1985/1986
2605	2.3	Human Rights International terrorism	1980/1986
2612	2.5.2	CEE political comity Asian group	1883/1986
2651	2.11.2	OTAN/Asian Group	1985/1986
2654	2.12	Commonwealth	1980/1986
2701	4.3	Relations USA/Asia-Pacific	1985/1986
2717	6.3.2	Relations ASEAN and its neighbours	1980/1986
2770	9.3.1	Forum of the Pacific 14th meeting in Canberra	August 1983

© The Editor(s) (if applicable) and The Author(s), under exclusive
license to Springer Nature Switzerland AG 2019
P. Soyez, *Australia and France's Mutual Empowerment*,
Studies in Diplomacy and International Relations,
https://doi.org/10.1007/978-3-030-13449-5

270 APPENDIX—LIST OF ARCHIVES

Australia

2838	4.1	National defence, weapons/military strategy	1980/1986
2841	6	Atomic questions	1980/1986
2842	6.1	Nuclear questions	1980/1986
	6.2	Aus. nuclear activities	1980/1982
2851	7.5	Multilateral eco coop Mines/oil/energy	1980/1986
2852	8.1	Foreign policies	1980/1986
2853	8.1	South Pacific Disarmament	1980/1986
2854	8.2	Relations with ASEAN	1980/1986
2855	8.3	Relations with Chine	1980/1986
2857	8.3	Relations with Japan and Indonesia	1980/1986
2858	8.3	Relations with UK	1980/1986
2859	8.4	Relations with USA	1980/1984
2860	8.4	Relations with USA	1985/1986
2864	9.4	Relations with France	1985/1986
2866	9.4	Consultation Fr-Aus Disarm and non-proliferation	February 1984
2868	9.4	Nuclear Testings	1985/1986
2869	9.4.1	New Caledonia	1985/1986

Economic division, economic and financial issues no. 77 1984–1986

2380	VI.655.7	Australia	1985

French Ministry of Foreign Affairs Archives Nantes

Consular Archives:
French Consulate, Melbourne 1854–1991

124	Military issue	1967–1991
125	Cultural issues (French–Australian relations)	1955–1988
131	General economic issues	1979–1988
	Political issues (French presence in Pacific)	1930–1951
132	Political issues (local reactions to French nuclear policies)	1966–1985

French Consulate, Melbourne 1989–1996

156	Economic and financial issues	1988–1996
157	Economic and financial issues	1989–1996
164	Culture and education	1987–1996

APPENDIX—LIST OF ARCHIVES 271

Multilateral Institutions:
French Embassy to the UN, New York, up to 1985

507 B.3.54.1.1	Conference on nuclear energy's peaceful uses	1983–1984
513 B.3.61.1	Pacific territories decolonisation	1978–1981
536 B.3.81.3	Comity preparing the UN conference on cooperation on nuclear energy's pacific uses	1981–1985
632	French nuclear testings and NPT	1975–1985
633	Idem + Nuclear free Pacific	1975–1985
694 B.8.2.2	Countries	1980–1985

French Embassy to the UN, Geneva, up to 1990

36	4th conf on nuclear energy's pacific uses	1971
37	Nuclear energy and nuclear testings	1958–1989
542	WHO in the Pacific region	1950–1989
616	About Secretariat of the Pacific Community	1970–1990
681 91	Australia	1982–1989

French Embassy to the ESCAP (Economic and Social Commission for Asia and the Pacific) up to 1999

19	38th–43rd meetings	1982–1987
20	44th meeting in Jakarta	1988
21	Idem	
22	Idem	
23	Idem	
24	45th meeting in Bangkok	1989
25	Idem	
26	46th meeting	1990
27	Idem	
28	Idem	
29	47th meeting	1991
30	48th meeting	1992
31	Idem	
32	49th meeting	1993
33	Idem	
34	50th meeting	1994
35	51st meeting	1995
36	52nd meeting	1996
37	53rd meeting	1997
38	54th meeting	1998
39	55th meeting	1999

272   APPENDIX—LIST OF ARCHIVES

79	Environmental issues	1985–1995
80	Environmental issues	1985–1990
81	Idem	1993–1997
98	Natural resources	1982–1983
99	Idem	1984–1987
100	Idem	1988–1998
101	16th meeting, natural resources	1991
105	Questions of energy	1986–1993

French Embassy to the Secretariat of the Pacific Community, Noumea, up to 1998

79	17th conference of the SPC	1977
141	26th and 27th conf in French Polynesia	1986–1987
142	28th conference in Rarotonga, Cooks Islands	1988
143	29th conference in Guam	1989
144	30th conference in Noumea	1990
145	31st conference in Tonga	1991
146	32nd and 33rd conference in Fiji and Noumea	1992–1993
147	34th, 35th, 36th conferences	1994–1996
148	37th conference in Canberra	1997
161	Issues of energy	1988–1997
164	French position to the SPC	1987–1988
167	Relations between SPC and Pacific Forum	1987–1997

French National Archives—Pierrefitte

Ministry of French Overseas Territories
Cabinet and divisions advising the Minister: Cabinet 1986–1988

	- Geographic Files	
	- New Caledonia	
19980589/9	Expulsion of the Australian General Consulate in Noumea	1986–1987
	- Thematic Files	
	- Contextual Matters	
19980589/6	SPC	1986

Cabinet and divisions advising the Minister: Cabinet 1988–1993

- Minister's archives
- International Relations

19940509/50	Bob Hawke's visit to New Caledonia	July 1990
19940509/51	South Pacific	1989–1990
19940509/52	Advisory notes for the reception of the French Ambassador to Australia	1991
	- States visits in French Overseas Territories	
19940509/41	Minister's visit to New Zealand	1992
	- Cabinet Directors' Archives: Alain Christnacht	
	- Geographic Files	
19940509/80	New Caledonia	1988–1991
19940509/81	New Caledonia and Polynesia	1988–1991
19940509/82	Polynesia	1987–1991
	- Foreign Policy	
19940509/95	Relations between France and other States of the South Pacific	1987–1990

Cabinet and divisions advising the Minister: Cabinet 1981–1995

	- Minister's Secretariat Archives	
	- Official visits overseas	
19970557/9	Minister's visit to Australia and New Zealand Meeting with Keating, Evans and Bilney	September 1994

Cabinet and divisions advising the Minister: Cabinet 1997–2000

	- Thierry Lataste's files as cabinet director	
	- Meetings	
20010326/5	Minister's meeting with French ambassador to the SPC	1997
	Minister's meeting with French ambassador to Australia	1997
	Minister's meeting with French Representative to the Forum about cooperation	1997
20010326/6	Minister's meeting with Australian ambassador to France	1997
	- Geographic files	
20010326/22	Documents dealing with the South Pacific	1997–1998

Political, administrative and financial division, sub-division for political matters

	- Relations with non-European States	
	- Pacific	
19980006/7	Nuclear issues	1980–1989
19980006/8	French–Australian relations	1983–1989
	- Nouvelle-Calédonie	

274 APPENDIX—LIST OF ARCHIVES

19980006/15	International reactions about tensions regarding independence	1986–1989
	- Relations with international organisations	
	-UN	
19980006/17	Discussions about the status of New Caledonia	1986–1987
	-SPC	
19980006/22	SPC's activities	1983–1992
	- Forum of the South Pacific	
19980006/21	Forum Meetings including one in Canberra	1981–1986
	- Regional cooperation	
	- Pacific	
19980006/32	International cooperation in the Pacific	1978–1987

Prime Minister

Prime Minister; Prime Minister Cabinet and dependent divisions 1988–1991

	- Documentations, visits and meetings	
19930409/3	Visit of Rocard to Australia	August 1989
19930409/4	Australia, meetings with Keating and Evans	1988–1991
	- South Pacific	
19930409/22	Secretariat of the Pacific Community Regional situation	1988–1991
	- Trade/environment	
19930409/27	Environmental protection in South Pacific	1989–1990

Prime Minister; Prime Minister Cabinet and dependent divisions; Cabinet; Council 1992–1993

| 19950484/2 | Soeharto's State visit to Mitterand | November 1992 |

Prime Minister; Prime Minister Cabinet and dependent divisions; Cabinet; Technical advisor 1992–1995

| 19970446/2 | Australia | 1992–1995 |

Prime Minister; Prime Minister Cabinet and dependent divisions; Cabinet; Technical advisor 1995–1997

| 20000310/2 | Australia | 1995–1997 |

APPENDIX—LIST OF ARCHIVES 275

Prime Minister; Prime Minister Cabinet and dependent divisions 1997–2002

20030440/4	Jospin's visit to New Caledonia	1998

Prime Minister; Prime Minister Cabinet and dependent divisions; Cabinet; Technical advisor 1997–2002

20050038/6	Description of Australia's diplomacy	1997–2002

Fonds Michel Rocard 1953–2013

	- MR, Minister	
	- Prime Minister	
680AP/22	Rocard's visit to the South Pacific	1989
	- MR, European Deputy	
	- Independent Groups	
680AP/40	*International Crisis Group*'s administration *Group*, report with Gareth Evans	2000
680AP/47	*Pacific Economic Cooperation Council*	1988–2008
	Rocard's visits and activity reports	
	- European and International affairs (thematic files, international questions, nuclear disarmament)	
680AP/118	Rocard's implication for nuclear disarmament, documents from the Australian government	1992–2011
	- European and International affairs (thematic files, crises and conflicts resolutions, international thematic files)	
680AP/93 à 97	Canberra Commission	1969–2009

National Australian Archives—Canberra

DFAT—Central Office—Agency CA 5987

- Series AWM260	Peacekeeping operation, miscellaneous records 1949–1988 (Australian War Memorial)

276   APPENDIX—LIST OF ARCHIVES

8721494	United Nations Truce Supervision Organisation Miscellaneous correspondence including Operations briefings, equipment recognition guide and unit recognition	1985–1988
8721493	United Nations Truce Supervision Organisation Miscellaneous correspondence, The Empty Page—Observer Group Lebanon official newsletter	1987–1989
8723971	Operation Fino—Vanuatu: Director-General, Operations and Plans—Army	1980–1981
8723970	Operation Fino—Vanuatu: Director-General, Operations and Plans—Army	1980
	- Series M2391	Folders containing copies of inward correspondence to Evans as Minister for Foreign Affairs and Trade 1971–1989

Study of folders 1–141

	- Series M3179	Papers relating to Evans overseas visits 1972–1999
5	Visit to New Caledonia	September 1988
8	Visit to Fiji	September 1988
10	Visit to South Pacific—Forum Issues	September 1988
11	Visit to New Zealand	September 1988
12	Visit to New York and Washington	October 1988
13	United Nations General Assembly 43rd Session	1988
14	UN General Assembly 43rd Session	1988
15	UNGA Overview, objectives and meeting with UN Secretary General	October 1988
16	UNGA—Part 2- Bilateral meetings	October 1988
34	Visit to China	January 1989
35	Japan—Country Brief	January 1989
50	Visit to Western Europe—Round Up Brief	March 1989
51	Visit to Western Europe—Background Papers	March 1989
55	Visit to France	March 1989
57	Visit to the European Community	March 1989
58	Brief for Meeting with UN Secretary General	March 1989
59	Brief for Visit to the United States Vol I Bilateral Issues and Background Notes—New York and Washington	March 1989
60	Brief for Visit to the US Vol 1 New York and Washington	March 1989
64	Visit to Western Europe—Round Up Brief	June 1989

APPENDIX—LIST OF ARCHIVES   277

65	Visit to Western Europe—Round Up Brief	June 1989
75	ASEAN Post Ministerial Conf—Aus Delegation Brief	July 1989
80	Visit to South Pacific—Regional Issues	July 1989
90	International Conference on Cambodia, Paris	August 1989
91	International Conference on Cambodia—Paris	August 1989
92	International Conference on Cambodia—Paris	August 1989
93	International Conference on Cambodia—Paris	August 1989
94	Visit to the 44th United Nations General Assembly	1989
95	UNGA Bilateral Meetings: Briefing Papers Part 1	1989
96	UNGA Bilateral Meetings: Briefing Papers Part 2	1989
97	UNGA Bilateral Meetings: Country Background Papers	1989
98	UNGA Bilateral Meetings: Country Background Papers	1989
99	UNGA Bilateral Meetings: Country Background Papers	1989
100	UNGA Bilateral Meetings: Country Background Papers	1989
110	Visit to Europe—NATO, G24 and Country Briefs	December 1989
111	Visit to Europe—NATO, G24 and Country Briefs	December 1989
300	New Caledonia	1988
312	EC-M1NS Brussels	June 1990
314	G24 Brussells	December 1989
315	Brussells	1989
438	Trip Files—France	August 1989
439	Trip files—France and Yugoslavia	August 1989

	- Series M3793	Papers relating to overseas visits 1960–1988	
Box	Record item		
1	[1]	Brief for the Counterpart Talks between the Foreign Ministers of Australia and Japan	January 1987
	[2]	9th Australia/Japan Ministerial Committee, Background Brief	January 1987
	[3]	Ninth Australia/Japan Ministerial Committee, Ministerial Brief	January 1987
	[4]	Visit of Mr. Bill Hayden, MP, to New Zealand, 10–13 December 1986, Brief	
	[5]	Visit of Mr. Bill Hayden, MP, to New Zealand, 10–13 December 1986, Background Brief	

278   APPENDIX—LIST OF ARCHIVES

	[6]	Brief Australia-European Communities Ministerial Consultation, Canberra	November 1986
	[7]	Mr. Bill Hayden, MP, Visit to Singapore, Brief	5–7 October 1986
	[8]	Mr. Bill Hayden, MP, Minister for Foreign Affairs, Bilateral Meetings at UNGA 41, Briefing Notes	9 October 1986
	[9]	ASEAN Post Ministerial Meeting Six Plus Six, Six Plus One, Singapore	June 1987
2	[10]	Aid Brief for Visit to PNG by Mr. Bill Hayden, MP	September 1986
	[11]	Brief for Visit to PNG by Hon Bill Hayden, MP, Minister for Foreign Affairs	September 1986
	[12]	Brief for Minister for DFAT, Vienna	September 1986
	[13]	Forum Ministerial Meeting on New Caledonia Auckland, <u>documents partly released only</u>	March 1987
	[14]	Visit by the Minister for Foreign Affairs Mr. Bill Hayden, MP, to Torres Strait	April 1987
	[16]	Thirty First Regular Session of the General Conference of the IAEA, Brief for the Australian Delegation	September 1987
	[17]	Documents Brief, OECD Ministerial Council Meeting 1987	
	[18]	Brief for the Minister for Foreign Affairs, Mr. Bill Hayden,MP, OECD Ministerial Council Meeting, Paris	May 1987
	[19]	Brief for the Minister for Foreign Affairs, Mr. Bill Hayden, MP, OECD Ministerial Council Meeting, Paris	May 1987
3	[21]	ASEAN Post Ministerial Conference (Bilateral Briefs and additional material), Singapore, Australian Delegation Brief, Vol 2	June 1987
	[22]	Briefing Notes for the Minister for FA, Mr. Bill Hayden, MP, OECD Ministerial Council Meeting, Paris	May 1984
	[23]	Visit to Europe and the USSR by Mr. Bill Hayden, 7 May 1984, International Issues	
	[25]	Briefing Notes for Mr. Bill Hayden, MP, Minister for Foreign Affairs, Visit to Tokyo	April 1984
	[26]	Minister's Brief, Australia–European Communities Ministerial Consultation, Canberra	March 1984

APPENDIX—LIST OF ARCHIVES **279**

	[27]	Submission to the Joint Committee on For Aff and Defence Sub-Committee on Aus. and ASEAN (draft)	March 1984
	[28]	ASEAN–Australia Foreign Ministers' Meeting, Jakarta,	July 1984
4	[37]	Visit to South Asia by the Minister for Foreign Affairs, Mr. Bill Hayden, India	1985
5	[40]	Brief for the Fortieth Session of the United Nations General Assembly	
	[42]	Review of ASEAN and ASEAN–Australia Relations	March 1985
	[43]	Visit to South Asia by the Minister for Foreign Affairs, Mr. Bill Hayden, MP, Pakistan	May 1985
	[45]	Australia/China Disarmament and Arms Control Talks, Canberra, Brief	July 1985
6	[50]	Brief for Mr. Hayden's Visit to Vietnam	March 1985
	[51]	Brief for Mr. Hayden's Visit to Malaysia	March 1985
	[52]	Regional Issues Brief for Mr. Hayden's visit to Malaysia, Singapore, Thailand, Laos and Vietnam	March 1985
	[53]	Brief for Mr. Hayden's Visit to Singapore	March 1985
	[54]	Background Brief for the Visit to Australia by His Exc Prof. Dr. Kusumaatmadja, Indonesian Foreign Minister	December 1985
	[55]	Issues Brief for the Visit to Australia by His Exc. Prof. Dr. Kusumaatmadja, Indonesian Foreign Minister	December 1985
	[57]	Brief for Mr. Bill Hayden's Visit to Washington, DC	October 1985
	[63]	Summary record (Australian Delegation) Australia–United States Ministerial Talks, Canberra	July 1985
9	[87]	Brief for the Australian Delegation to the Fifteenth Special Session of the UN General Assembly, 3rd Special Session Devoted to Disarmament, New York	June 1988
	[88]	Briefing Notes for the Minister for DFAT Mr. Bill Hayden MP, OECD Ministerial Council Meeting, Paris,	May 1988
	[89]	Briefing Notes for the Minister for Foreign Affairs and Trade, Mr. Bill Hayden, MP, OECD Council Meeting, Paris, Policy Papers Brief	May 1988

280 APPENDIX—LIST OF ARCHIVES

	[90]	Australia–EC Annual Consultations, Canberra, Background Brief	May 1988
	[91]	Briefing for Mr. Hayden's Visit to Italy	May 1988
	[92]	Visit to Australia by the Hon Donald Kalpokas, Minister of Foreign Aff and Judicial Services of the Rep of Vanuatu	June 1988
	[93]	Documents Brief, OECD Ministerial Council Meeting	1988
	[94]	Briefing for Mr. Hayden's Visit to Norway	May 1988
	[95]	Issues Brief for the Visit to China of Mr. Bill Hayden, Minister for Foreign Affairs and Trade and Mrs. Hayden	July 1988
	[96]	Australia–EC Annual Consultations, Canberra, Ministerial Brief	May 1988
	[97]	Background Briefing for Minister for Trade Negotiations, Foreign Policy Issues Part 1	July 1987
	[98]	Background Briefing for Minister for Trade Negotiations, Foreign Policy Issues Part 2	July 1987
10	[99]	Background briefing for Minister for Trade Negotiations, Foreign Policy Issues Part 3	1987
	[100]	Briefing for Mr. Hayden's Visit to Italy	1988
	[101]	Briefing for Mr. Hayden's Visit to Poland	November 1987
	[102]	South Pacific Heads of Mission, Chairman's Brief, Canberra, ~~document partly released only~~	November 1987
	[103]	Brief for Mr. Bill Hayden, MP, for the Visit to Australia by Hon Russell Marshall, New Zealand Minister of Foreign Affairs and Minister for Disarmament, Canberra	October 1987
	[104]	Brief for Mr. Bill Hayden, MP, Minister for Foreign Affairs and Trade, Visit by Lord Glenarthur, Minister of State at the Foreign and Commonwealth Office	October 1987
	[106]	Itinerary, Mr. Bill Hayden, MP, Minister for Foreign Affairs, visit to United Kingdom, France, The Netherlands, Hungary, Soviet Union, India and Thailand	June 1984
	[108]	Australia–EC Annual Consultations, Brussels, Ministerial Brief	October 1987
13	[138]	Ministerial Brief US/Australia Ministerial Trade Talks, Canberra	January 1988
14	[145]	Brief for the 41st Session of the UN General Assembly 1986	

APPENDIX—LIST OF ARCHIVES   281

	[147]	Discussions between Mr. Bill Hayden, MP, and Canadian Secretary of State for External Affairs, the Rt Hon Joe Clarke, Vancouver	August 1986
	[148]	Australian Joint Party Delegation Visit to Washington	July 1986
	[149]	Volume 1 ASEAN Post Ministerial Conference (Six Plus Six, Six Plus One, and Bilateral Meetings) Manila, Australian Delegation Brief	June 1986
	[150]	Volume 2 ASEAN Post Ministerial Conference (Background) Manila, Australian Delegation Brief	June 1986
15	[161]	Country Brief: Mr. Hayden's Visit to the South Pacific, Solomon Islands	May 1986
	[162]	Mr. Hayden's Visit to the South Pacific, General Background Brief	May 1986
	[163]	Mr. Hayden's Visit to the South Pacific Country Brief: Tonga	May 1986
	[166]	Blue folder entitled "Mr. Eglis Burtmanis" Australia–United States Ministerial Talks, San Francisco	August 1986
	[167]	Australia–United States Ministerial Talks, SF	August 1986
	[168]	Background Brief for the Minister for Foreign Aff, Mr. Bill Hayden, MP, Visit to Malaysia	March 1986
	[169]	Issues Brief for the Minister for Foreign Affairs, Mr. Bill Hayden, MP, Visit to Malaysia	March 1986
	[170]	Issues Brief for the Minister for Foreign Affairs, Mr. Bill Hayden, MP, Visit to Indonesia	March 1986
	[171]	Background Brief for the Minister for Foreign Affairs Mr. Bill Hayden, MP, Visit to Indonesia	March 1986
	[172]	Issues Brief for the Minister for Foreign Affairs, Mr. Bill Hayden, MP, Visit to Singapore	March 1986
	[173]	Mr. Hayden's Visit to the South Pacific, Country Brief: Fiji	March 1986
16	[190]	Visit to Canberra of Dr. Blix, Director General, IAEA, General Brief	1988
17	[194]	Visit to Japan by Mr. Bill Hayden, MP, Minister for Foreign Affairs and Trade, Part 2, Background Papers	April 1988

282   APPENDIX—LIST OF ARCHIVES

	[195]	Visit to Japan by Mr. Bill Hayden, MP, Minister for Foreign Affairs and Trade and Mrs. Hayden, Part 1, Brief	April 1988
	[198]	Visit to the Republic of Korea by Mr. Bill Hayden, MP, Minister for Foreign Affairs and Trade	April 1988
	[199]	Visit to the Republic of Korea by Mr. Bill Hayden, MP, Minister for Foreign Affairs and Trade,	April 1988
22	[238]	Prime Minister's Brief, 18th South Pacific Forum, Apia,	1987
23	[246]	Brief for Australia/US Ministerial Talks, Volume 1, HMAS Watson, Sydney,	June 1987
	[247]	Records of Prime Minister's Conversations 1985—Background notes on Cambodia for Debate on 19 March—Papers re: Ministerial responsibility	
	[248]	ASEAN Post Ministerial Conference, Australian Delegation Brief, Bangkok	July 1988
	[249]	Joint communique after Australian–United States Ministerial talks at Sydney	June 1987
	[250]	Brief for Australia/US Ministerial talks, Volume 1, HMAS Watson, Sydney	June 1987
	[252]	ASEAN Post Ministerial Conference, Australian Delegation Brief, Bilateral Meetings, Bangkok	July 1988
24	[253]	Review of the Aus–NZ Closed Economic Relations Trade Agreement, Ministerial Meeting Minister's Brief	1988
-	Series M4438	Subject correspondence maintained as Deputy Prime Minister and Minister for Trade 1996–1999	
-	Series M4439	Subject correspondence maintained as Deputy Prime Minister and Minister for Trade 1996–1999	
-	Series M4570	Correspondence on trade and agreements 1996–1999	
-	Series M4591	General correspondence maintained as Minister of Trade 1996–1999	

	- Series A9737 Correspondence files	1925–1992
8266994	France—Political and General	1987–1991
30710948	International trade law—science and tech agreements	1987–1992
8265824	USA—Disarmament and Arms Control	1987–1988
8259934	Fiji—Immigration Policy	1987–1991
8263539	Peace Research Including SIPRI (Stockholm International Peace Research Institute) and UNIDIR (United Nations Institute for Disarmament Research)	1987–1992
8262608	ASEAN—Summit Meeting	1987–1989
8266867	USA—Australian Defence Cooperation—Australian Liaison with CINCPAC (Commander in Chief, Pacific Command)	1987–1988

APPENDIX—LIST OF ARCHIVES **283**

30713362	New Caledonia—political developments	1987–1988
30710141	Major power relations—international economy	1987–1989
30712957	Norway—Australia relations	1987–1989
30712920	France—relations with New Zealand	1987–1990
8269342	Defence—Relations with Australia—USA	1987–1989
8259758	New Caledonia—Economic Developments (including policy and assessments)	1987–1992
8258064	South Pacific Regional Organisations—FFA Policy Membership Meetings	1987–1988
8259514	Aid to PNG	1987–1988
8266603	Vanuatu—Counter Terrorism—Relations with Australia	1987–1988
30712964	United Kingdom—representation in Australia	1987–1993
8255562	European Community—Pol Coordination Cooperation	1987–1988
30714561	France disarmament and arms control	1987–1988
8253011	France—New Caledonia—UN Re-Inscription	1987–1991
8259790	New Caledonia—UN Aspects	1987/1988
8260161	Australia Relations with New Zealand—COCOM (Coordinating Committee on Multilateral Export Controls)	1987/1989
30713348	New Caledonia—assessments and briefing material	1987–1988
30710110	Major power relations—North Asia incl Northern Territories	1987–1993
8257368	Political Matters—USA	1987–1990
8258547	United Nations Disarmament—Nuclear Free Zone	1987–1988
8266872	USA—Australian Defence Cooperation—USA Projects in Australia—General Policy Considerations	1987–1988
30713732	ANZUS_NZS (NZ security)	1987–1988
30713358	New Caledonia—South Pacific forum bilateral relations	
8264844	Indonesia—Relations with ASEAN	1987–1990
8266819	PNG (Papua New Guinea)—Relations with Australia	1987–1988
8268946	France—Relations with South Pacific	1987–1988
8266579	Counter Terrorism—Cooperation with other countries	1987–1988
30709643	Defence Cooperation with PNG (Papua New Guinea)	1987–1990

Department of the Prime Minister and Cabinet—Agency CA 1401

	- Series M3571	1983–1991
	Foreign Affairs and Defence papers containing some classified material maintained by the PM	
163	New Zealand Ship Visits	1984–1991
339	Defence Matters	1983–1985
340	ANZUS	1985
342	Media releases, Interviews and Correspondence regarding the Fiji Coup	1987

284 APPENDIX—LIST OF ARCHIVES

	- Series M3856	1983–1991
	Overseas visits, background notes, letters of thanks, transcripts of speeches	
55	Overseas Trips—South Pacific Forum	5 June 1987
56	South Pacific Forum, Draft Forum Communique	May 1987
60	Overseas visit, CHOGM, Vancouver	October 1987
96	Supplementary briefs for PM's visit to France, UK USA, the Federal Republic of Germany and Hungary	June 1989
97	Overseas trips, France, UK, USA, Hungary, Germany	June 1989
98	Briefs visit France, UK, USA, Hungary, Germany	July 1989
116	Overseas visit by the Hon RJL Hawke to France	1983
122	Visit to Papua New Guinea by the Hon RJL Hawke	September 1985
124	Overseas visit by the Hon RJL Hawke to Washington DC	April 1986
125	Overseas visit by the Hon RJL Hawke to Brussels	April 1986
126	Program of the visit to Italy of the Hon Hawke, Rome	April 1986
131	Overseas visit by the Hon.RJL Hawke to South Pacific Forum, Apia, Western Samoa	May 1987
136	Overseas visit by the Hon RIL Hawke France, United Kingdom, United States of America, Federal Republic of Germany, Peoples Republic of Hungary	June 1989
137	Overseas visit by the Hon RJL Hawke to the South Pacific Forum	July 1989

BIBLIOGRAPHY

Aldrich, R 1994, *France and the South Pacific Since 1940*, Macmillan, London.

Alomes, S & Provis, M 1998, *French Worlds—Pacific Worlds, French Nuclear Testing in Australia's Backyard*, Two Rivers Press, Melbourne.

Althaus, C, Bridgman, P & Davis, G 2013, *The Australian Policy Handbook*, Allen & Unwin, Sydney.

Al Wardi, S, Regnault, J-M & Sabouret, J-F 2017, *L'Océanie convoitée, Histoire, géopolitique et sociétés*, CNRS Éditions, Paris.

Anderson, B 1983, *Imagined Communities*, Verso, London.

Angleviel, F 2015, *Un drame de la colonisation, Ouvéa, Nouvelle-Calédonie, mai 1988*, Vendémiaire, Paris.

Antheaume, B & Bonnemaison, J 1988, *Atlas des îles des États du Pacifique Sud*, GIP Reclus/Publisud, Paris.

Argounès, F 2006, *Géopolitique de l'Australie*, Complexe, Bruxelles.

Argounès, F 2011, 'L'Australie, entre puissance moyenne et puissance régionale: une analyse réaliste néoclassique', Thesis (Ph.D.), Université Bordeaux 4, Bordeaux, France.

Argounès, F 2012, 'L'Australie: la tentation de la puissance régionale', *Pouvoirs*, vol. 2, no. 141, pp. 103–116.

AusAID 2006, *Pacific 2020: Challenges and Opportunities for Growth*, AusAID, Canberra.

Australian Department of Defence 2016, *Defence White Paper*, Australian Department of Defence, Canberra.

© The Editor(s) (if applicable) and The Author(s), under exclusive license to Springer Nature Switzerland AG 2019
P. Soyez, *Australia and France's Mutual Empowerment*,
Studies in Diplomacy and International Relations,
https://doi.org/10.1007/978-3-030-13449-5

286 BIBLIOGRAPHY

Australian Department of Foreign Affairs and Trade 2016, 'Wallis and Futuna Country Brief', viewed 17th July 2017, http://dfat.gov.au/geo/wallis-futuna/Pages/wallis-and-futuna-country-brief.aspx.

Australian Department of Foreign Affairs and Trade 2017, *Foreign Policy White Paper*, Australian Department of Foreign Affairs and Trade, Canberra.

Badel, L 2006, 'Pour une histoire de la diplomatie économique de la France', *Revue d'histoire du Vingtième siècle*, vol. 2, no. 90, pp. 169–185.

Baldino, D 2005, 'Australia and the World', in C Aulich & R Wettenhall (eds), *Howard's Second and Third Governments*, Australian National University Press, Canberra, pp. 189–207.

Baldino, D, Carr, A & Langlois, AJ 2014, *Australian Foreign Policy, Controversies and Debates*, Oxford University Press, Oxford.

Ball, D & Richelson, JT 1985, *The Ties That Bind*, Allen & Unwin, Sydney.

Bandel, N, Blanchard, P & Lemaire, S 2005, *La Fracture coloniale: la société française au prisme de l'héritage colonial*, La Découverte, Paris.

Bayne, N & Woolcock, S 2011, *New Economic Diplomacy, Decision-Making and Negotiation in International Economic Relations*, Ashgate, London.

Beasley, C 2014, 'The Breaking of the "Great Australian Silence": How and Why the Writing of Indigenous Australian History Has Changed Over the Last 40 Years', *The ANU Undergraduate Research Journal*, vol. 5, Australian National University Press, Canberra.

Beazley, K 2003, 'The Hawke Years: Foreign Affairs and Defence', in S Ryan & T Bramston (eds), *The Hawke Government, a Critical Retrospective*, Pluto Press, Melbourne, pp. 347–366.

Beeson, M 2003, 'Australia's Relationship with the United States: The Case for Greater Independence', *Australian Journal of Political Science*, vol. 38, no. 3, pp. 387–405.

Beeson, M 2008, *Institutions of the Asia-Pacific, ASEAN, APEC, and Beyond*, Routledge, London and New York.

Beeson, M 2014, 'The Rise of the Indo-Pacific', *The Conversation*, 3 May, viewed 30 October 2017, http://theconversation.com/the-rise-of-the-indo-pacific-26271.

Beeson, M & Hameiri, S 2017, *Navigating the New International Disorder, Australia in World Affairs 2011–2015*, Oxford Press, Oxford.

Bevir, M & Rhodes, R 2012, 'Interpretivism and the Analysis of Traditions and Practices', *Critical Policy Studies*, vol. 6, no. 2, pp. 201–208.

Bizley, N 2017, 'Julie Bishop's Washington Mission: Find Out Who's Running the Show', *The Interpreter*, 22 February, viewed 1 November 2017, https://www.lowyinstitute.org/the-interpreter/julie-bishops-washington-mission-find-out-whos-running-show.

Blainey, G 1983, *The Tyranny of Distance*, Sun Books, Sydney.

BIBLIOGRAPHY 287

Boniface, P 1995, 'Dissuasion et non-prolifération: un équilibre difficile, nécessaire mais rompu', *Politique étrangère*, vol. 60, no. 3, pp. 707–721.

Boniface, P 1998, *La France est-elle encore une grande puissance?* Presses de Sciences Po, Paris.

Botterill, L 2003, *From Back Jack McEwen to the Cairns Group Reform in Australian Agricultural Policy*, Australian National University Center for European Studies, Canberra.

Bourke, J 2005, *Fear, a cultural History*, Virago, London.

Boyce, J 2011, *1835 The Founding of Melbourne and the Conquest of Australia*, Black Inc., Carlton.

Bozo, F 2012, *La politique étrangère de la France depuis 1945*, Flammarion, Paris.

Brenner, N 1999, 'Globalisation as Reterritorialization: The Re-scaling of Urban Governance in the European Union', *Urban Studies*, vol. 36, no. 3, pp. 431–451.

Broinowski, A 2003, *Howard's War*, Scribe, Melbourne.

Broinowski, A 2007, *Allied and Addicted*, Scribe, Melbourne.

Brown, P 2005, 'Australie-France: année de grandes rencontres', *L'Année Francophone Internationale 2015–2016*, viewed 28th November 2017, http://www.agora-francophone.org/afi/afi-no24-2015-2016/pays-regions-24/article/australie-par-peter-brown.

Brown, A 2010, 'The Gorbachev Revolution and the End of the Cold War', in MP Leffler & OA Westad (eds), *The Cambridge History of the Cold War, Endings*, Vol. III, Cambridge University Press, Cambridge, pp. 244–266.

Brown, P 2013, 'Negotiating Postcolonial Identities in the Shadow of the EU: New Caledonia', in R Adler-Nissen & UP Gad (eds), *European Integration and Postcolonial Sovereignty Games: The EU Overseas Countries and Territories*, Routledge, London, pp. 169–186.

Buzan, B, Wæver, O & de Wilde, J 1998, *Security, a New Framework for Analysis*, Lynne Riener Publishers, Boulder.

Carr, A & Robert, C 2010, 'Foreign Policy', in C Aulich & M Evans (eds), *The Rudd Government*, Australian National University Press, Canberra, pp. 241–258.

Chappell, D 1999, 'The Noumea Accord: Decolonisation Without Independence in New Caledonia?', *Pacific Affairs*, vol. 72, no. 3, pp. 373–391.

Checkel, J 1998, 'The Constructivist Turns in International Relations Theory', *World Politics*, vol. 50, no. 2, pp. 324–348.

Choi, Y 2007, 'L'importance de l'Union européenne dans les territoires français du Pacifique' *Pouvoir(s) et politique(s) en Océanie, actes du XIXe colloque CORAIL*, L'Harmattan, Paris, pp. 151–163.

288 BIBLIOGRAPHY

Clark, M & Pietsch, J 2012, 'Democratisation and Indonesia's Changing Perceptions of ASEAN and Its Alternatives', in D Novotny & C Portela (eds), *EU–ASEAN Relations in the 21st Century: Strategic Partnership in the Making*, Palgrave Macmillan, Basingstoke and New York, pp. 45–61.

Colás, A 2002, *International Civil Society, Social Movements in World Politics*, Polity Press, Cambridge.

Commissions des Affaires étrangères de l'Assemblée nationale 1995, *Rapport d'information sur les réactions internationales à la reprise par la France des essais nucléaires*, Assemblée nationale française, Paris.

Commissions des Affaires étrangères, de la Défense et des Forces armées du Senat français 1997, 'L'Australie et la Nouvelle-Zélande, têtes de pont de la présence française dans la région Asie-Pacifique?', *Rapport d'information no. 290*, Sénat français, Paris.

Commissions des Affaires étrangères du Sénat français 2017, 'Australie : le rôle de la France dans le nouveau monde', *Rapport d'information no. 222*, Sénat français, Paris.

Commission des Finances du Sénat français 1997, Un «océan de fertilité» pour l'économie française? Leçons d'une mission sur le commerce extérieur au Japon, en Australie et en Nouvelle-Zélande, *Rapport d'information no. 27*, Sénat français, Paris.

Cook, M & Dalrymple, R 2014, 'Relations with Indonesia', in D Baldino, A Carr, AJ Langlois (eds), *Australian Foreign Policy, Controversies and Debates*, Oxford University Press, Oxford, pp. 155–173.

Coquery-Vidrovitch, C 2011, 'Colonisation, racisme et roman national en France', *Canadian Journal of African Studies*, vol. 45, no. 1, pp. 17–44.

Cordonnier, I 1995, *La France dans le Pacifique sud: approche géostratégique*, Publisud, Paris.

Cot, JP 1973, 'Affaire des Essais nucléaires (Australie c. France et Nouvelle-Zélande c. France). Demandes en indication de mesures conservatoires. Ordonnances du 22 juin 1973', *Annuaire français de droit international*, vol. 19, pp. 252–271.

Cotton, J & Ravenhill, J 2007, *The National Interest in a Global Era, Australia in World Affairs 2001–2005*, Oxford University Press, Oxford.

Crouzet, C 2009, 'L'outre-mer coûte près de sept milliards à l'État', *Le Figaro*, 11 February, viewed 17 July 2017, http://www.lefigaro.fr/economie/2009/02/11/04001-20090211ARTFIG00602-l-outre-mer-coute-pres-de-sept-milliards-a-l-etat-.php.

Dancer, M 2017, 'La France attire de plus en plus d'investissements étrangers', *La Croix*, 23 May, viewed 8 November 2017, https://www.la-croix.com/Economie/France/France-attire-dinvestissements-etrangers-2017-05-23-1200849374.

Danielsson, B & M-T 1993, *Mururoa, notre bombe coloniale: histoire de la colonisation nucléaire de la Polynésie française*, L'Harmattan, Paris.

David, D 1995, 'La France et le monde: inventaire après essais', *Études*, vol. 383, no. 6, pp. 581–590.

Davies, A 2017, 'A Fall-Back Option for the Future Submarines?', *ASPI The Strategist*, 3 October, viewed 8 November 2017, https://www.aspistrategist. org.au/a-fall-back-option-for-the-future-submarines/.

Davis Cross, MK 2011, 'Europe, a Smart Power?', *International Politics*, vol. 48, no. 6, pp. 691–706.

Davison, R & Khan, S 2014, 'ANZUS and the Rise of China', in D Baldino, A Carr, AJ Langlois (eds), *Australian Foreign Policy, Controversies and Debates*, Oxford University Press, Oxford, pp. 136–154.

De Montbrial, T & Gomart, T 2017, *Notre intérêt national, quelle politique étrangère pour la France?* Odile Jacob, Paris.

Derville, G 1996, 'Quand la machine médiatique s'emballe', *Communication et langages*, vol. 109, no. 1, pp. 17–32.

Deutsch, K 1968, *The Analysis of International Relations*, Prentice Hall International, Englewood Cliffs.

Devin, G 2002, 'Les diplomaties de la politique étrangère', in F Chatillon (ed), *Politique étrangère, nouveaux regards*, Presses de Sciences Po, Paris, pp. 223–225.

Di Méo, G 1996, *Les territoires du quotidien*, L'Harmattan, Paris.

Dinnie, K 2016, *Nation Branding, Concepts, Issues, Practice*, Routledge, London.

Downer, A 2000, 'Australia's Global Agenda, Speech to French Institute of International Affairs', 31 January, viewed 1st August 2017, http://foreign-minister.gov.au/speeches/2000/000131_aust_global_agenda.html.

Downer, A 2001, 'Australian Foreign POLICY, a Liberal Perspective', *Australian Journal of International Affairs*, vol. 55, no. 3, pp. 337–341.

Downer, A 2005, 'Securing Australia's Interests: Australian Foreign Policy Priorities', *Australian Journal of International Affairs*, Canberra, vol. 59, no. 1, pp. 7–12.

Dumoulin, A & Wasinski, C 2010, 'Justifier l'arme nucléaire. Le cas français pendant les années 1990', *Études internationals*, vol. 41, no. 1, pp. 79–96.

Eck, J-F 2006, *La France dans la nouvelle économie mondiale*, Presses Universitaires de France, Paris.

Evans, G & Grant, B 1995, *Australia's Foreign Relations*, The University of Melbourne Press, Melbourne.

Falk, J, Green, J & Mudd, G 2006, 'Australia, Uranium and Nuclear Power', *International Journal of Environmental Studies*, Melbourne, vol. 63, no. 6, pp. 845–857.

Farge, A 2002, 'Penser et définir l'événement en histoire. Approche des situations et des acteurs sociaux', *Terrain*, no. 38, pp. 69–78.

Finlayson, A 2007, 'From Belief to Argument: Interpretive Methodology and Rhetorical Political Analysis', *British Journal of Politic and International Relations*, vol. 9, no. 4, pp. 545–563.

290 BIBLIOGRAPHY

Firth, S 2011, *Australia in International Politics*, Allen & Unwin, Sydney.

Firth, S 2016, 'Australia's Detention Centre and the Erosion of Democracy in Nauru', *The Journal of Pacific History*, vol. 51, no. 3, pp. 286–300.

Fisher, D 2013, *France in the South Pacific: Power and Politics*, Australian National University Press, Canberra.

Frank, R, Haba, K & Momose, H 2009, *The End of the Cold War and the Regional Integration*, Aoyama Gakuin University Press, Tokyo.

Fry, G 2015, 'Recapturing the Spirit of 1971: Toward a New Regional Political Settlement in the Pacific', *SSGM Discussion Paper*, vol. 3, Australian National University Press, Canberra, pp. 1–16.

Gallois, D & Taix, C 2016, 'Sous-marins vendus par DCNS à l'Australie: les coulisses d'un contrat 'historique', *Le Monde*, 26 April, viewed 17th July 2017, http://www.lemonde.fr/entreprises/article/2016/04/26/le-francais-dcns-remporte-un-megacontrat-de-sous-marins-a-34-milliards-d-euros-en-australie_4908510_1656994.html.

Garnaut, R 1989, *Australia and the Northeast Asian Ascendancy*, Australian Government Publishing Service, Canberra.

Garran, R 2004, *True Believer, John Howard, George Bush & the American alliance*, Allen & Unwin, Sydney.

Grand, C 1997, 'La diplomatie nucléaire du Président Chirac', *Relations internationales et stratégiques*, no. 25, pp. 157–169.

Gruen, F & Grattan, M 1993, *Managing Government, Labor's Achievements and Failures*, Longman Cheshire, Melbourne.

Guéhenno, J-M 1999, 'Américanisation du monde ou mondialisation de l'Amérique ?', *Politique Étrangère*, vol. 64, no. 1, pp. 7–20.

Gyngell, A 2017, *Fear of Abandonment*, Black Inc., Melbourne.

Gyngell, A & Wesley, M 2007, *Making Australian Foreign Policy*, Cambridge University Press, Cambridge.

Haas, P & Haas, E 2002, 'Pragmatic Constructivism and the Study of International Institutions', *Millennium*, vol. 31, no. 3, pp. 573–602.

Henningham, S 1992, *France and the South Pacific: A Contemporary History*, Allen & Unwin, Sydney.

Henningham, S 1996, 'Testing Times: France's Underground Nuclear Tests and Its Relations with Asia-Pacific', *Modern and Contemporary France*, vol. 4, no. 1, pp. 81–92.

Henningham, S 2017, 'The Limits of Influence: Australia and the Future of New Caledonia, 1975 to 1988', *The Journal of Pacific History*, vol. 2, no. 4, pp. 482–500.

Holm, U 2013, 'French Concepts of State: Nation, *patrie*, and the Overseas', in R Adler-Nissen & UP Gad (eds), *European Integration and Postcolonial Sovereignty Games: The EU Overseas Countries and Territories*, Routledge, London, pp. 145–151.

Hymans, JEC 2000, 'Isotopes and Identity: Australia and the Nuclear Weapons Option, 1949–1999', *The Nonproliferation Review*, vol. 7, no. 1, pp. 1–23.

Hynek, N & Teti, A 2010, 'Saving Identity from Postmodernism? The Normalisation of Constructivism in International Relations', *Contemporary Political Theory*, vol. 9, no. 2, pp. 171–199.

Institut d'Emission d'Outre-Mer 2008, *Wallis et Futuna en 2007*, Institut d'Emission d'Outre-Mer, Paris.

Jennings, P 2017, 'Australia-EU Cooperation on Security, Foreign Policy and Development', *Australian Outlook*, 5 June, viewed 3 November 2017, http://www.internationalaffairs.org.au/australianoutlook/australia-eu-security-cooperation/.

Kelly, P 1994, *The End of Certainty*, Allen & Unwin, Sydney.

Kenyon, D & Kunkel, J 2005, 'Australia and the European Union in the World Trade Organisation: Partners or Adversaries?', *Australian Journal of International Affairs*, vol. 59, no. 1, pp. 55–69.

Kessler, MC 1999, *La Politique étrangère de la France, Acteurs et processus*, Presses de Sciences Po, Paris.

Kevin, T 2004, 'Foreign Policy', in R Manne (ed), *The Howard Years*, Black Inc. Agenda, Melbourne, pp. 291–313.

Kuhn, T 1979, 'Metaphor in Science', in A Ortony (ed), *Metaphor and Thought*, Cambridge University Press, Cambridge, pp. 409–419.

Langmore, J 2005, *Dealing with America: The UN, the US and Australia*, University of New South Wales Press, Sydney.

Langmore, J 2013, 'Australia's Campaign for Security Council Membership', *Australian Journal of Political Science*, vol. 48, no. 1, pp 101–111.

Langmore, J, Frydenberg, J & Parke, M 2014, 'The Liberal/Labor Tradition', in D Baldino, A Carr, AJ Langlois (eds), *Australian Foreign Policy, Controversies and Debates*, Oxford University Press, Oxford, pp. 19–38.

Le Corre, P & O'Hanlon, M 2016, 'France's Pivot to Asia: It's More Than Just Submarines', *The National Interest*, 9 May, viewed 17th July 2017, http://nationalinterest.org/print/feature/frances-pivot-asia-its-more-just-submarines-16117.

Le Quintrec, G 1998, *La France dans le monde depuis 1945*, Seuil, Paris.

Lévy, J & Lussault, M 2009, *Dictionnaire de la géographie et de l'espace des sociétés*, Belin, Paris.

Maclellan, N 2014a, 'François Hollande Says France Wants to Remain a Pacific Power: Is It Wishful Thinking?', *The Guardian*, 18 November, viewed 1st August 2017, https://www.theguardian.com/commentisfree/2014/nov/18/francois-hollande-says-france-wants-to-remain-a-pacific-power-is-it-wishful-thinking.

Maclellan, N 2014b, 'The Complicated Politics of a French Defence Treaty', *The Crickey*, 19 November, viewed 1st August 2017, https://www.crikey.com.au/2014/11/19/the-complicated-politics-of-a-french-defence-treaty/.

292 BIBLIOGRAPHY

Maclellan, N 2015, 'Transforming the Regional Architecture: New Players and Challenges for the Pacific Islands', *Asia Pacific Issues*, no. 118, pp. 1–8.

Maclellan, N 2016, 'France and the Forum', *Inside Story*, 13 October, viewed 17th July 2017, http://insidestory.org.au/france-and-the-forum.

Maclellan, N & Chesnaux, J 1998, *La France dans le Pacifique, de Bougainville à Mururoa*, La Découverte, Paris.

Mainguet, Y 2016, 'À part entière dans le Forum du Pacifique', *Les nouvelles calédoniennes*, 2 November, viewed 17th July, http://www.lnc.nc/article/pays/politique/a-part-entiere-dans-le-forum-du-pacifique.

Mallatrait, C 2009, *La France, puissance inattendue au XXIe siècle dans le Pacifique sud: éléments pour une approche géopolitique de l'Océanie*, L'Harmattan, Paris.

Manne, R 2004, *The Howard Years*, Black Inc. Agenda, Melbourne.

Mathew, P & Harley, T 2016, *Refugees, Regionalism and Responsibility*, Edward Elgar Publishing, Cheltenham.

McAllister, I & Ravenhill, J 1998, 'Australian Attitudes Towards Closer Engagement with Asia', *The Pacific Review*, vol. 11, no. 1, pp. 119–141.

McCallum, W 1992, 'European Loyalist and Polynesian Political Dissent in New Caledonia: The Other Challenge to RPCR Orthodoxy', *Pacific Studies*, vol. 15, no. 3, pp. 39–40.

McDougall, D 2009, *Australian Foreign Relations, Entering the 21st Century*, Pearson, Sydney.

Medcalf, R & Townshend, A 2016, 'Shifting Water: China's New Passive Assertiveness in Asian Maritime Security', *Lowy Institute Reports*, 29 April, viewed 17th July 2017, https://www.lowyinstitute.org/publications/shifting-waters-china-s-new-passive-assertiveness-asian-maritime-security.

Messerlin, P 2017, 'Politique commerciale et "intérêt national"', in T de Montbrial & T Gomart (eds), *Notre intérêt national, quelle politique étrangère pour la France?* Odile Jacob, Paris, pp. 269–281.

Michel, B 1995, *Histoire de l'Australie, de 1770 à nos jours, naissance d'une nation du Pacifique*, L'Harmattan, Paris.

Ministère français de la Défense 2013, *Livre Blanc, Défense et sécurité nationale*, Ministère français de la Défense, Paris.

Mohamed-Gaillard, S 2010a, 'Les relations franco-australiennes en Océanie: représentations croisées de deux politiques régionales', *Outre-mers*, vol. 97, no. 366, pp. 123–133.

Mohamed-Gaillard, S 2010b, *L'archipel de la puissance? La politique de la France dans le Pacifique Sud de 1946 à 1998*, P. Lang, Bruxelles.

Mokaddem, H 2005, *Kanaky et/ou Nouvelle-Calédonie*, Expressions, Marseille.

Monlouis-Félicité, F 2017, 'Les grandes entreprises et la politique étrangère française', in T de Montbrial & T Gomart (eds), *Notre intérêt national, quelle politique étrangère pour la France?* Odile Jacob, Paris, pp. 255–268.

Monnoyer, L 1997, 'La légitimation par la science: un défi pour la démocratie', *Hermès*, vol. 1, no. 21, pp. 157–169.

BIBLIOGRAPHY 293

Morgan, W 2014, 'Regional Trade Negotiations and the Construction of Policy Choice in the Pacific Islands Forum (1994–2004)', Thesis (Ph.D.), The University of Melbourne, Melbourne, Australia.

Morgan, W 2017, 'Coal Comfort: Pacific Islands on Collision Course with Australia Over Emissions', *The Conversation*, 1 March, viewed 17th July 2017, https://theconversation.com/coal-comfort-pacific-islands-on-collision-course-with-australia-over-emissions-73662.

Mrgudovic, N 2008, *La France dans le Pacifique sud: les enjeux de la puissance*, L'Harmattan, Paris.

Murray, P 2013, 'Problems of Symmetry and Summitry in the EU–Australian Relationship', in S Lawson (ed), *Europe and the Asia-Pacific, Culture, Identity and Representations of Region*, Routledge, New York, pp. 66–85.

Murray, P 2016, 'EU–Australia Relations: A Strategic Partnership in All but Name', *Cambridge Review of International Affairs*, vol. 29, no. 1, pp. 171–191.

Murray, P & Benvenuti, A 2014, 'EU–Australia Relations at Fifty: Reassessing a Troubled Relationship', *Australian Journal of Politics and History*, vol. 60, no. 3, pp. 431–448.

Murray, P & Matera, M 2016, 'Brexit and Australia, the Way Forward', *Pursuit*, 2 July, viewed 17 July 2017, https://pursuit.unimelb.edu.au/articles/brexit-and-australia-the-way-forward.

Murray, P, Warleigh-Lack, A & He, B 2014, 'Awkward States and Regional Organisations: The United Kingdom and Australia Compared', *Comparative European Politics*, vol. 12, no. 3, pp. 279–300.

Nederveen Pieterse, J 1994, 'Globalisation as Hybridization', *International Sociology*, vol. 9, no. 2, pp. 161–184.

Nossal, KR & Vivian, C 1997, *A Brief Madness: Australia and the Resumption of French Nuclear Testing*, Australian National University Press, Canberra.

Nye, JS 2011, *The Future of Power*, Public Affairs, New York.

Odell, JS 2000, *Negotiating the World Economy*, Cornell University Press, Ithaca.

Offenstadt, N 2006, *Les mots de l'historien*, Presses Universitaires du Mirail, Toulouse.

Ohff, HJ 2017, 'Nuclear Versus Diesel-Electric: The Case for Conventional Submarines for the RAN', *ASPI The Strategist*, 11 July, viewed on 8 November 2017, https://www.aspistrategist.org.au/nuclear-versus-diesel-electric-case-conventional-submarines-ran/.

O'Keefe, M 2007, 'Australia and the Fragile States in the Pacific', in J Ravenhill & J Cotton (eds), *Trading on Alliance Security, Australia in World Affairs 2001–2005*, Oxford University Press, Melbourne, 2007, pp 131–149.

Oliver, A & Shearer, A 2011, *Diplomatic Disrespair, Rebuilding Australia's International Policy Infrastructure*, Lowy Institute, Sydney, 2011.

O'Malley, N 2013, 'Mali Crisis Is Australian's Big UN Test, Says Envoy', *Sydney Morning Herald*, 16 January, viewed 3 November 2017, http://www.smh.

294 BIBLIOGRAPHY

com.au/world/mali-crisis-is-australias-big-un-test-says-envoy-20130115-2crlv.html.

Pacific Islands Forum 2016, 'Forum Communiqué', 10 September, viewed 17th July 2017, http://www.forumsec.org/resources/uploads/embeds/file/2016-communique-working-19-09-2016.pdf.

Pan, C 2002, 'A Case for Pragmatism and Self-Reflection in Australia's Asia Thinking and Engagement', *Australia in the Asian Century White Paper*, Department of Foreign Affairs and Trade, Canberra.

Perkins, DD & Zimmerman, MA 1995, 'Empowerment Theory, Research and Application', *American Journal of Community Psychology*, vol. 23, no. 5, pp. 569–579.

Piketty, T 2013, *Le Capital au XXIᵉsiècle*, Seuil, Paris.

Piquet, M 2000, *Cold War in Warm Waters: Reflections on Australian and French Mutual Misunderstandings in the Pacific*, The University of Melbourne Press, Melbourne.

Piquet, M 2004, *Australie plurielle*, L'Harmattan, Paris.

Poirine, B 2013, 'Will the EU and the Euro Lead to More Sovereignty? French Polynesia', in R Adler-Nissen & UP Gad (eds), *European Integration and Postcolonial Sovereignty Games: The EU Overseas Countries and Territories*, Routledge, London, pp. 152–168.

Pons, X 1988, *Le géant du Pacifique*, Economic, Paris.

Pons, X 2000, *L'Australie, entre Occident et Orient*, La Documentation française, Paris.

Puissochet, JP 1991, 'Le Protocole au Traité sur l'Antarctique, relatif à la protection de l'environnement', *Annuaire français de droit international*, vol. 37, no. 1, pp. 755–773.

Purnendra, J 2006, 'Japan-Australia Security Ties and the United States: The Evolution of the Trilateral Dialogue Process and Its Challenges', *Australian Journal of International Affairs*, vol. 60, no. 4, pp. 521–535.

Ravenhill, J & Cotton, J 2007, *Trading on Alliance Security, Australia in the World Affairs 2001–2005*, Oxford Press, Oxford.

Regaud, N 2016, *France and Security in the Asia-Pacific, from the End of the First Indochina Conflict to Today*, ASPI Strategic Insights, Canberra.

Reynolds, H 1999, *Why Weren't We Told?* Penguin Books Australia, Ringwood.

Ricklefs, MC 2004, 'Australia and Indonesia', in R Manne (ed), *The Howard Years*, Black Inc. Agenda, Melbourne, pp. 267–290.

Riecker, P 2017, *French Foreign Policy in a Changing World, Practising Grandeur*, Palgrave Macmillan, Melbourne.

Robinson, R 1996, *Pathways to Asia, The Politics of Engagement*, Allen & Unwin, Sydney.

Ruggie, J 1998, 'What Makes the World Hang Together? Neo-utilitarianism and the Social Constructivist Challenge',*International Organization*, vol. 52, no. 4, pp. 855–885.

Sassen, S 2011, 'Sociology, Globalization, and the Re-shaping of the National', *Theory Talk #43*, 6 September, viewed 17 July 2017, http://www.theory-talks.org/2011/09/theory-talk-43.html.

Schultz, J 2012, 'Overseeing and Overlooking: Australian Engagement with the Pacific Islands 1988–2007', Thesis (Ph.D.), The University of Melbourne, Melbourne, Australia.

Schultz, J & Wallis, J 2014, 'Australia in the Pacific', in D Baldino, A Carr & AJ Langlois (eds), *Australian Foreign Policy, Controversies and Debates*, Oxford University Press, Oxford, pp. 174–192.

Snyder, GH 1997, *Alliance Politics*, Cornell University Press, Ithaca.

Soyez, P 2016, 'French-Indian Relations Take Off', *ASPI The Strategist*, 28 October, viewed 17 July 2017, https://www.aspistrategist.org.au/french-indian-relations-take-off/.

Soyez, P 2017, 'Macron and Turnbull Clarify Their Common Ambitions', *ASPI The Strategist*, 27 July, viewed 30 July, https://www.aspistrategist.org.au/macron-turnbull-clarify-common-ambitions/.

Stanner, WEH 1968, *The Boyer Lectures 1968—After the Dreaming*, Australian Broadcasting Commission, Sydney.

Steinmetz, L 2014, 'L'État, l'Union européenne, la Nouvelle-Calédonie: leur représentation réciproque', in I Amiot & Y Tommasini (eds), *L'éducation civique en Nouvelle-Calédonie*, SCÉRÉN – Vice Rectorat de la Nouvelle-Calédonie, Nouméa, pp. 53–66.

Stewart, A 2014, 'How Fiji Outsmarted Australia',*Lowy Institute The Interpreter*, 27 August, viewed 17 July 2017, https://www.lowyinstitute.org/the-interpreter/how-fiji-outsmarted-australia.

Swedberg, R & Agevall, O 2005, *The Max Weber Dictionary*, Stanford University Press, Stanford.

Synder, CA 1998, 'Australia's Pursuit of Regional Security into the 21st Century', *Journal of Strategic Studies*, vol. 21, no. 4, pp. 1–17.

Tarte, S 2004, 'Regionalism and Changing Regional Order in the Pacific Islands', *Asia & the Pacific Policy Studies*, vol. 1, no. 2, pp. 312–324.

Thibault, H & Philip, B 2016, 'Mer de Chine: les Philippines attendent que la Chine lui rende ses bancs de sable', *Le Monde*, 11 July, viewed 17th July 2017, http://www.lemonde.fr/asie-pacifique/article/2016/07/11/mer-de-chine-arbitrage-attendu-sur-le-conflit-entre-pekin-et-manille_4967793_3216.html.

Toa, E 2017, 'Bilateral Approach for Issues with Maritime Borders', *Vanuatu Independent*, 17 September, viewed 17th July, https://vanuatuindependent.com/2016/09/17/bilateral-approach-for-issues-with-maritime-borders/.

United Nations Development Program 2018, *Human Development Report*, United Nations, New York.

Védrine, H 2001, *France in an Age of Globalisation*, Brookings Institution Press, Washington.

BIBLIOGRAPHY

Walker, D 1999, *Anxious Nation: Australia and the Rise of Asia 1850–1939*, The University of Queensland Press, Brisbane.

Wallis, J 2017, 'Crowded and Complex: The Changing Geopolitics of the South Pacific', *ASPI The Strategist*, 24 April, viewed 17 July 2017, https://www.aspistrategist.org.au/crowded-complex-changing-geopolitics-south-pacific/.

Wallis, J & Dalsgaard, S 2016, 'Money, Manipulation and Misunderstanding on Manus Island', *The Journal of Pacific History*, vol. 51, no. 3, pp. 301–329.

Wendt, A 1992, 'Anarchy Is What States Make of It: The Social Construction of Power Politics', *International Organization*, vol. 46, no. 2, pp. 391–425.

Wendt, A 1999, *Social Theory of International Politics*, Cambridge University Press, Cambridge.

Wendt, A 2003, 'Why a State World Is Inevitable', *European Journal of International Relations*, vol. 9, no. 4, pp. 491–542.

Wesley, M 2007, *The Howard Paradox, Australian Diplomacy in Asia 1996–2006*, Australia Broadcast Corporation, Sydney.

Wesley, M & Warren, T 2000, 'Wild Colonial Ploys? Currents of Thought in Australian Foreign Policy', *Australian Journal of Political Science*, vol. 35, no. 1, pp. 9–18.

Wheeler, NJ 2013, 'Investigation Diplomatic Transformations', *International Affairs*, vol. 89, no. 2, pp. 477–496.

Wheeler, NJ & Booth, K 2008, *The Security Dilemma: Fear, Cooperation and Trust in World Politics*, Palgrave Macmillan, New York.

White, H 2010, 'Power Shift: Australia's Future Between Washington and Beijing', *Quaterly Essay*, no. 39, pp. 1–74.

White, H 2017, 'The United States or China: "We Don't Have to Choose"', in M Beeson & S Hameiri (eds), *Navigating the New International Disorder, Australia in World Affairs 2011–2015*, Oxford Press, Oxford, pp. 93–108.

Widmaier, W 2004, 'Theory as a Factor and the Theorist as an Actor: The 'Pragmatist Constructivist' Lessons of John Dewey and John Kenneth Galbraith', *International Studies Review*, vol. 6, no. 3, pp. 427–445.

Wilson, EJ 2008, 'Hard Power, Soft Power, Smart Power', *The Annals of the American Academic of Political and Social Sciences*, vol. 616, pp. 110–124.

Windschuttle, K 2002, *The Fabrication of Aboriginal History: Van Diemen's Land 1803–1847*, Macleay Press, Sudney.

Wolfers, A 1962, *Discord and Collaboration, Essays on International Politics*, The John Hopkins University Press, Baltimore.

INDEX

A

Aid programs, 192, 216, 222, 232, 238, 241, 242, 244, 245, 251

Asia-Pacific Economic Cooperation (APEC), 12, 35, 64

Association of Southeast Asian Nations (ASEAN), 12, 35, 63, 141, 143, 144, 239, 242, 243

Australia-New Zealand-United States (ANZUS), 12, 110–112, 119, 123, 139, 145, 150, 159, 168, 211

Awkward partner, 13, 42

B

Bishop, Julie, 91, 139, 162, 239

C

Cairns Group, 83–85, 88, 89, 97, 158, 264

China, 3, 4, 11, 13, 14, 19, 43, 45, 82, 97–99, 107, 120, 124, 126, 134, 140, 146, 147, 162, 163, 166, 167, 170, 174, 204, 209, 215, 218, 228, 235–239, 246, 252, 254–256, 265, 266

Chirac, Jacques, 41, 75, 101, 119, 182, 191, 195, 197, 214, 225, 252

Colonial history, 179, 184, 203, 217, 218, 233, 257, 267

Common Agricultural Policy (CAP), 5, 17, 83–88, 95, 97, 261, 264

Constructivism, 8, 23, 28, 32, 46, 262

D

Deutsch, Karl, 17, 27, 28, 154, 162, 247

© The Editor(s) (if applicable) and The Author(s), under exclusive license to Springer Nature Switzerland AG 2019
P. Soyez, *Australia and France's Mutual Empowerment*, Studies in Diplomacy and International Relations, https://doi.org/10.1007/978-3-030-13449-5

298 INDEX

E

Economic diplomacy, 9, 17, 38, 55–57, 60–69, 77, 80, 162, 263

European Union (EU), 4, 9, 17, 34, 40, 43, 56, 76, 79, 84–86, 88–92, 94–98, 161, 162, 170, 214, 221, 228, 240–245, 254, 264, 266, 267

Evans, Gareth, 11, 34, 36, 43, 45, 47, 82, 101, 108, 119, 120, 126, 130, 134, 151, 155, 157–159, 186–192, 198, 199, 203, 231–233, 248

F

Fiji, 19, 106, 110, 134, 188, 195, 200, 201, 204, 207, 209, 216, 224, 243, 251

Forces armées de la Nouvelle-Calédonie/Armed Forces of New Caledonia (FANC), 228, 251, 253

France-Australia-New Zealand (FRANZ), 167, 251

Free Trade Agreement (FTA), 12, 17, 56, 82, 89–97, 143, 161, 264, 267

French Polynesia, 19, 20, 40, 101, 114–116, 124–129, 133, 181, 182, 192, 212, 215, 220, 223–227, 229, 242, 244–246, 250, 258, 264

H

Hollande, François, 1, 59, 67, 68, 79, 89, 92, 96, 97, 127, 128, 161, 162, 172, 218, 222, 234

I

Identity, 3, 5, 7–11, 15, 25–27, 45, 121, 138, 175, 182, 184, 217, 218, 225, 238, 257, 262, 263

Indian Ocean, 15, 16, 19, 108, 162, 163, 174, 183, 212, 221, 239, 253–256, 267

Indonesia, 4, 98, 134, 140–145, 162, 169, 175, 188, 209, 221, 235, 238

Indo-Pacific region, 9, 10, 14, 15, 19, 24–27, 38, 39, 94, 139, 143, 153, 161, 215, 221, 222, 235, 236, 240, 243, 262, 263, 266, 267

International Atomic Energy Agency (IAEA), 104–107, 110, 120, 129, 132, 134

J

Japan, 4, 44, 63, 70, 82, 93, 97, 99, 111, 112, 126, 130, 131, 140, 145–147, 158, 159, 172, 201, 202, 218, 228, 230, 234, 238, 245, 255

L

Le Drian, Jean-Yves, 162, 163, 172, 174, 238

M

Macron, Emmanuel, 10, 89, 95, 152, 160, 162, 164, 209, 250, 267

Melanesia, 15, 19, 194, 195, 219, 220

Middle power, 2, 4, 7, 9, 15, 25, 37–39, 41, 42, 45, 47, 102, 123, 130, 159, 211, 221, 231, 261, 262, 267, 268

Moruroa, 106, 114–116, 118, 120, 125–130, 158, 193, 219
Multilateralism, 35, 37
Mutual empowerment, 1, 5, 25, 26, 37, 153, 154, 167, 256, 257, 261–263, 265–267

N
Naval Group, 18, 59, 73, 74, 161, 170–174, 236, 244, 255
New Caledonia, 5, 6, 18, 19, 26, 36, 40, 41, 46, 74, 80, 113, 116, 118, 120, 122, 145, 146, 155, 157, 158, 179–199, 202, 204–208, 212, 213, 215, 218–220, 222–229, 233, 238, 239, 242, 244–246, 249–252, 256, 261, 263, 267
New Zealand, 15, 46, 84, 106, 107, 110–112, 116, 117, 119, 121, 125, 127, 129, 134, 150, 151, 159, 167, 176, 182, 184, 204, 209, 213, 216, 219, 224, 230, 231, 234, 241, 244, 245, 249, 252

O
Outre-mer, 15, 19, 185, 212, 224, 225, 228, 229, 239

P
Pacific Community (PC), 33, 35, 37, 115, 116, 134, 223, 230, 233, 249, 250
Pacific Island Countries (PICs), 13, 15, 17, 110, 115, 116, 121, 129, 130, 141, 147, 148, 150, 199, 200, 204, 215, 216, 218, 219,

221, 222, 227, 230–233, 240, 241, 251, 252, 256, 266, 267
Pacific Islands Forum (PIF), 15, 35, 115, 188, 189, 194, 199, 200, 216, 223, 227, 233, 244
Papua New Guinea (PNG), 19, 112, 116, 129, 140, 200, 204, 206, 209, 211, 215, 224, 230, 235, 249
Political legitimacy, 18, 176, 208, 267
Politique de grandeur, 7, 8, 42, 114, 185, 265

R
Regional integration, 11, 12, 17, 19, 38, 140, 182, 183, 186, 212, 215, 223, 224, 227, 229, 230, 243, 245, 256
Rocard, Michel, 6, 34, 88, 108, 134, 149–151, 155, 157–159, 185, 186, 198, 214, 231, 248

S
Scientific cooperation, 247, 248, 250
Smart power, 1, 16–19, 23–27, 30, 32, 45, 114, 120, 121, 153, 154, 169, 171, 214, 251, 262, 263, 265, 267, 268
South China Sea, 147, 162, 236, 237
Strategic narrative, 10, 16, 19, 39, 212, 218, 221, 230, 267
Strategic partnership, 1, 5, 14, 17, 18, 24, 25, 27, 29, 38, 40, 45, 59, 77, 133, 138, 143, 146, 148, 152–154, 160–164, 169, 170, 174, 203, 208, 212, 215, 235, 236, 239, 244, 247, 256, 261, 262, 264, 267

300 INDEX

T

Terrorism, 18, 102, 106, 137, 143, 153, 161, 162, 164–166, 168–170, 175, 188, 235, 257, 265

Turnbull, Malcolm, 1, 73, 102, 160, 163, 172–174, 206, 240, 241

U

United Nations (UN), 10, 11, 18, 33, 35, 36, 43, 47, 62, 74, 89, 102, 106–109, 112, 114, 115, 121, 124, 129, 133, 142, 146, 148, 159, 164, 165, 182, 190–192, 198, 199, 209, 215, 221, 225, 226, 233, 236, 240, 241, 257

Uranium diplomacy, 102, 131

V

Vanuatu, 19, 112, 116, 129, 188, 195, 200, 207, 209, 211, 215, 219, 220, 224, 226, 249

W

Wallis and Futuna, 19, 20, 127, 212, 220, 229, 238, 246, 249